THAT TIME I GOT REINCARNATED AS A

SLIME

8

Author: FUSE

Artist: TAIKI KAWAKAMI

Character design: MITZ VAH

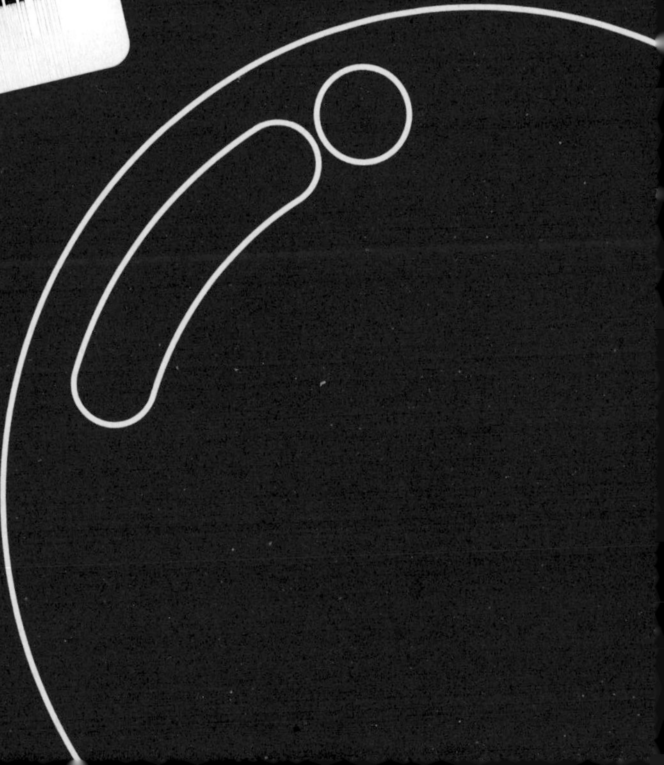

World Map

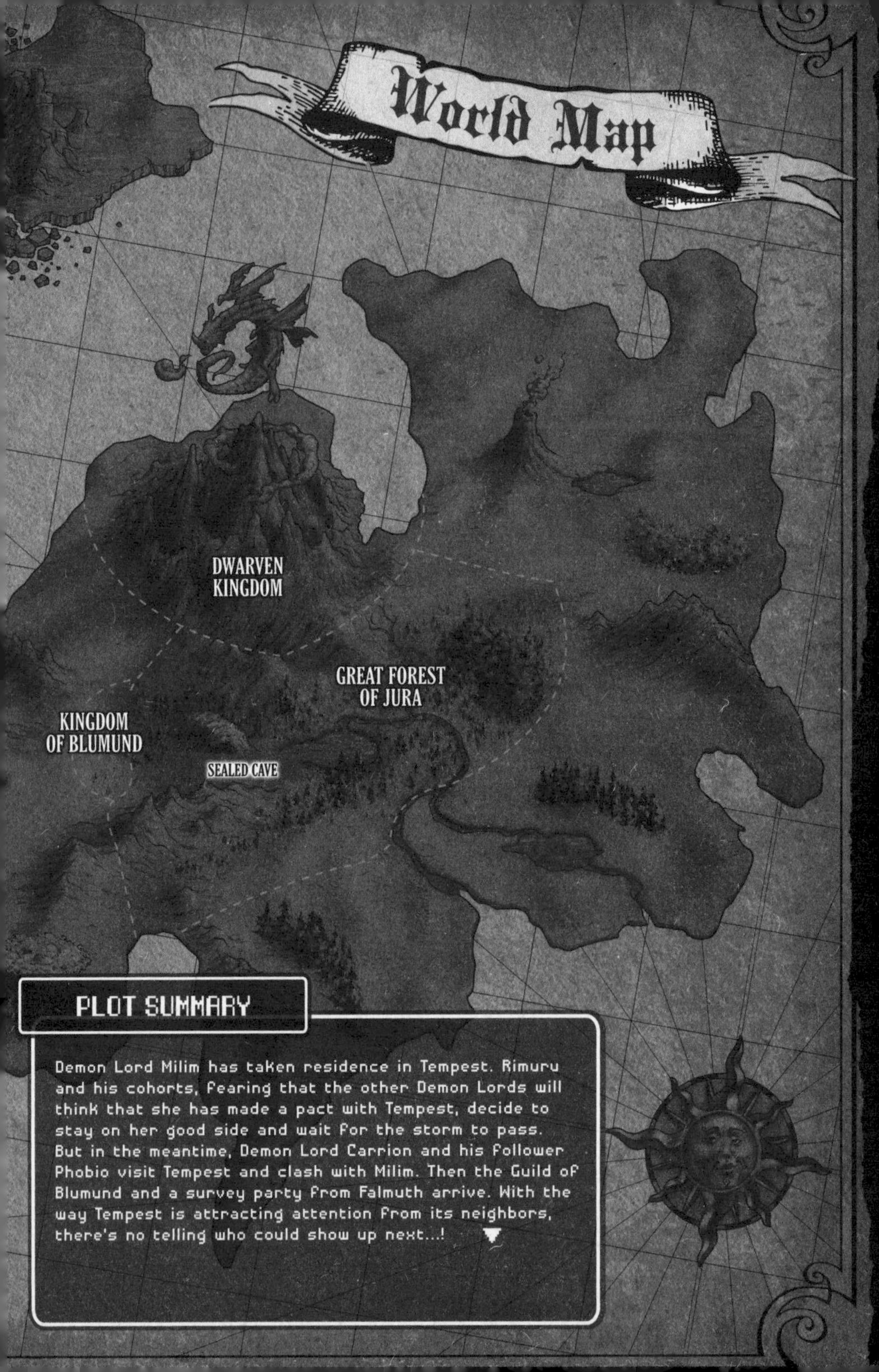
DWARVEN KINGDOM
GREAT FOREST OF JURA
KINGDOM OF BLUMUND
SEALED CAVE

PLOT SUMMARY

Demon Lord Milim has taken residence in Tempest. Rimuru and his cohorts, fearing that the other Demon Lords will think that she has made a pact with Tempest, decide to stay on her good side and wait for the storm to pass. But in the meantime, Demon Lord Carrion and his follower Phobio visit Tempest and clash with Milim. Then the Guild of Blumund and a survey party from Falmuth arrive. With the way Tempest is attracting attention from its neighbors, there's no telling who could show up next...!

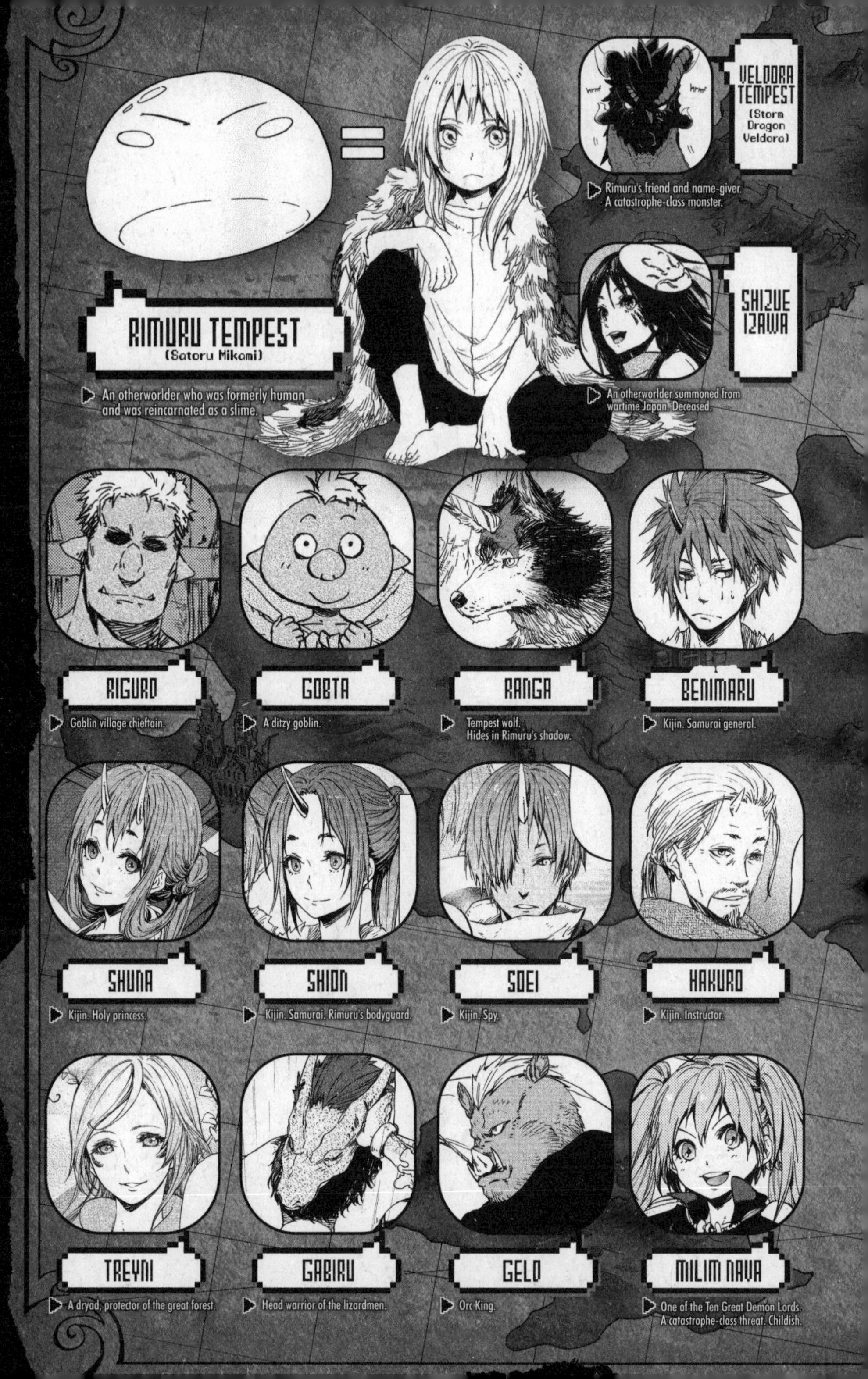

RIMURU TEMPEST
(Satoru Mikami)

▷ An otherworlder who was formerly human and was reincarnated as a slime.

VELDORA TEMPEST
(Storm Dragon Veldora)

▷ Rimuru's friend and name-giver. A catastrophe-class monster.

SHIZUE IZAWA

▷ An otherworlder summoned from wartime Japan. Deceased.

RIGURD

▷ Goblin village chieftain.

GOBTA

▷ A ditzy goblin.

RANGA

▷ Tempest wolf. Hides in Rimuru's shadow.

BENIMARU

▷ Kijin. Samurai general.

SHUNA

▷ Kijin. Holy princess.

SHION

▷ Kijin. Samurai. Rimuru's bodyguard.

SOEI

▷ Kijin. Spy.

HAKURO

▷ Kijin. Instructor.

TREYNI

▷ A dryad, protector of the great forest.

GABIRU

▷ Head warrior of the lizardmen.

GELD

▷ Orc King.

MILIM NAVA

▷ One of the Ten Great Demon Lords. A catastrophe-class threat. Childish.

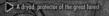

CONTENTS

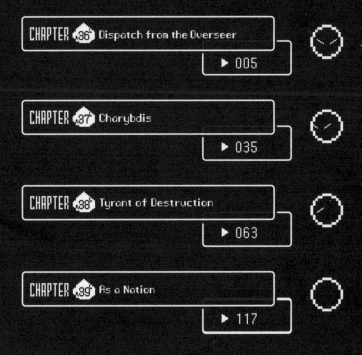

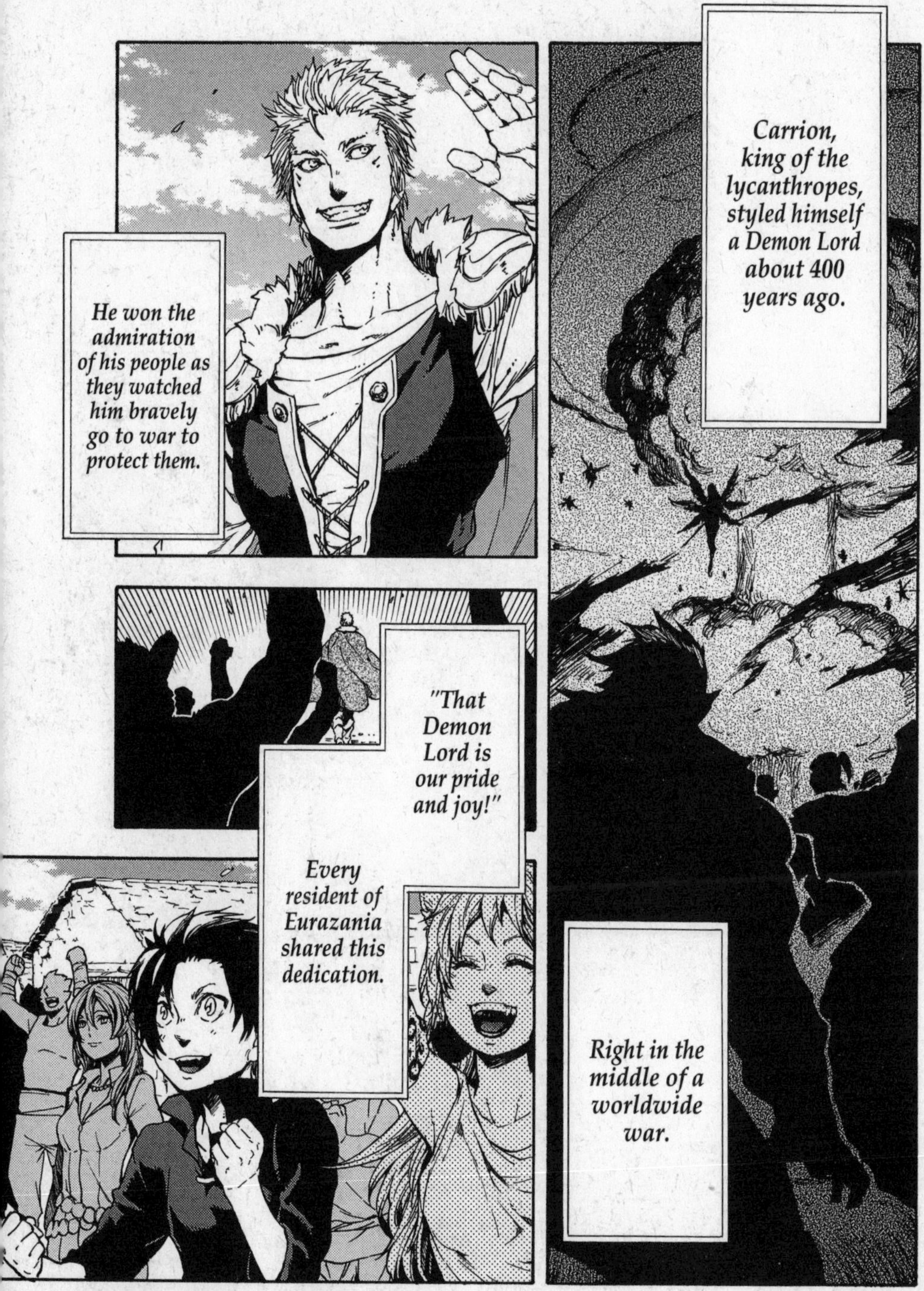
Carrion, king of the lycanthropes, styled himself a Demon Lord about 400 years ago.
Right in the middle of a worldwide war.
He won the admiration of his people as they watched him bravely go to war to protect them.
"That Demon Lord is our pride and joy!"
Every resident of Eurazania shared this dedication.

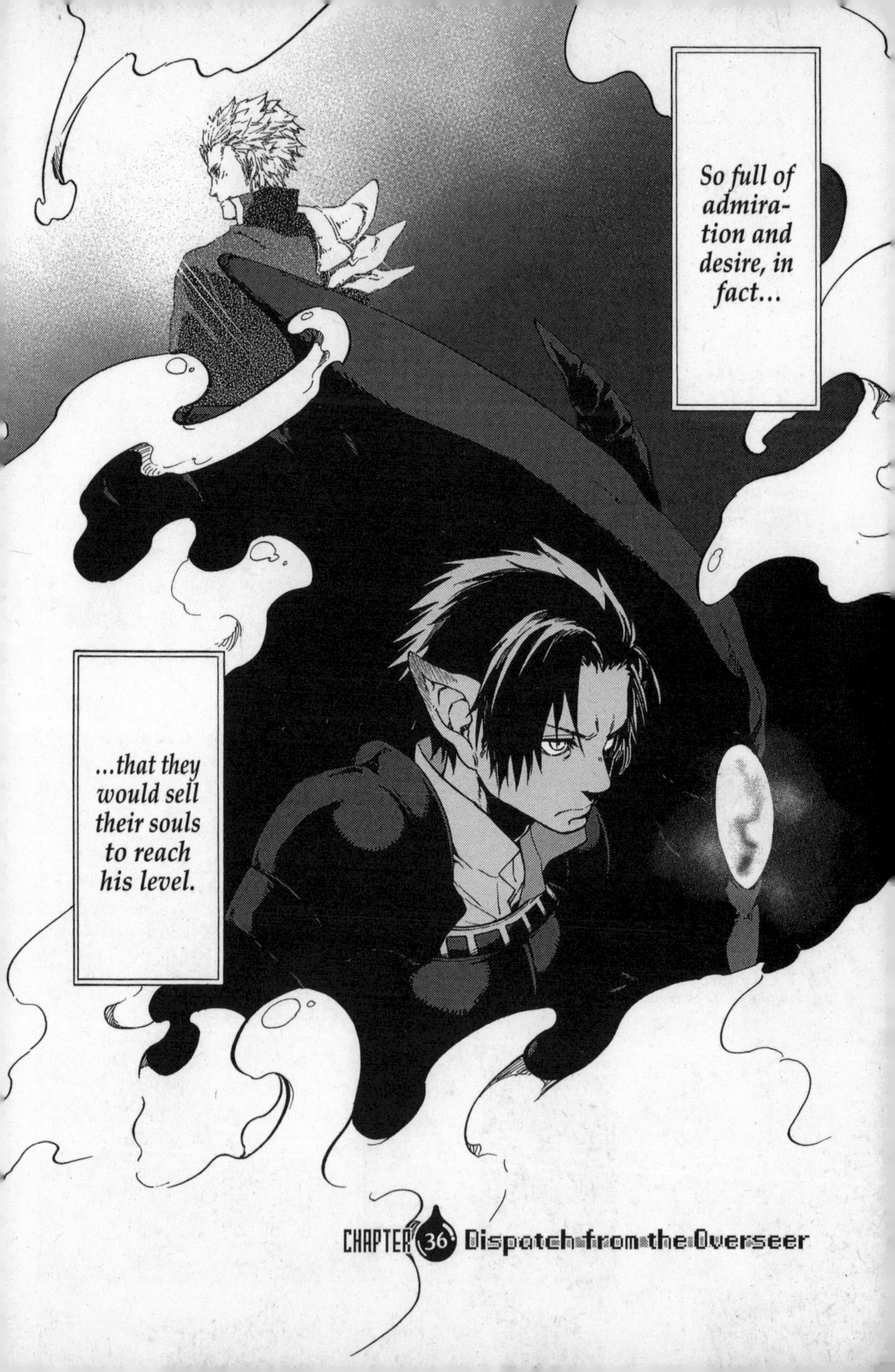
So full of admiration and desire, in fact…
…that they would sell their souls to reach his level.
CHAPTER 36 Dispatch from the Overseer

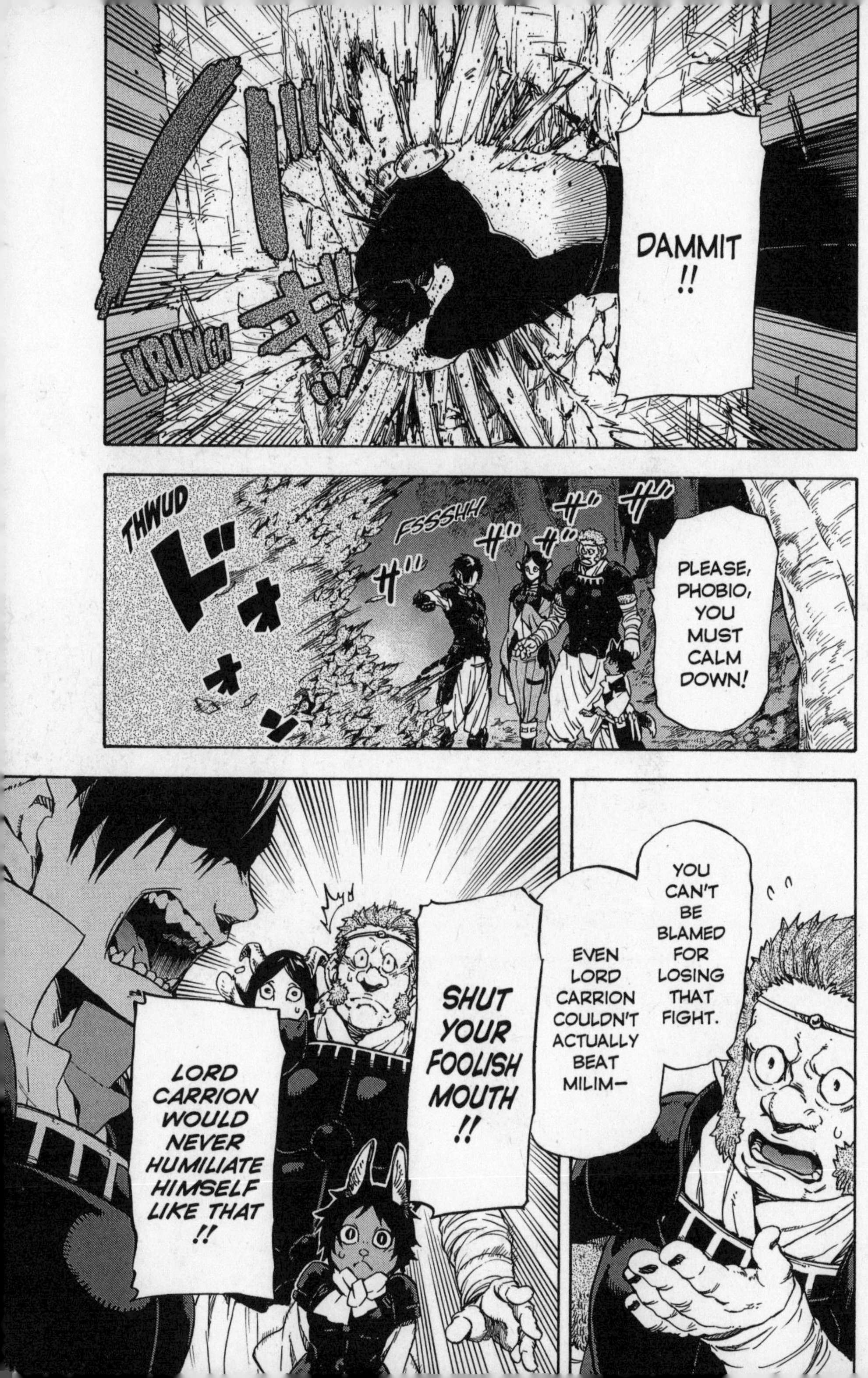
DAMMIT!!
KRUNCH
PLEASE, PHOBIO, YOU MUST CALM DOWN!
FSSSHH
THWUD
YOU CAN'T BE BLAMED FOR LOSING THAT FIGHT.
EVEN LORD CARRION COULDN'T ACTUALLY BEAT MILIM—
SHUT YOUR FOOLISH MOUTH!!
LORD CARRION WOULD NEVER HUMILIATE HIMSELF LIKE THAT!!

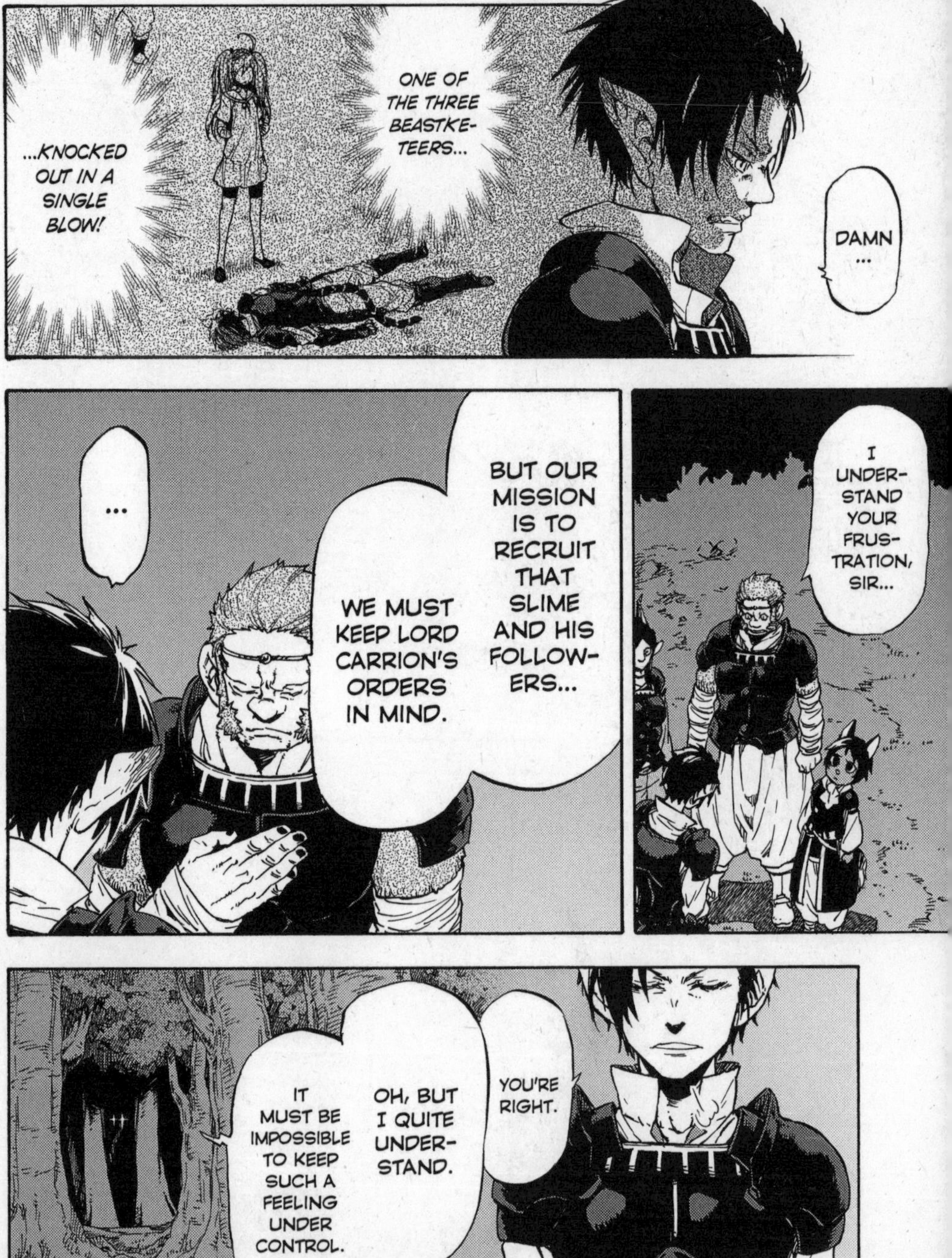
DAMN...
ONE OF THE THREE BEASTKETEERS...
...KNOCKED OUT IN A SINGLE BLOW!
I UNDERSTAND YOUR FRUSTRATION, SIR...
BUT OUR MISSION IS TO RECRUIT THAT SLIME AND HIS FOLLOWERS...
WE MUST KEEP LORD CARRION'S ORDERS IN MIND.
...
YOU'RE RIGHT.
OH, BUT I QUITE UNDERSTAND.
IT MUST BE IMPOSSIBLE TO KEEP SUCH A FEELING UNDER CONTROL.

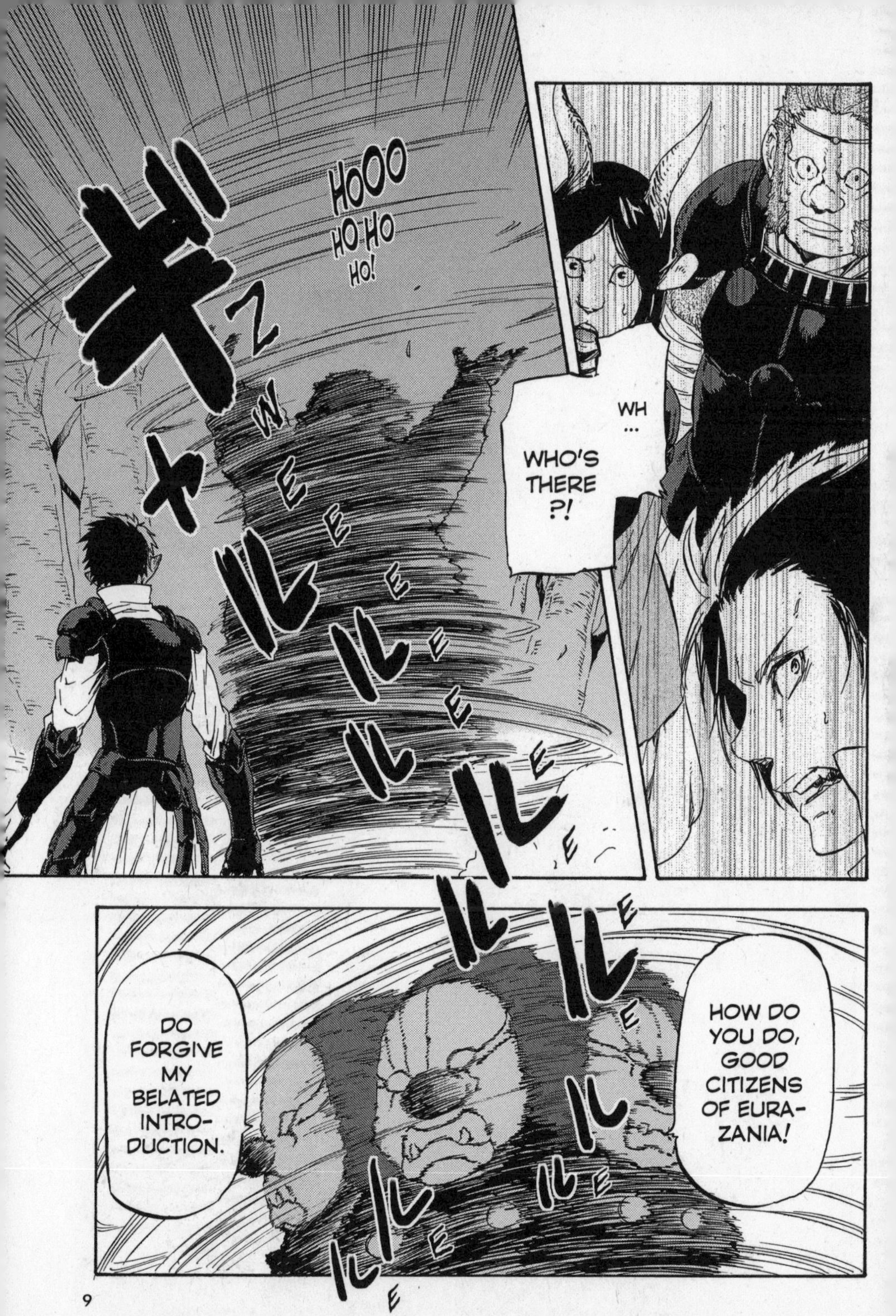
WH... WHO'S THERE?!
HOOO HO HO HO!
HOW DO YOU DO, GOOD CITIZENS OF EURA-ZANIA!
DO FORGIVE MY BELATED INTRO-DUCTION.

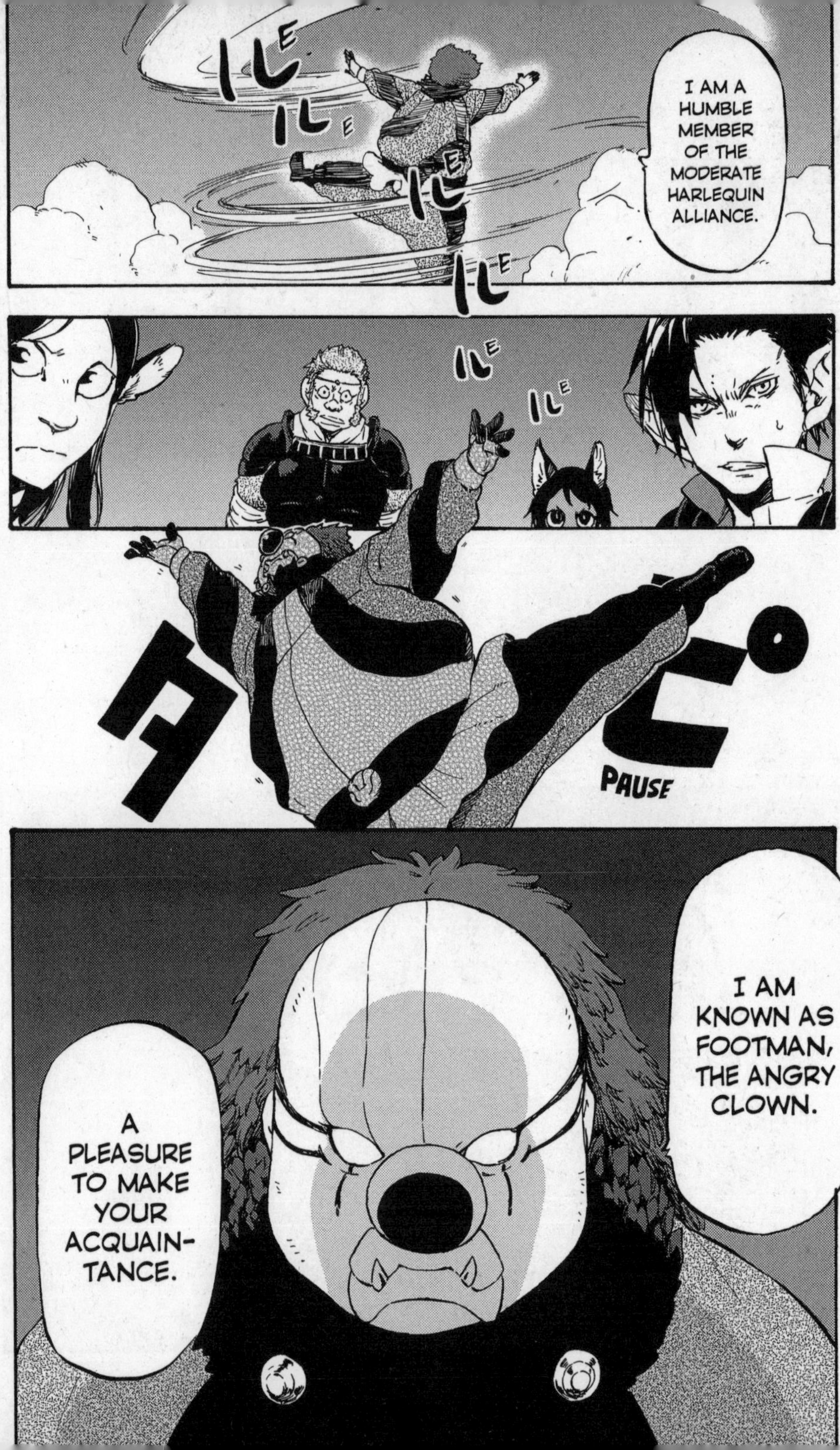
I AM A HUMBLE MEMBER OF THE MODERATE HARLEQUIN ALLIANCE.
PAUSE
I AM KNOWN AS FOOTMAN, THE ANGRY CLOWN.
A PLEASURE TO MAKE YOUR ACQUAIN-TANCE.

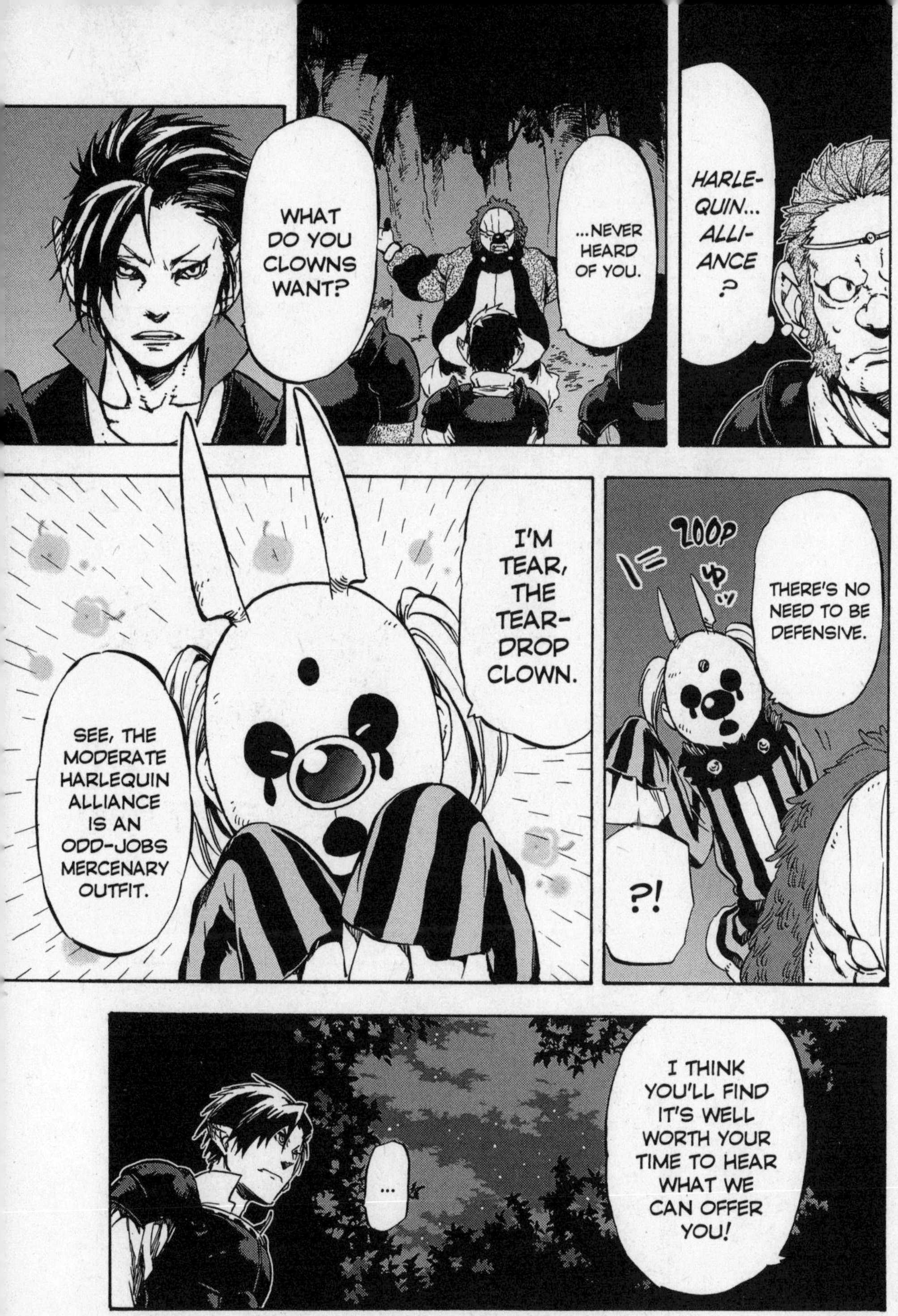
HARLEQUIN... ALLIANCE?
...NEVER HEARD OF YOU.
WHAT DO YOU CLOWNS WANT?
ZOOP
THERE'S NO NEED TO BE DEFENSIVE.
?!
I'M TEAR, THE TEARDROP CLOWN.
SEE, THE MODERATE HARLEQUIN ALLIANCE IS AN ODD-JOBS MERCENARY OUTFIT.
I THINK YOU'LL FIND IT'S WELL WORTH YOUR TIME TO HEAR WHAT WE CAN OFFER YOU!
...

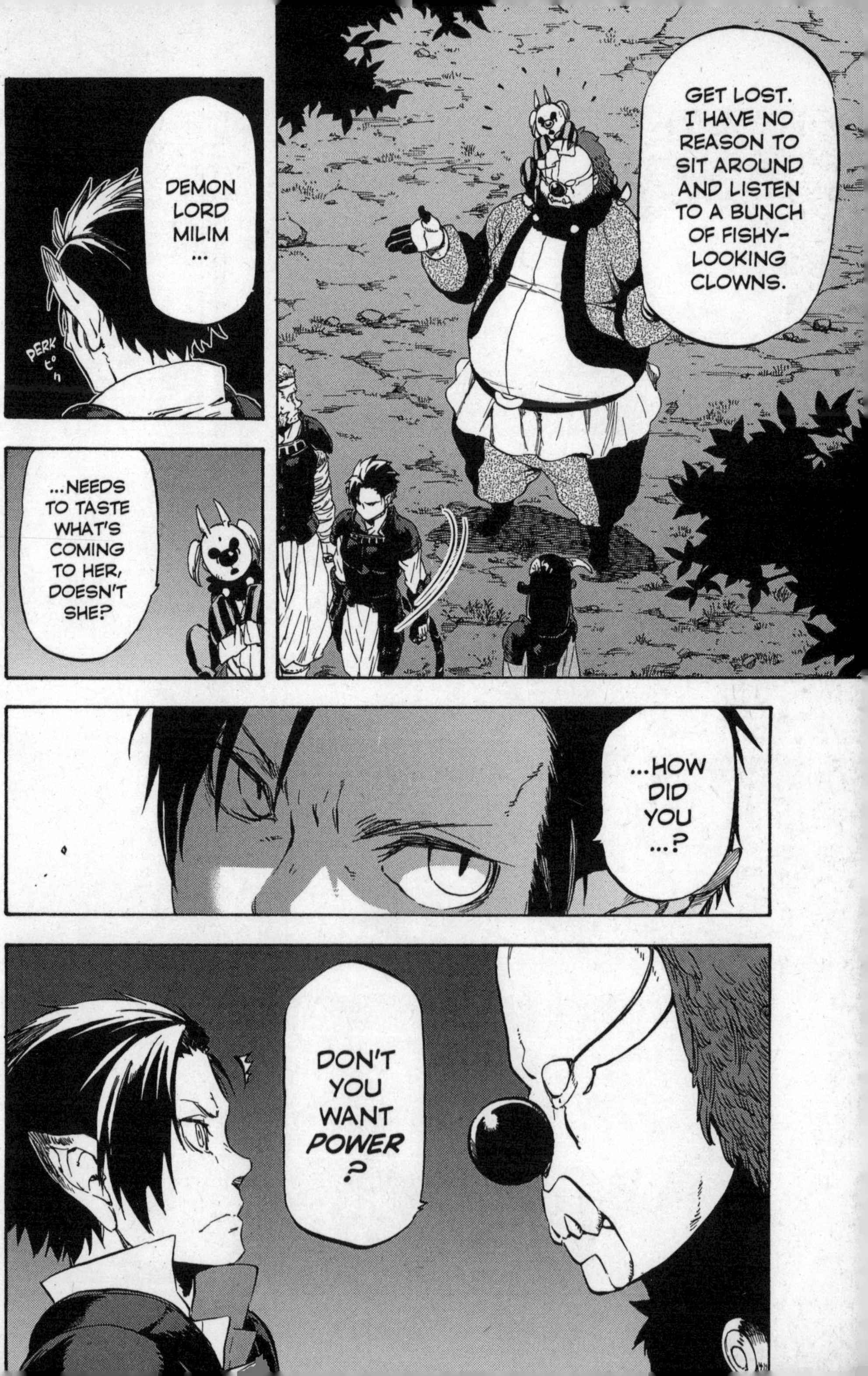
GET LOST. I HAVE NO REASON TO SIT AROUND AND LISTEN TO A BUNCH OF FISHY-LOOKING CLOWNS.
DEMON LORD MILIM ...
PERK
...NEEDS TO TASTE WHAT'S COMING TO HER, DOESN'T SHE?
...HOW DID YOU ...?
DON'T YOU WANT *POWER* ?

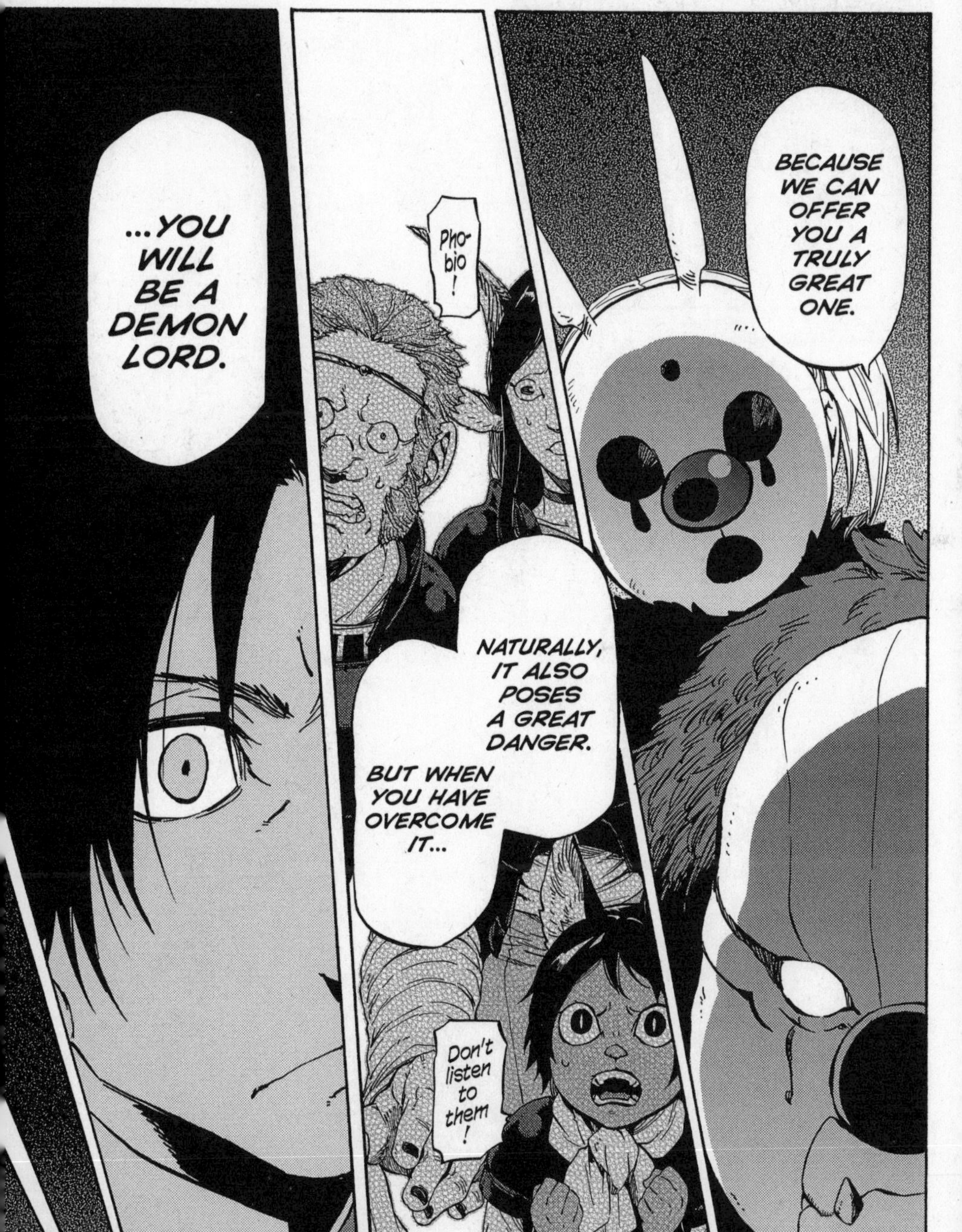
BECAUSE WE CAN OFFER YOU A TRULY GREAT ONE.
Pho-bio!
NATURALLY, IT ALSO POSES A GREAT DANGER.
BUT WHEN YOU HAVE OVERCOME IT...
Don't listen to them!
...YOU WILL BE A DEMON LORD.

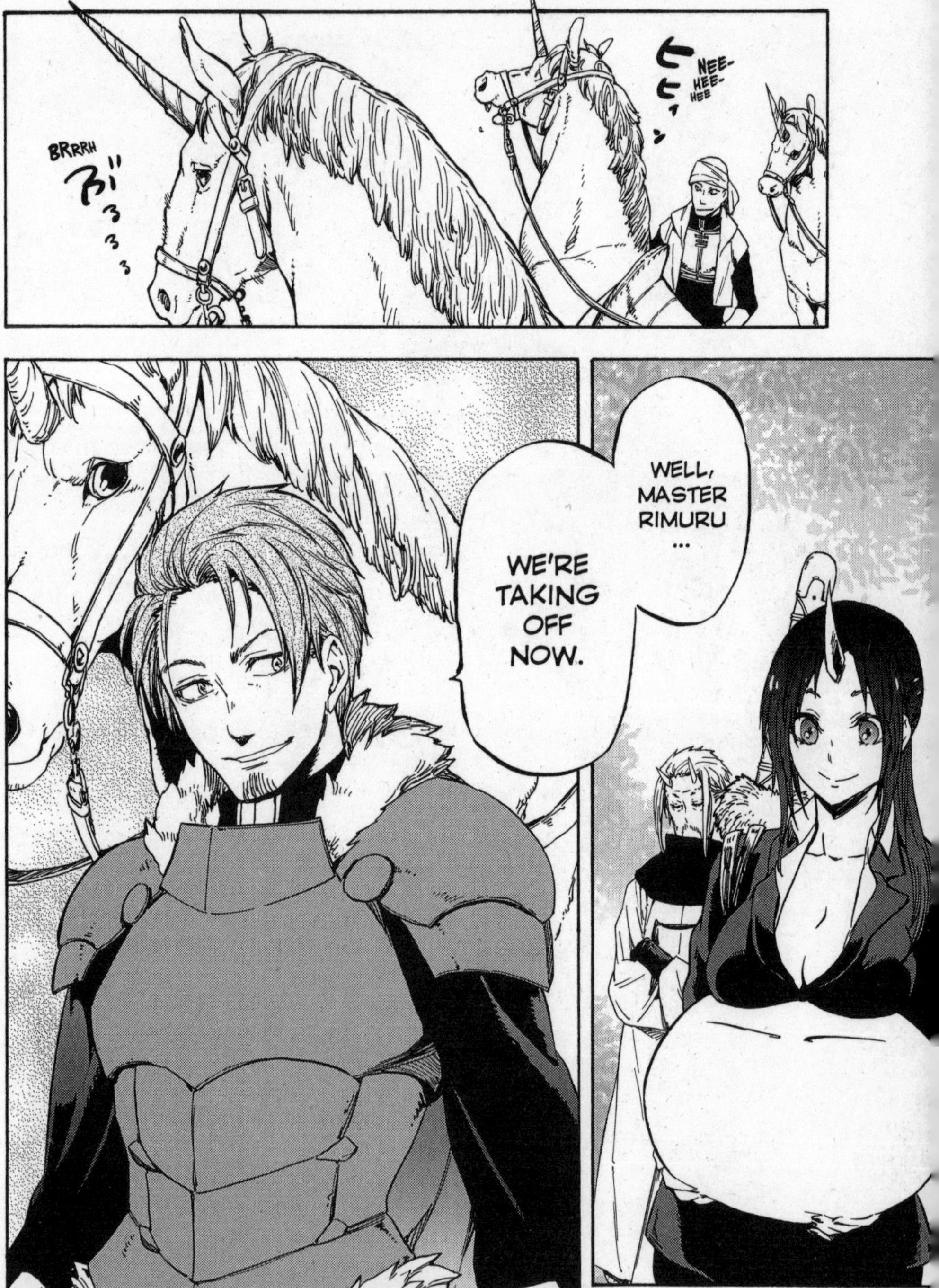
ヒヒン
NEE-HEE-HEE
ぶるるる
BRRRH
WELL, MASTER RIMURU ...
WE'RE TAKING OFF NOW.

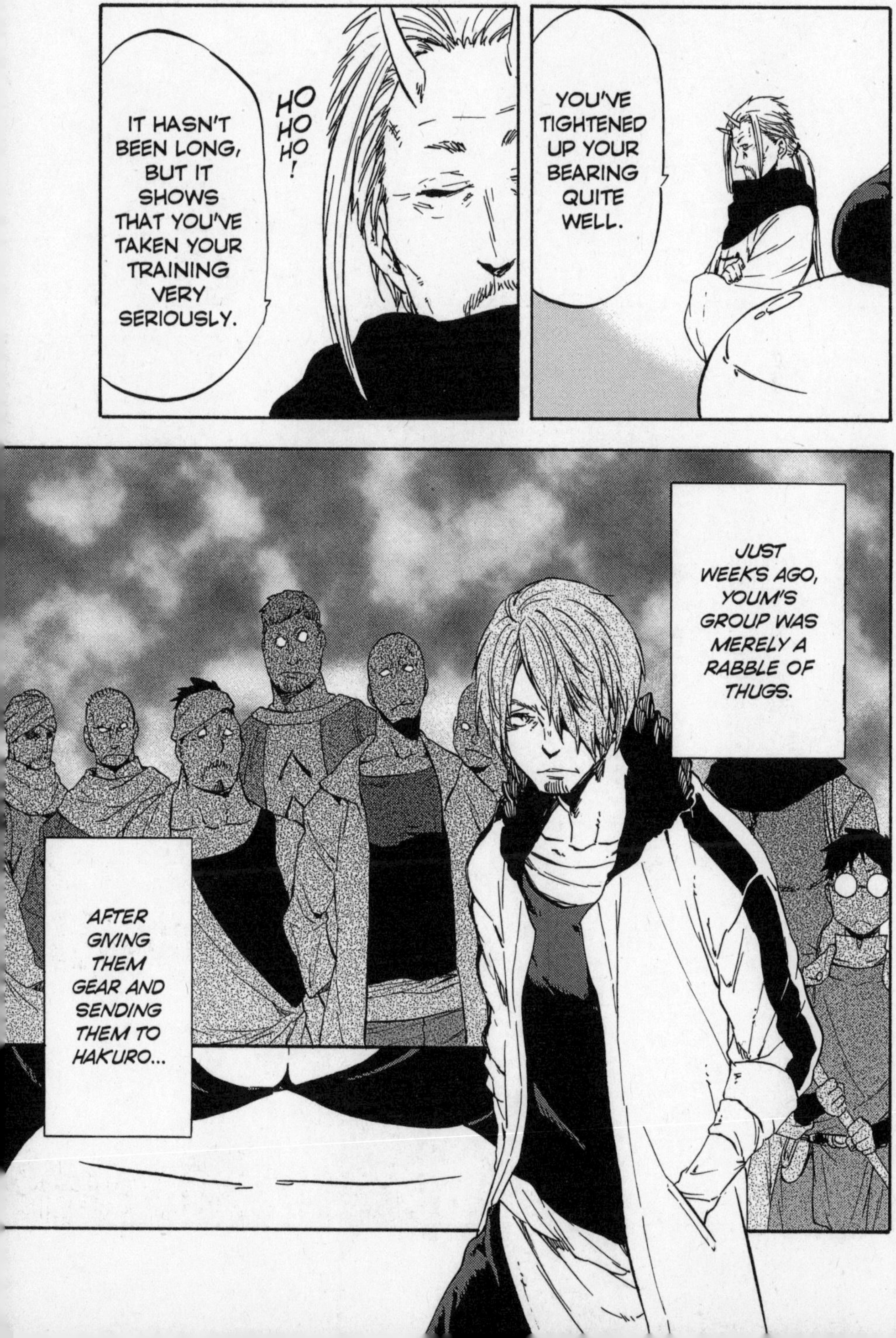
YOU'VE TIGHTENED UP YOUR BEARING QUITE WELL.
HO HO HO!
IT HASN'T BEEN LONG, BUT IT SHOWS THAT YOU'VE TAKEN YOUR TRAINING VERY SERIOUSLY.
JUST WEEKS AGO, YOUM'S GROUP WAS MERELY A RABBLE OF THUGS.
AFTER GIVING THEM GEAR AND SENDING THEM TO HAKURO...

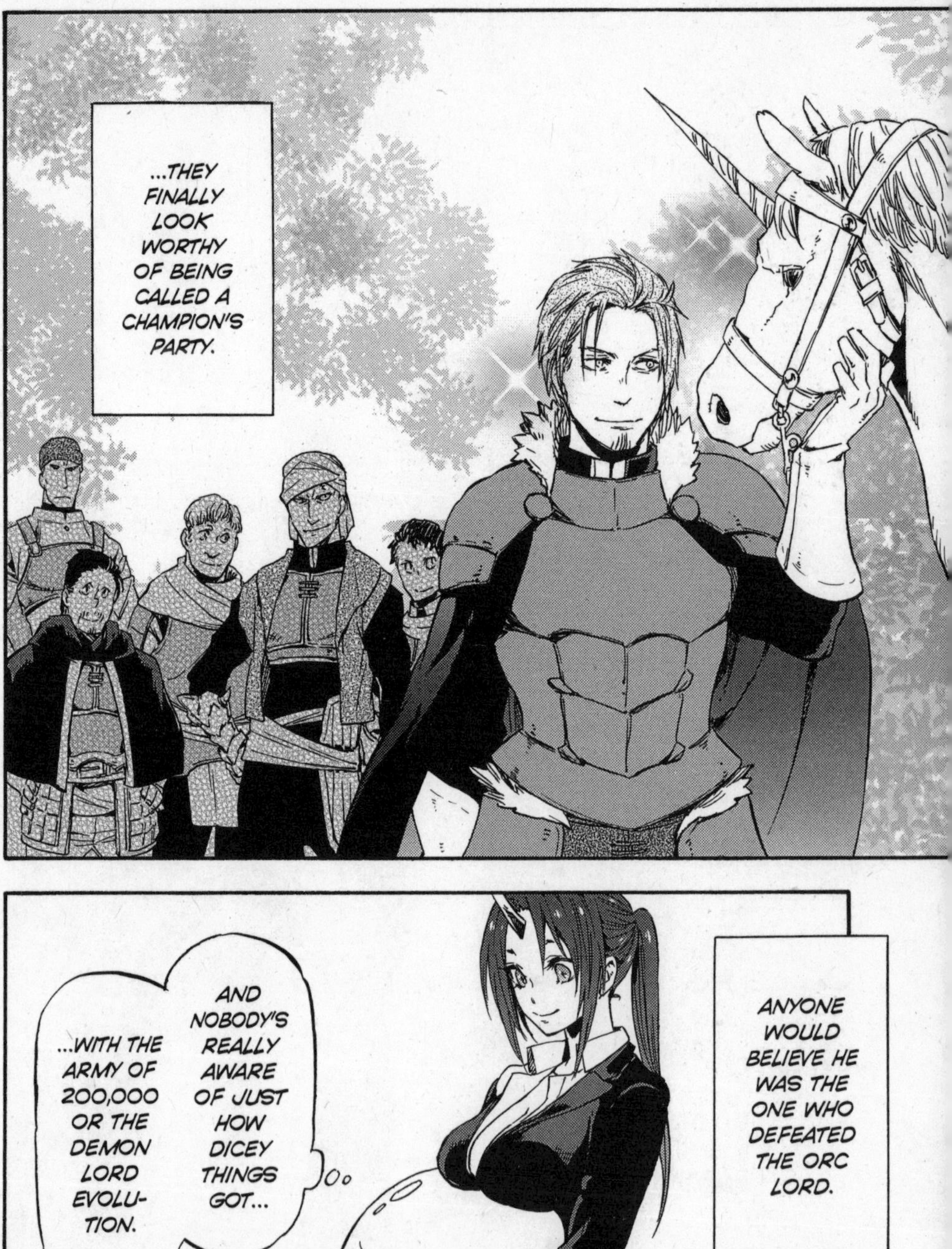
...THEY FINALLY LOOK WORTHY OF BEING CALLED A CHAMPION'S PARTY.
ANYONE WOULD BELIEVE HE WAS THE ONE WHO DEFEATED THE ORC LORD.
AND NOBODY'S REALLY AWARE OF JUST HOW DICEY THINGS GOT...
...WITH THE ARMY OF 200,000 OR THE DEMON LORD EVOLUTION.

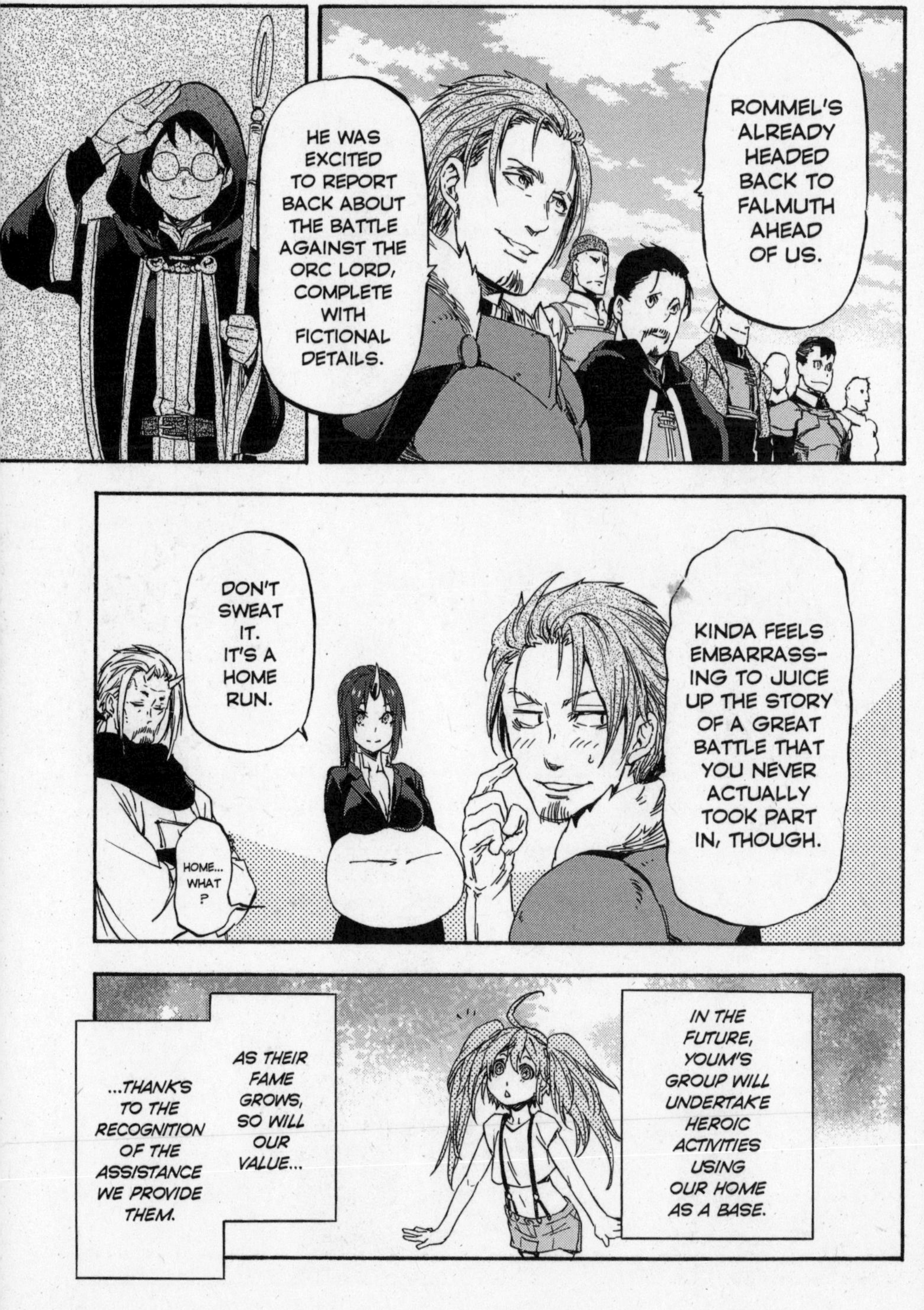
ROMMEL'S ALREADY HEADED BACK TO FALMUTH AHEAD OF US.
HE WAS EXCITED TO REPORT BACK ABOUT THE BATTLE AGAINST THE ORC LORD, COMPLETE WITH FICTIONAL DETAILS.
KINDA FEELS EMBARRASS-ING TO JUICE UP THE STORY OF A GREAT BATTLE THAT YOU NEVER ACTUALLY TOOK PART IN, THOUGH.
DON'T SWEAT IT. IT'S A HOME RUN.
HOME... WHAT?
IN THE FUTURE, YOUM'S GROUP WILL UNDERTAKE HEROIC ACTIVITIES USING OUR HOME AS A BASE.
AS THEIR FAME GROWS, SO WILL OUR VALUE...
...THANKS TO THE RECOGNITION OF THE ASSISTANCE WE PROVIDE THEM.

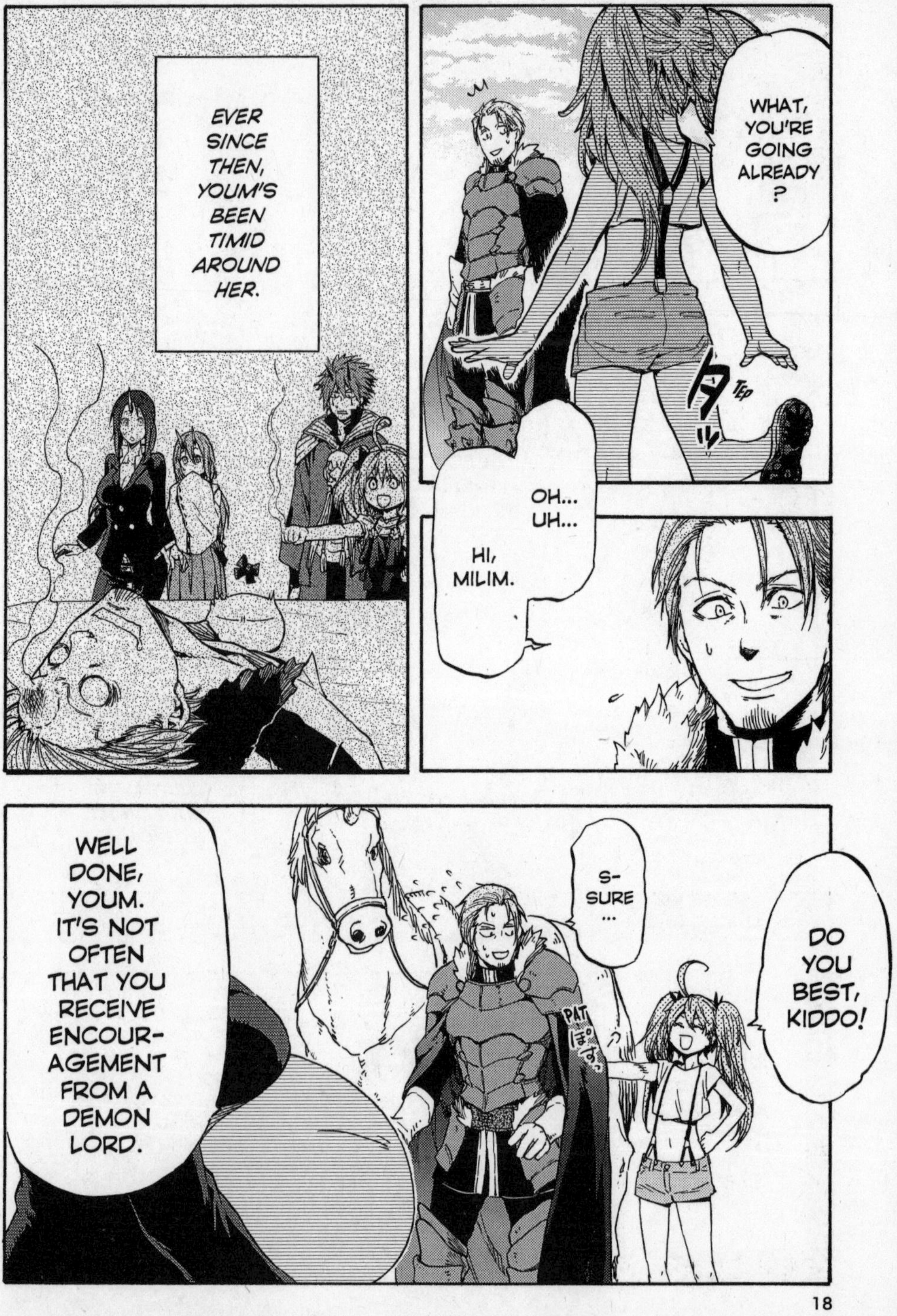
WHAT, YOU'RE GOING ALREADY?
TEP
OH... UH...
HI, MILIM.
EVER SINCE THEN, YOUM'S BEEN TIMID AROUND HER.
DO YOU BEST, KIDDO!
PAT
ぽすっ
S-SURE...
WELL DONE, YOUM. IT'S NOT OFTEN THAT YOU RECEIVE ENCOURAGEMENT FROM A DEMON LORD.

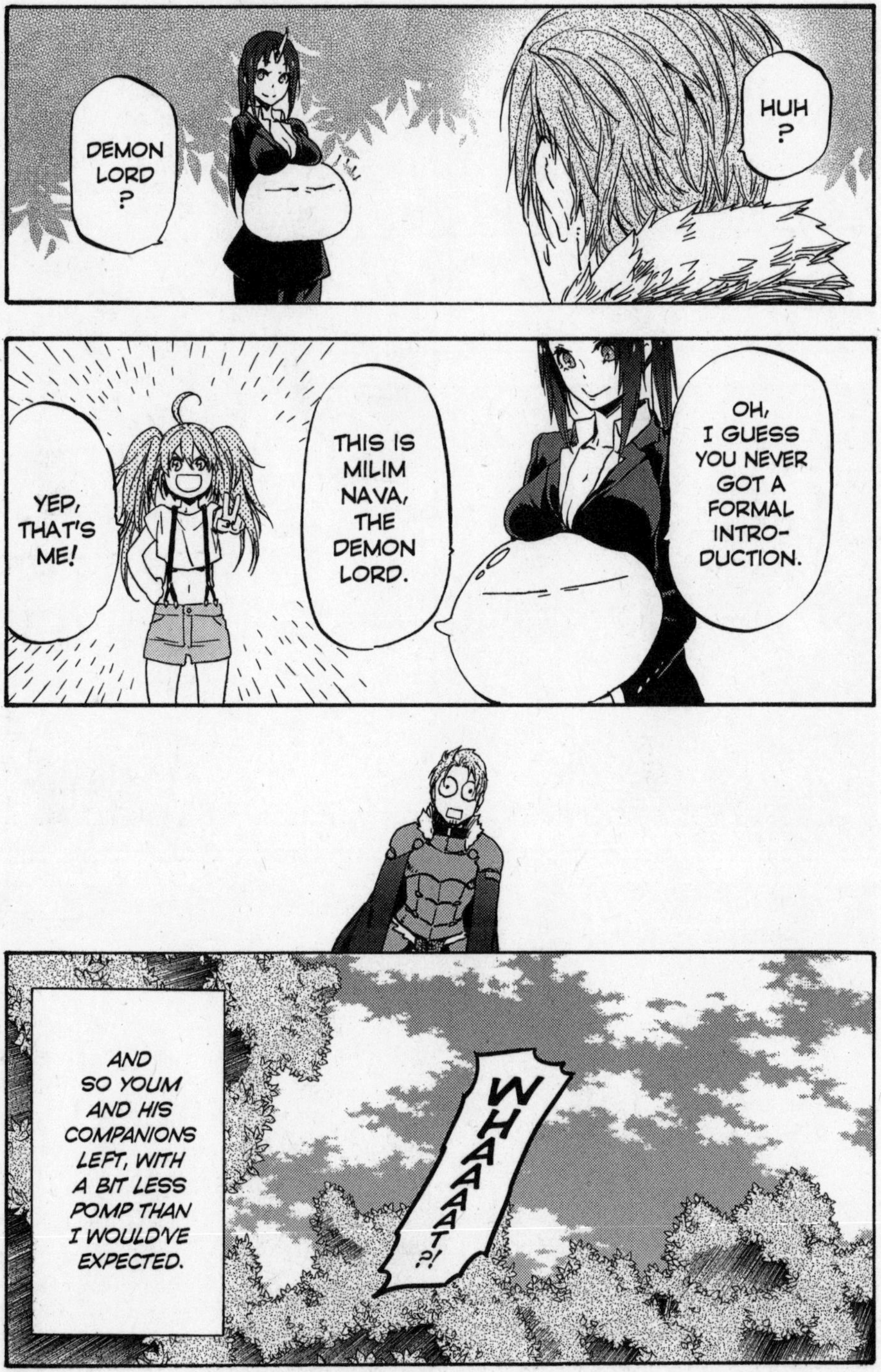
HUH?
DEMON LORD?
OH, I GUESS YOU NEVER GOT A FORMAL INTRO-DUCTION.
THIS IS MILIM NAVA, THE DEMON LORD.
YEP, THAT'S ME!
WHAAAAAT?!
AND SO YOUM AND HIS COMPANIONS LEFT, WITH A BIT LESS POMP THAN I WOULD'VE EXPECTED.

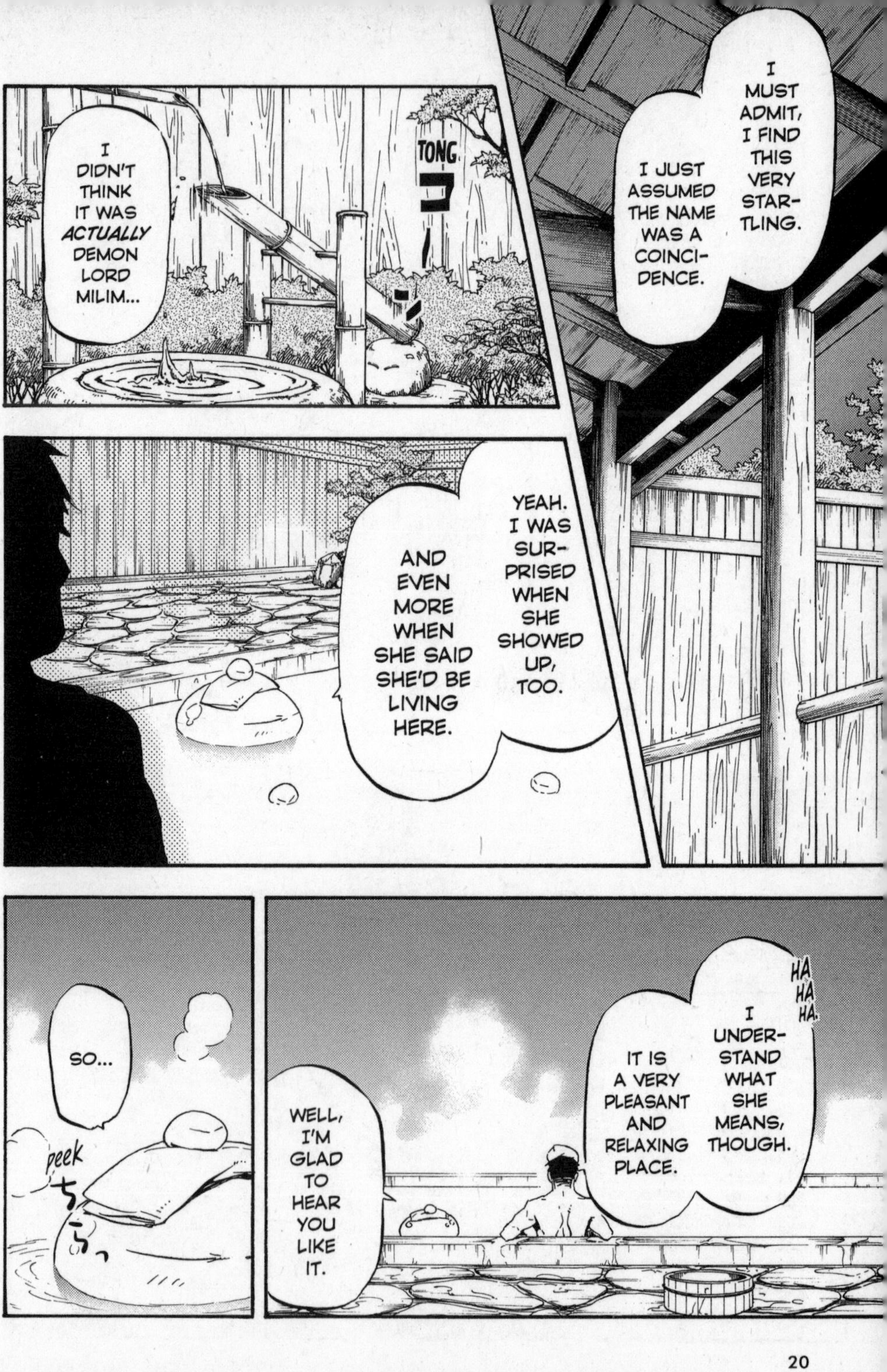
I MUST ADMIT, I FIND THIS VERY STARTLING.
I JUST ASSUMED THE NAME WAS A COINCIDENCE.
I DIDN'T THINK IT WAS *ACTUALLY* DEMON LORD MILIM...
TONG
YEAH. I WAS SURPRISED WHEN SHE SHOWED UP, TOO.
AND EVEN MORE WHEN SHE SAID SHE'D BE LIVING HERE.
HA HA HA.
I UNDERSTAND WHAT SHE MEANS, THOUGH.
IT IS A VERY PLEASANT AND RELAXING PLACE.
WELL, I'M GLAD TO HEAR YOU LIKE IT.
SO...
peek

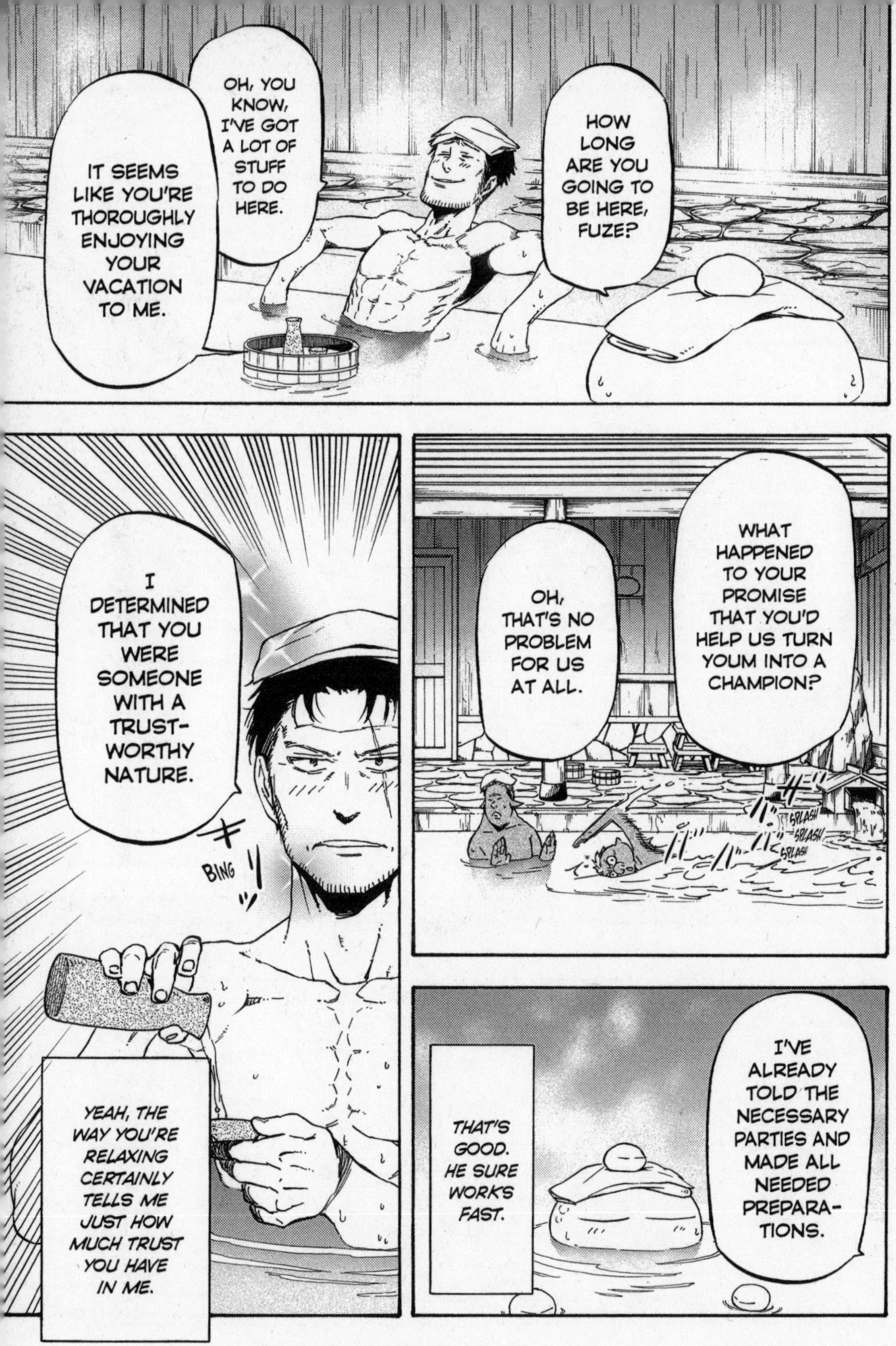
HOW LONG ARE YOU GOING TO BE HERE, FUZE?
OH, YOU KNOW, I'VE GOT A LOT OF STUFF TO DO HERE.
IT SEEMS LIKE YOU'RE THOROUGHLY ENJOYING YOUR VACATION TO ME.
WHAT HAPPENED TO YOUR PROMISE THAT YOU'D HELP US TURN YOUM INTO A CHAMPION?
OH, THAT'S NO PROBLEM FOR US AT ALL.
SPLASH
SPLASH
SPLASH
I'VE ALREADY TOLD THE NECESSARY PARTIES AND MADE ALL NEEDED PREPARATIONS.
THAT'S GOOD. HE SURE WORKS FAST.
I DETERMINED THAT YOU WERE SOMEONE WITH A TRUST-WORTHY NATURE.
BING
YEAH, THE WAY YOU'RE RELAXING CERTAINLY TELLS ME JUST HOW MUCH TRUST YOU HAVE IN ME.

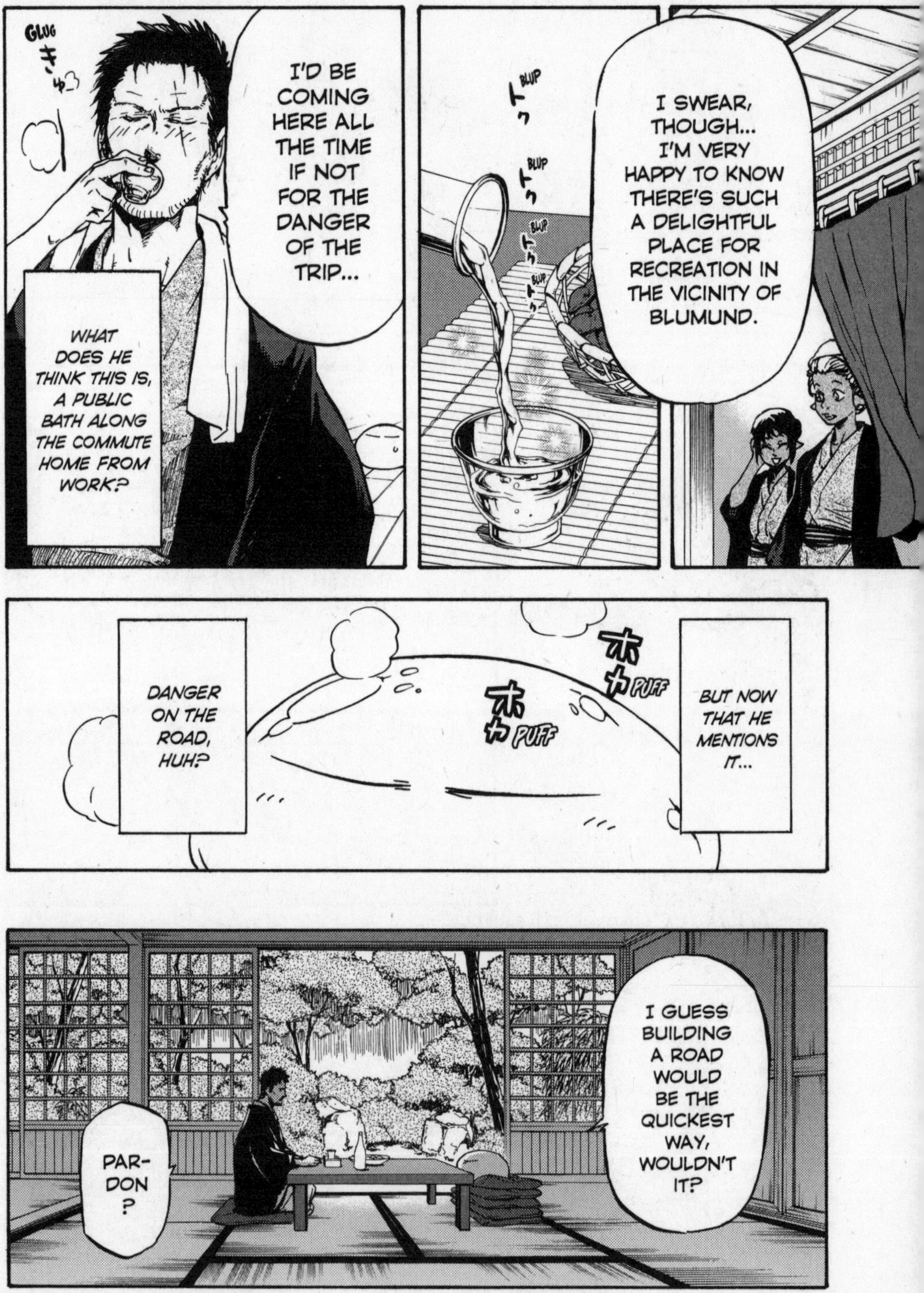

I SWEAR, THOUGH... I'M VERY HAPPY TO KNOW THERE'S SUCH A DELIGHTFUL PLACE FOR RECREATION IN THE VICINITY OF BLUMUND.
BLUP
BLUP
BLUP
BLUP
GLUG
I'D BE COMING HERE ALL THE TIME IF NOT FOR THE DANGER OF THE TRIP...
WHAT DOES HE THINK THIS IS, A PUBLIC BATH ALONG THE COMMUTE HOME FROM WORK?
BUT NOW THAT HE MENTIONS IT...
PUFF
PUFF
DANGER ON THE ROAD, HUH?
I GUESS BUILDING A ROAD WOULD BE THE QUICKEST WAY, WOULDN'T IT?
PAR-DON?

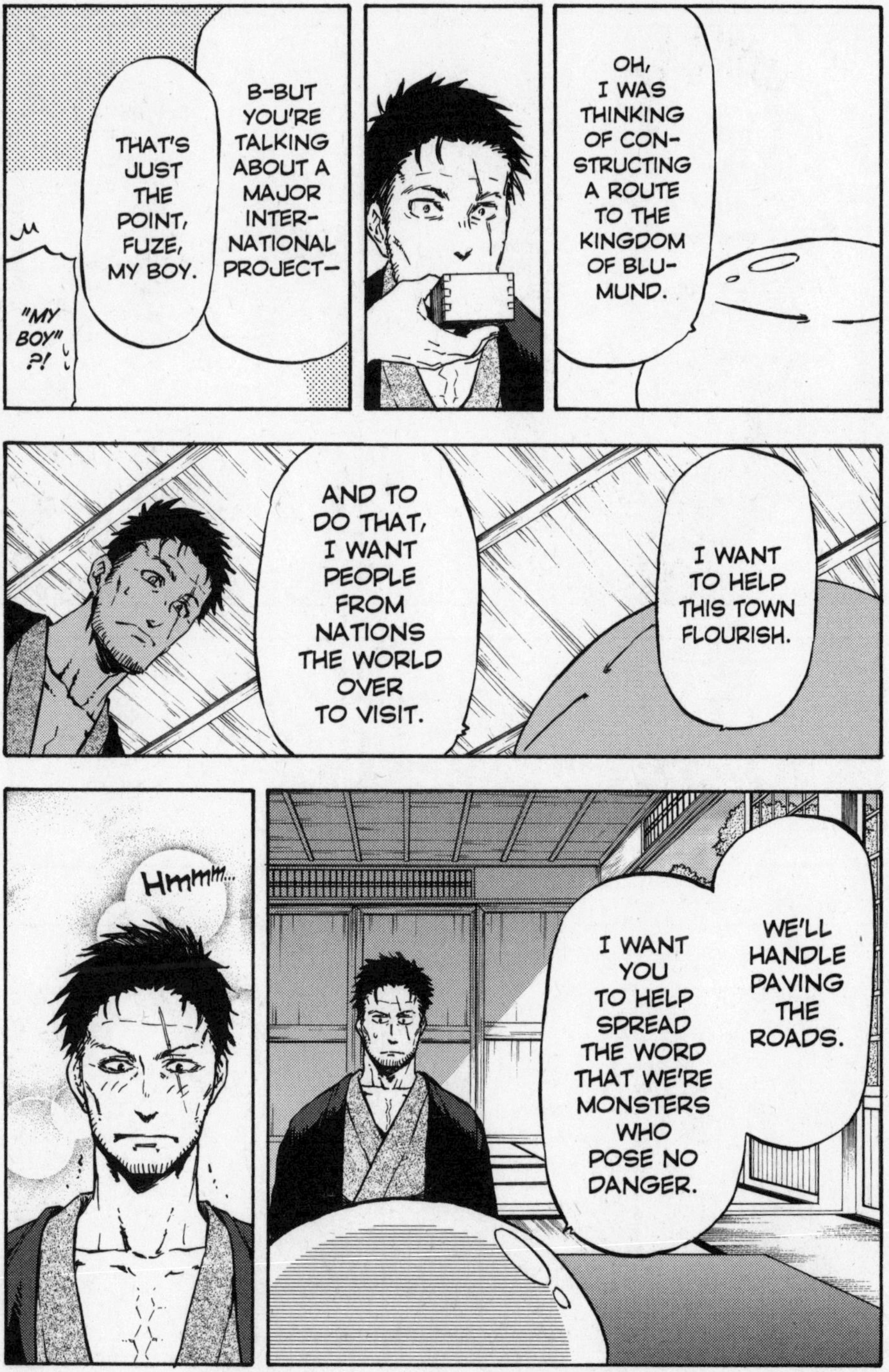
OH, I WAS THINKING OF CONSTRUCTING A ROUTE TO THE KINGDOM OF BLUMUND.
B-BUT YOU'RE TALKING ABOUT A MAJOR INTERNATIONAL PROJECT—
THAT'S JUST THE POINT, FUZE, MY BOY.
"MY BOY"?!
I WANT TO HELP THIS TOWN FLOURISH.
AND TO DO THAT, I WANT PEOPLE FROM NATIONS THE WORLD OVER TO VISIT.
WE'LL HANDLE PAVING THE ROADS.
I WANT YOU TO HELP SPREAD THE WORD THAT WE'RE MONSTERS WHO POSE NO DANGER.
Hmmm...

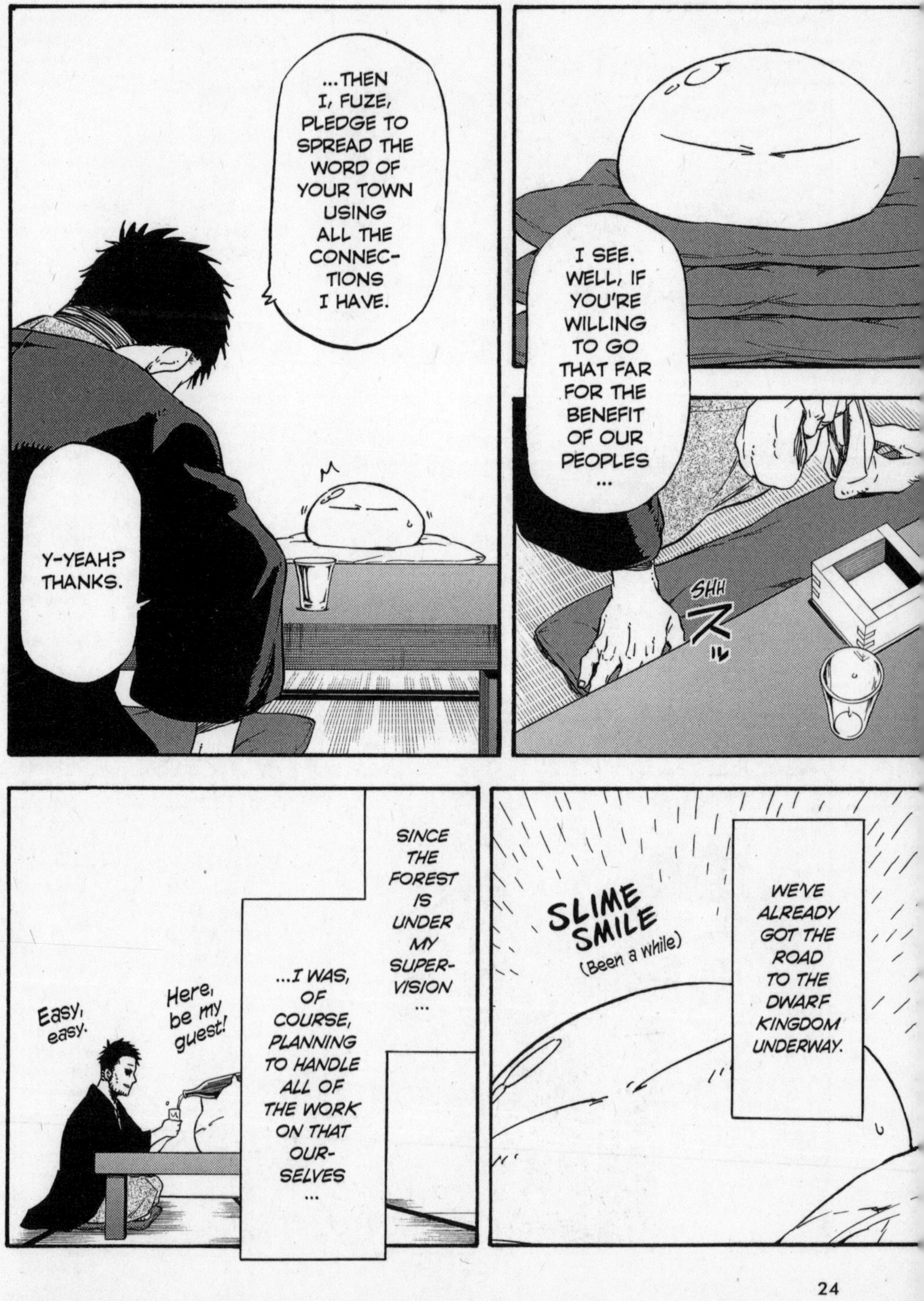
I SEE. WELL, IF YOU'RE WILLING TO GO THAT FAR FOR THE BENEFIT OF OUR PEOPLES ...
SHH
...THEN I, FUZE, PLEDGE TO SPREAD THE WORD OF YOUR TOWN USING ALL THE CONNECTIONS I HAVE.
Y-YEAH? THANKS.
WE'VE ALREADY GOT THE ROAD TO THE DWARF KINGDOM UNDERWAY.
SLIME SMILE
(Been a while)
SINCE THE FOREST IS UNDER MY SUPERVISION ...
...I WAS, OF COURSE, PLANNING TO HANDLE ALL OF THE WORK ON THAT OURSELVES ...
Here, be my guest!
Easy, easy.

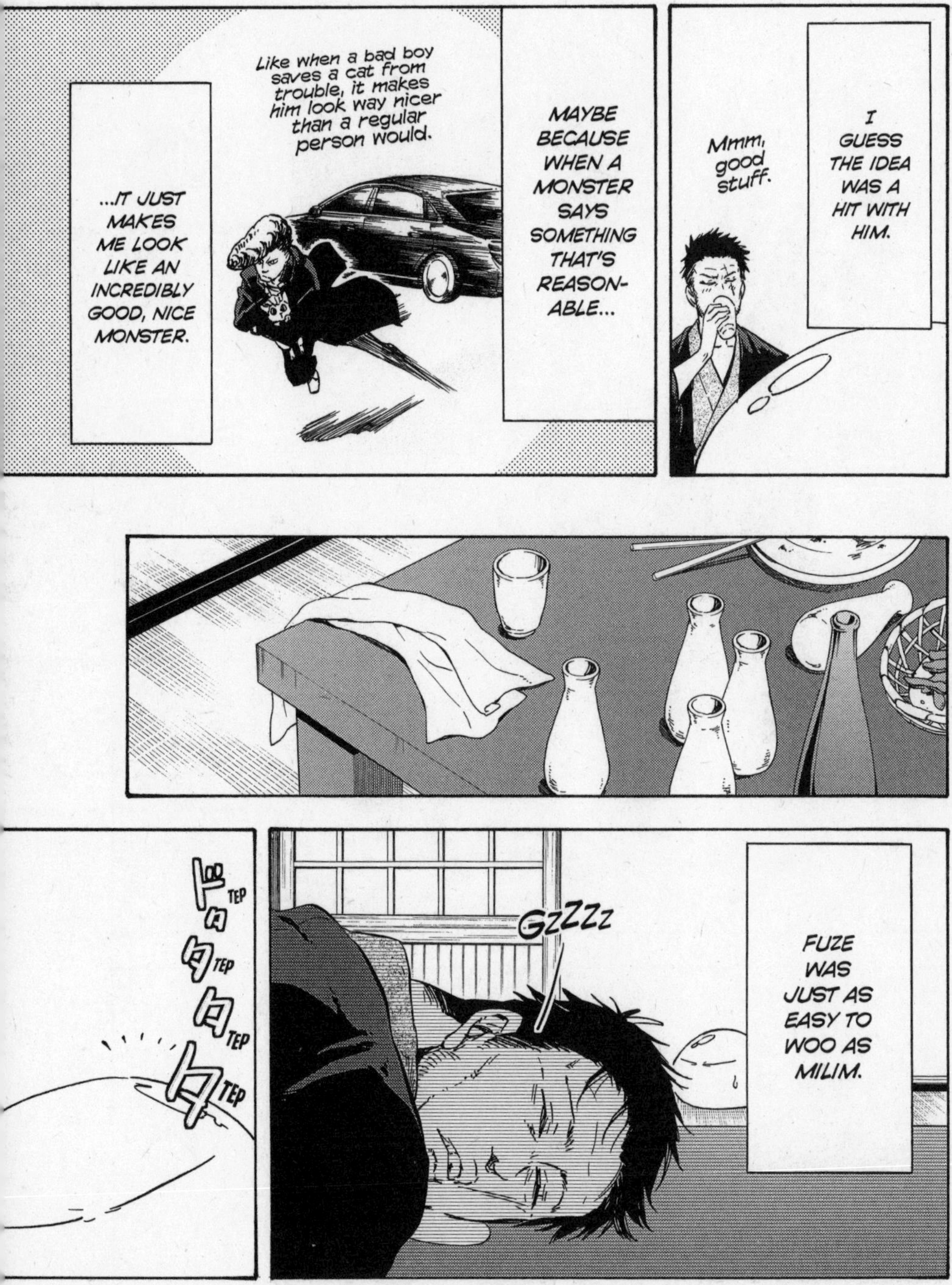
I GUESS THE IDEA WAS A HIT WITH HIM.
Mmm, good stuff.
MAYBE BECAUSE WHEN A MONSTER SAYS SOMETHING THAT'S REASON-ABLE...
Like when a bad boy saves a cat from trouble, it makes him look way nicer than a regular person would.
...IT JUST MAKES ME LOOK LIKE AN INCREDIBLY GOOD, NICE MONSTER.
FUZE WAS JUST AS EASY TO WOO AS MILIM.
GZZZz
TEP
TEP
TEP
TEP

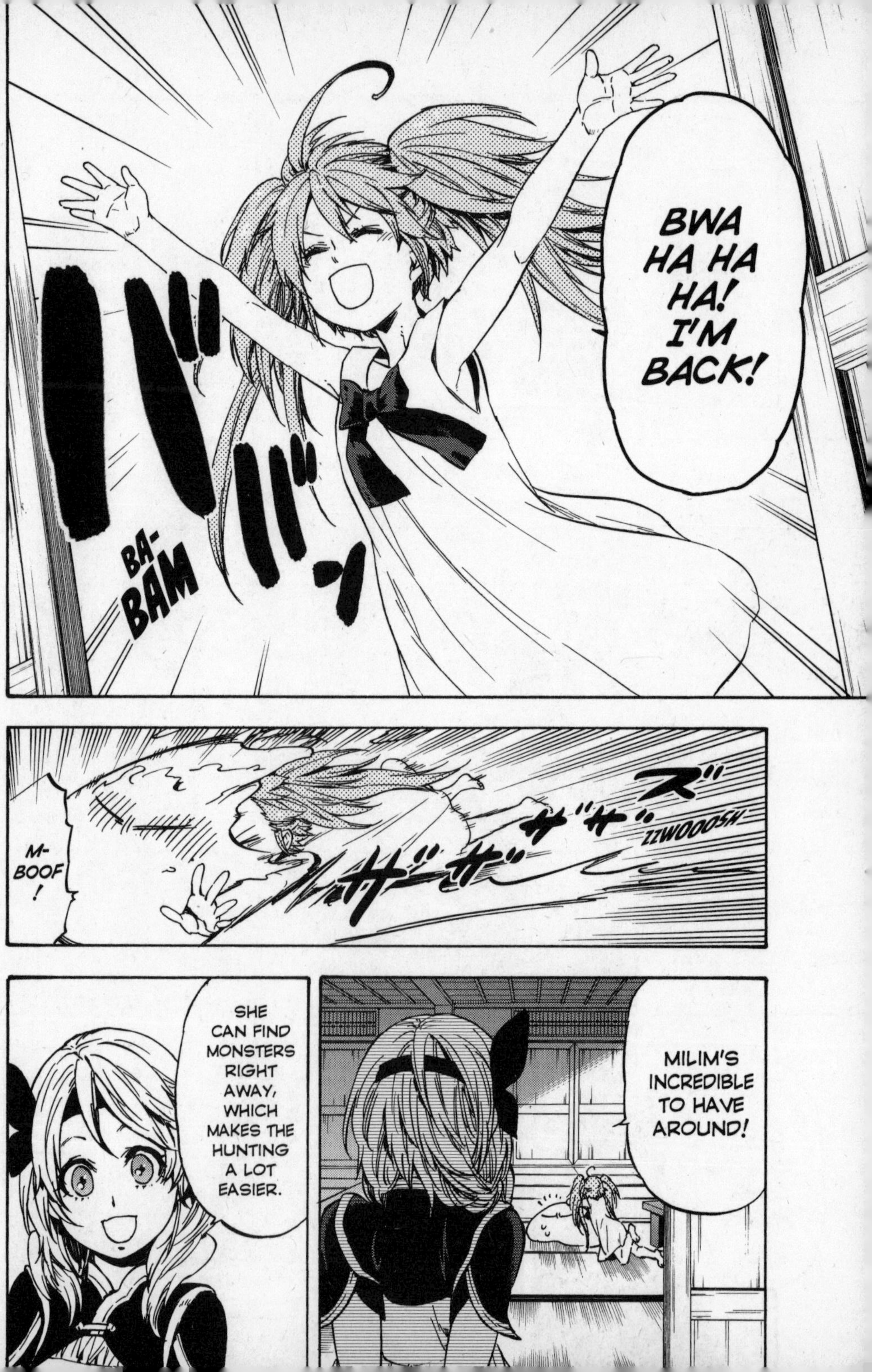
BWA HA HA HA! I'M BACK!
BA-BAM
ZZWOOOSH
M-BOOF!
MILIM'S INCREDIBLE TO HAVE AROUND!
SHE CAN FIND MONSTERS RIGHT AWAY, WHICH MAKES THE HUNTING A LOT EASIER.

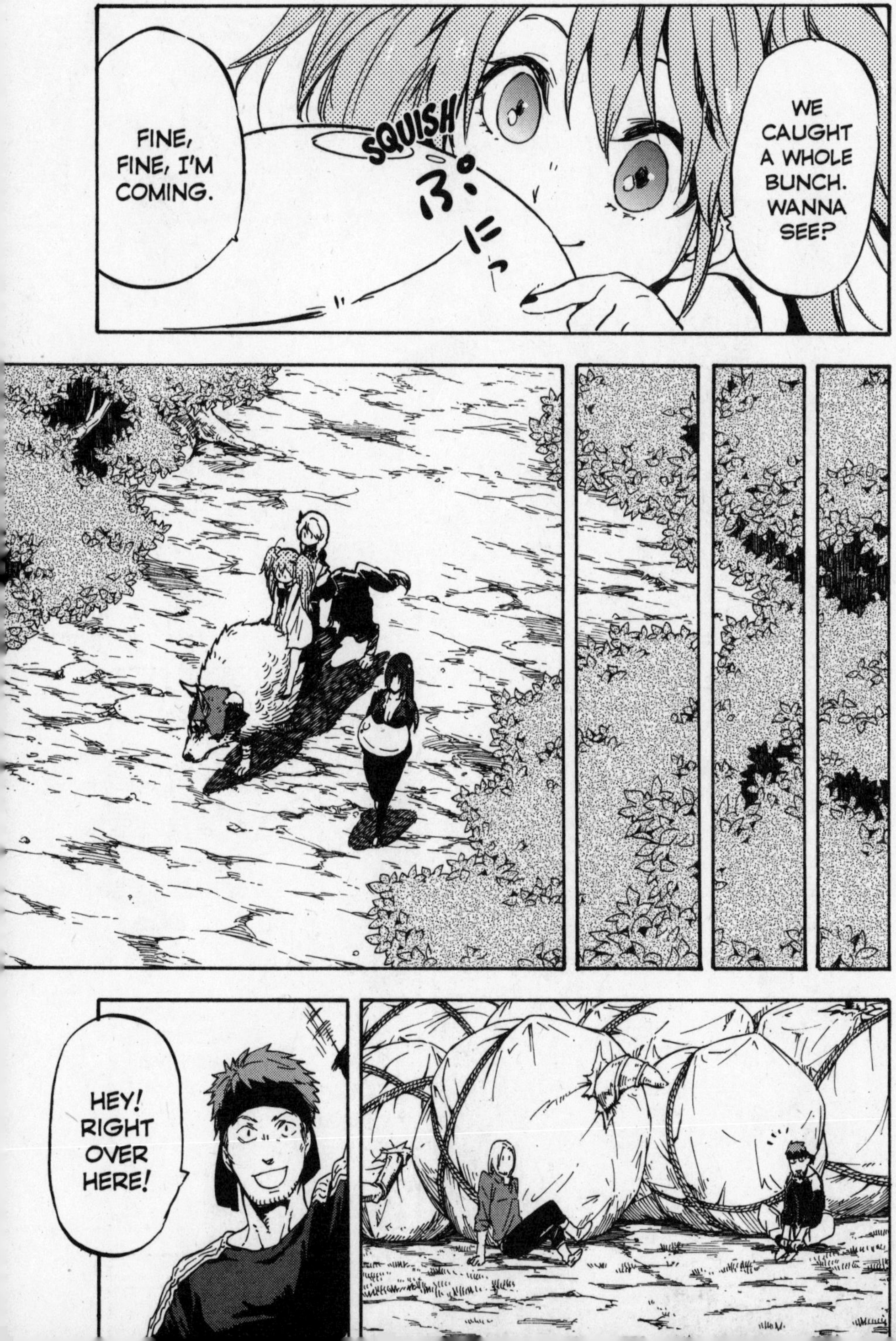
WE CAUGHT A WHOLE BUNCH. WANNA SEE?
SQUISH
ぷにっ
FINE, FINE, I'M COMING.
HEY! RIGHT OVER HERE!

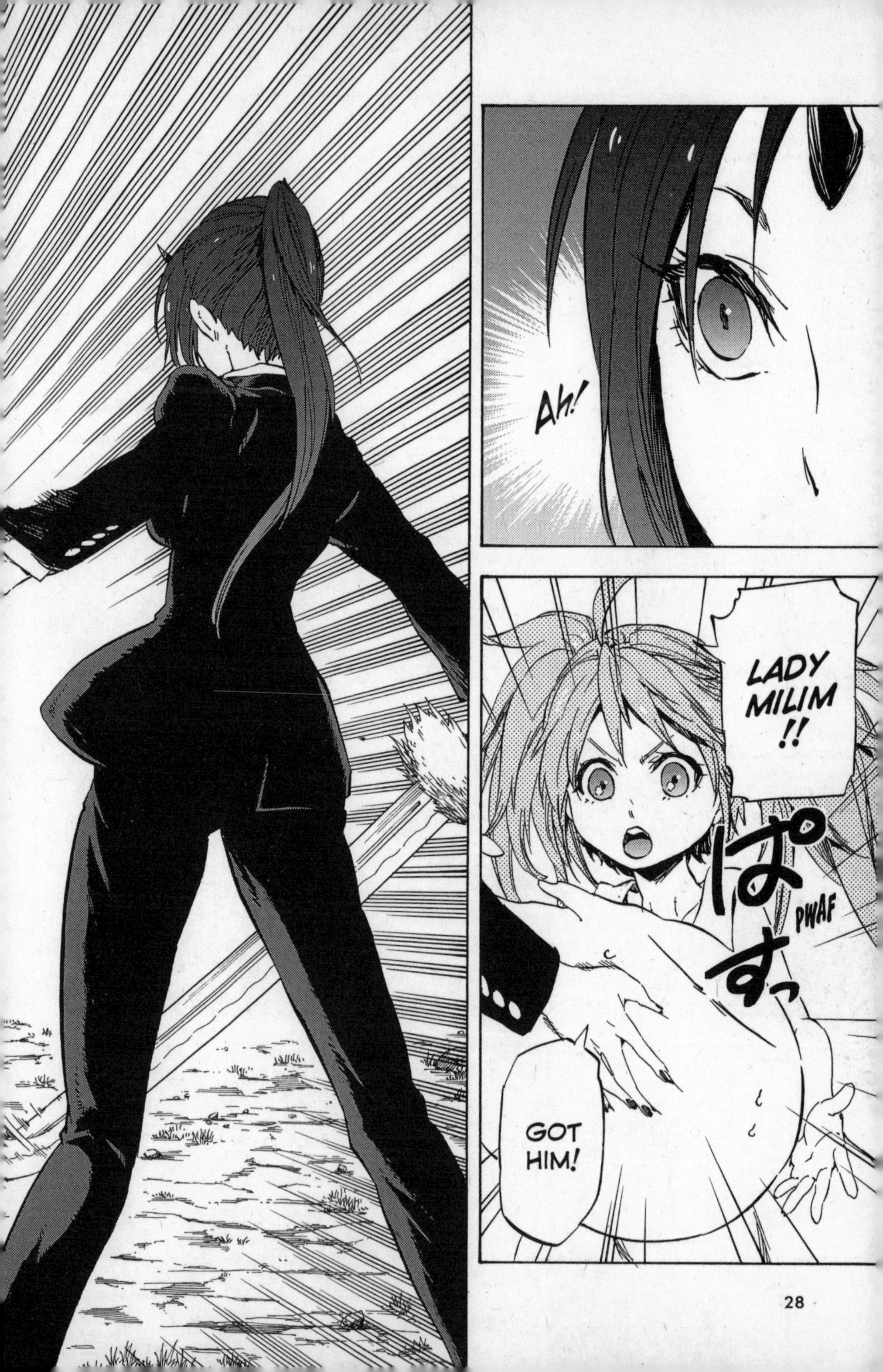
Ah!
LADY MILIM!!
ぱすっ
PWAF
GOT HIM!

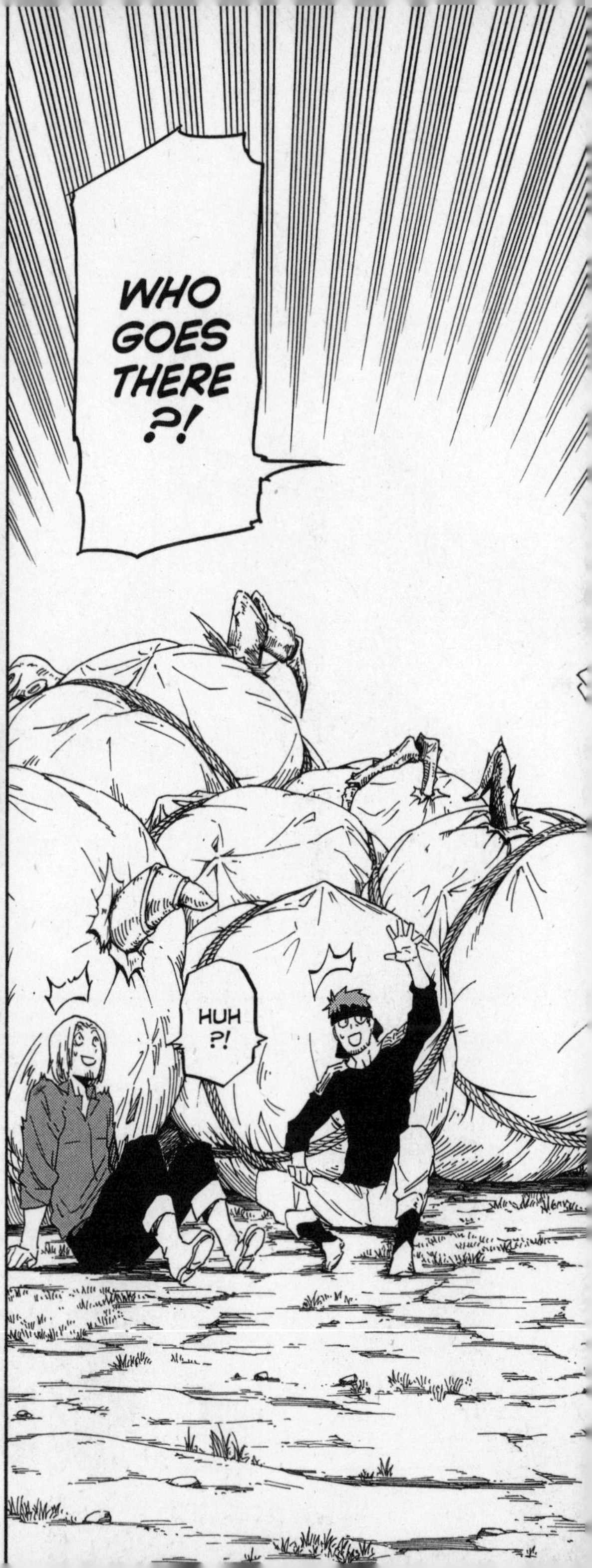
WHO GOES THERE?!
HUH?!

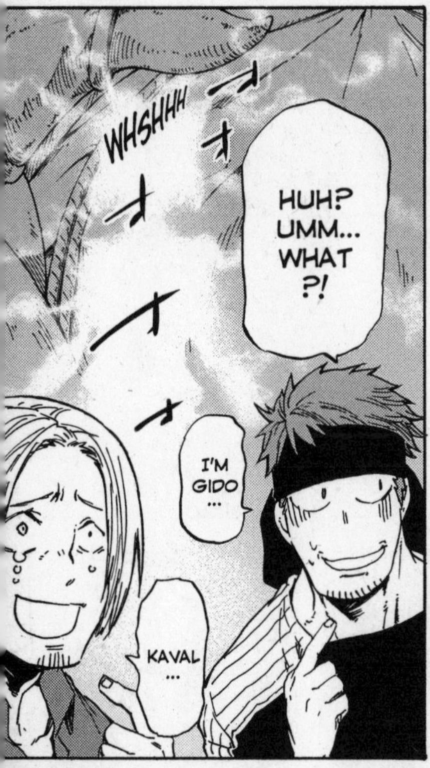
WHSHHH
HUH? UMM... WHAT?!
I'M GIDO...
KAVAL...

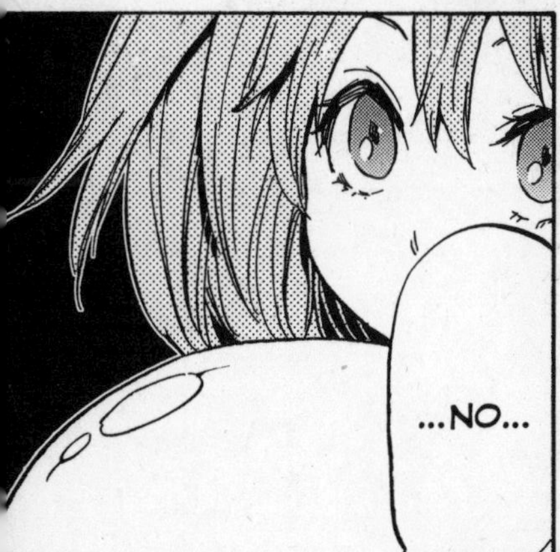
...NO...

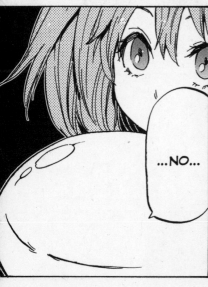

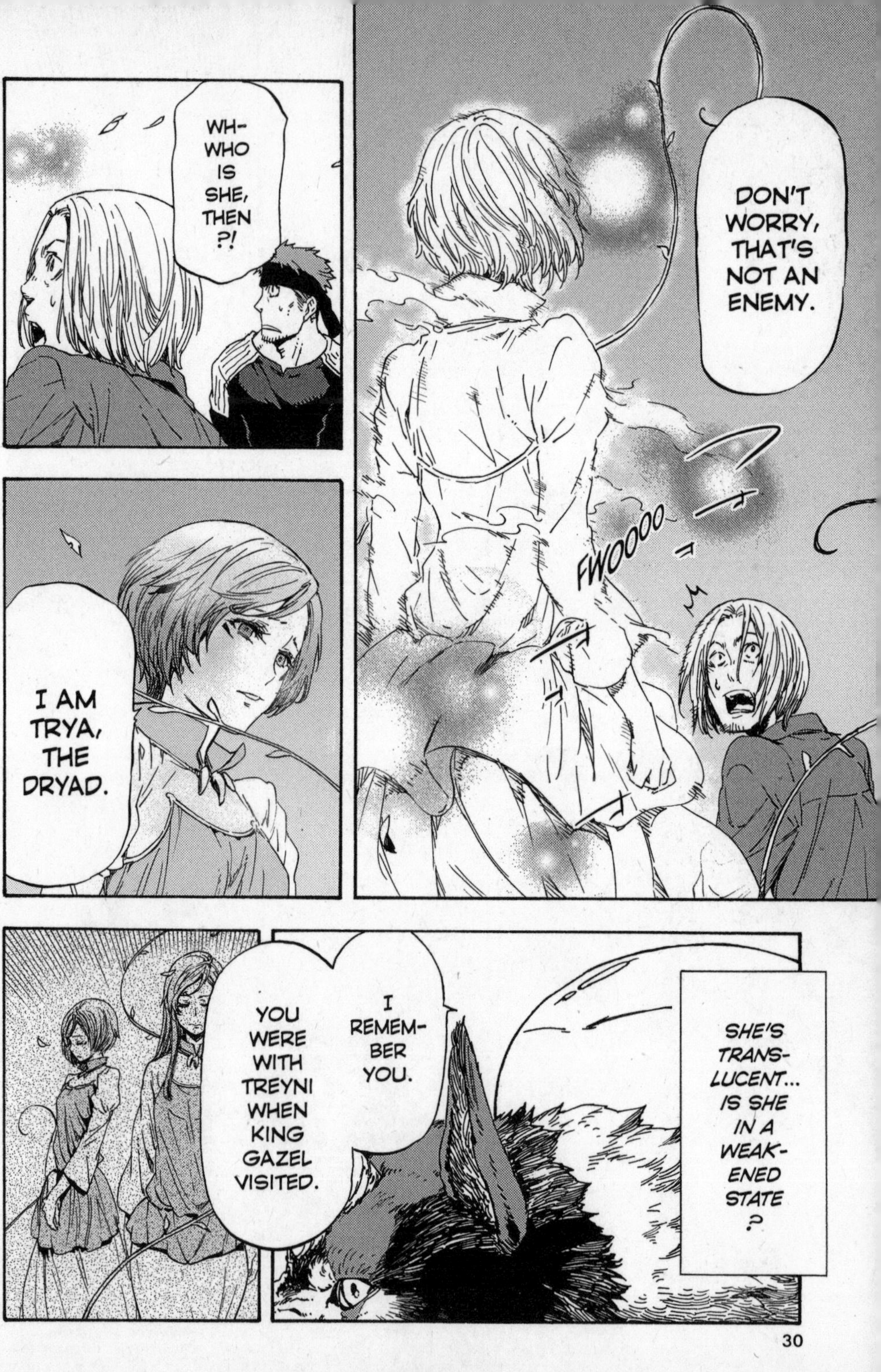
DON'T WORRY, THAT'S NOT AN ENEMY.
FWOOOO
WH-WHO IS SHE, THEN?!
I AM TRYA, THE DRYAD.
SHE'S TRANSLUCENT... IS SHE IN A WEAKENED STATE?
I REMEMBER YOU.
YOU WERE WITH TREYNI WHEN KING GAZEL VISITED.

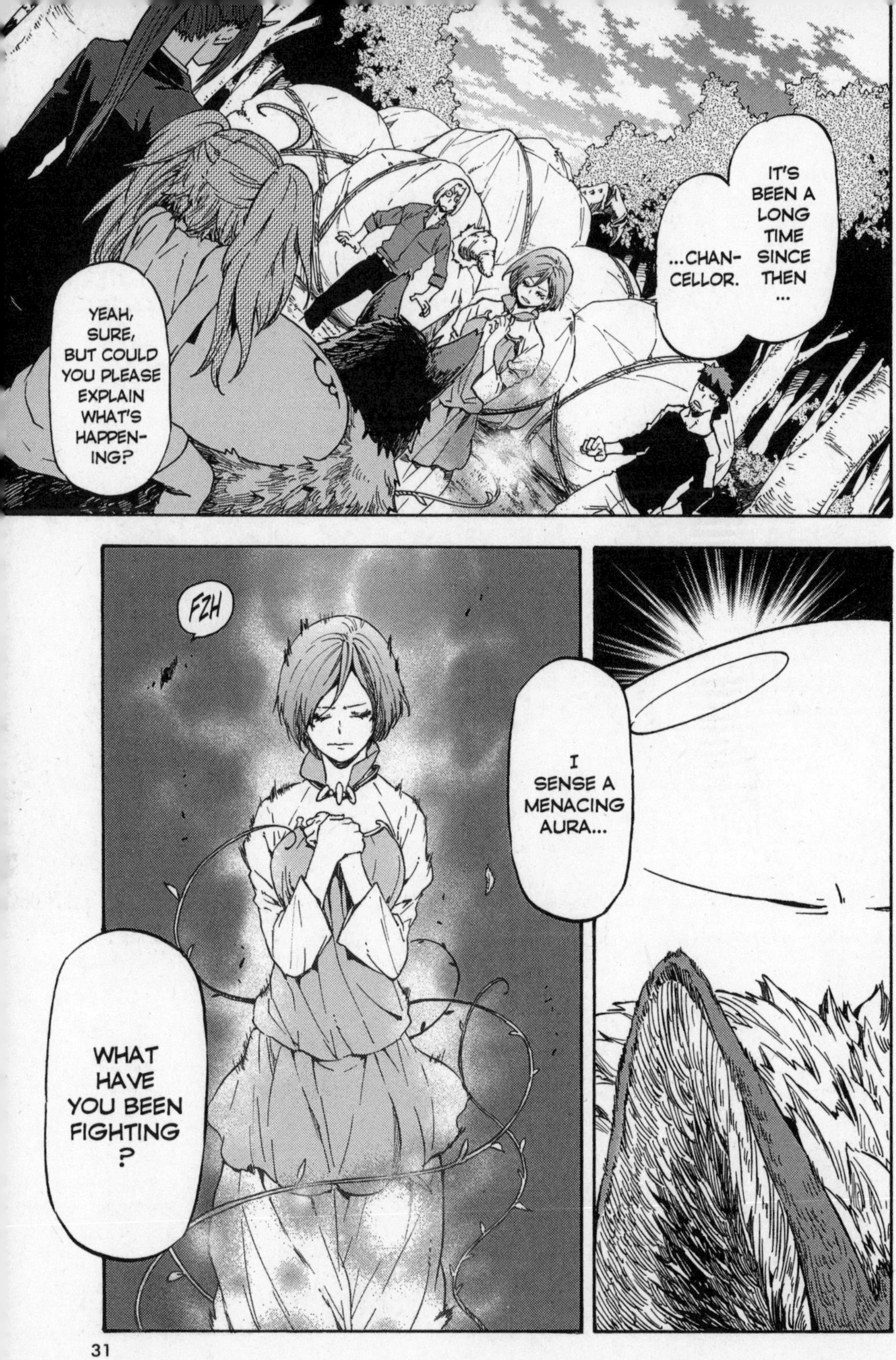
IT'S BEEN A LONG TIME SINCE THEN ...
...CHANCELLOR.
YEAH, SURE, BUT COULD YOU PLEASE EXPLAIN WHAT'S HAPPENING?
I SENSE A MENACING AURA...
FZH
WHAT HAVE YOU BEEN FIGHTING?

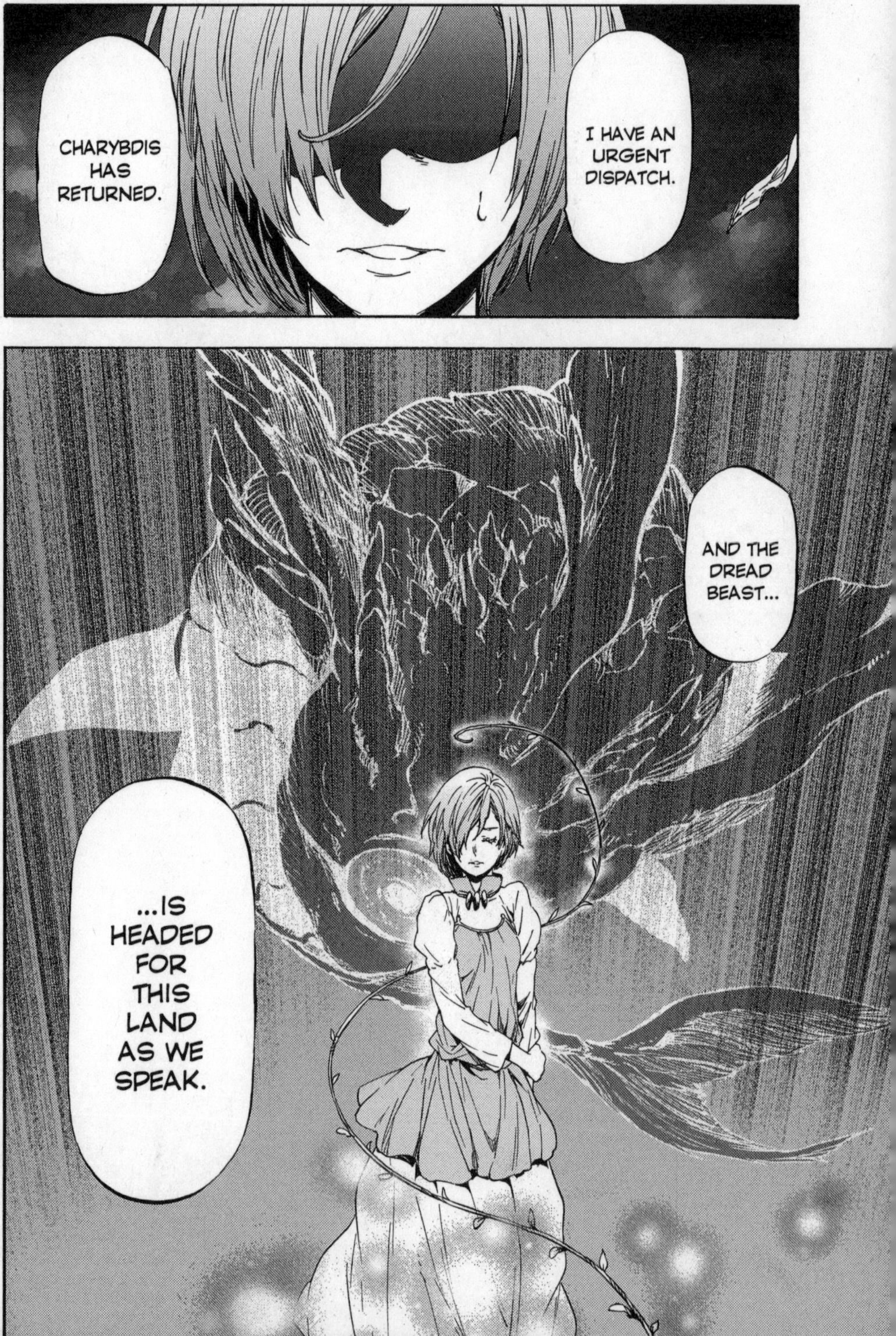
I HAVE AN URGENT DISPATCH.
CHARYBDIS HAS RETURNED.
AND THE DREAD BEAST...
...IS HEADED FOR THIS LAND AS WE SPEAK.

In the city of Tempest

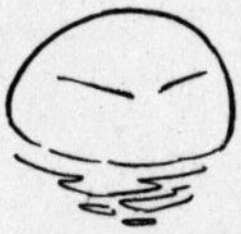

is

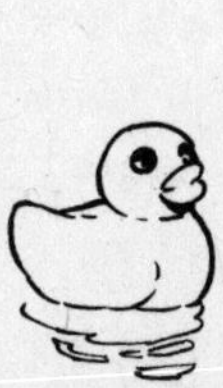

when floating in the bath

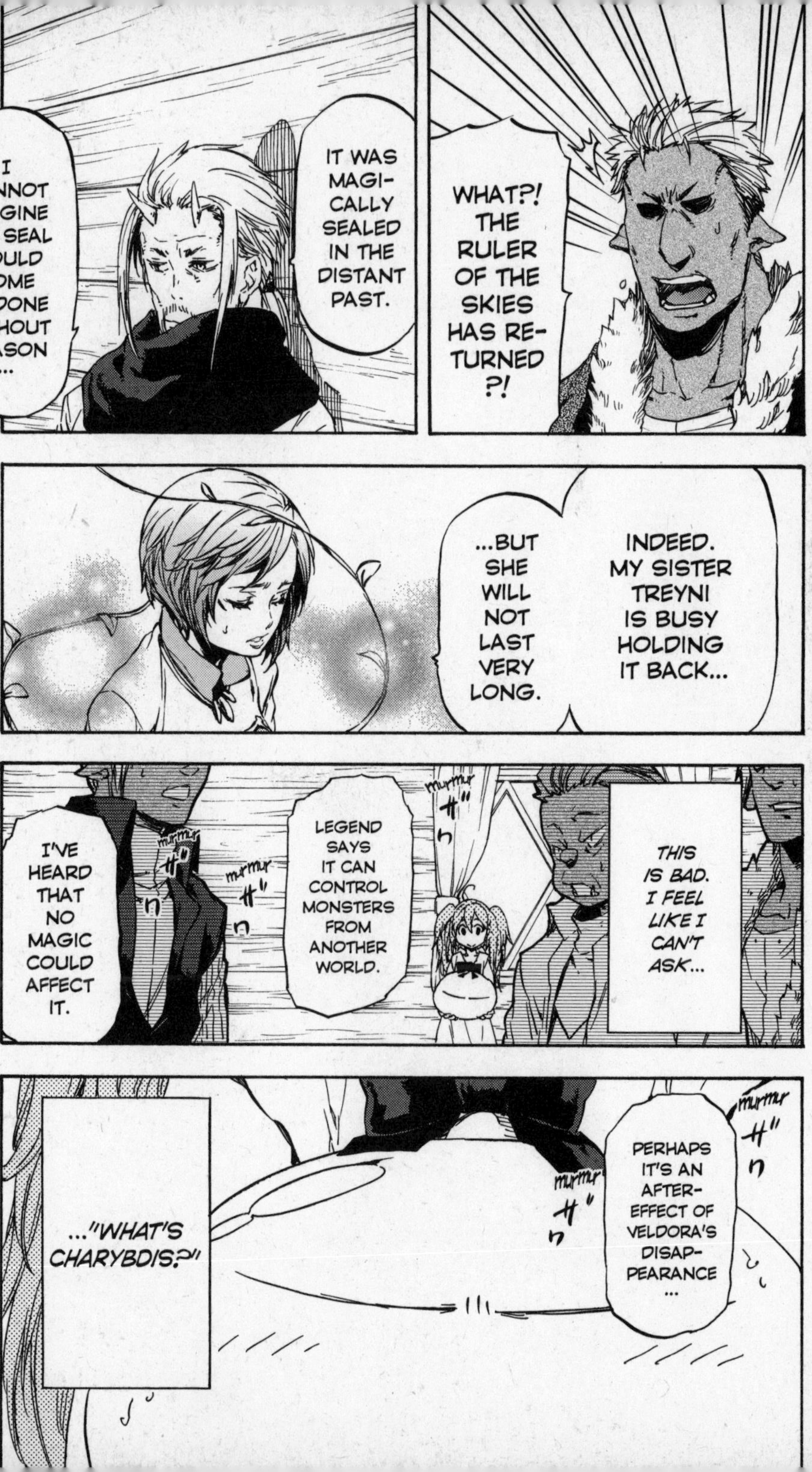
WHAT?! THE RULER OF THE SKIES HAS RE-TURNED?!
IT WAS MAGI-CALLY SEALED IN THE DISTANT PAST.
I CANNOT IMAGINE THE SEAL WOULD COME UNDONE WITHOUT REASON...
INDEED. MY SISTER TREYNI IS BUSY HOLDING IT BACK...
...BUT SHE WILL NOT LAST VERY LONG.
THIS IS BAD. I FEEL LIKE I CAN'T ASK...
murmur
LEGEND SAYS IT CAN CONTROL MONSTERS FROM ANOTHER WORLD.
murmur
murmur
I'VE HEARD THAT NO MAGIC COULD AFFECT IT.
murmur
PERHAPS IT'S AN AFTER-EFFECT OF VELDORA'S DISAP-PEARANCE...
murmur
..."WHAT'S CHARYBDIS?"

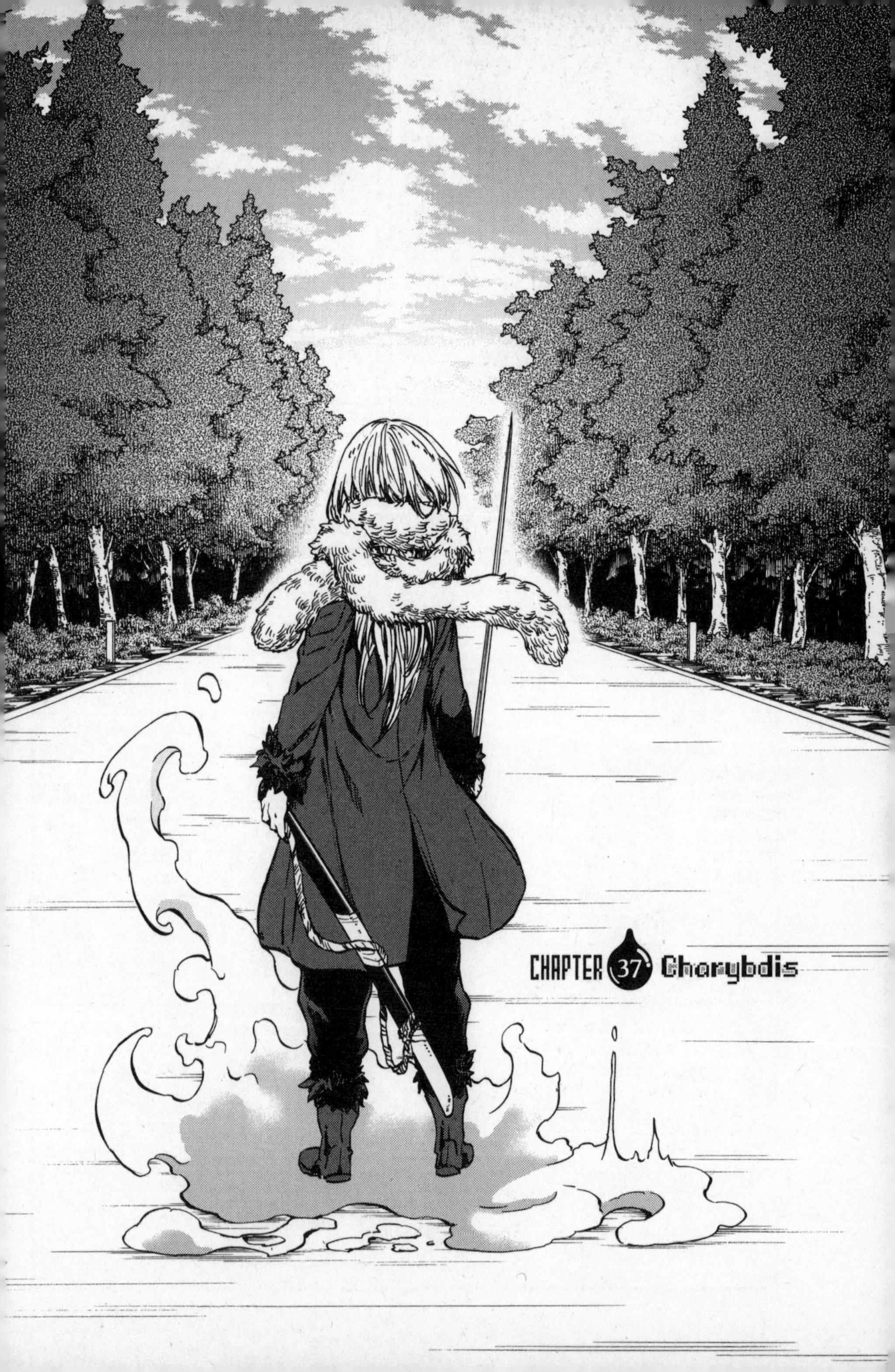
CHAPTER 37 Charybdis

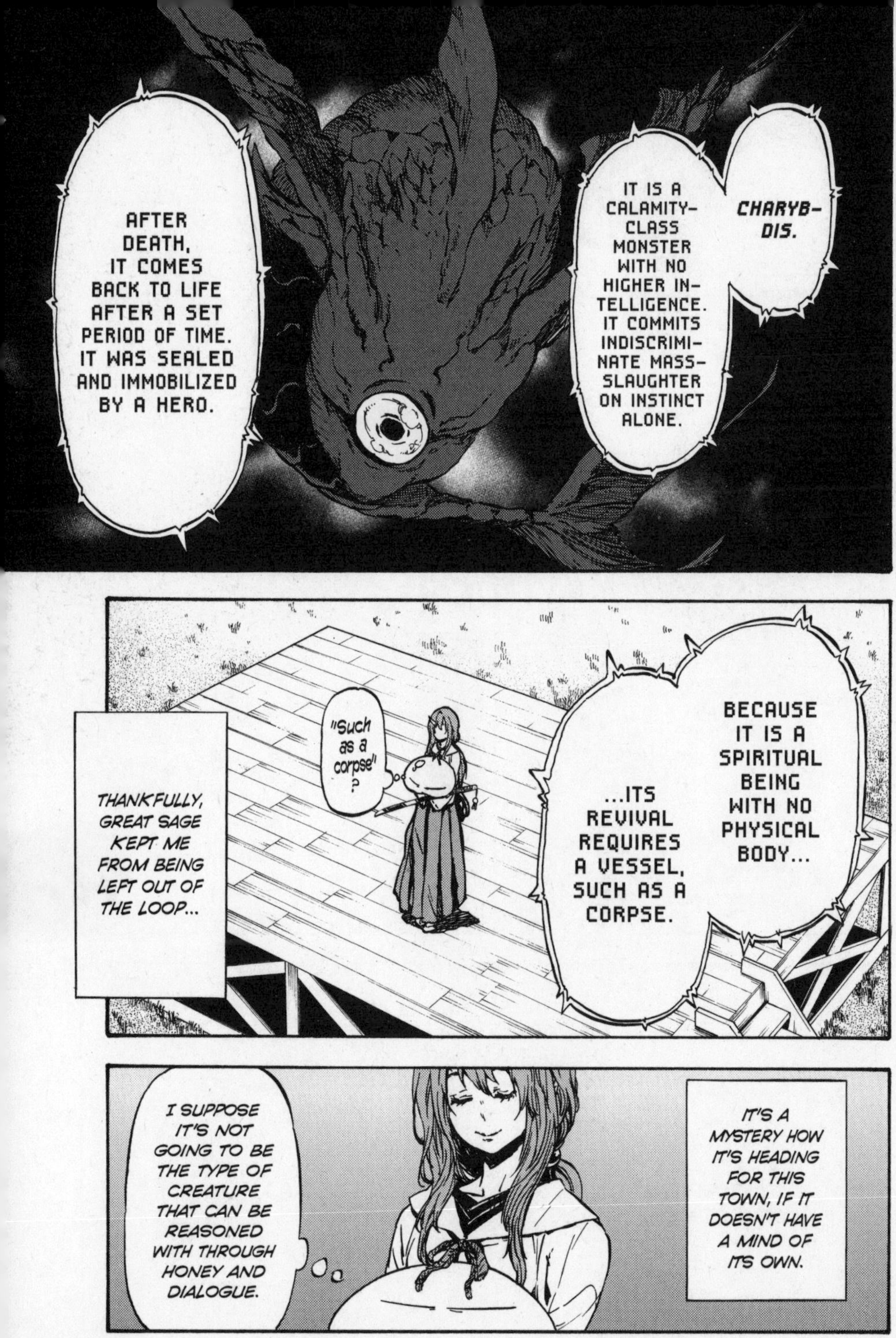
CHARYBDIS.
IT IS A CALAMITY-CLASS MONSTER WITH NO HIGHER INTELLIGENCE. IT COMMITS INDISCRIMINATE MASS-SLAUGHTER ON INSTINCT ALONE.
AFTER DEATH, IT COMES BACK TO LIFE AFTER A SET PERIOD OF TIME. IT WAS SEALED AND IMMOBILIZED BY A HERO.
BECAUSE IT IS A SPIRITUAL BEING WITH NO PHYSICAL BODY...
...ITS REVIVAL REQUIRES A VESSEL, SUCH AS A CORPSE.
"Such as a corpse"?
THANKFULLY, GREAT SAGE KEPT ME FROM BEING LEFT OUT OF THE LOOP...
IT'S A MYSTERY HOW IT'S HEADING FOR THIS TOWN, IF IT DOESN'T HAVE A MIND OF ITS OWN.
I SUPPOSE IT'S NOT GOING TO BE THE TYPE OF CREATURE THAT CAN BE REASONED WITH THROUGH HONEY AND DIALOGUE.

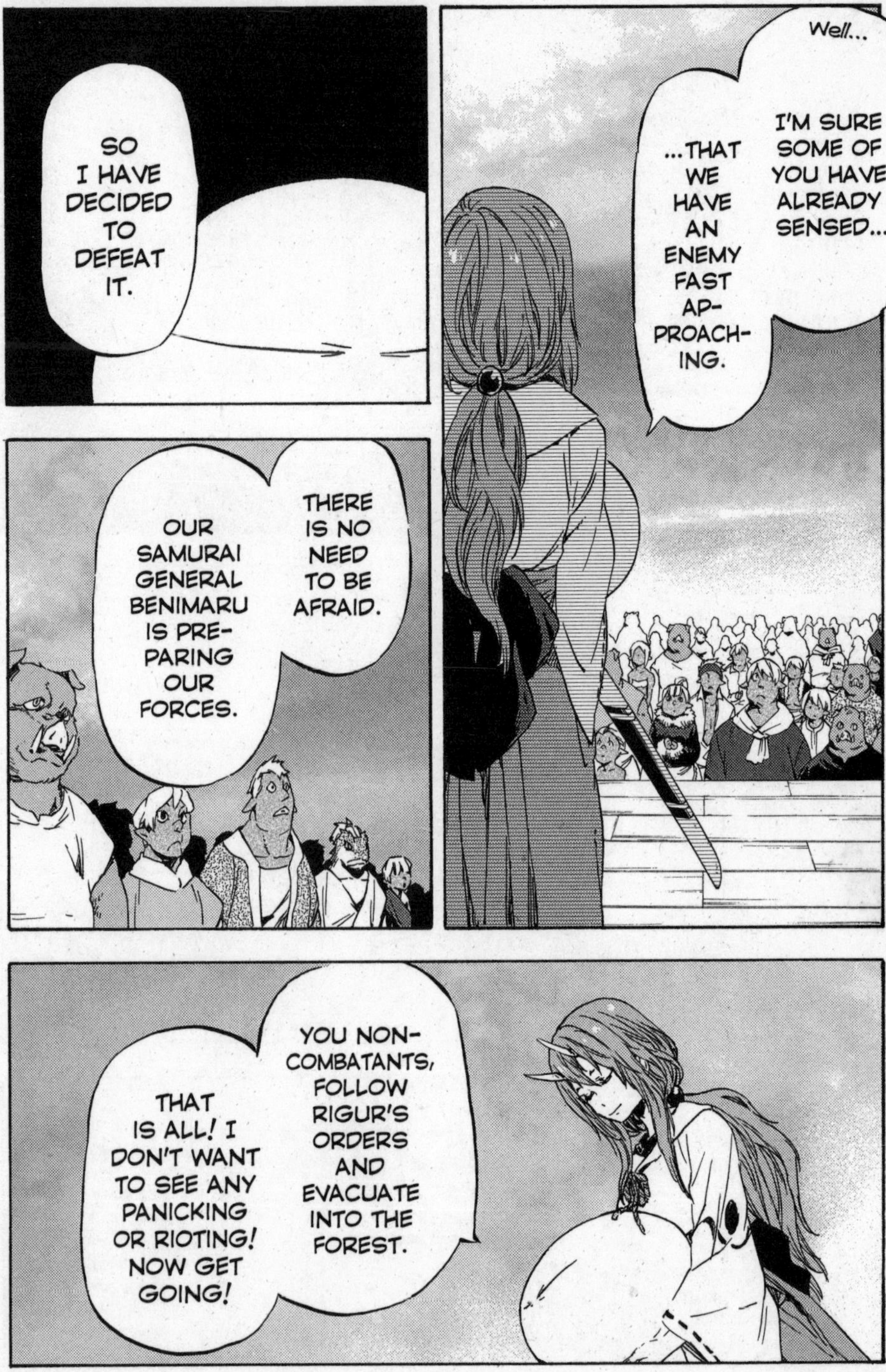
Well...
I'M SURE SOME OF YOU HAVE ALREADY SENSED...
...THAT WE HAVE AN ENEMY FAST APPROACHING.
SO I HAVE DECIDED TO DEFEAT IT.
THERE IS NO NEED TO BE AFRAID.
OUR SAMURAI GENERAL BENIMARU IS PREPARING OUR FORCES.
YOU NON-COMBATANTS, FOLLOW RIGUR'S ORDERS AND EVACUATE INTO THE FOREST.
THAT IS ALL! I DON'T WANT TO SEE ANY PANICKING OR RIOTING! NOW GET GOING!

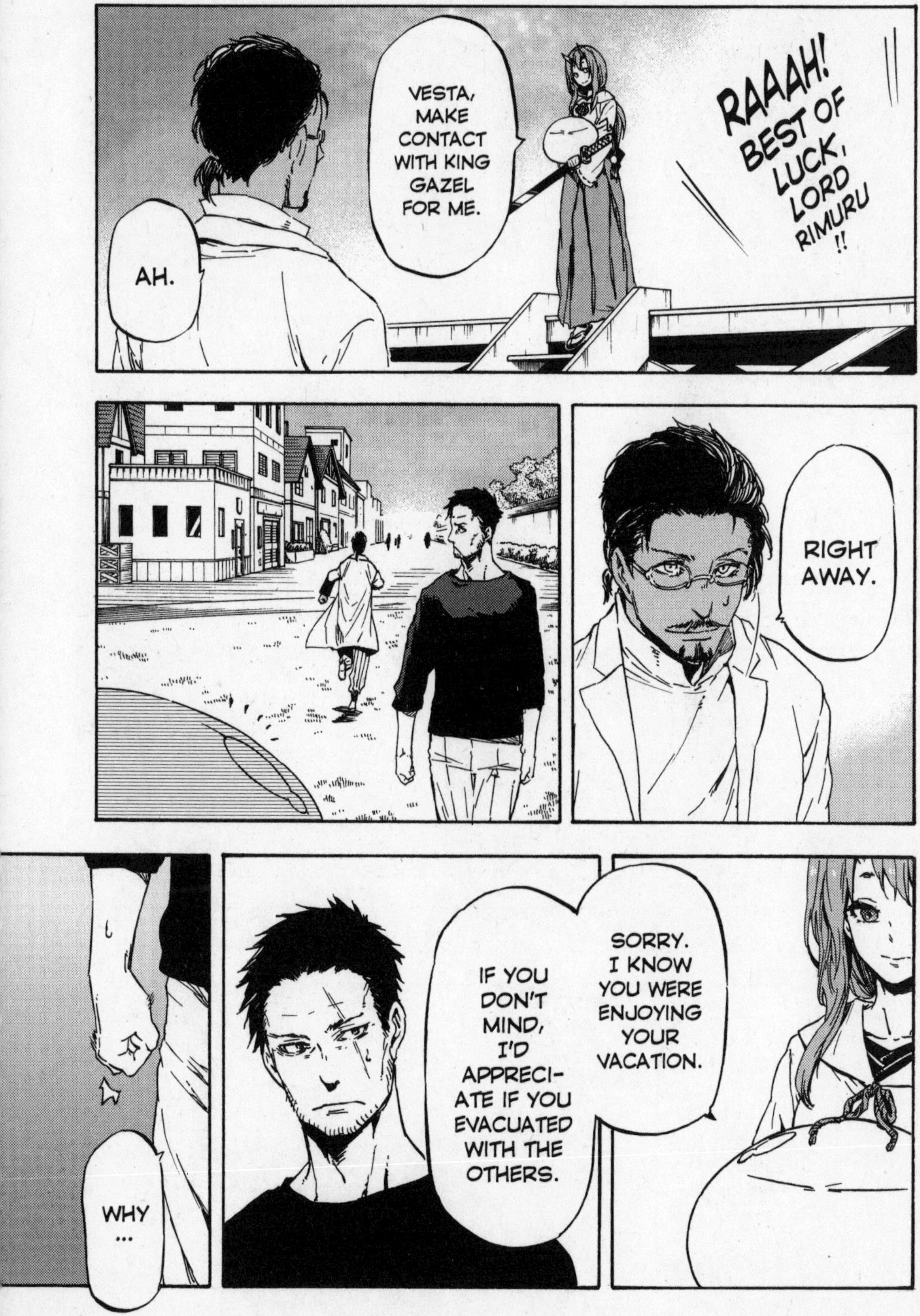
RAAAH! BEST OF LUCK, LORD RIMURU!!
VESTA, MAKE CONTACT WITH KING GAZEL FOR ME.
AH.
RIGHT AWAY.
SORRY. I KNOW YOU WERE ENJOYING YOUR VACATION.
IF YOU DON'T MIND, I'D APPRECI-ATE IF YOU EVACUATED WITH THE OTHERS.
WHY ...

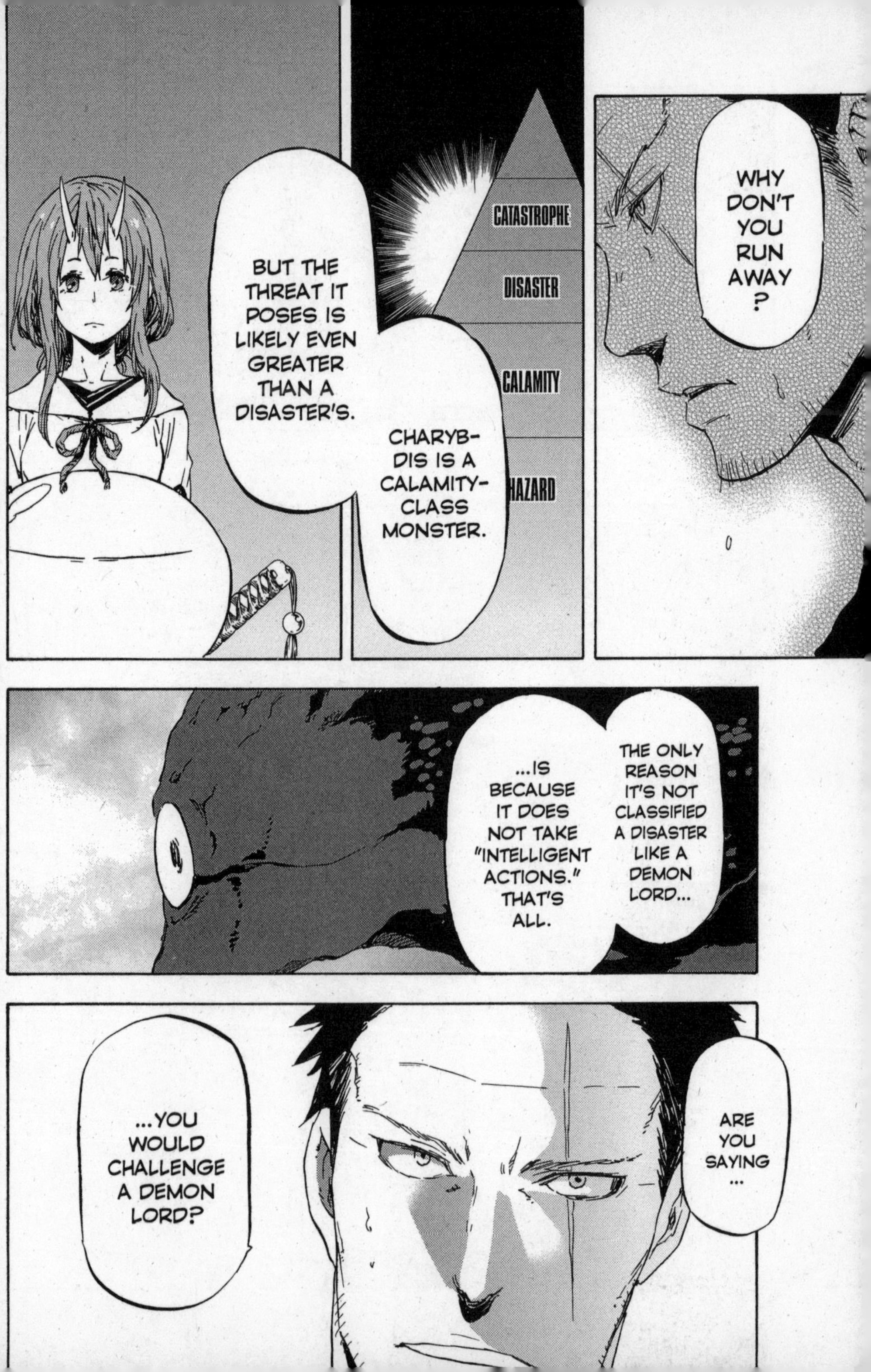
WHY DON'T YOU RUN AWAY?
CATASTROPHE
DISASTER
CALAMITY
HAZARD
CHARYB-DIS IS A CALAMITY-CLASS MONSTER.
BUT THE THREAT IT POSES IS LIKELY EVEN GREATER THAN A DISASTER'S.
THE ONLY REASON IT'S NOT CLASSIFIED A DISASTER LIKE A DEMON LORD...
...IS BECAUSE IT DOES NOT TAKE "INTELLIGENT ACTIONS." THAT'S ALL.
ARE YOU SAYING...
...YOU WOULD CHALLENGE A DEMON LORD?

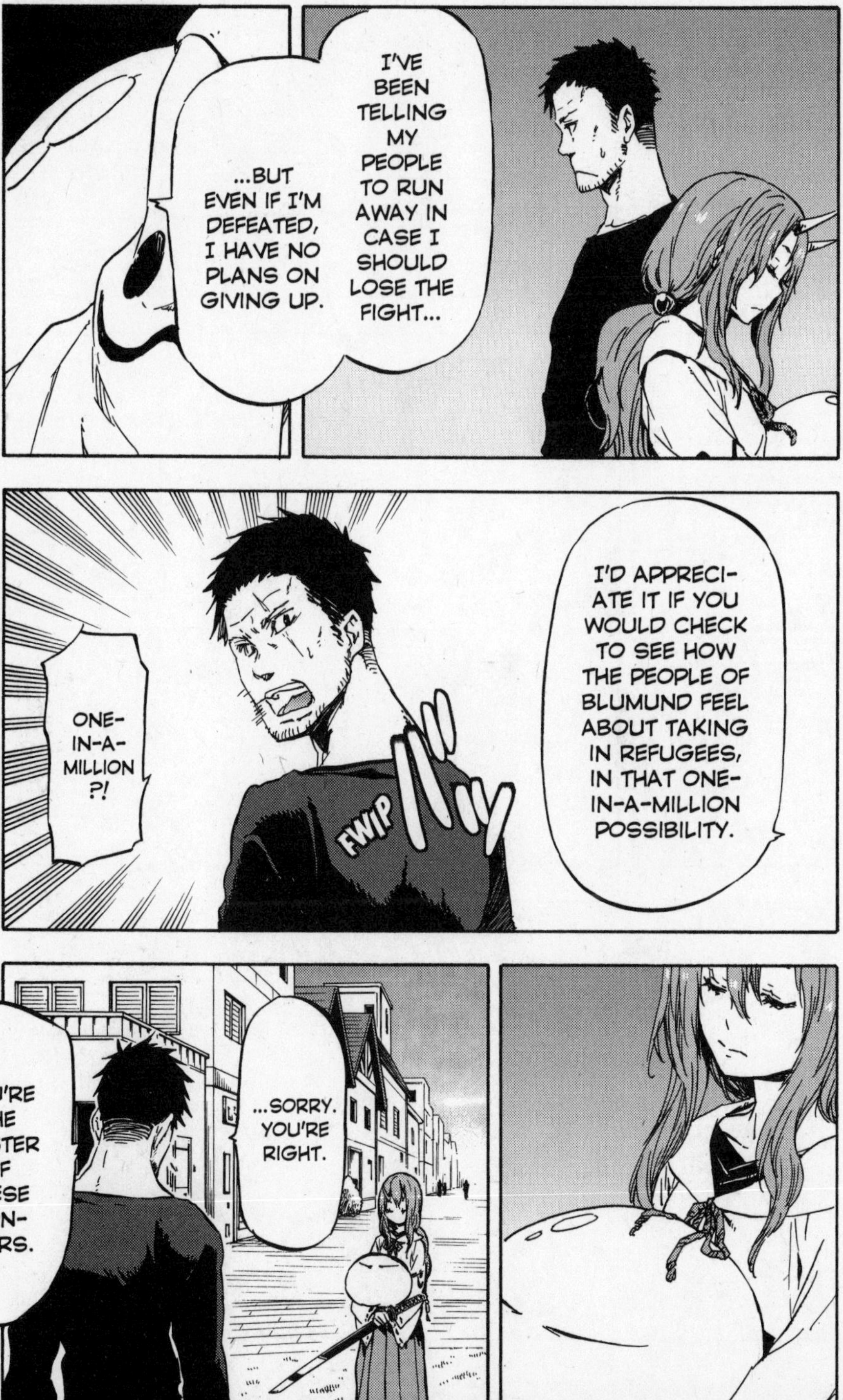
I'VE BEEN TELLING MY PEOPLE TO RUN AWAY IN CASE I SHOULD LOSE THE FIGHT...
...BUT EVEN IF I'M DEFEATED, I HAVE NO PLANS ON GIVING UP.
I'D APPRECIATE IT IF YOU WOULD CHECK TO SEE HOW THE PEOPLE OF BLUMUND FEEL ABOUT TAKING IN REFUGEES, IN THAT ONE-IN-A-MILLION POSSIBILITY.
ONE-IN-A-MILLION?!
FWIP
...SORRY. YOU'RE RIGHT.
YOU'RE THE MASTER OF THESE MONSTERS.

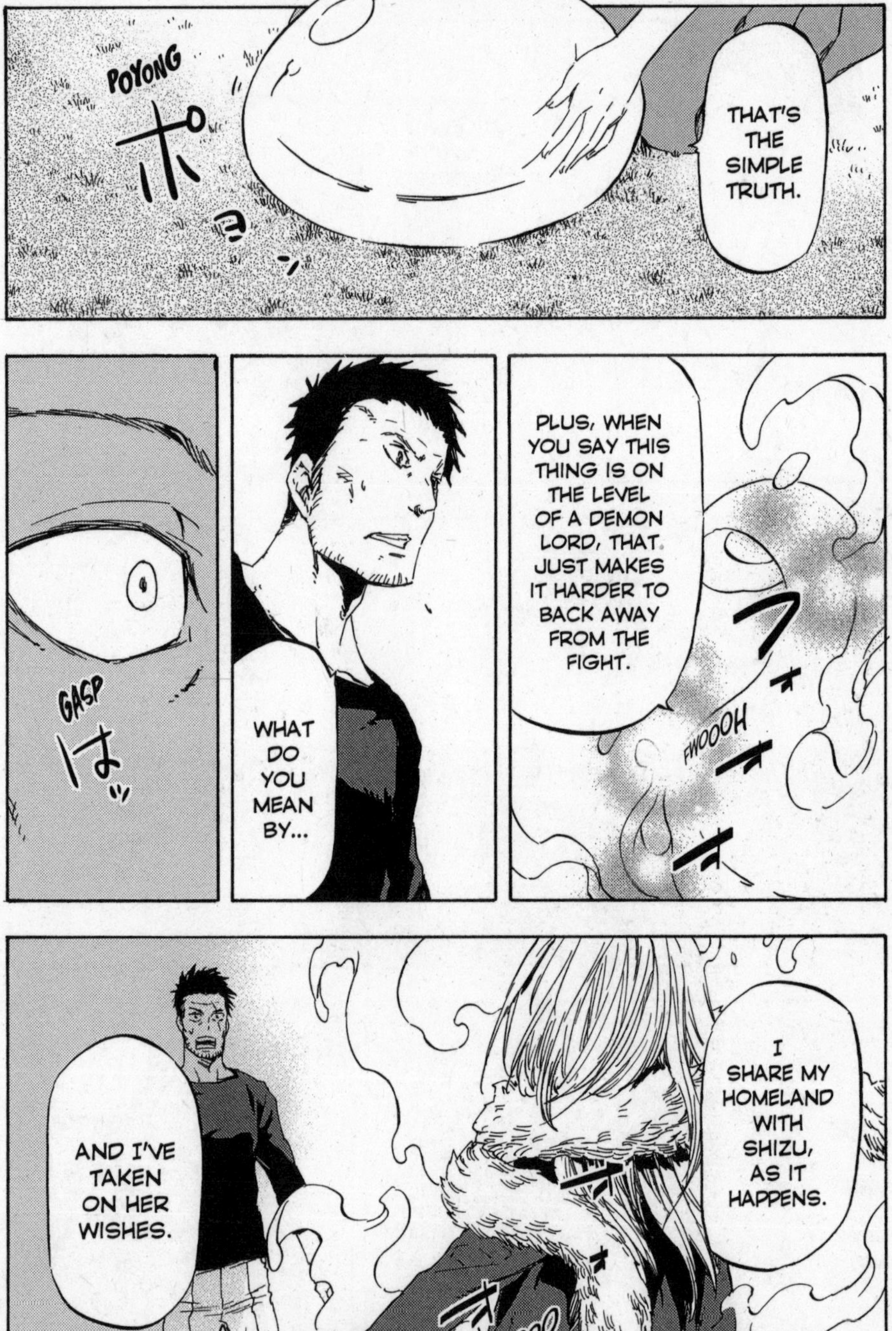
POYONG
THAT'S THE SIMPLE TRUTH.
PLUS, WHEN YOU SAY THIS THING IS ON THE LEVEL OF A DEMON LORD, THAT JUST MAKES IT HARDER TO BACK AWAY FROM THE FIGHT.
FWOOOH
WHAT DO YOU MEAN BY...
GASP
I SHARE MY HOMELAND WITH SHIZU, AS IT HAPPENS.
FWOOO
AND I'VE TAKEN ON HER WISHES.

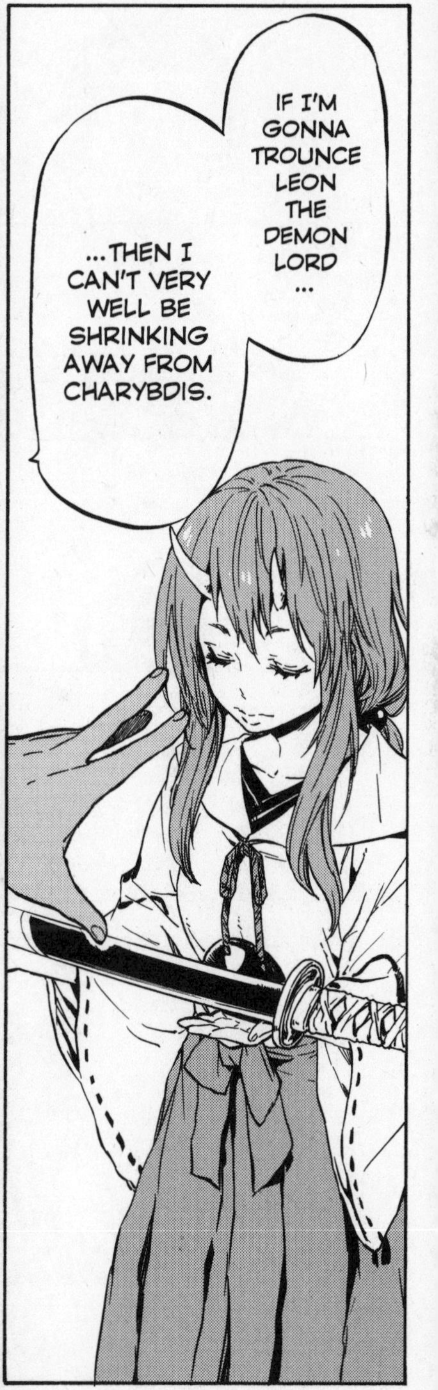
IF I'M GONNA TROUNCE LEON THE DEMON LORD ...
...THEN I CAN'T VERY WELL BE SHRINKING AWAY FROM CHARYBDIS.

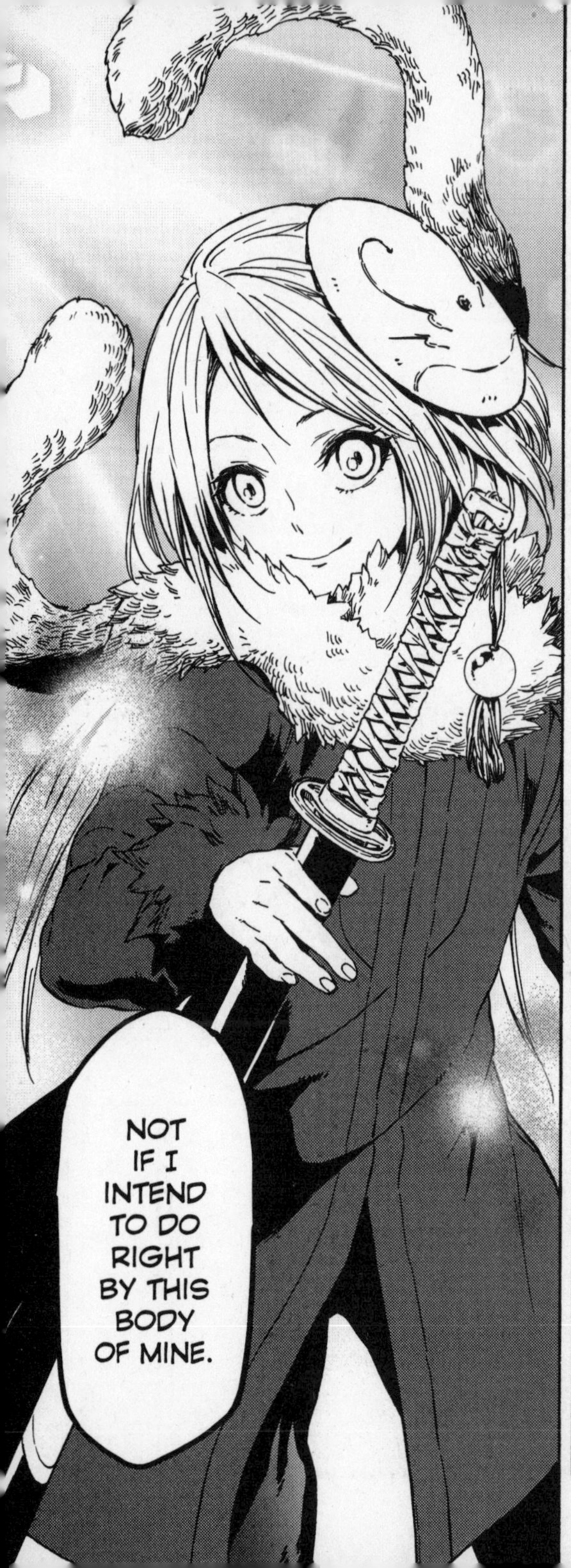
NOT IF I INTEND TO DO RIGHT BY THIS BODY OF MINE.

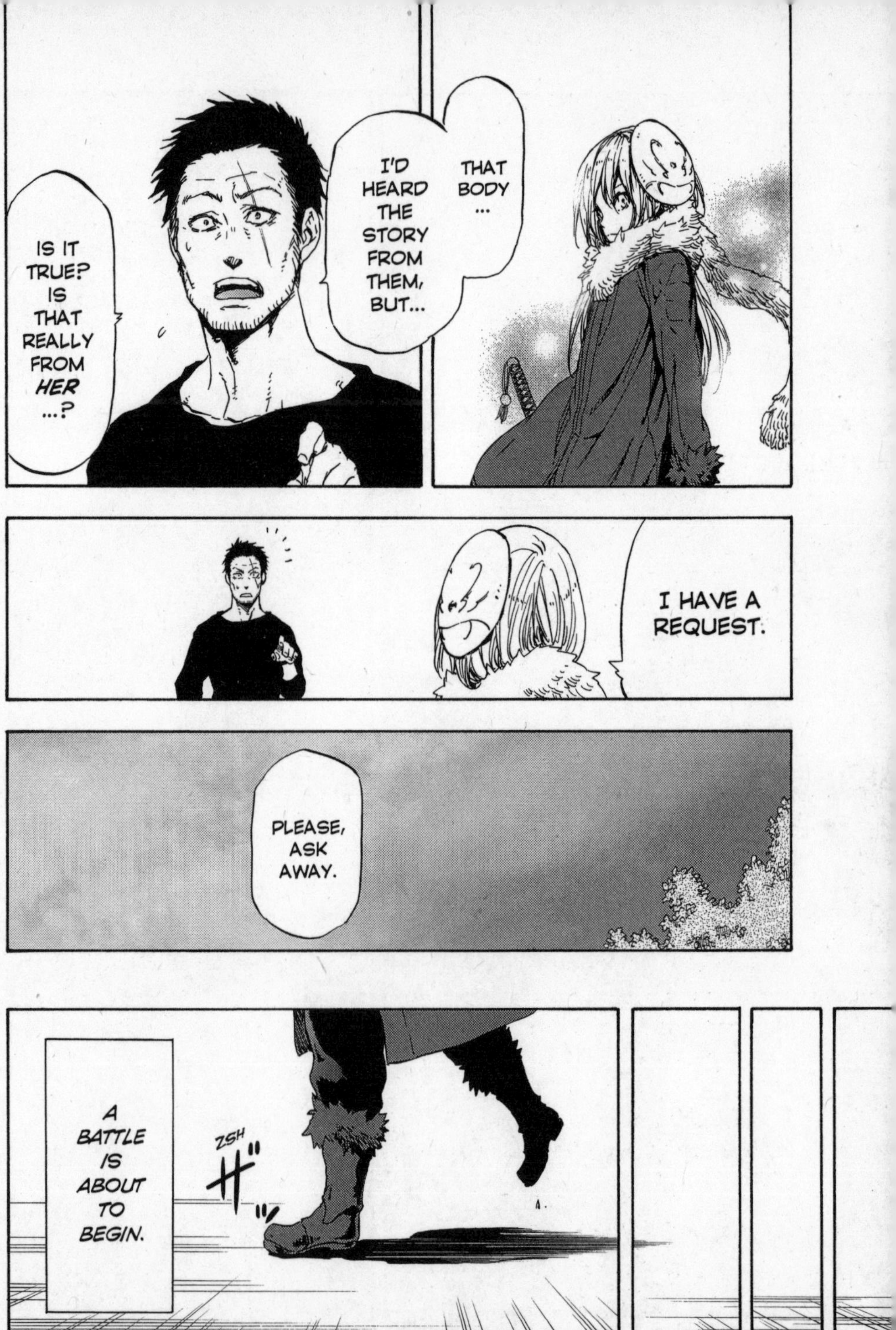
THAT BODY ...
I'D HEARD THE STORY FROM THEM, BUT...
IS IT TRUE? IS THAT REALLY FROM *HER* ...?
I HAVE A REQUEST.
PLEASE, ASK AWAY.
ZSH
A BATTLE IS ABOUT TO BEGIN.

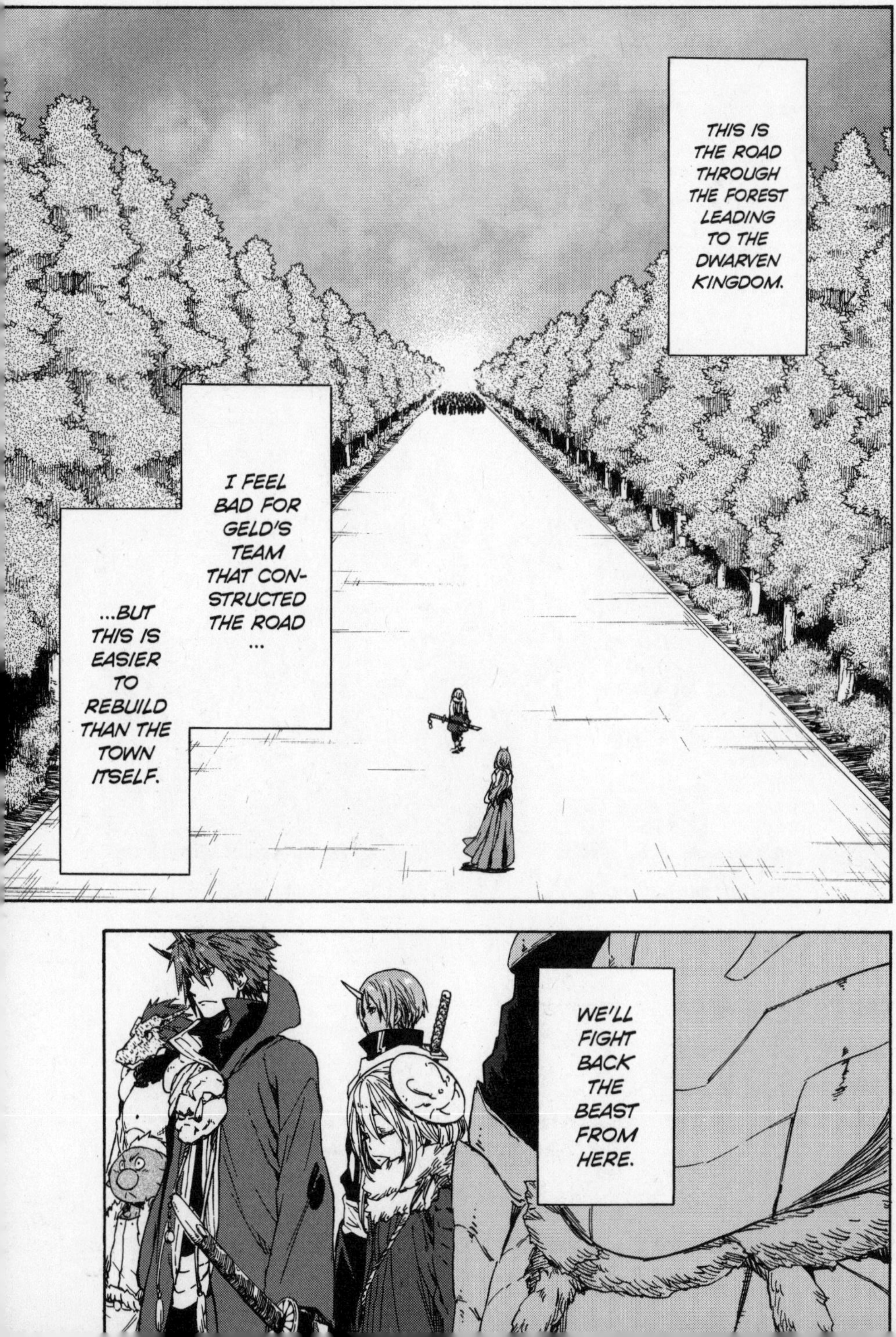
THIS IS THE ROAD THROUGH THE FOREST LEADING TO THE DWARVEN KINGDOM.
I FEEL BAD FOR GELD'S TEAM THAT CONSTRUCTED THE ROAD...
...BUT THIS IS EASIER TO REBUILD THAN THE TOWN ITSELF.
WE'LL FIGHT BACK THE BEAST FROM HERE.

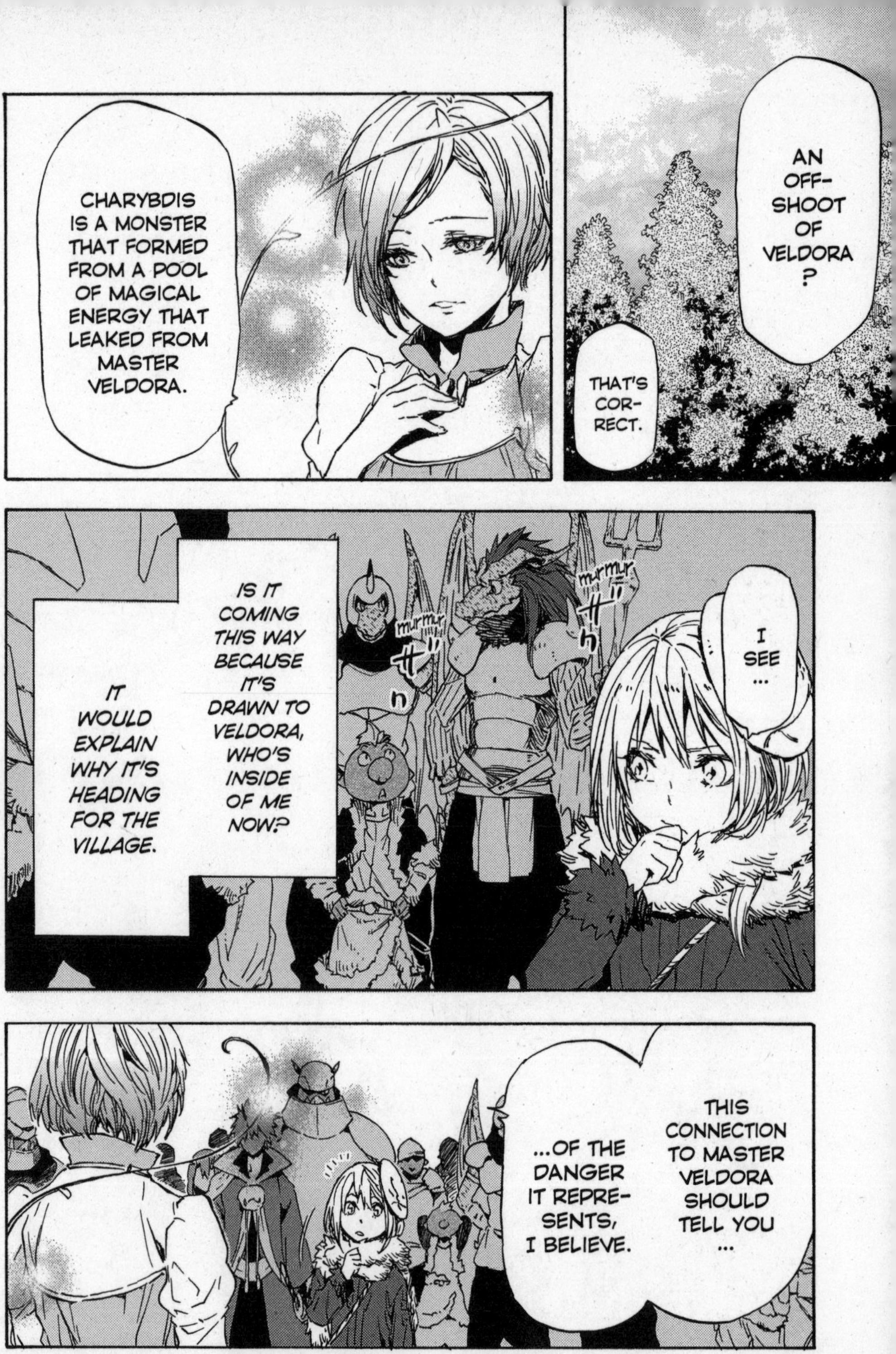
AN OFF-SHOOT OF VELDORA ?
THAT'S COR-RECT.
CHARYBDIS IS A MONSTER THAT FORMED FROM A POOL OF MAGICAL ENERGY THAT LEAKED FROM MASTER VELDORA.
I SEE ...
murmur
murmur
IS IT COMING THIS WAY BECAUSE IT'S DRAWN TO VELDORA, WHO'S INSIDE OF ME NOW?
IT WOULD EXPLAIN WHY IT'S HEADING FOR THE VILLAGE.
THIS CONNECTION TO MASTER VELDORA SHOULD TELL YOU ...
...OF THE DANGER IT REPRE-SENTS, I BELIEVE.

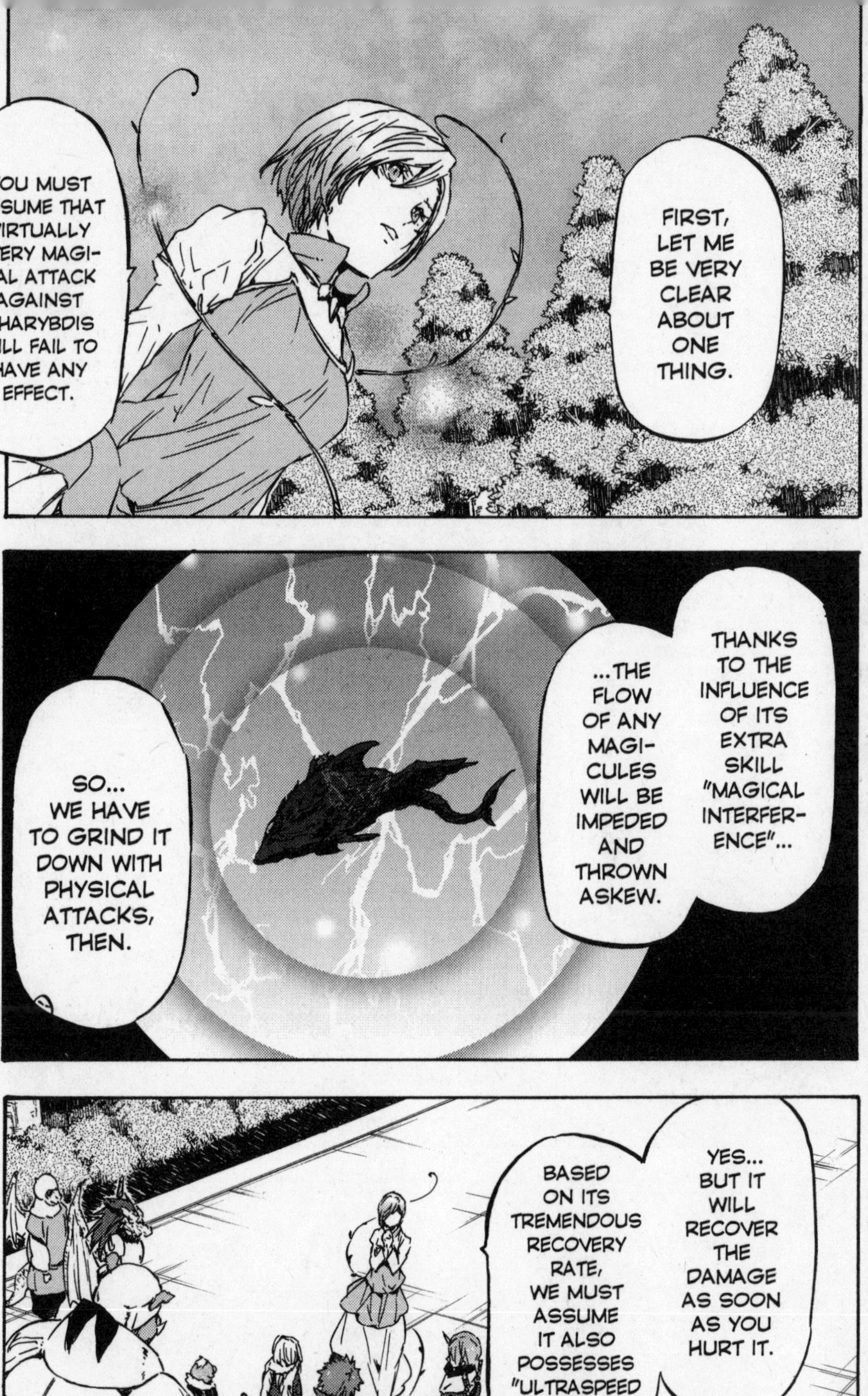
FIRST, LET ME BE VERY CLEAR ABOUT ONE THING.
YOU MUST ASSUME THAT VIRTUALLY EVERY MAGICAL ATTACK AGAINST CHARYBDIS WILL FAIL TO HAVE ANY EFFECT.
THANKS TO THE INFLUENCE OF ITS EXTRA SKILL "MAGICAL INTERFERENCE"...
...THE FLOW OF ANY MAGICULES WILL BE IMPEDED AND THROWN ASKEW.
SO... WE HAVE TO GRIND IT DOWN WITH PHYSICAL ATTACKS, THEN.
YES... BUT IT WILL RECOVER THE DAMAGE AS SOON AS YOU HURT IT.
BASED ON ITS TREMENDOUS RECOVERY RATE, WE MUST ASSUME IT ALSO POSSESSES "ULTRASPEED REGENERATION"...

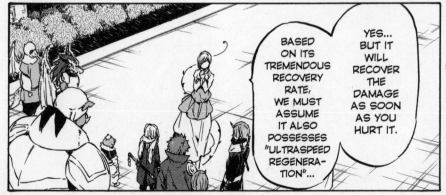

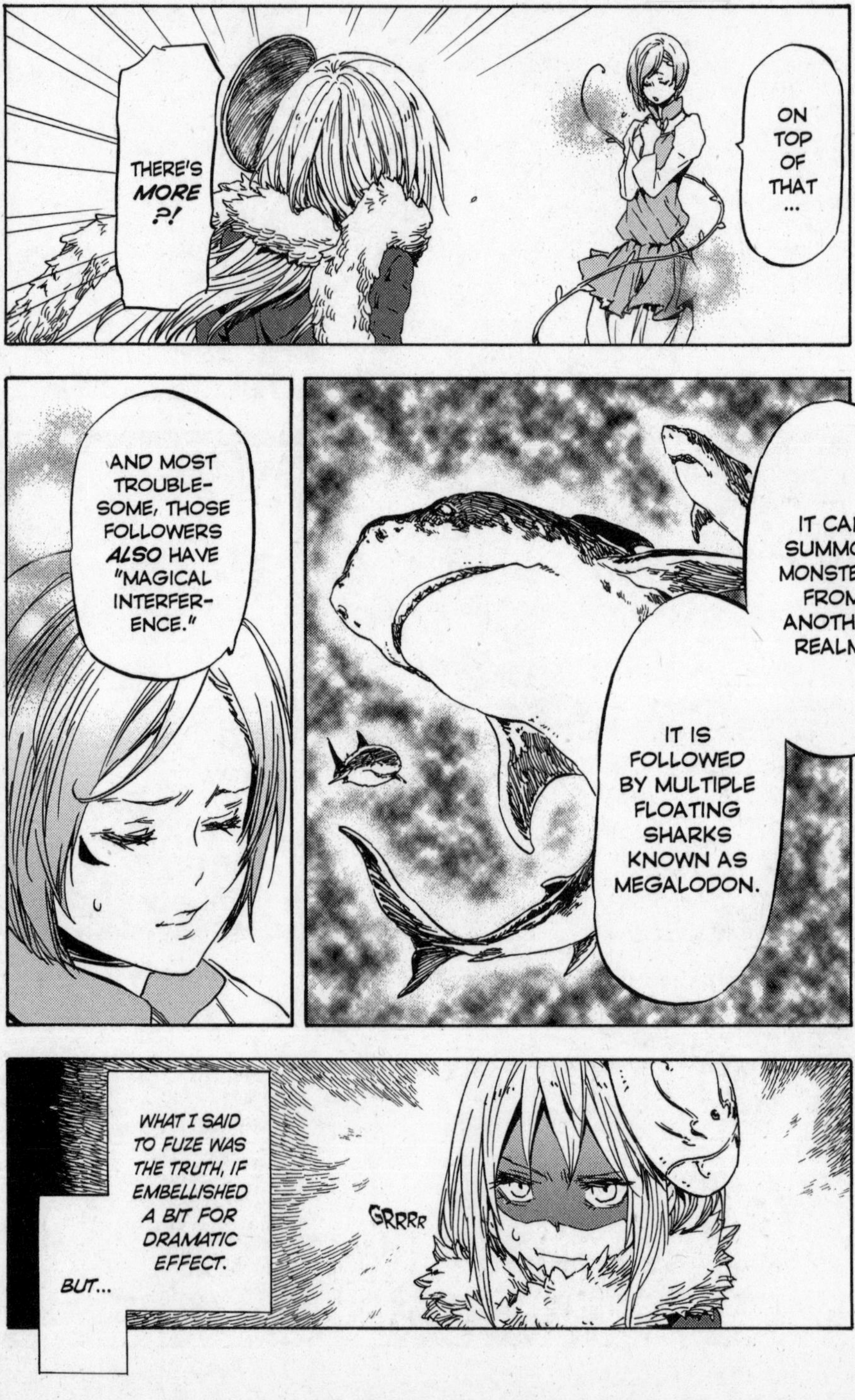
ON TOP OF THAT...
THERE'S *MORE* ?!
IT CAN SUMMON MONSTERS FROM ANOTHER REALM.
IT IS FOLLOWED BY MULTIPLE FLOATING SHARKS KNOWN AS MEGALODON.
AND MOST TROUBLE-SOME, THOSE FOLLOWERS *ALSO* HAVE "MAGICAL INTERFER-ENCE."
WHAT I SAID TO FUZE WAS THE TRUTH, IF EMBELLISHED A BIT FOR DRAMATIC EFFECT.
BUT...
GRRRR

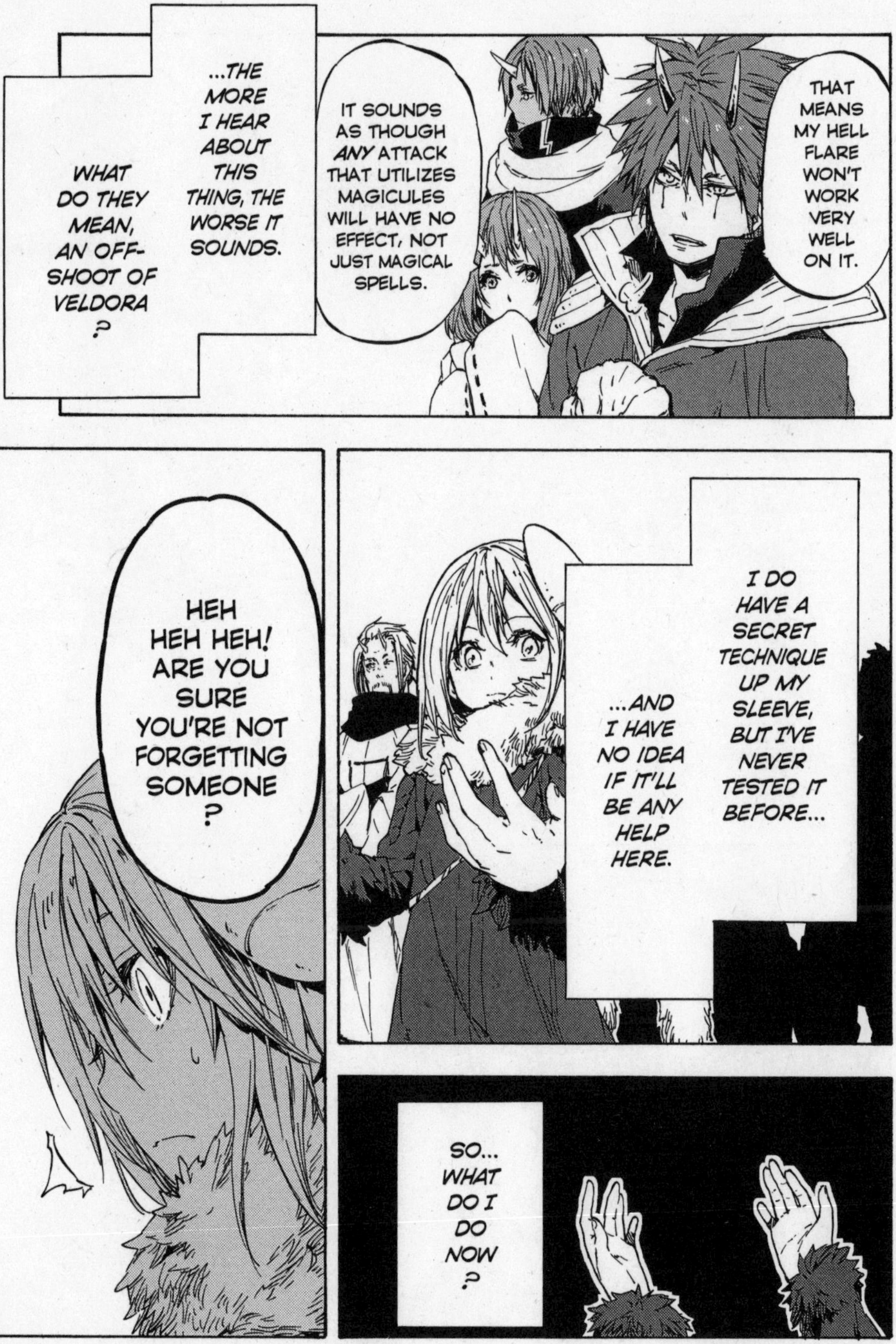
THAT MEANS MY HELL FLARE WON'T WORK VERY WELL ON IT.
IT SOUNDS AS THOUGH *ANY* ATTACK THAT UTILIZES MAGICULES WILL HAVE NO EFFECT, NOT JUST MAGICAL SPELLS.
...THE MORE I HEAR ABOUT THIS THING, THE WORSE IT SOUNDS.
WHAT DO THEY MEAN, AN OFF-SHOOT OF VELDORA?
I DO HAVE A SECRET TECHNIQUE UP MY SLEEVE, BUT I'VE NEVER TESTED IT BEFORE...
...AND I HAVE NO IDEA IF IT'LL BE ANY HELP HERE.
SO... WHAT DO I DO NOW?
HEH HEH HEH! ARE YOU SURE YOU'RE NOT FORGETTING SOMEONE?

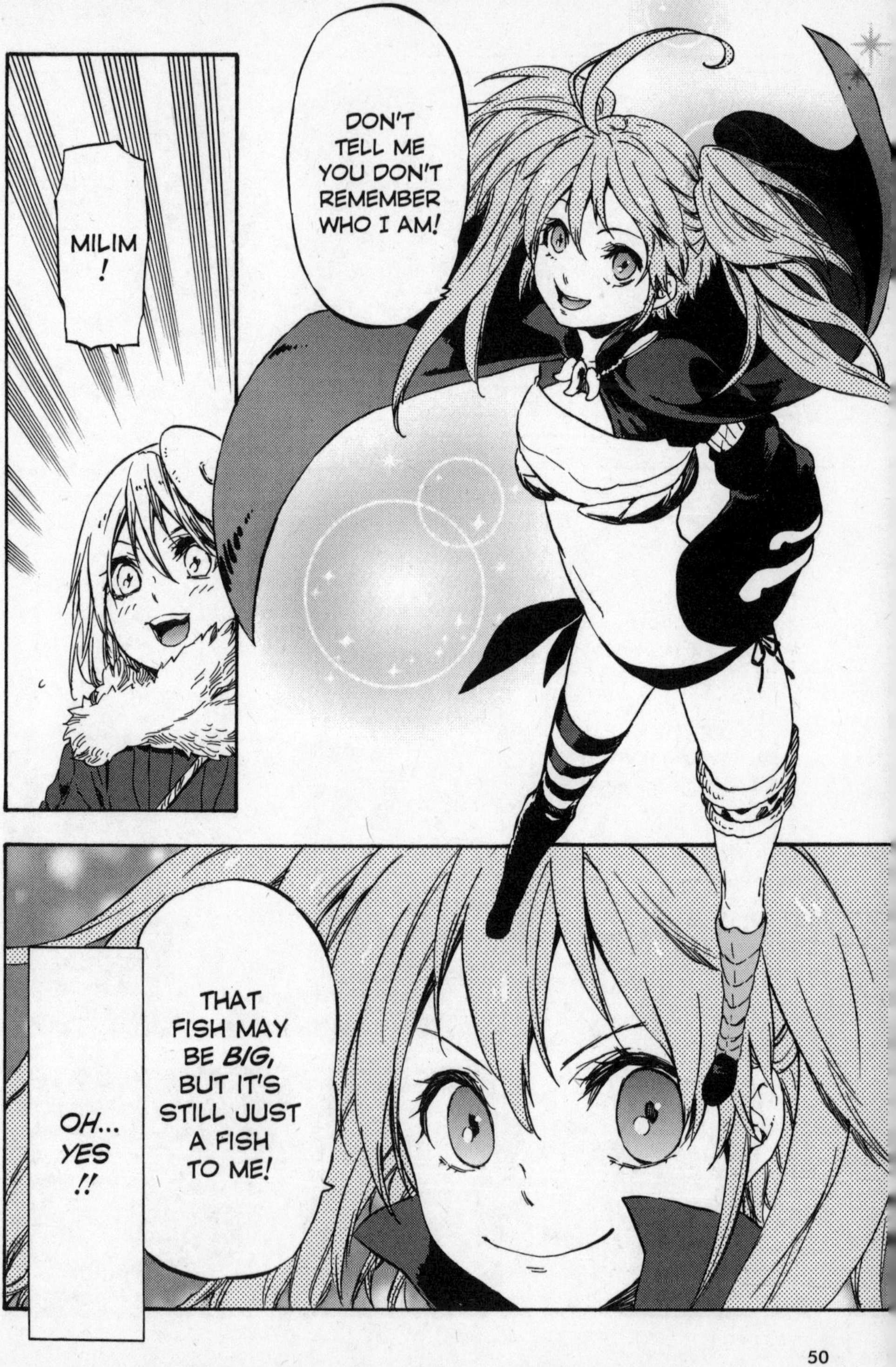
DON'T TELL ME YOU DON'T REMEMBER WHO I AM!
MILIM!
THAT FISH MAY BE *BIG*, BUT IT'S STILL JUST A FISH TO ME!
OH... YES!!

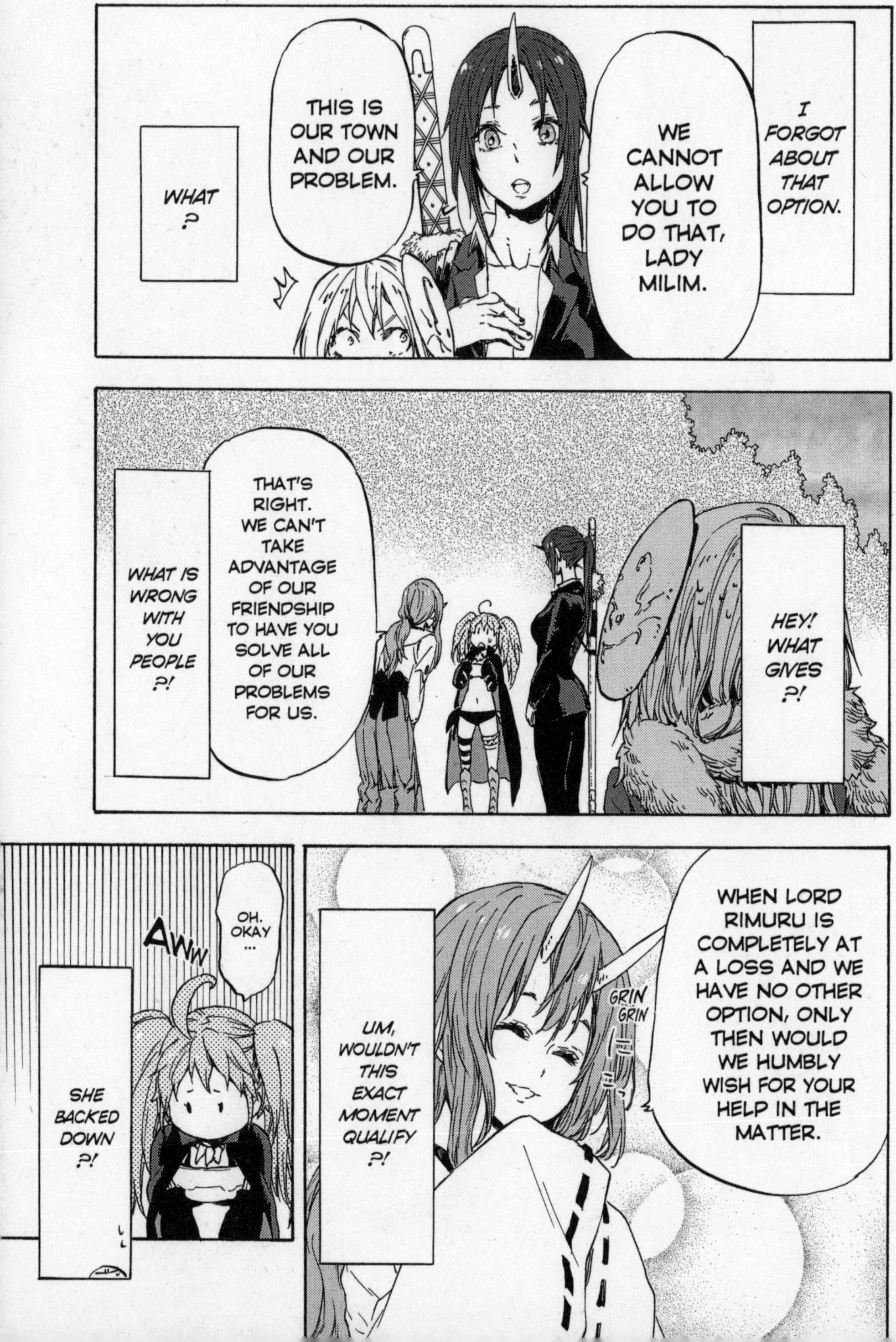
I FORGOT ABOUT THAT OPTION.
WE CANNOT ALLOW YOU TO DO THAT, LADY MILIM.
THIS IS OUR TOWN AND OUR PROBLEM.
WHAT ?
HEY! WHAT GIVES ?!
THAT'S RIGHT. WE CAN'T TAKE ADVANTAGE OF OUR FRIENDSHIP TO HAVE YOU SOLVE ALL OF OUR PROBLEMS FOR US.
WHAT IS WRONG WITH YOU PEOPLE ?!
WHEN LORD RIMURU IS COMPLETELY AT A LOSS AND WE HAVE NO OTHER OPTION, ONLY THEN WOULD WE HUMBLY WISH FOR YOUR HELP IN THE MATTER.
GRIN GRIN
UM, WOULDN'T THIS EXACT MOMENT QUALIFY ?!
OH. OKAY ...
AWW
SHE BACKED DOWN ?!

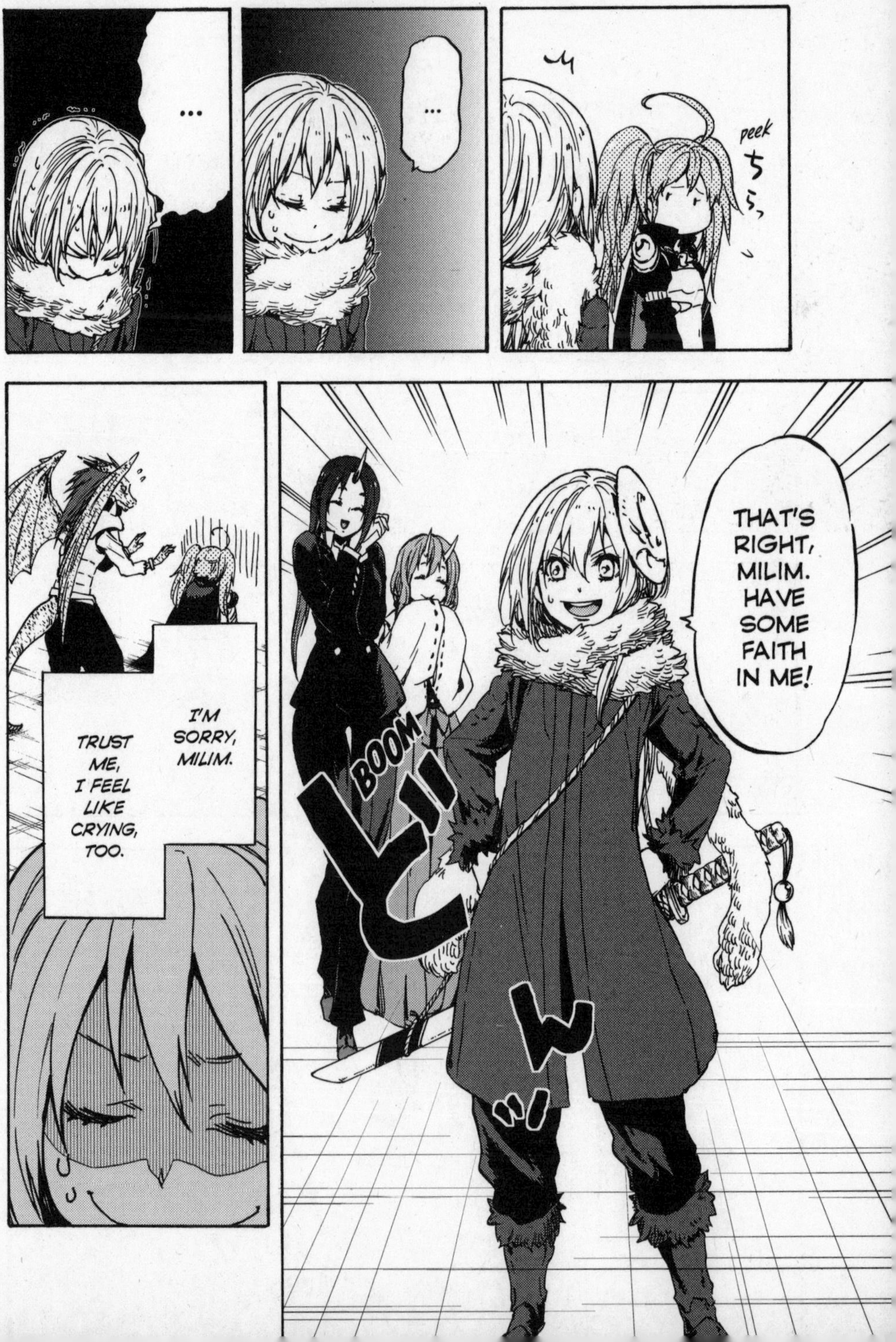

peek
...
...
THAT'S RIGHT, MILIM. HAVE SOME FAITH IN ME!
BOOM
I'M SORRY, MILIM.
TRUST ME, I FEEL LIKE CRYING, TOO.

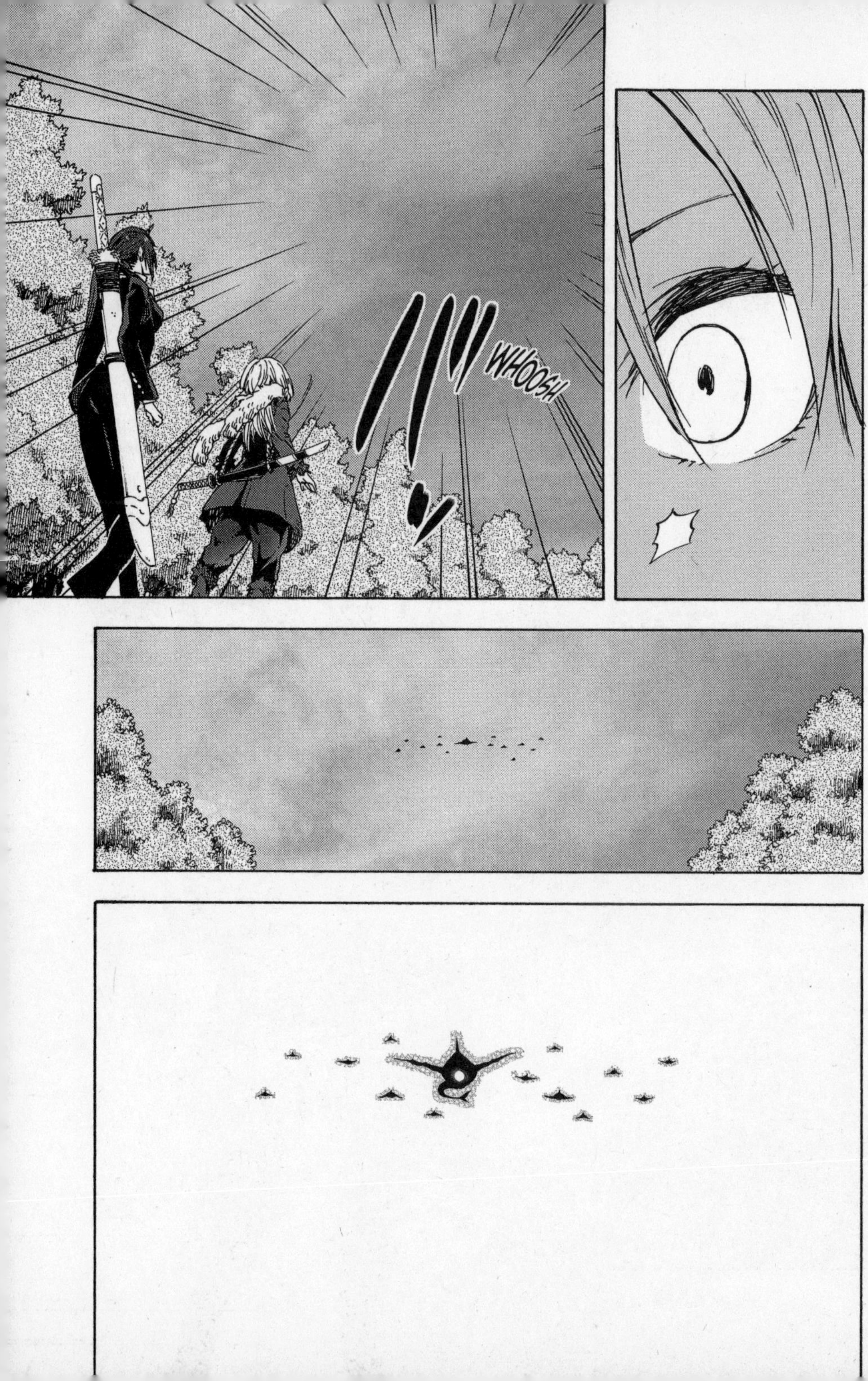
WHOOSH

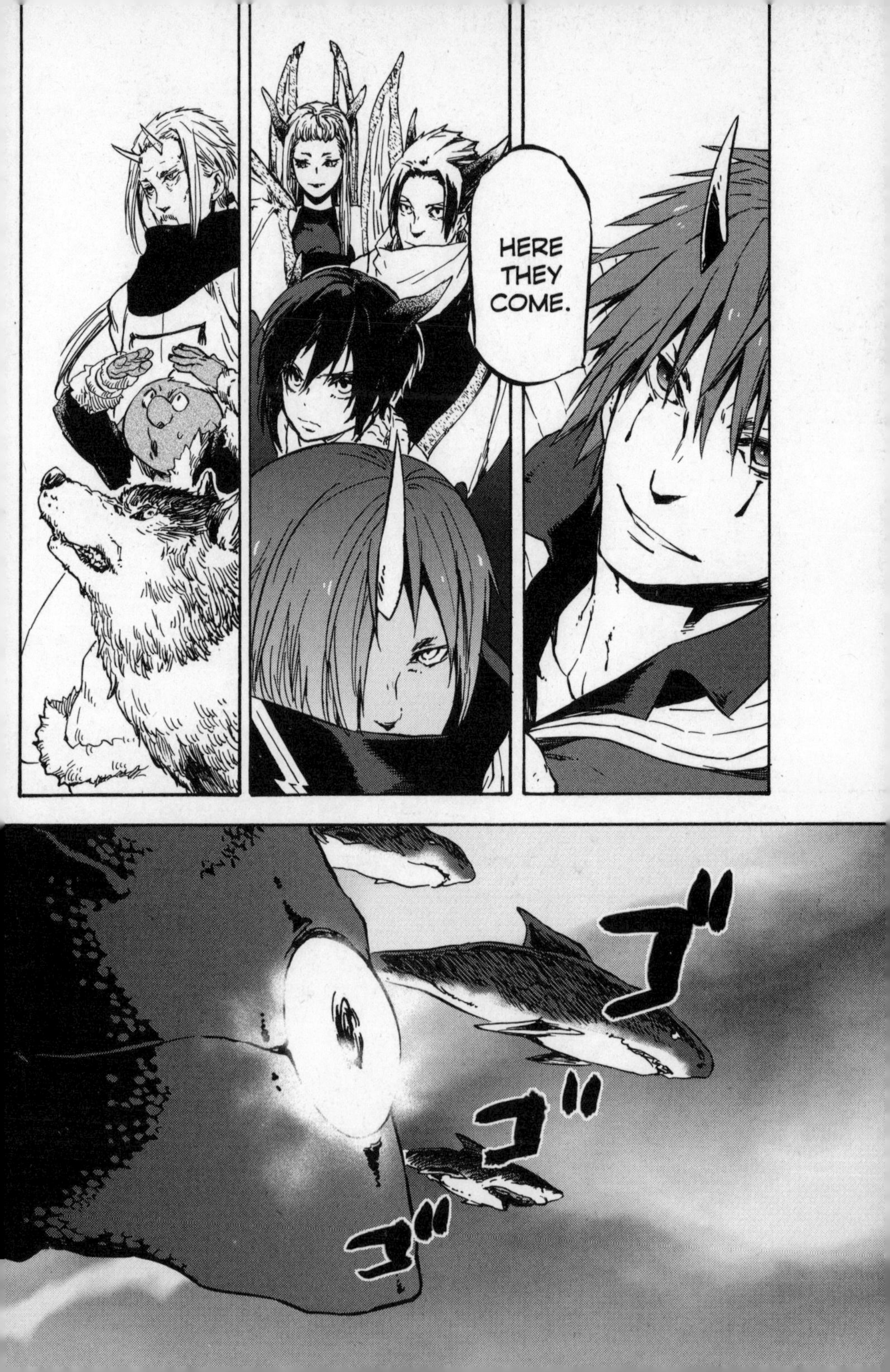
HERE THEY COME.
ゴゴゴ

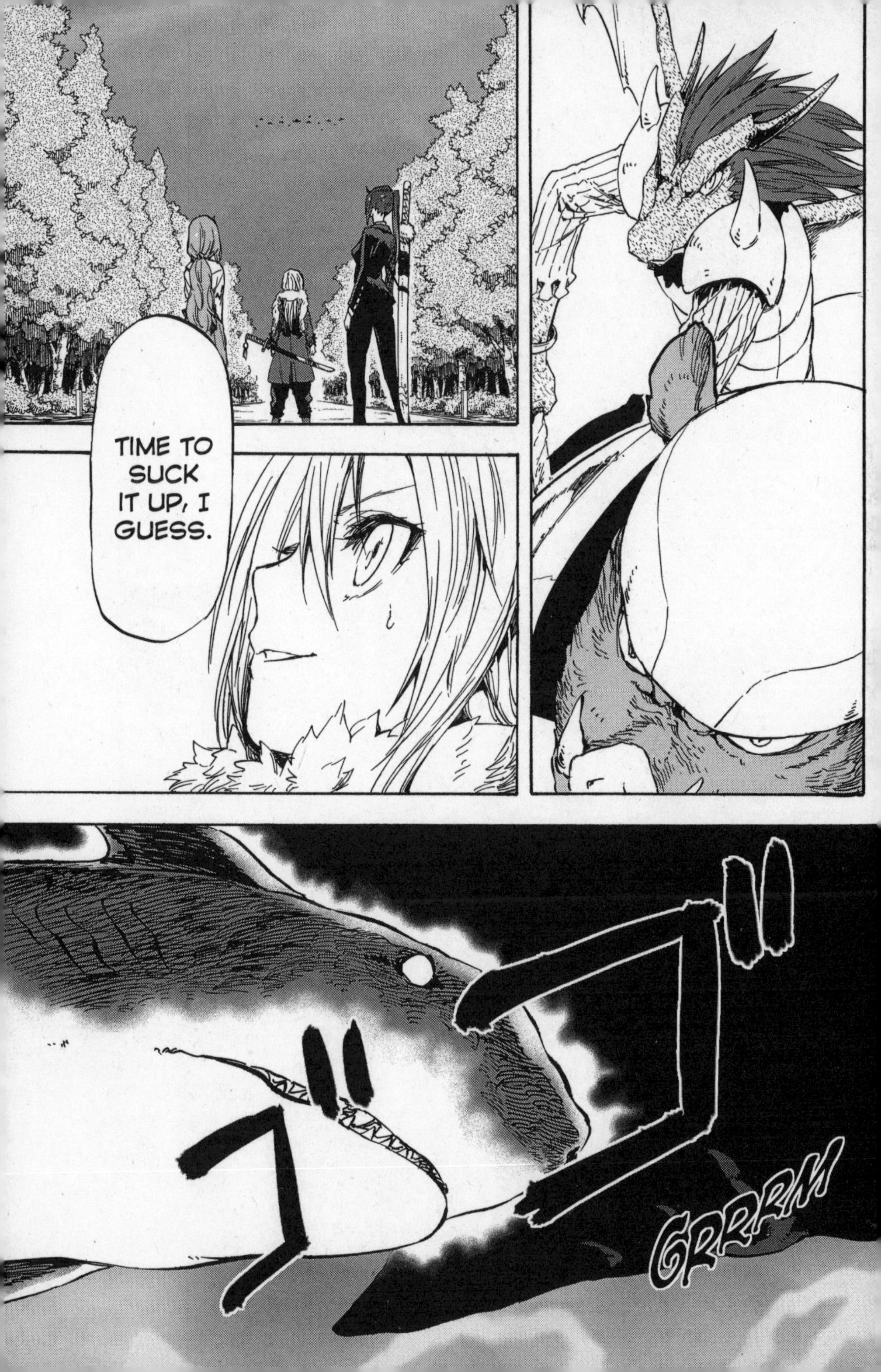
TIME TO SUCK IT UP, I GUESS.
GRRRM

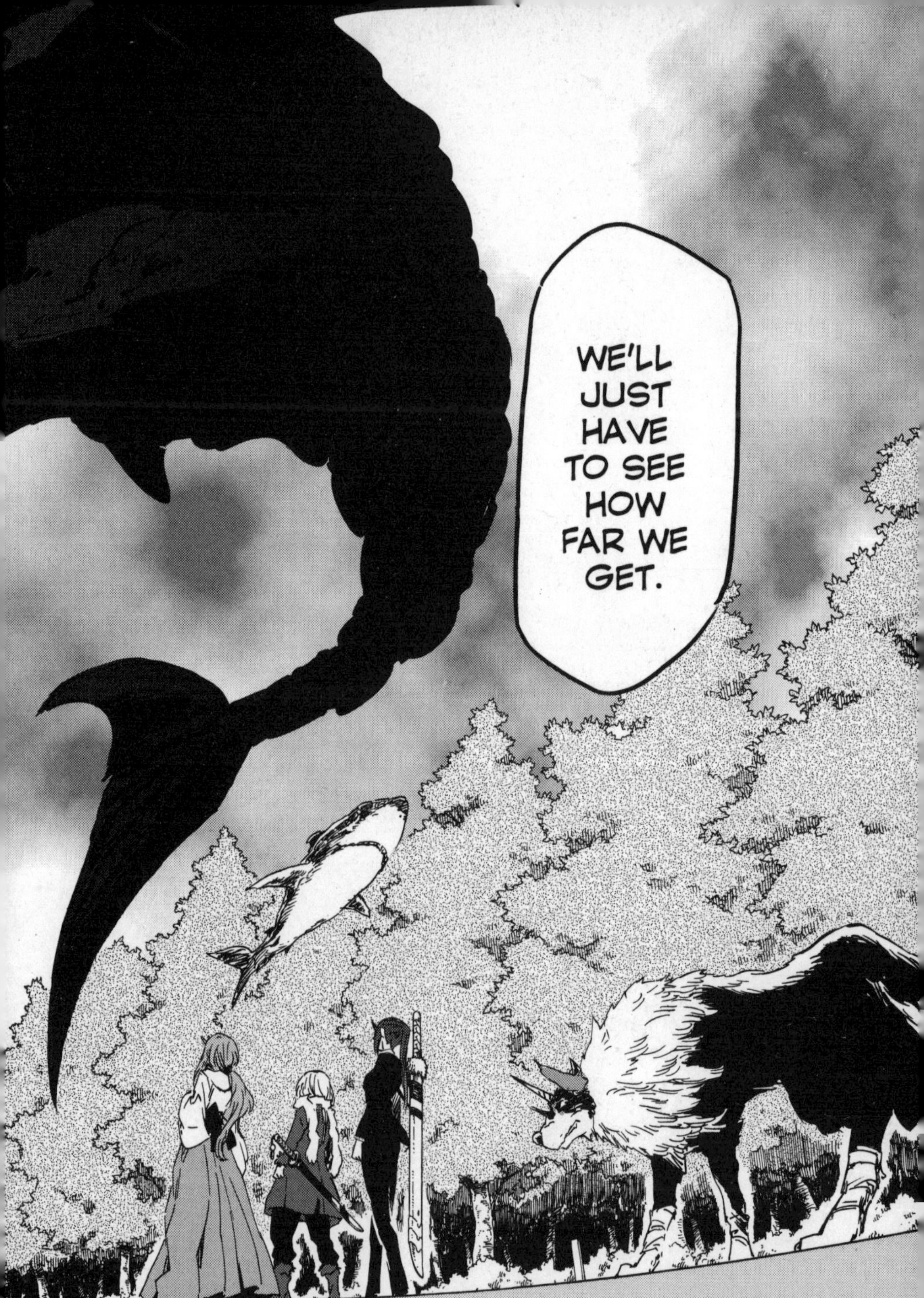
WE'LL JUST HAVE TO SEE HOW FAR WE GET.

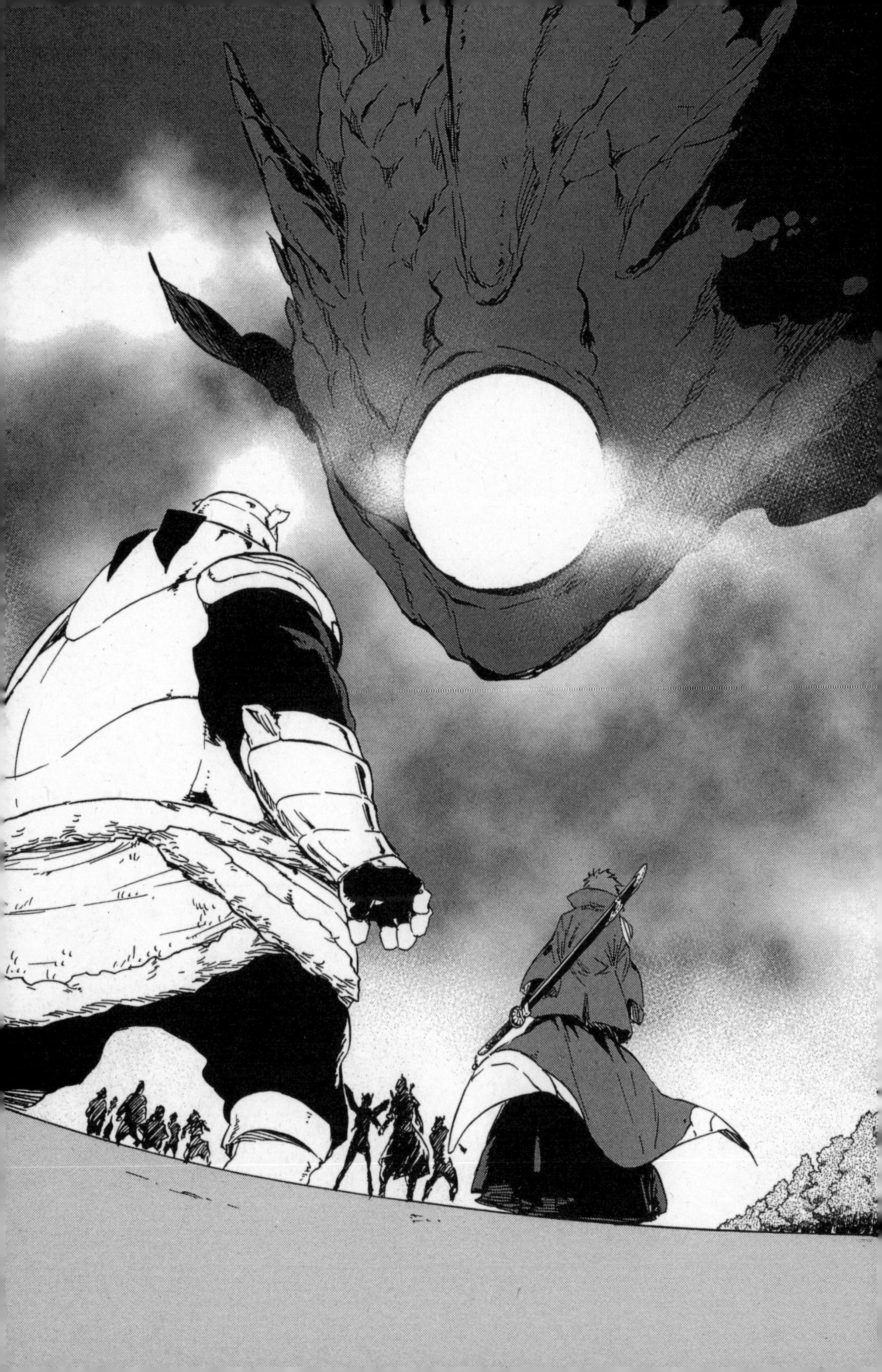

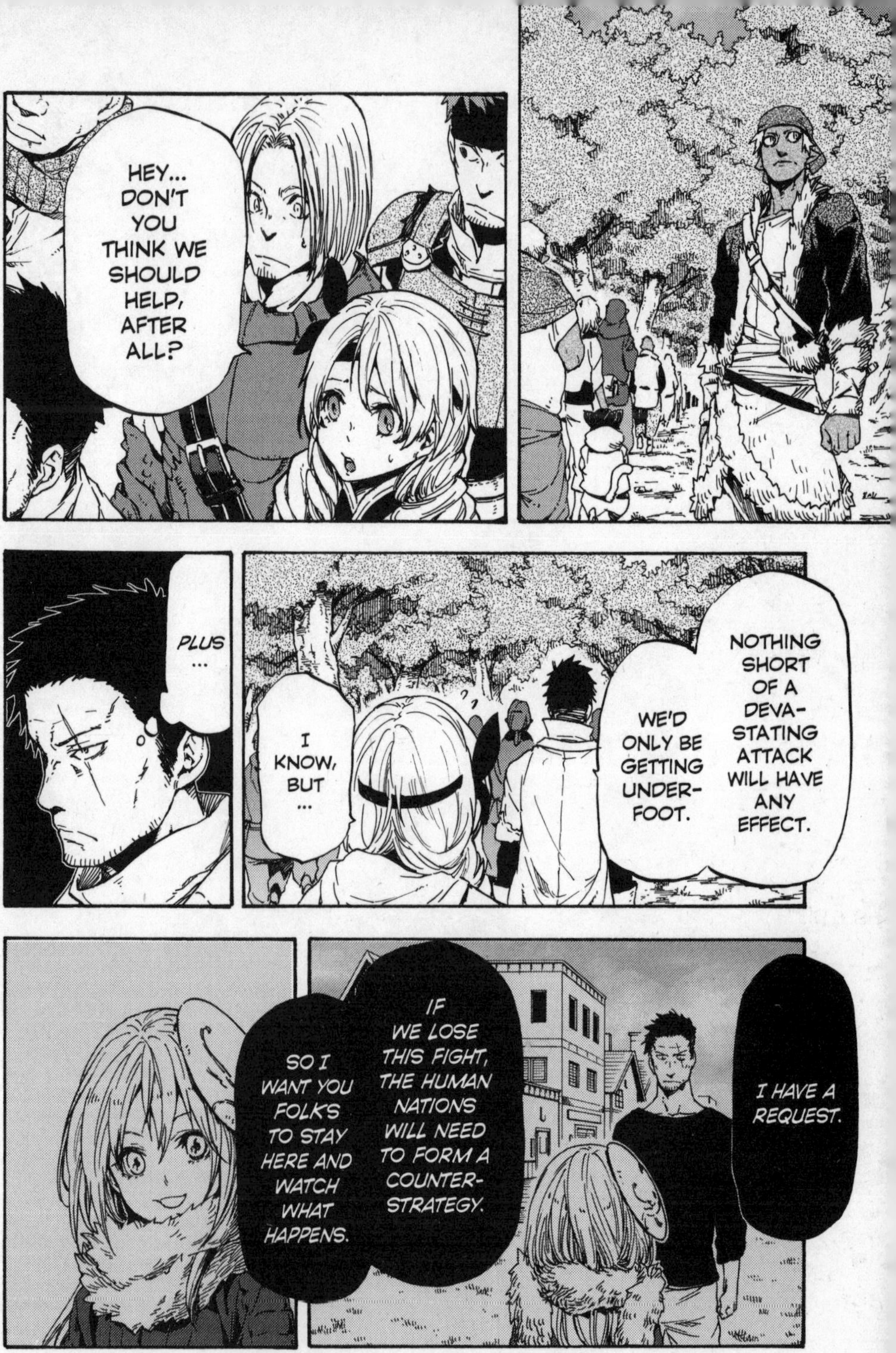
HEY... DON'T YOU THINK WE SHOULD HELP, AFTER ALL?
NOTHING SHORT OF A DEVA-STATING ATTACK WILL HAVE ANY EFFECT.
WE'D ONLY BE GETTING UNDER-FOOT.
I KNOW, BUT ...
PLUS ...
I HAVE A REQUEST.
IF WE LOSE THIS FIGHT, THE HUMAN NATIONS WILL NEED TO FORM A COUNTER-STRATEGY.
SO I WANT YOU FOLKS TO STAY HERE AND WATCH WHAT HAPPENS.

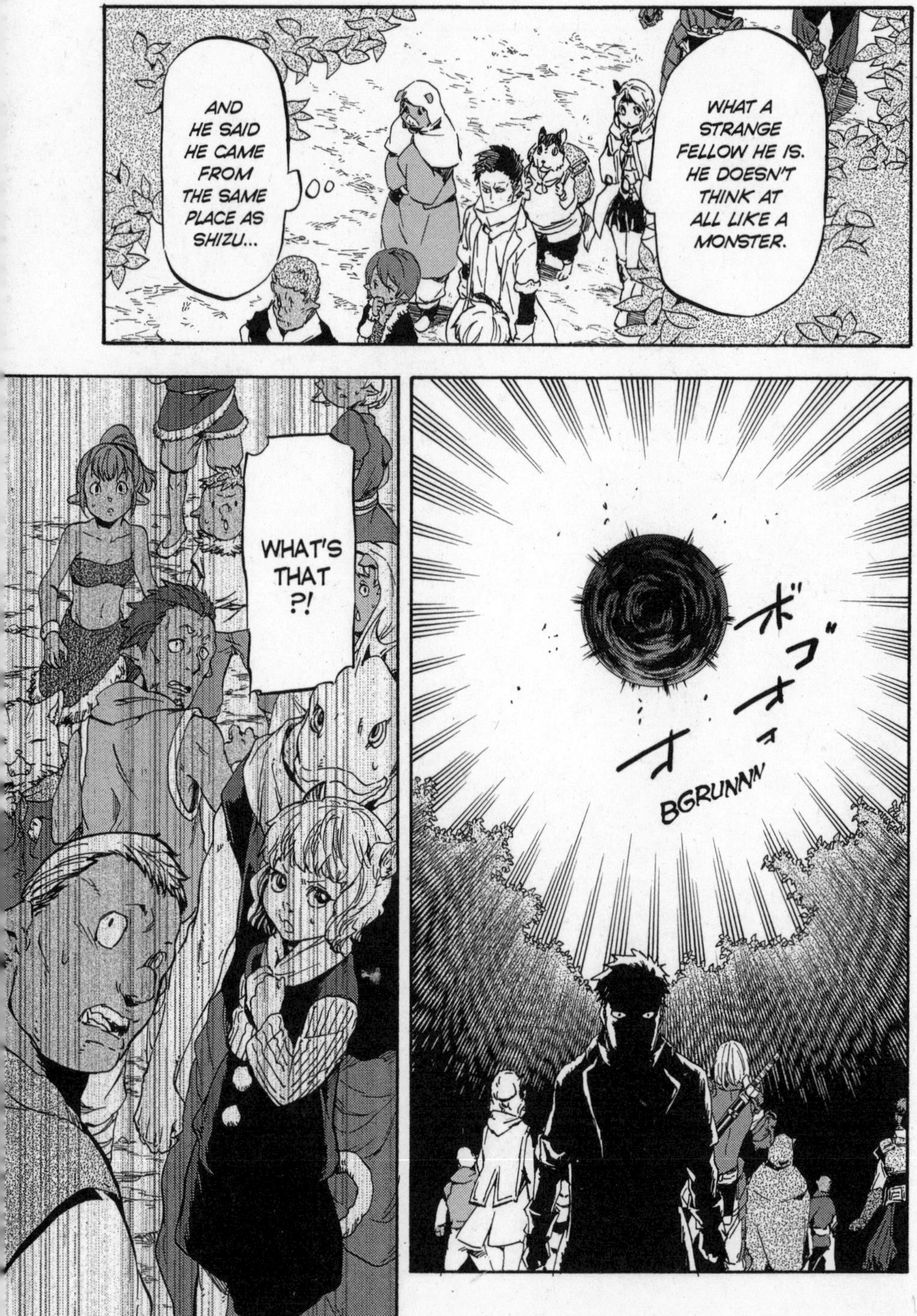
WHAT A STRANGE FELLOW HE IS. HE DOESN'T THINK AT ALL LIKE A MONSTER.
AND HE SAID HE CAME FROM THE SAME PLACE AS SHIZU...
ボゴォォオ
BGRUNNN
WHAT'S THAT ?!

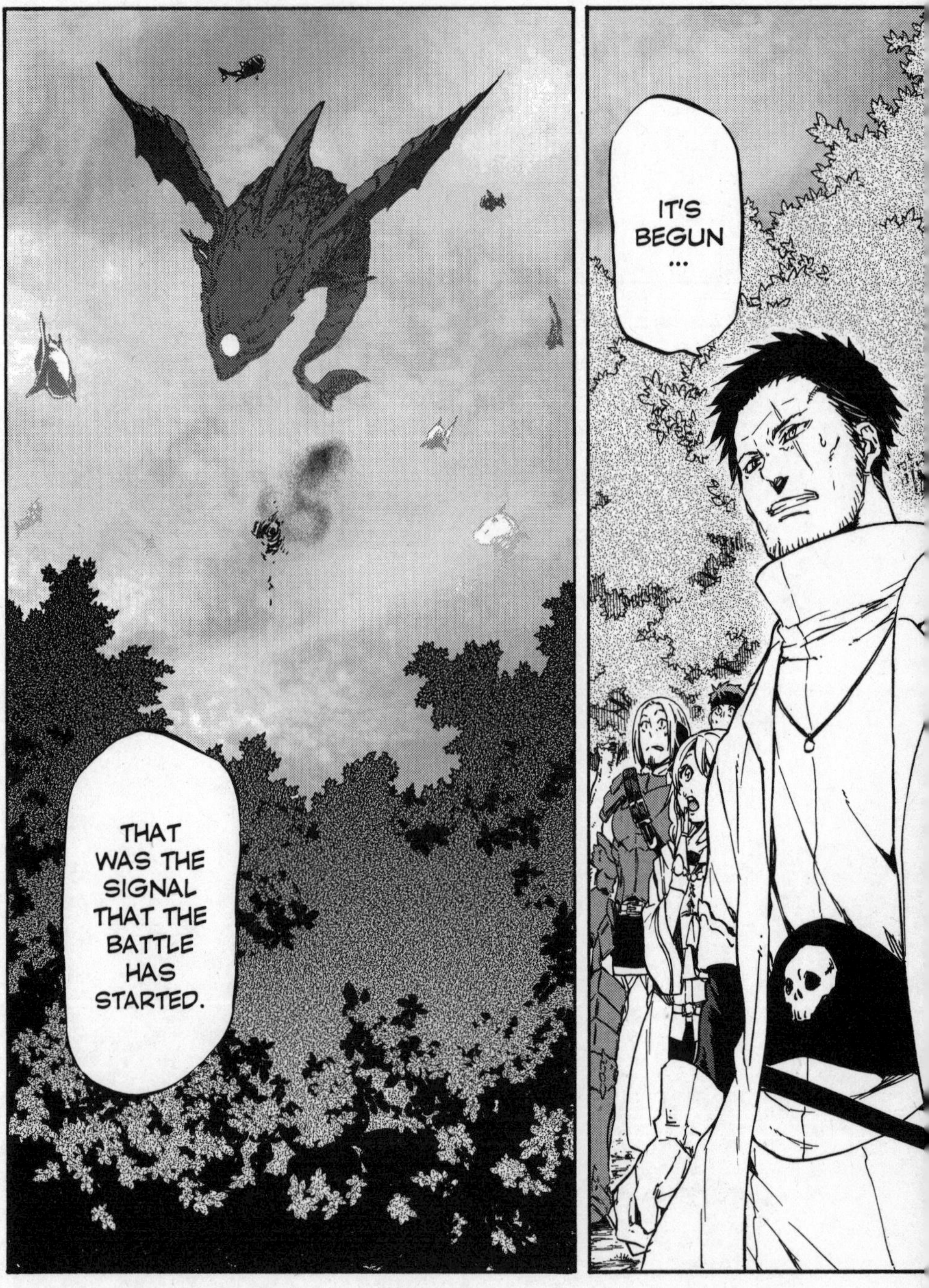
IT'S BEGUN ...
THAT WAS THE SIGNAL THAT THE BATTLE HAS STARTED.

Bored
Milim

CHAPTER 38 Tyrant of Destruction

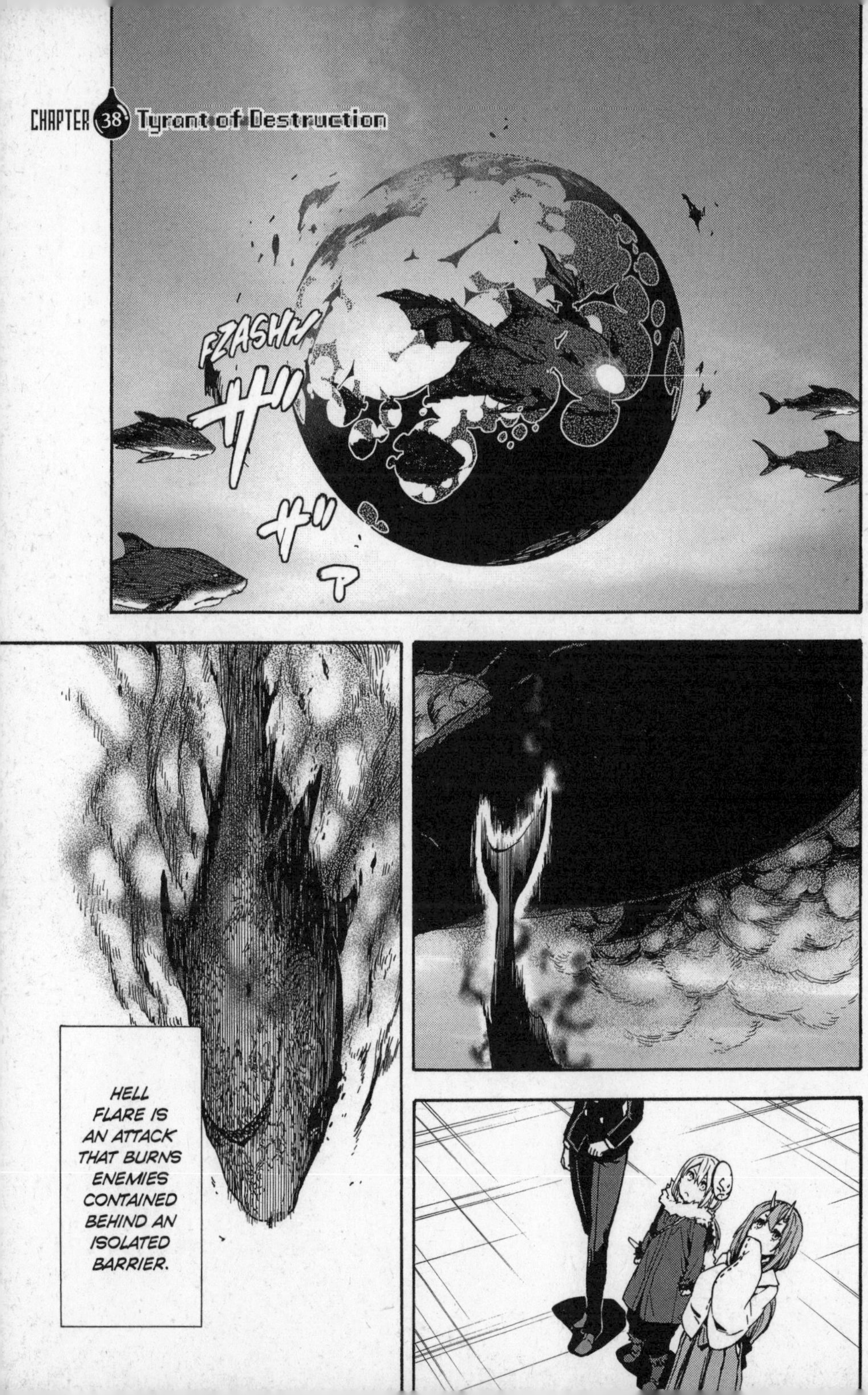
FZASHH
HELL FLARE IS AN ATTACK THAT BURNS ENEMIES CONTAINED BEHIND AN ISOLATED BARRIER.

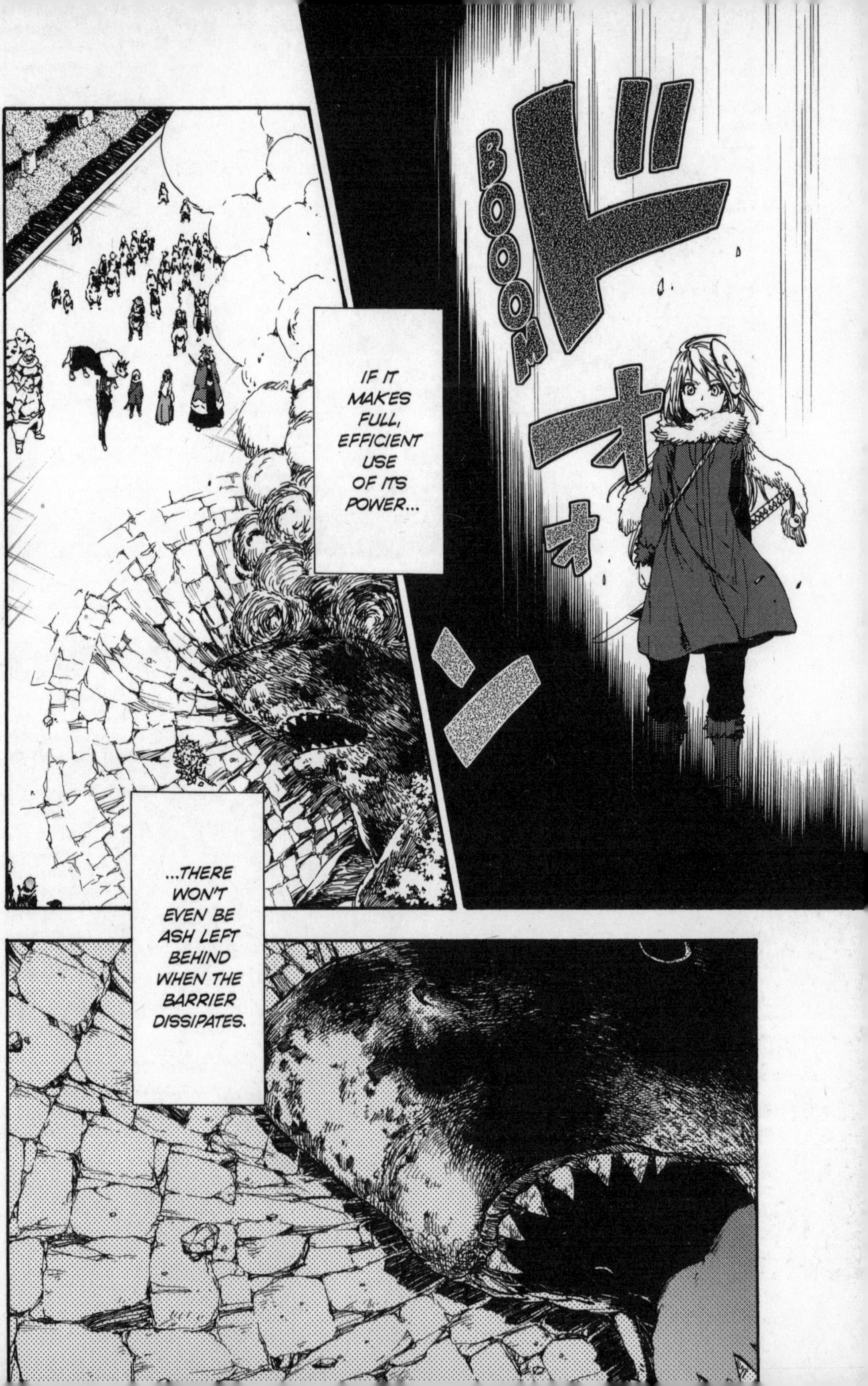

BOOOM
ドオオン
IF IT MAKES FULL, EFFICIENT USE OF ITS POWER...
...THERE WON'T EVEN BE ASH LEFT BEHIND WHEN THE BARRIER DISSIPATES.

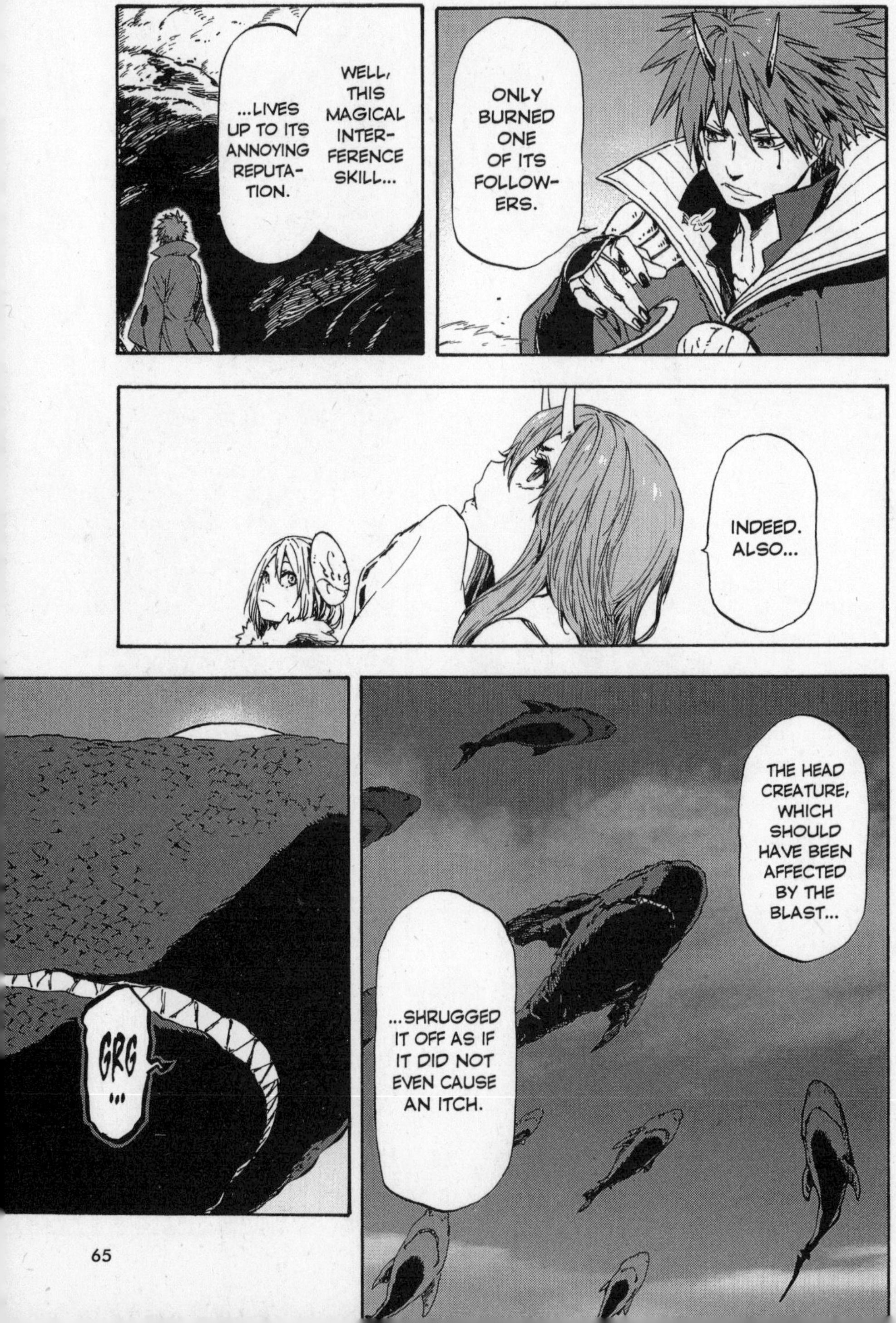
ONLY BURNED ONE OF ITS FOLLOWERS.
WELL, THIS MAGICAL INTERFERENCE SKILL...
...LIVES UP TO ITS ANNOYING REPUTATION.
INDEED. ALSO...
THE HEAD CREATURE, WHICH SHOULD HAVE BEEN AFFECTED BY THE BLAST...
...SHRUGGED IT OFF AS IF IT DID NOT EVEN CAUSE AN ITCH.
GRG...

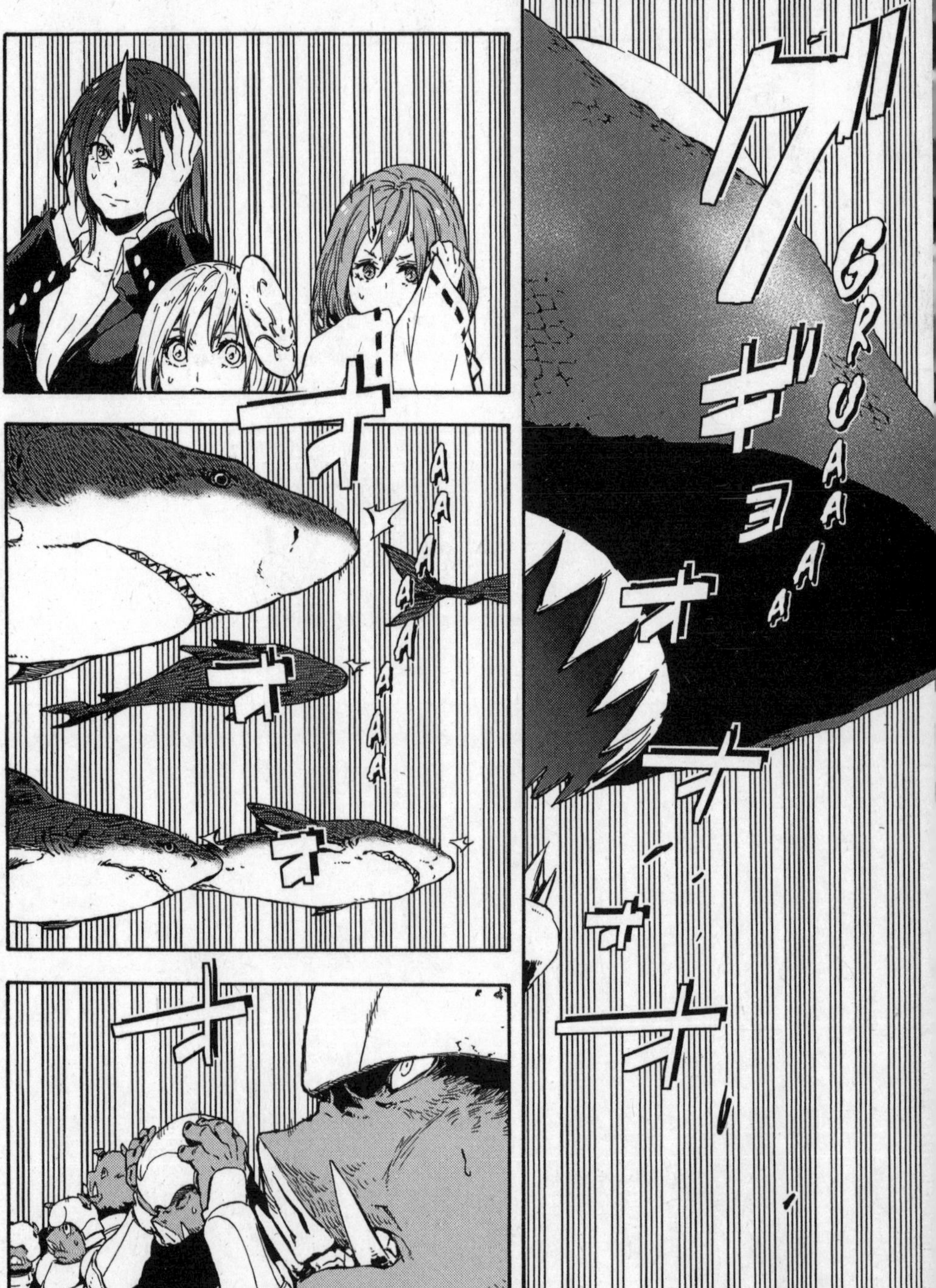

GRUAAAAAA
AAAAAAAAAA

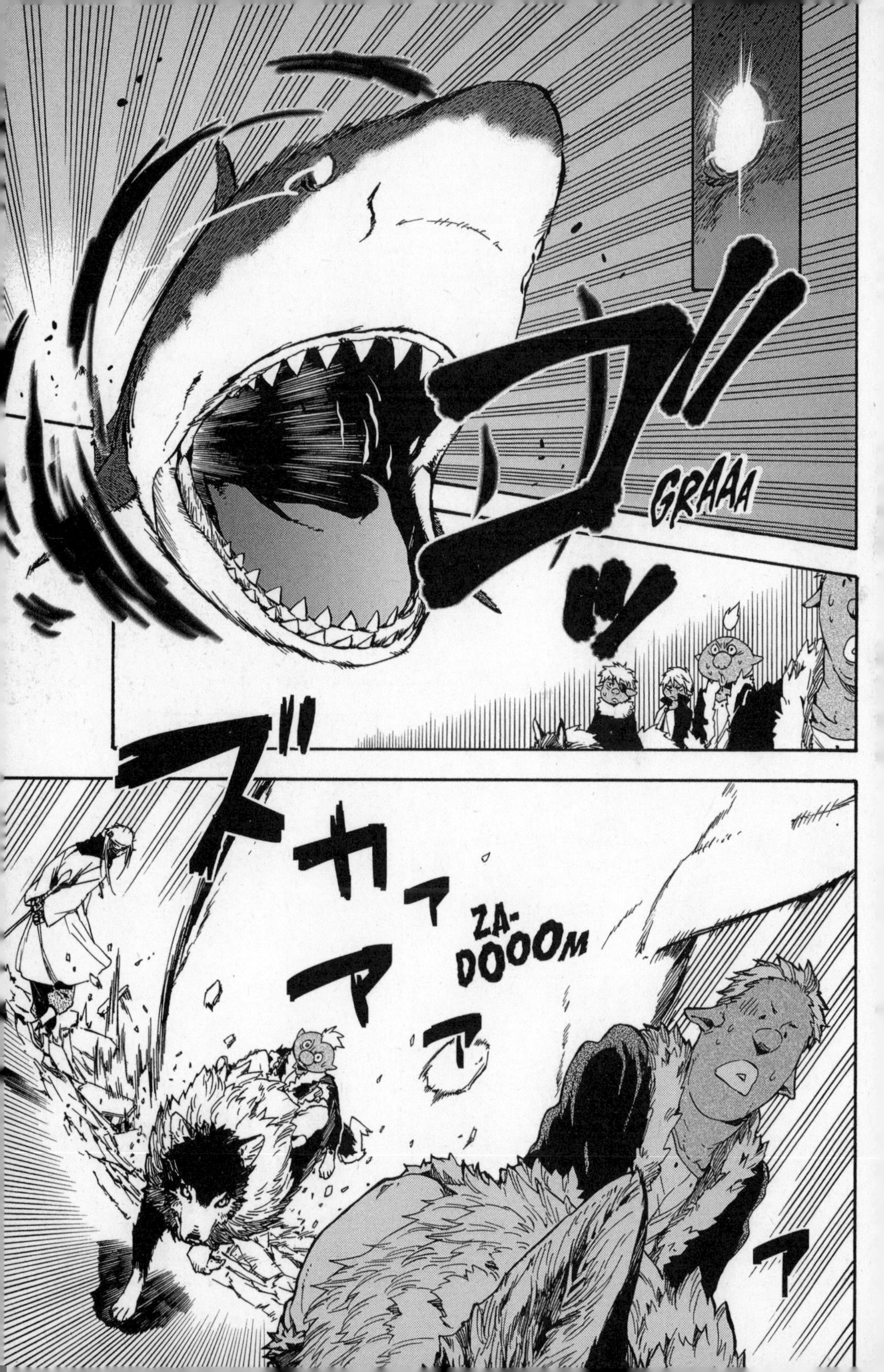
ゴッ
GRAAA
ズザァァァ
ZA-DOOOM

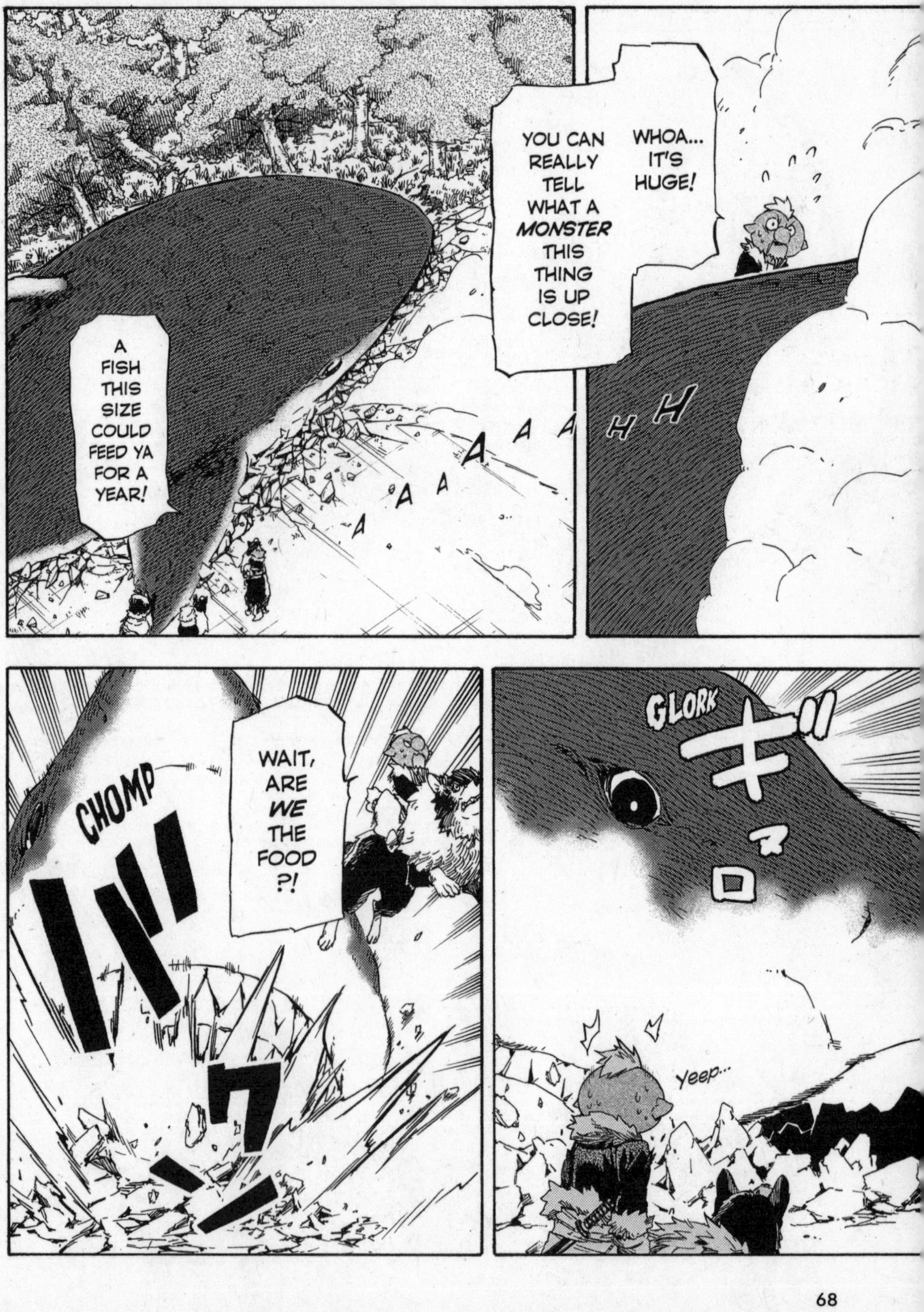
WHOA... IT'S HUGE!
YOU CAN REALLY TELL WHAT A *MONSTER* THIS THING IS UP CLOSE!
A FISH THIS SIZE COULD FEED YA FOR A YEAR!
GLORK
Yeep...
WAIT, ARE *WE* THE FOOD?!
CHOMP

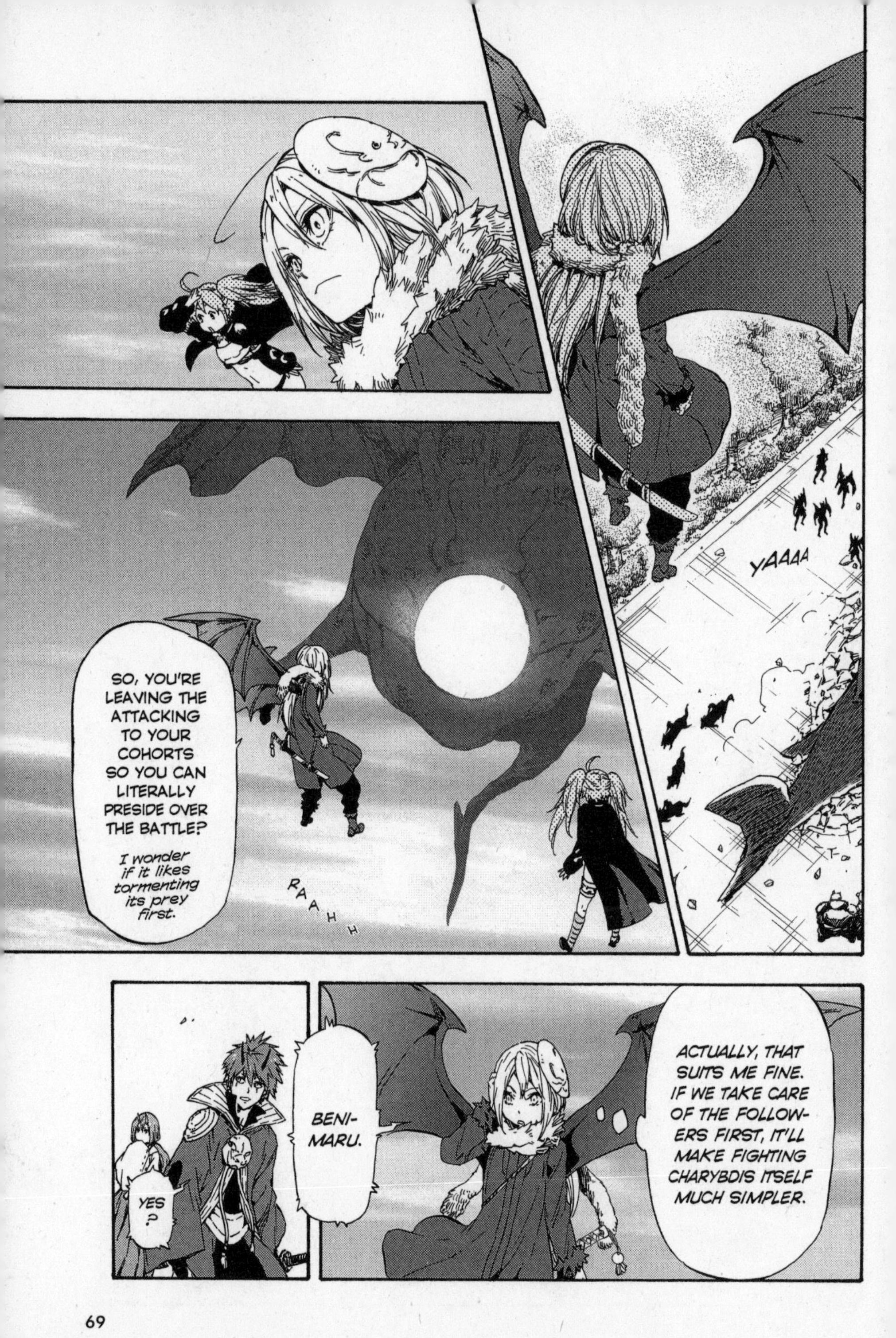
YAAAA
SO, YOU'RE LEAVING THE ATTACKING TO YOUR COHORTS SO YOU CAN LITERALLY PRESIDE OVER THE BATTLE?
I wonder if it likes tormenting its prey first.
RAAHH
ACTUALLY, THAT SUITS ME FINE. IF WE TAKE CARE OF THE FOLLOW-ERS FIRST, IT'LL MAKE FIGHTING CHARYBDIS ITSELF MUCH SIMPLER.
BENI-MARU.
YES?

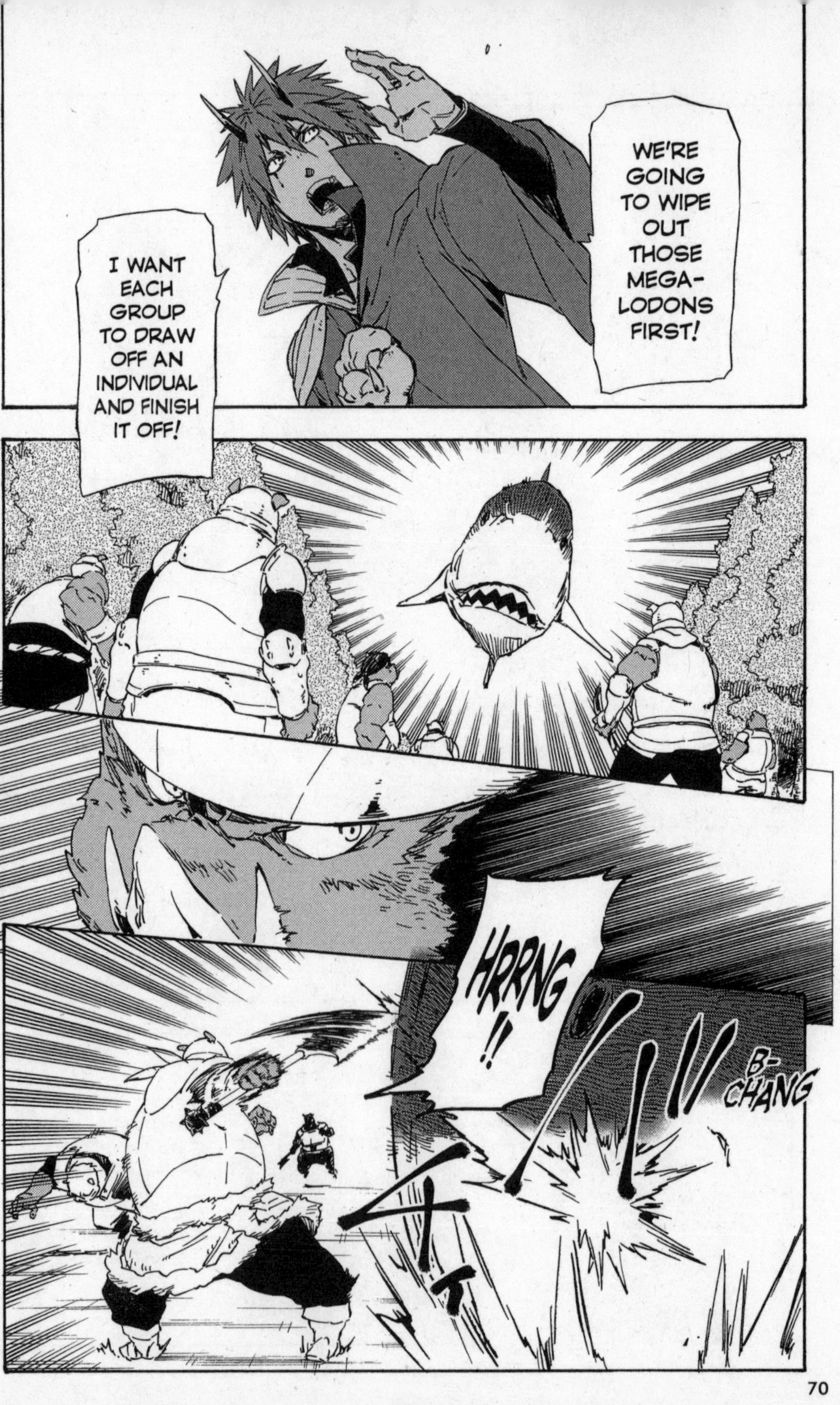
WE'RE GOING TO WIPE OUT THOSE MEGA-LODONS FIRST!
I WANT EACH GROUP TO DRAW OFF AN INDIVIDUAL AND FINISH IT OFF!
HRRNG!!
B-CHANG

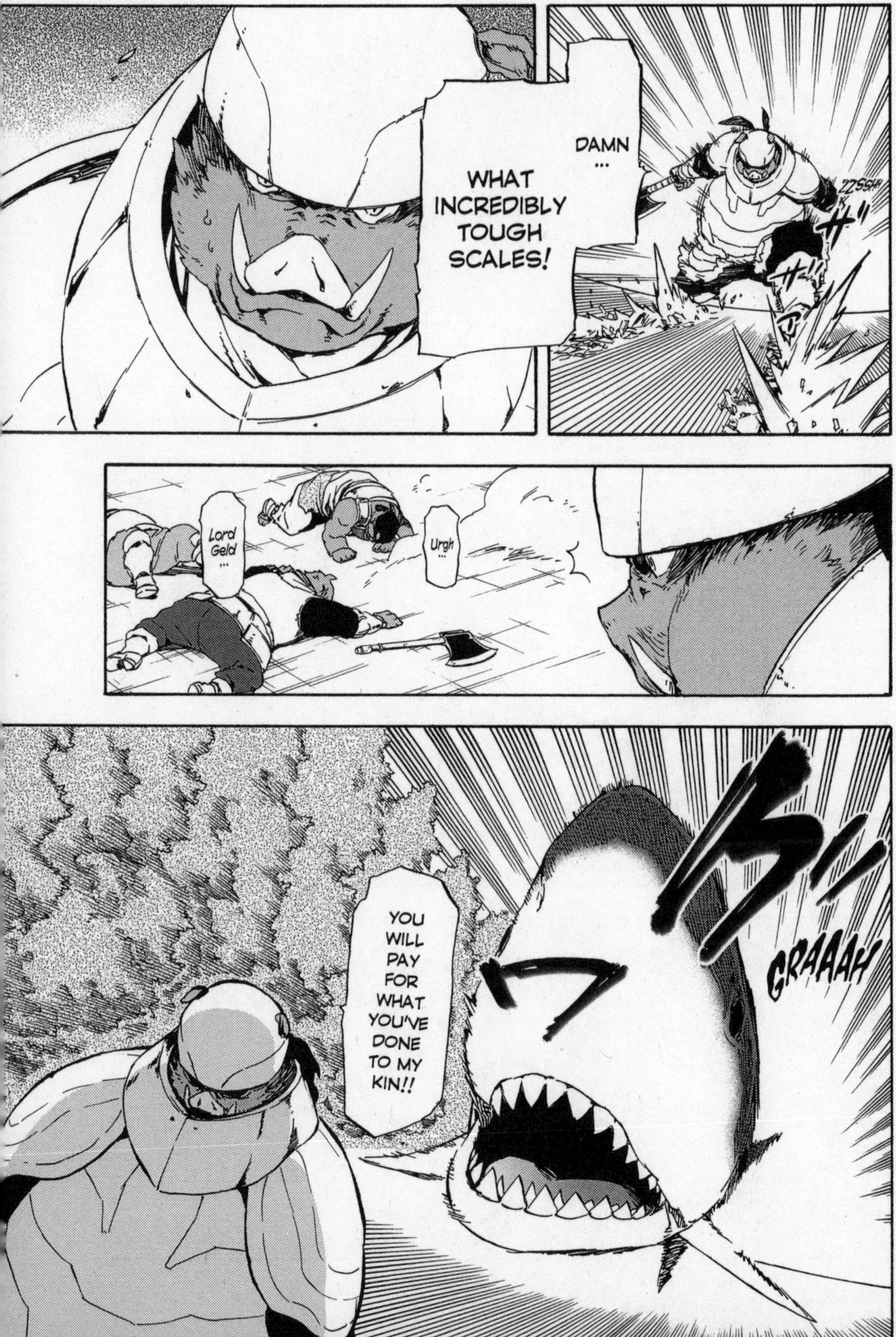
DAMN ...
WHAT INCREDIBLY TOUGH SCALES!
ZZSSH
Urgh ...
Lord Geld ...
GRAAAH
YOU WILL PAY FOR WHAT YOU'VE DONE TO MY KIN!!

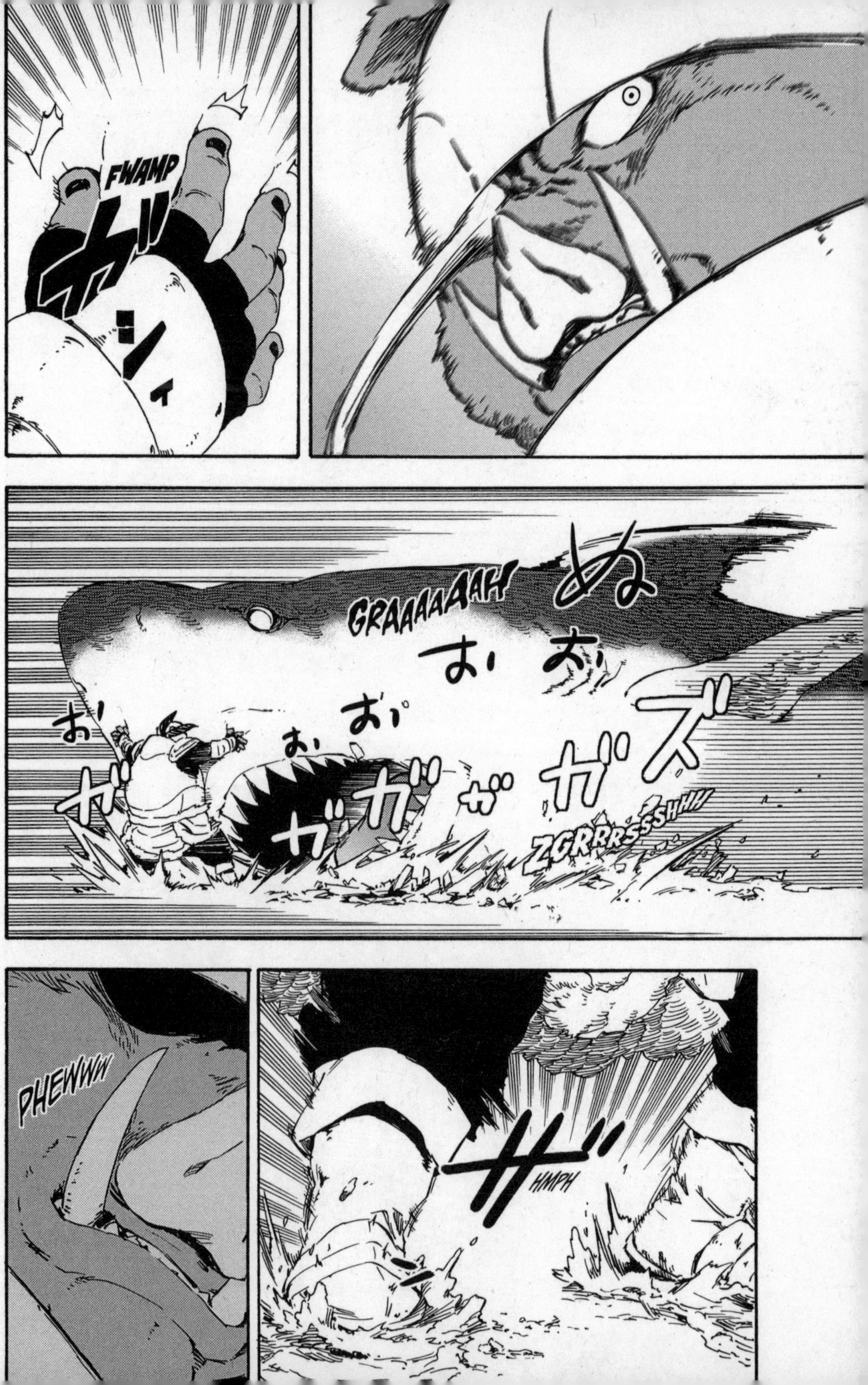
FWAMP
GRAAAAAAH
ZGRRRSSSHHH
HMPH
PHEWWW

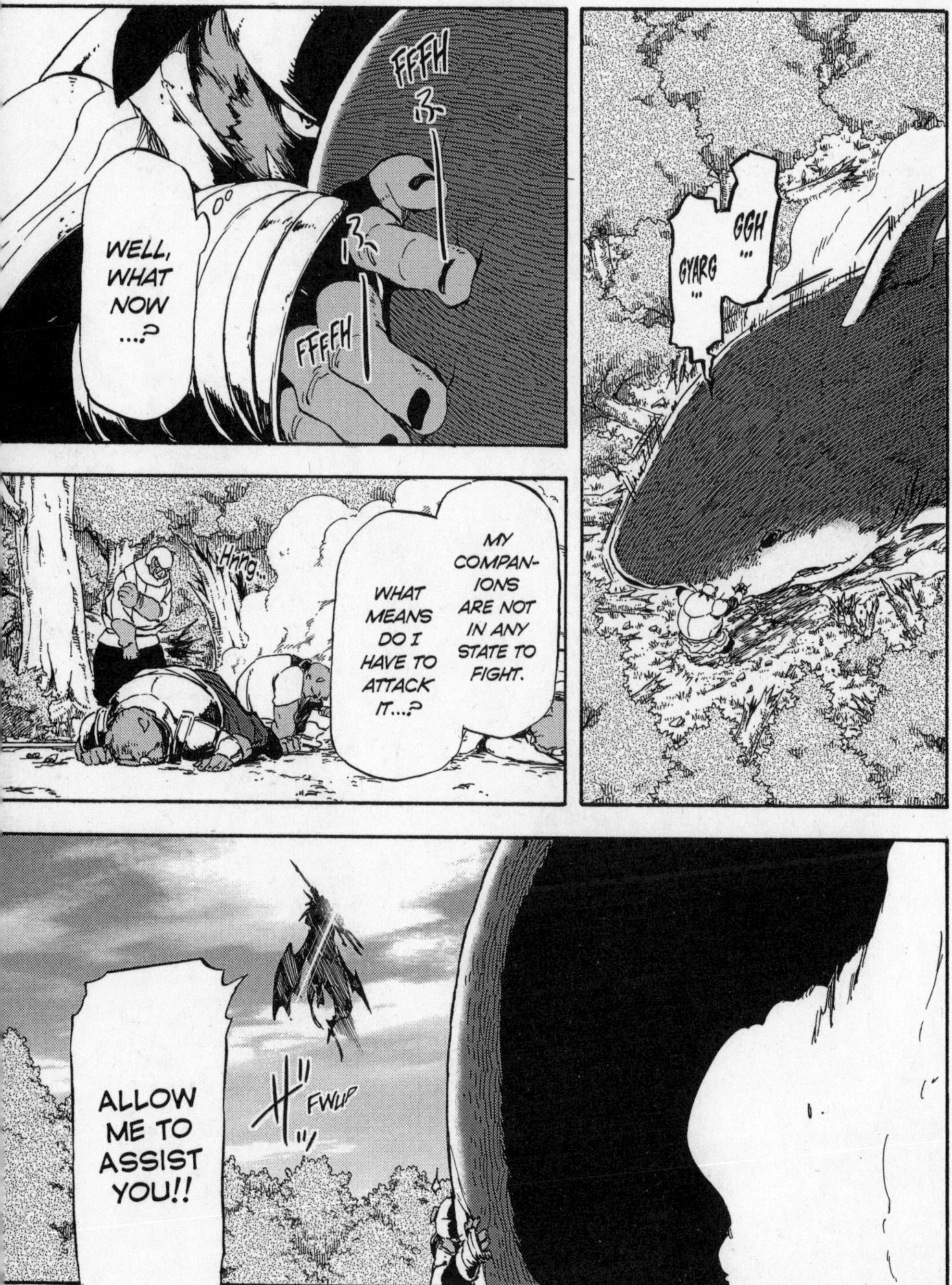
GYARG...
GGH...
FFFH
ふー
ふー
FFFFH
WELL, WHAT NOW ...?
MY COMPANIONS ARE NOT IN ANY STATE TO FIGHT.
WHAT MEANS DO I HAVE TO ATTACK IT...?
Hnng...
FWUP
ALLOW ME TO ASSIST YOU!!

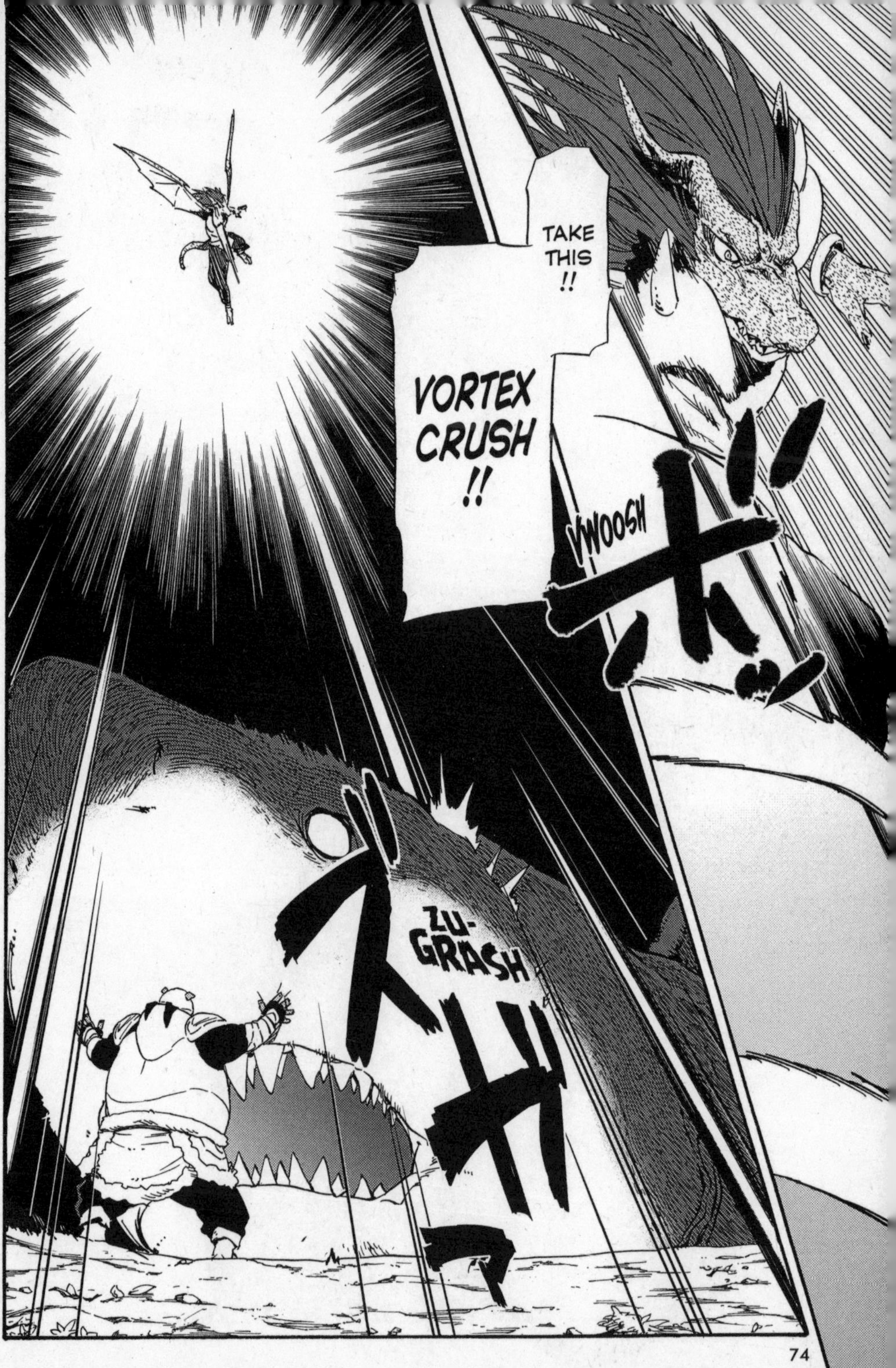
TAKE THIS !!
VORTEX CRUSH !!
VWOOSH
ZU-GRASH

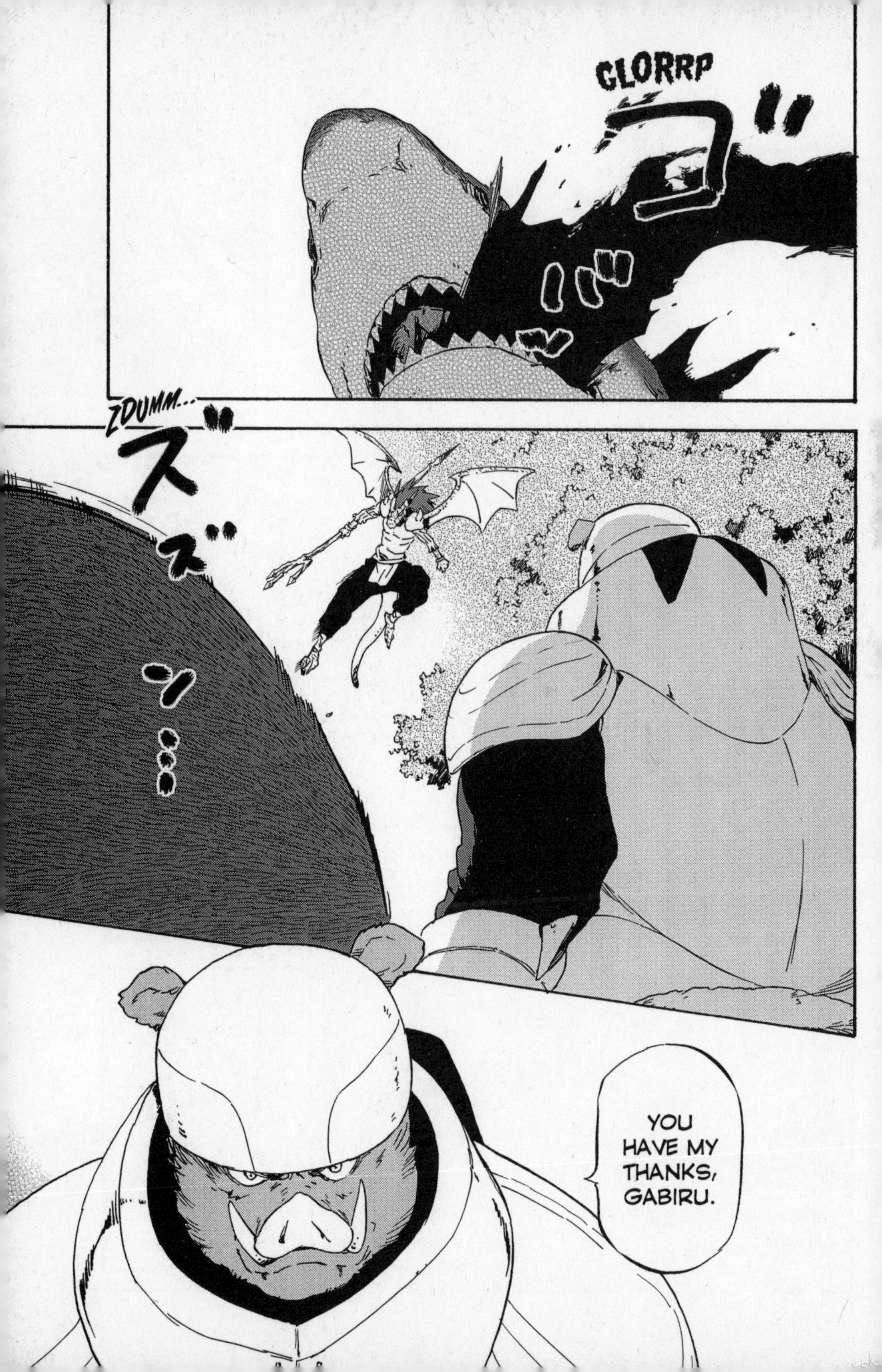
GLORRP
ZDUMM...
YOU HAVE MY THANKS, GABIRU.

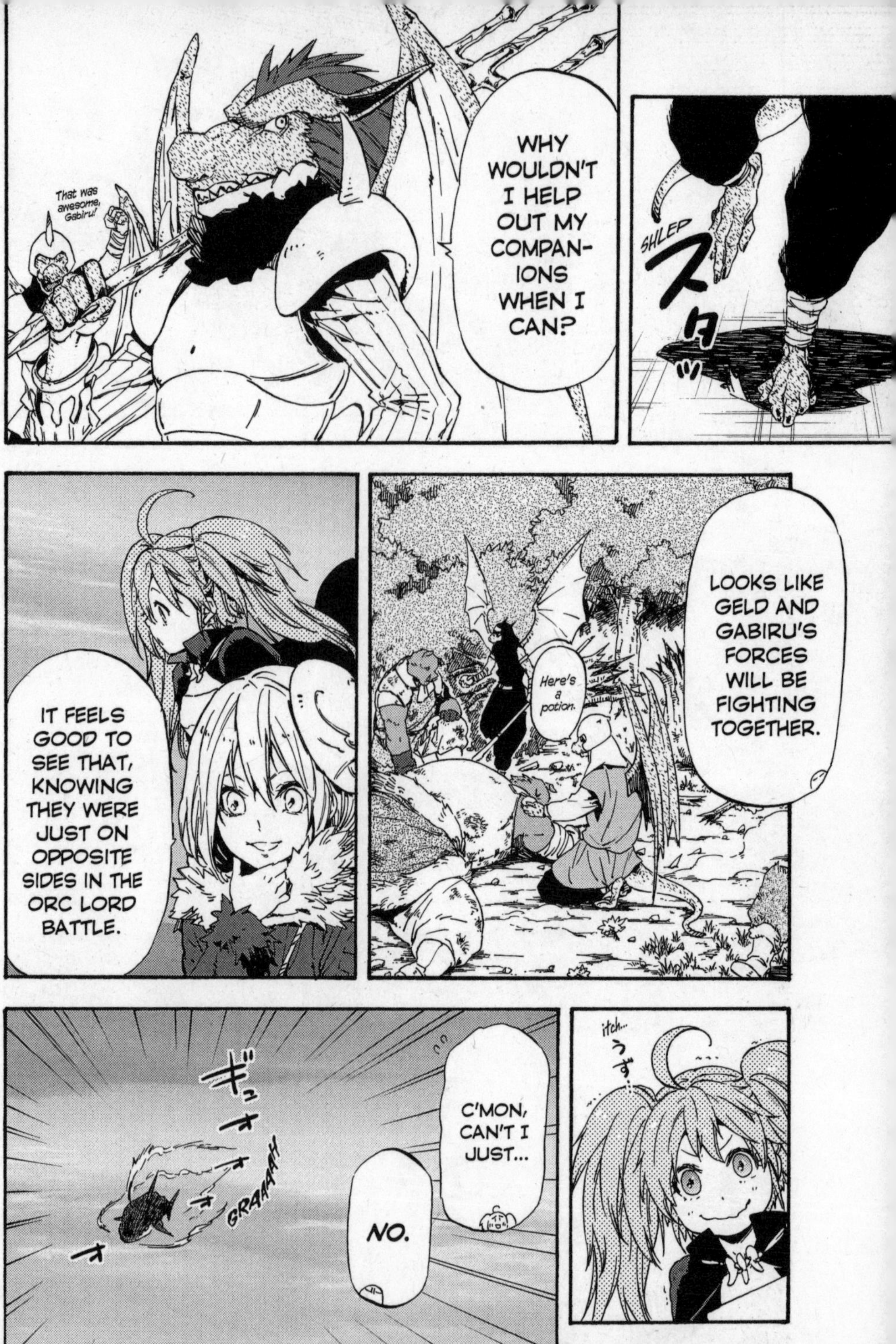
SHLEP
スタッ
WHY WOULDN'T I HELP OUT MY COMPANIONS WHEN I CAN?
That was awesome, Gabiru!
LOOKS LIKE GELD AND GABIRU'S FORCES WILL BE FIGHTING TOGETHER.
Here's a potion.
IT FEELS GOOD TO SEE THAT, KNOWING THEY WERE JUST ON OPPOSITE SIDES IN THE ORC LORD BATTLE.
itch...
うず…
C'MON, CAN'T I JUST...
NO.
ギュオォォォ
GRAAAAH

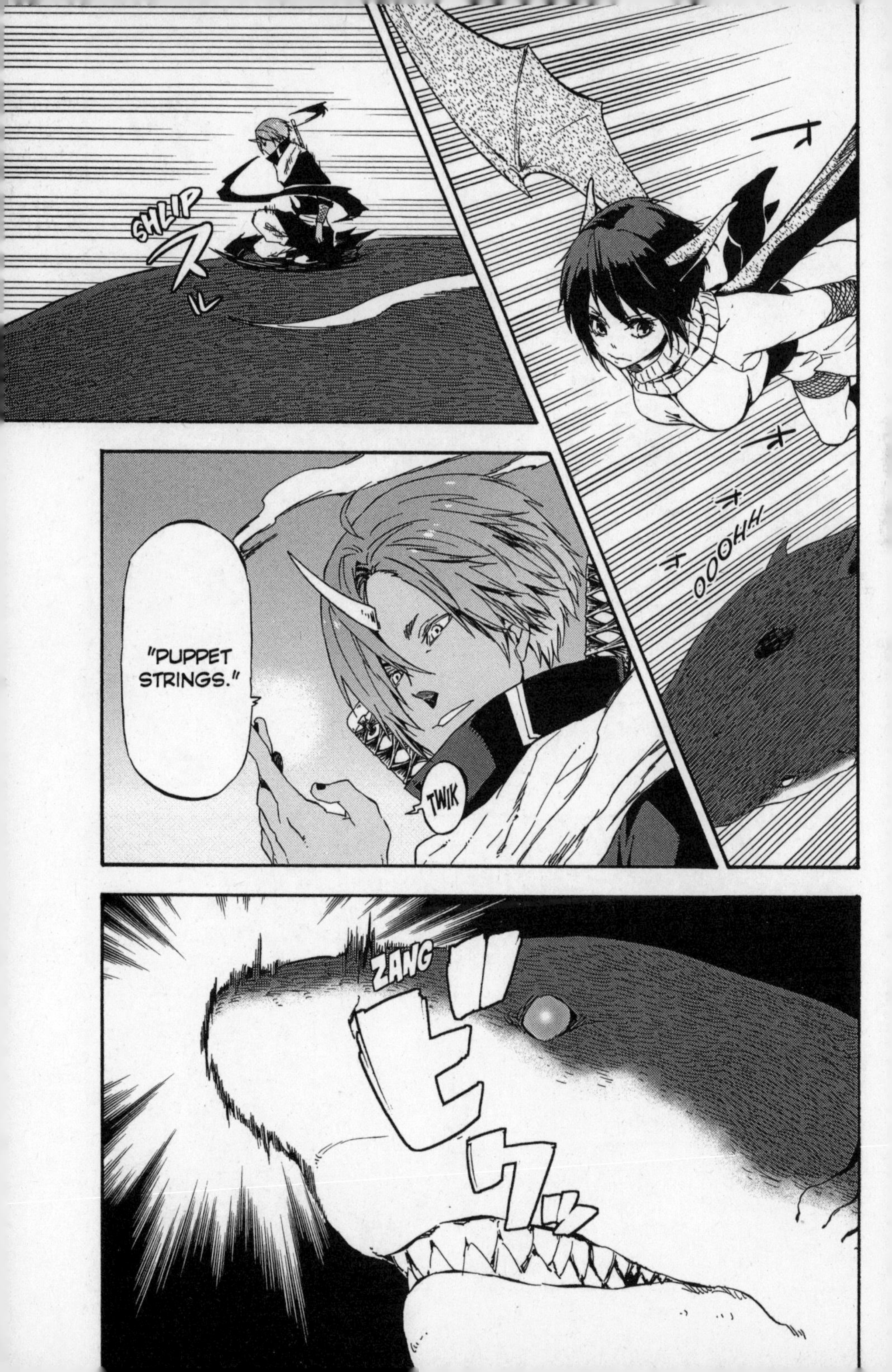
OOOHH
SHLIP
"PUPPET STRINGS."
TWIK
ZANG

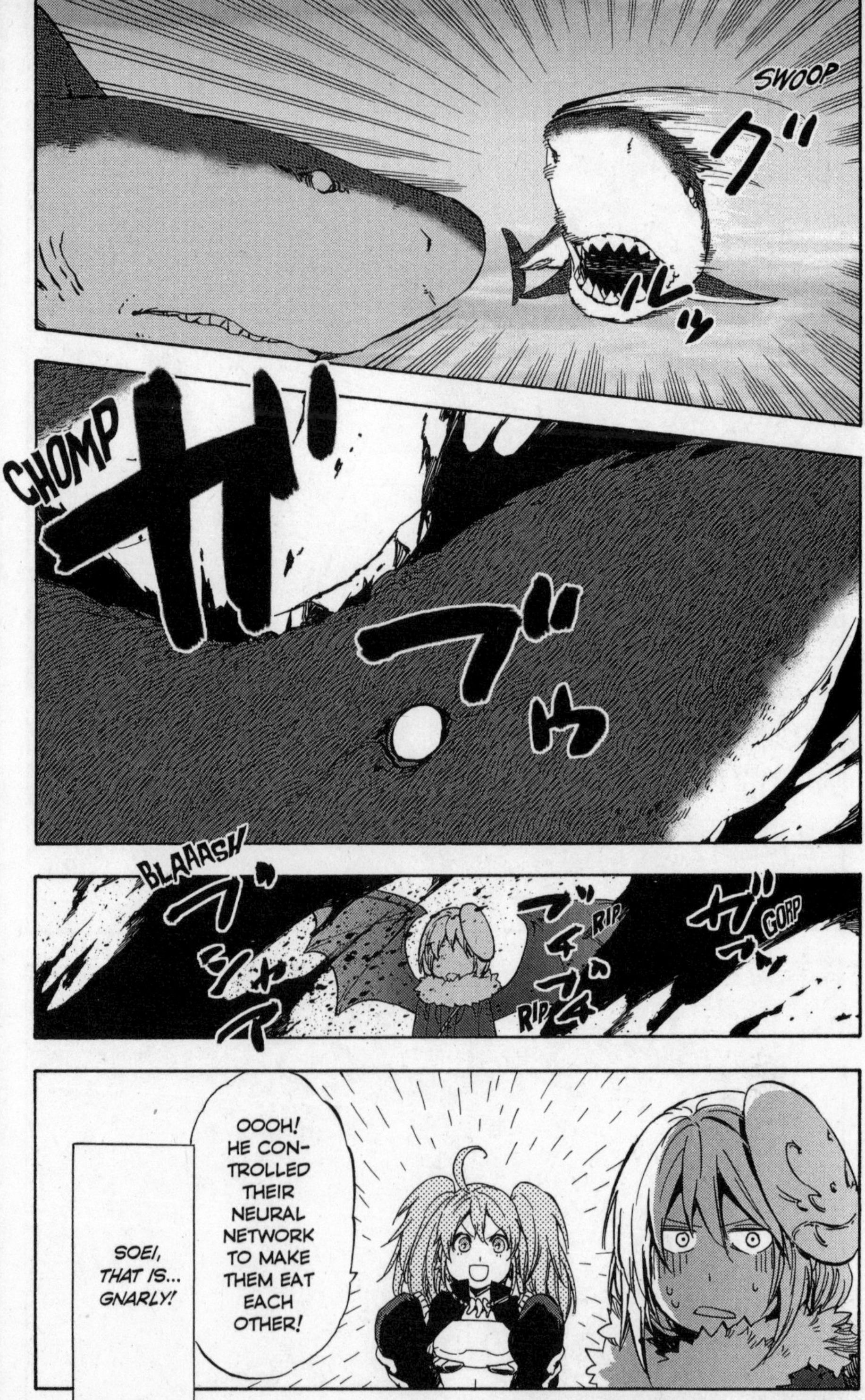
SWOOP
CHOMP
GORP
RIP
RIP
BLAAASH
OOOH! HE CONTROLLED THEIR NEURAL NETWORK TO MAKE THEM EAT EACH OTHER!
SOEI, THAT IS... GNARLY!

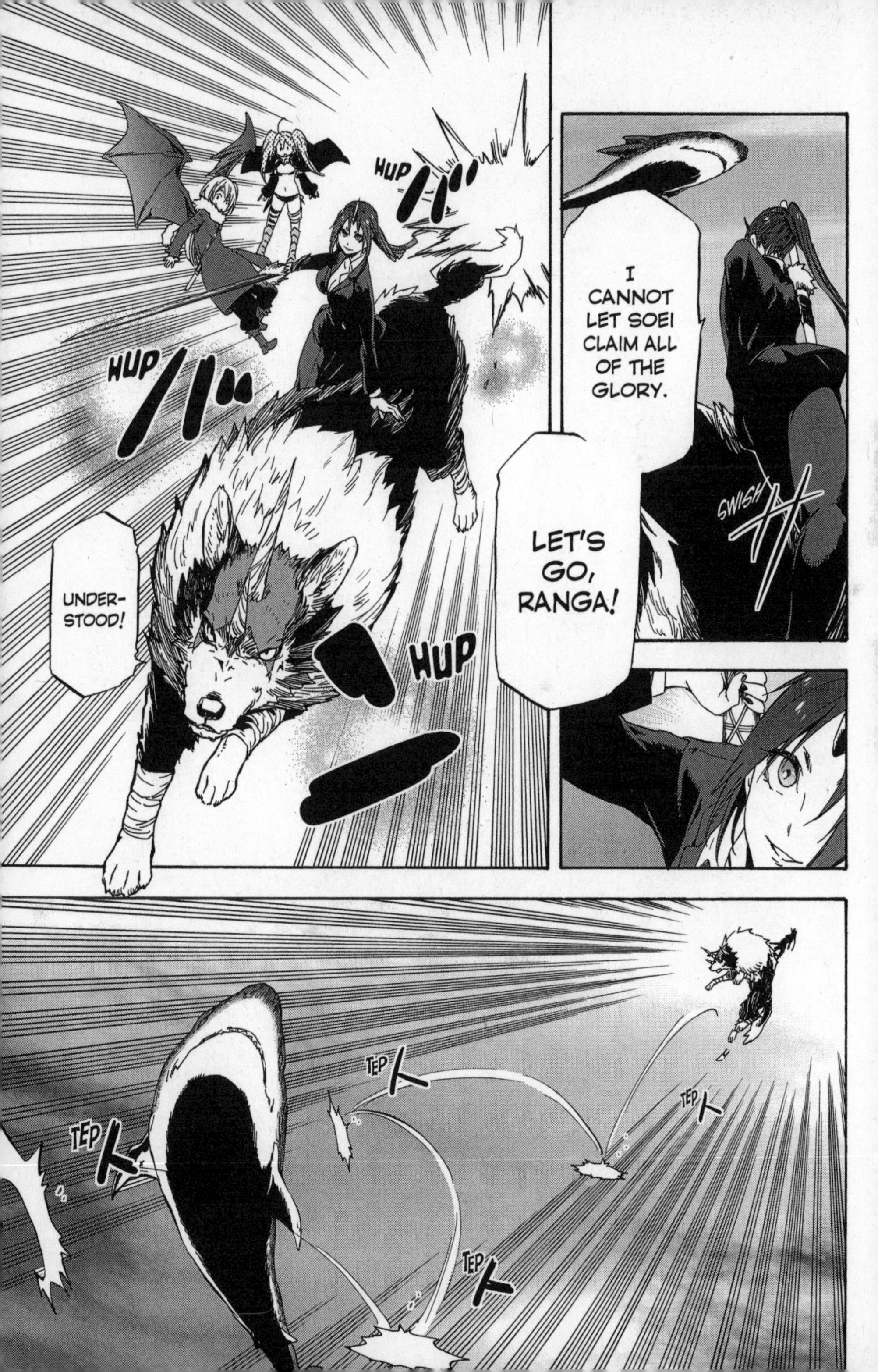
I CANNOT LET SOEI CLAIM ALL OF THE GLORY.
SWISH
LET'S GO, RANGA!
HUP
HUP
UNDERSTOOD!
HUP
TEP
TEP
TEP
TEP

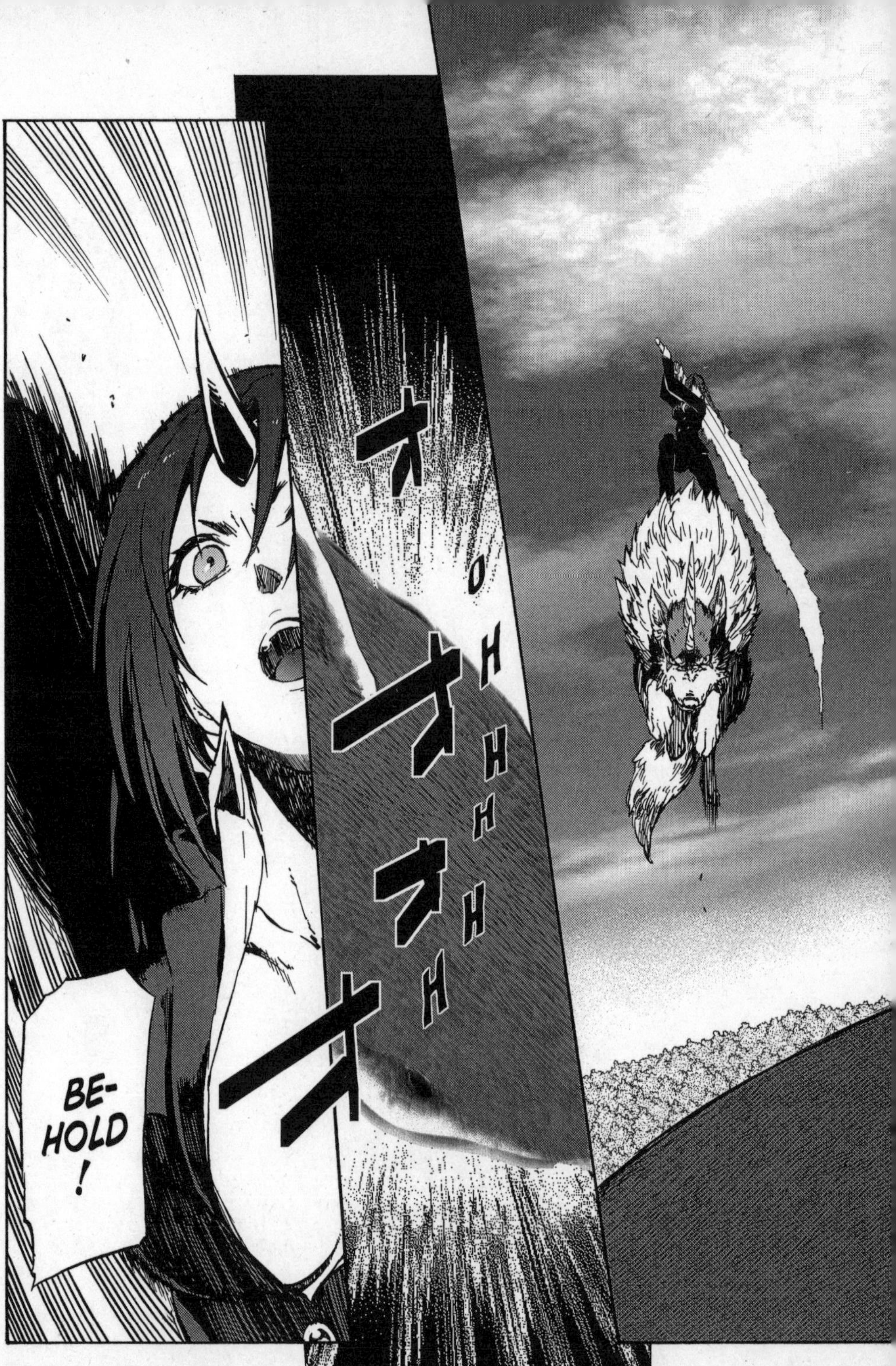
OHHHHH
BE-HOLD!

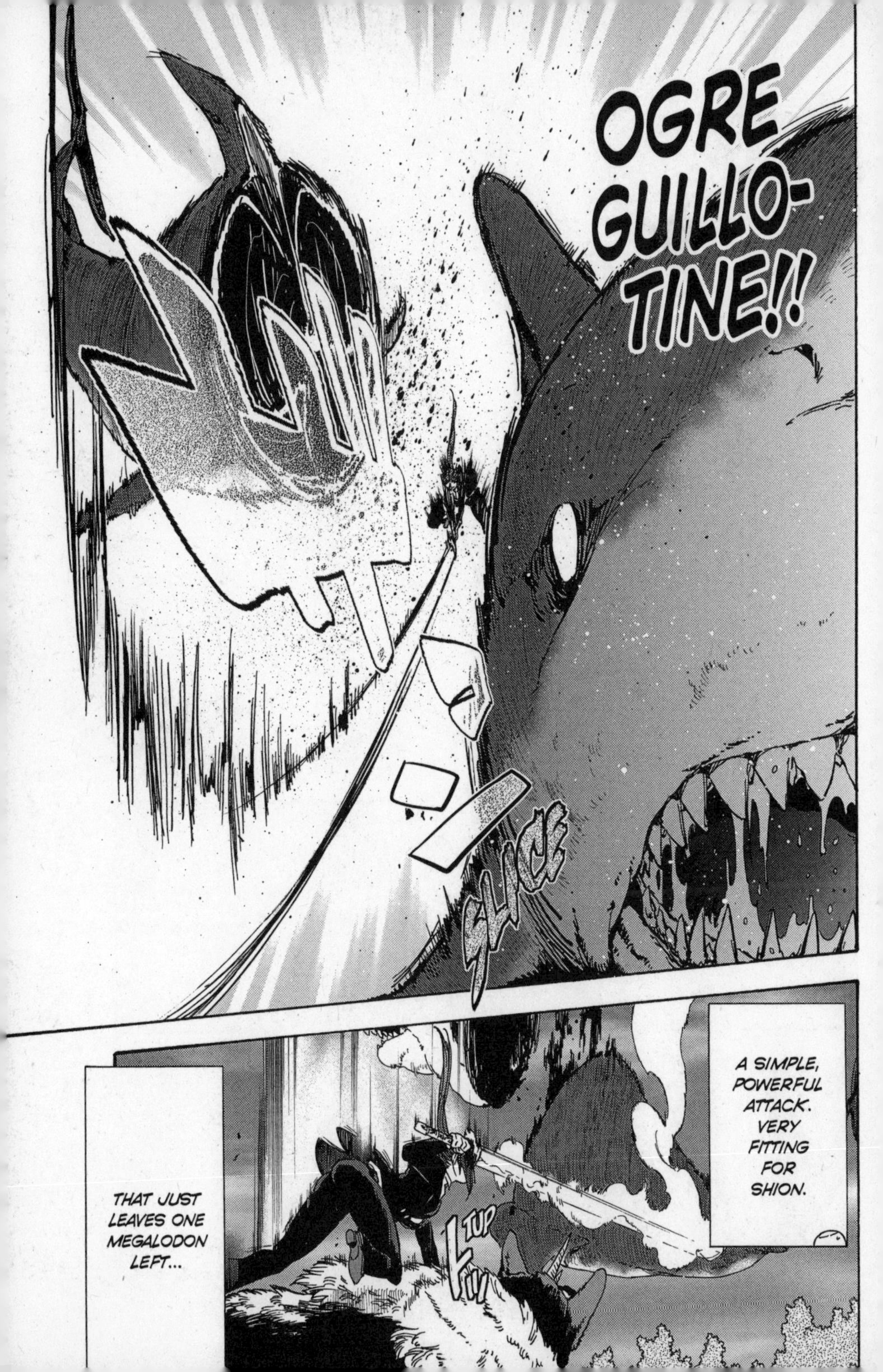
OGRE GUILLO-TINE!!
SLICE
A SIMPLE, POWERFUL ATTACK. VERY FITTING FOR SHION.
THAT JUST LEAVES ONE MEGALODON LEFT...

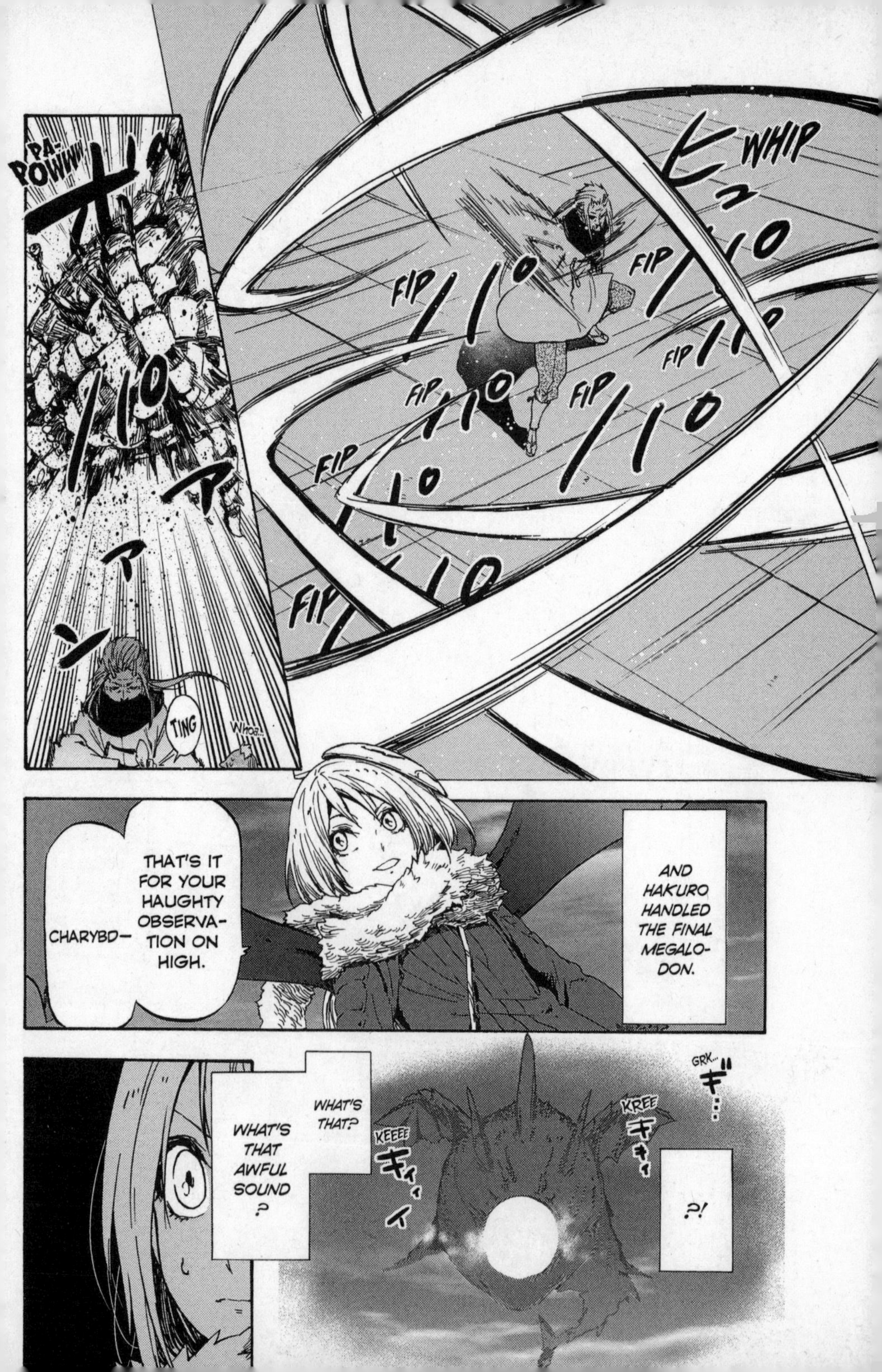
WHIP
FIP
FIP
FIP
FIP
FIP
FIP
FIP
FIP
PA-POWWW
TING
Whoa...
AND HAKURO HANDLED THE FINAL MEGALODON.
THAT'S IT FOR YOUR HAUGHTY OBSERVATION ON HIGH.
CHARYBD—
GRK...
KREE
?!
KEEEE
WHAT'S THAT?
WHAT'S THAT AWFUL SOUND?

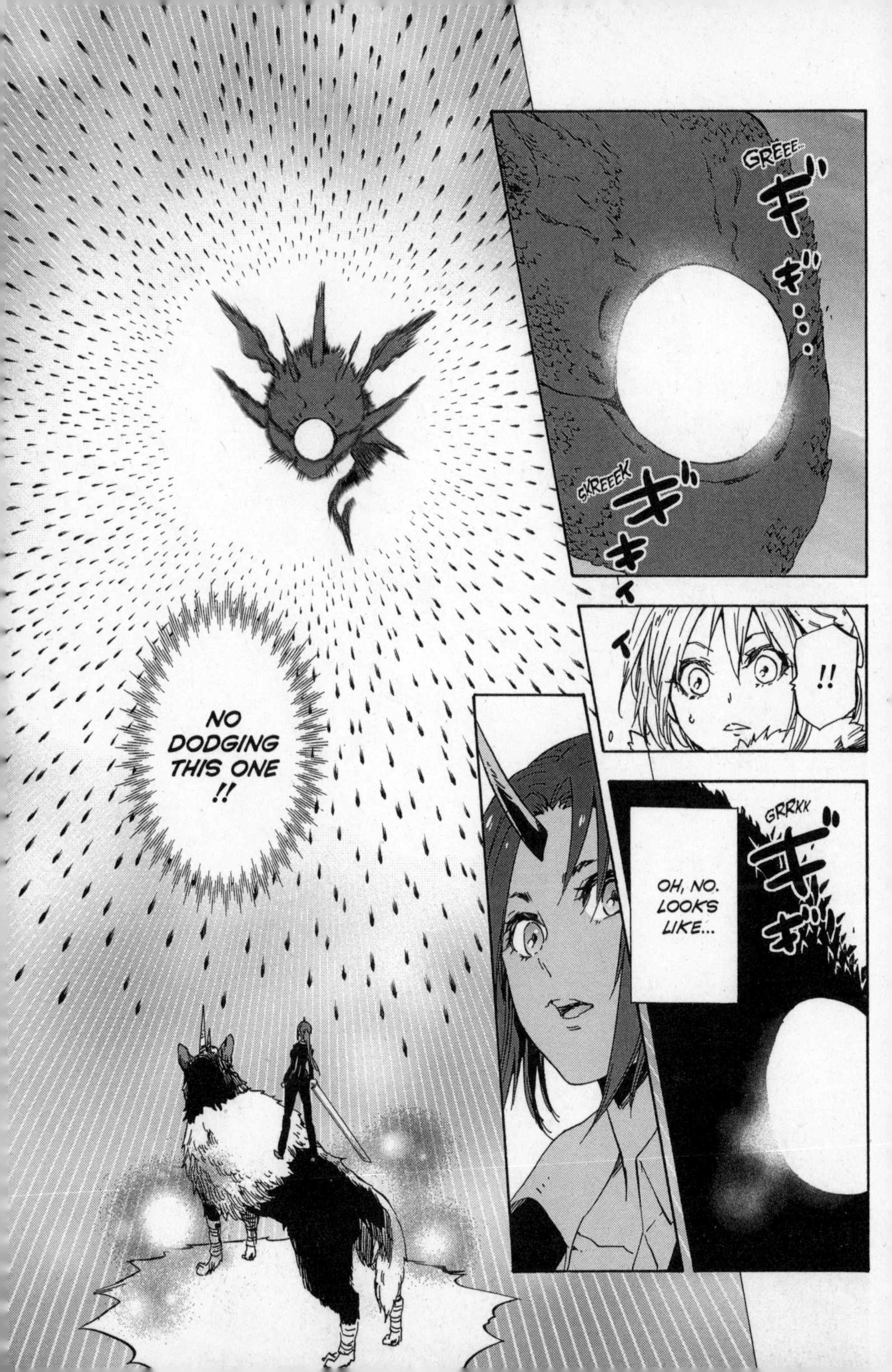
GREEE...
SKREEEK
!!
GRRKK
OH, NO. LOOKS LIKE...
NO DODGING THIS ONE !!

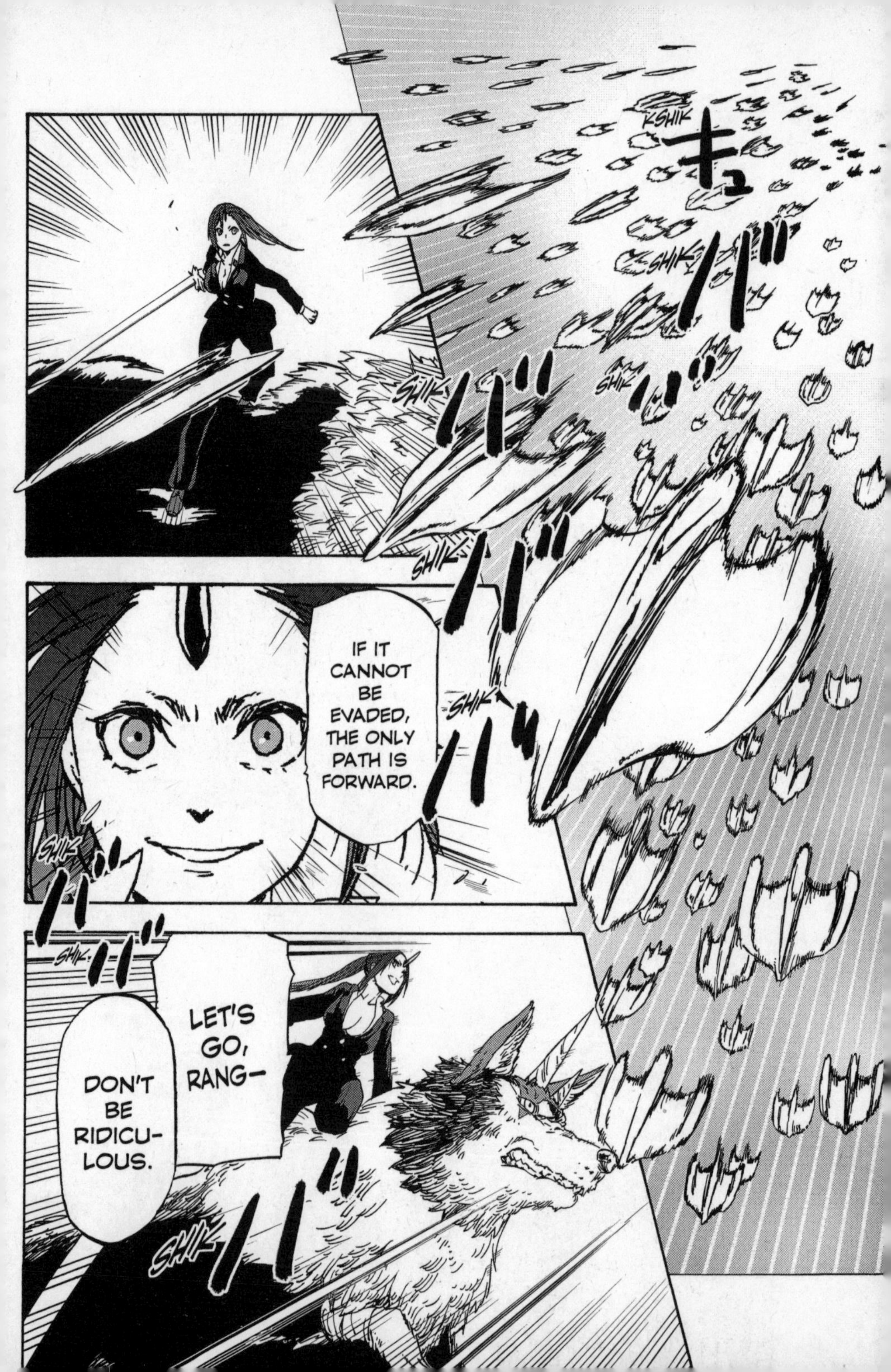
KSHIK
キュ
SHIK
バ
IF IT CANNOT BE EVADED, THE ONLY PATH IS FORWARD.
LET'S GO, RANG—
DON'T BE RIDICULOUS.

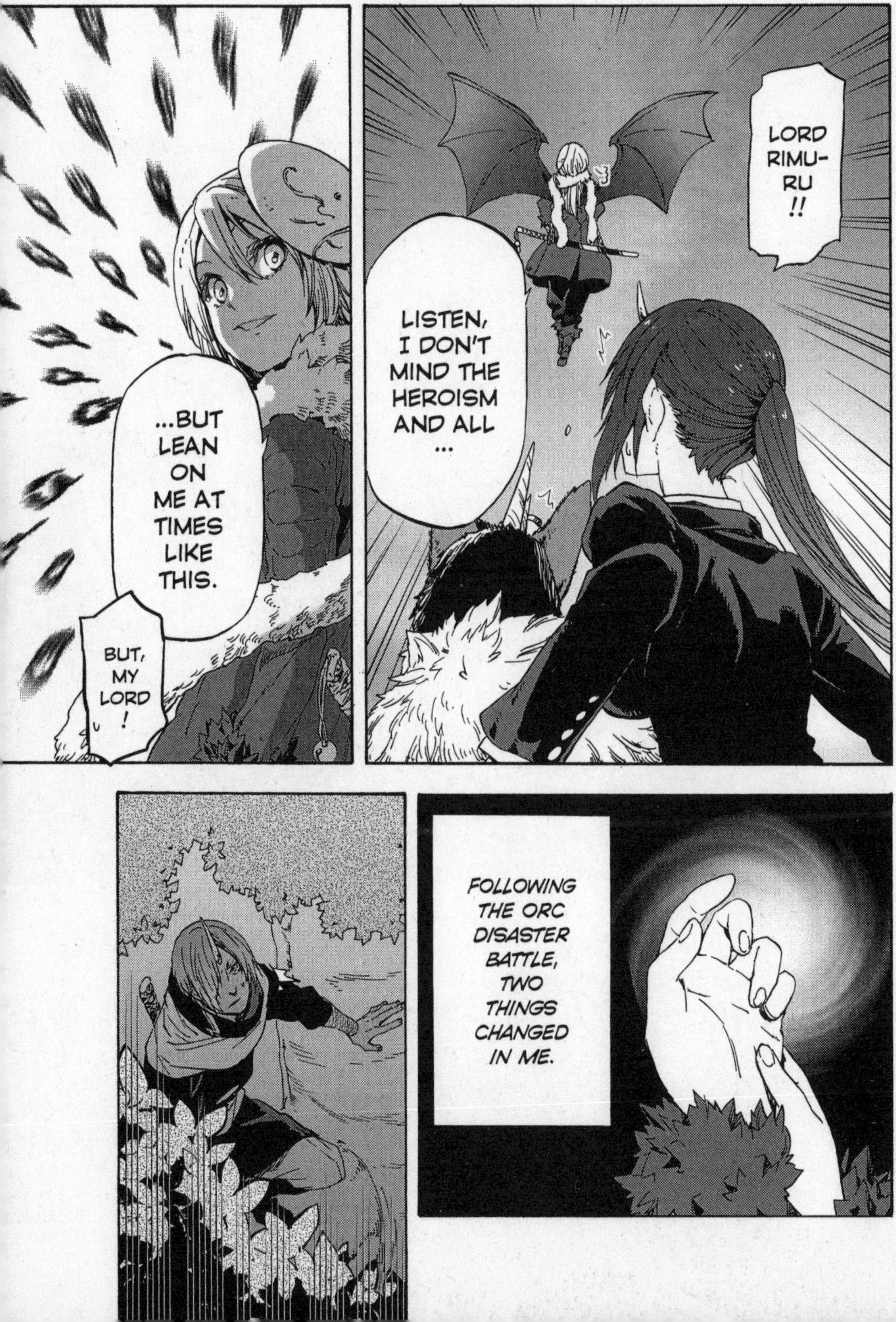
LORD RIMU-RU !!
LISTEN, I DON'T MIND THE HEROISM AND ALL ...
...BUT LEAN ON ME AT TIMES LIKE THIS.
BUT, MY LORD !
FOLLOWING THE ORC DISASTER BATTLE, TWO THINGS CHANGED IN ME.

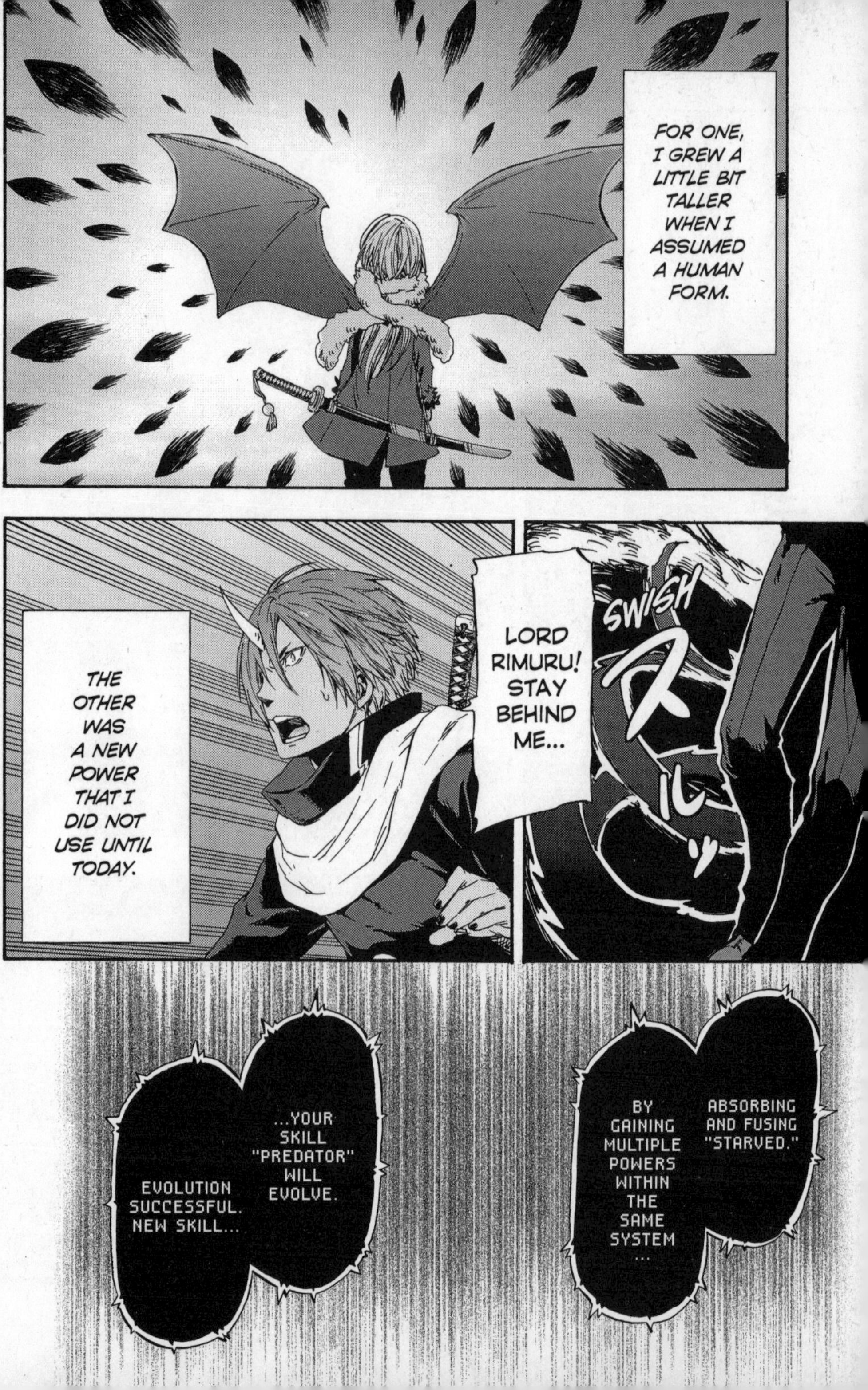
FOR ONE, I GREW A LITTLE BIT TALLER WHEN I ASSUMED A HUMAN FORM.
SWISH
スルッ
LORD RIMURU! STAY BEHIND ME...
THE OTHER WAS A NEW POWER THAT I DID NOT USE UNTIL TODAY.
ABSORBING AND FUSING "STARVED."
BY GAINING MULTIPLE POWERS WITHIN THE SAME SYSTEM ...
...YOUR SKILL "PREDATOR" WILL EVOLVE.
EVOLUTION SUCCESSFUL. NEW SKILL...

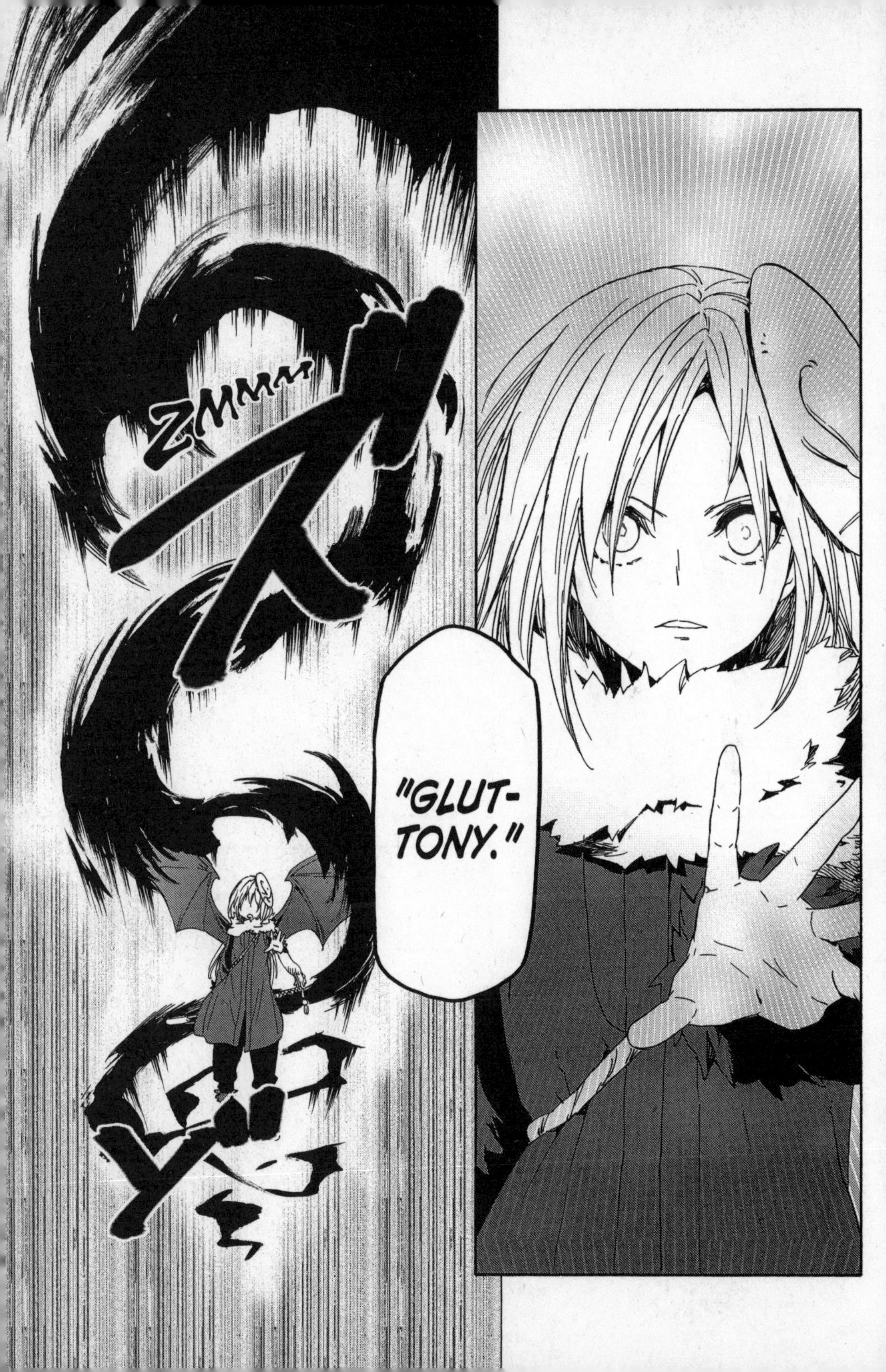
"GLUT-
TONY."
ZMMM

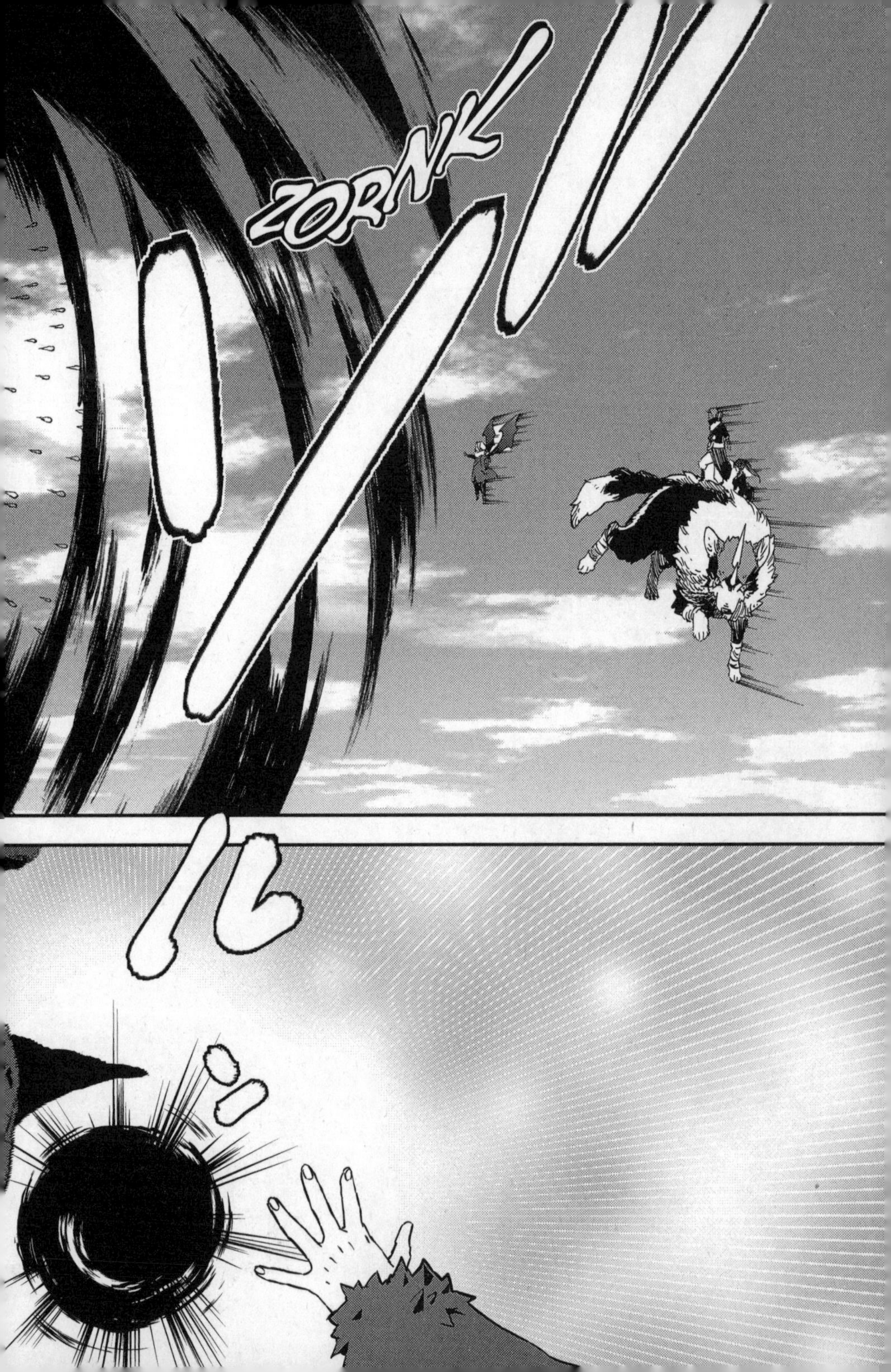
ZORNK!

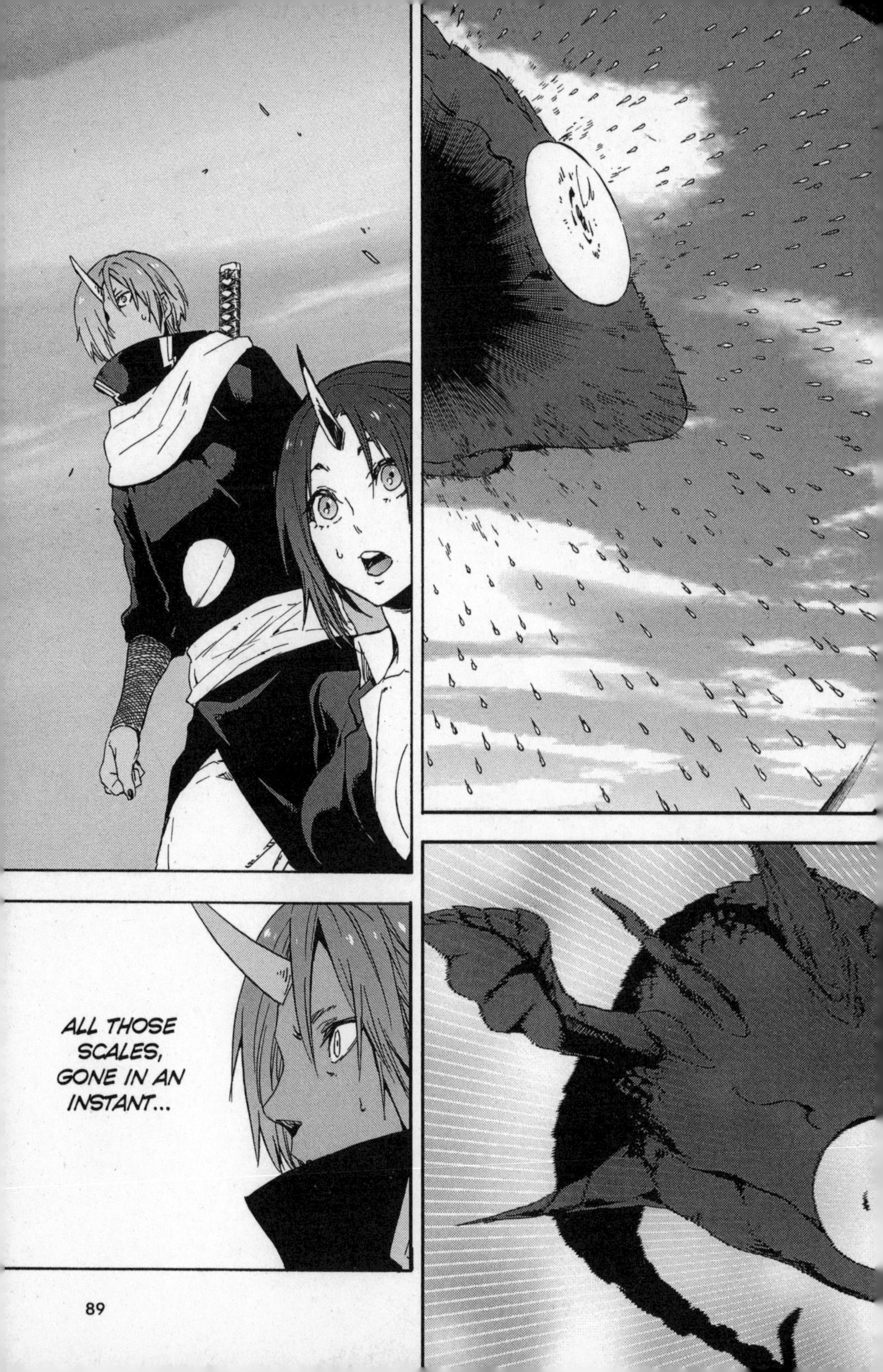
ALL THOSE SCALES, GONE IN AN INSTANT...

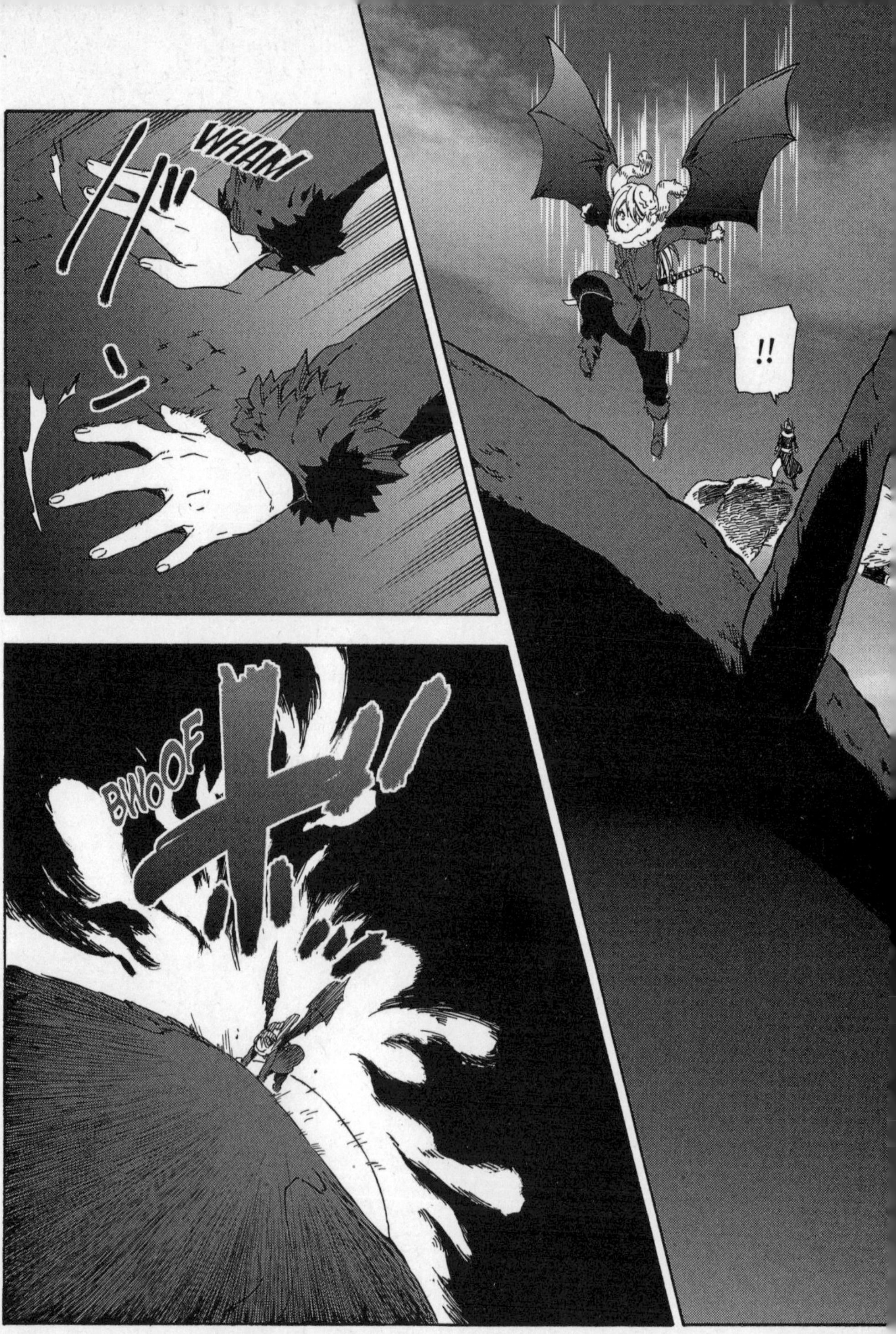
!!
WHAM
BWOOF

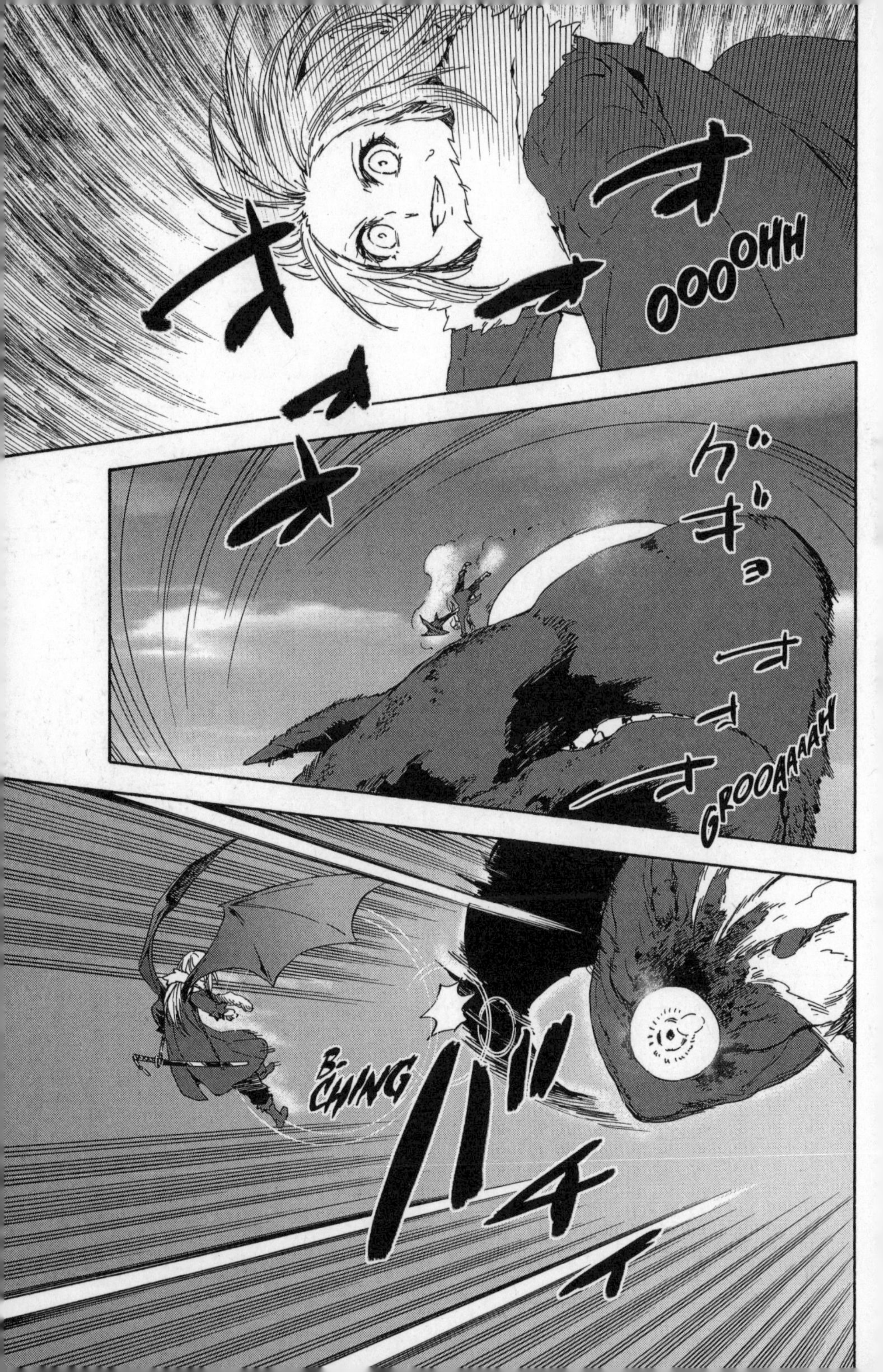
OOOOHH
GROOAAAAAH
B-CHING

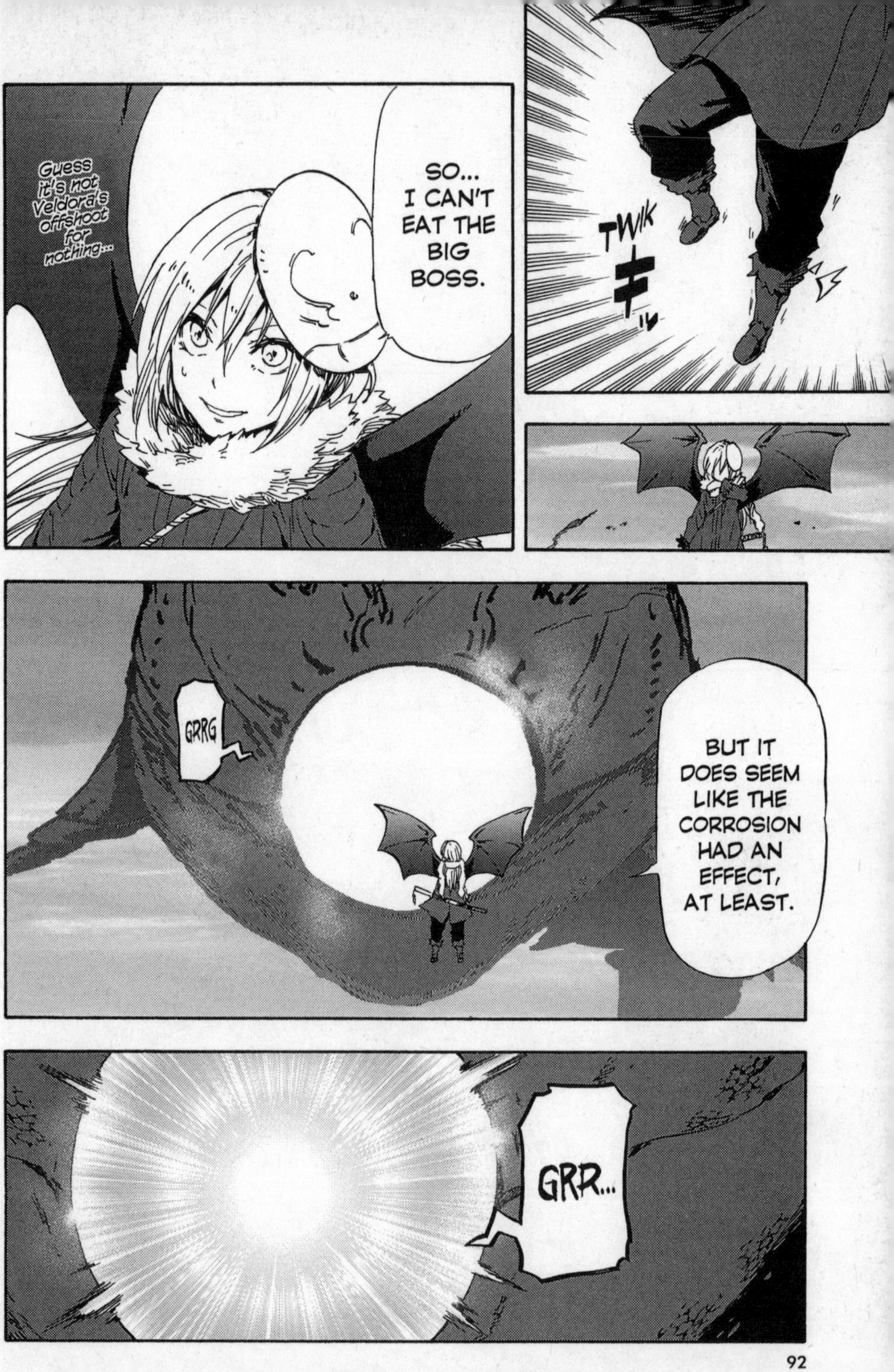
TWIK
SO... I CAN'T EAT THE BIG BOSS.
Guess it's not Veldora's offshoot for nothing...
BUT IT DOES SEEM LIKE THE CORROSION HAD AN EFFECT, AT LEAST.
GRRG
GRR...

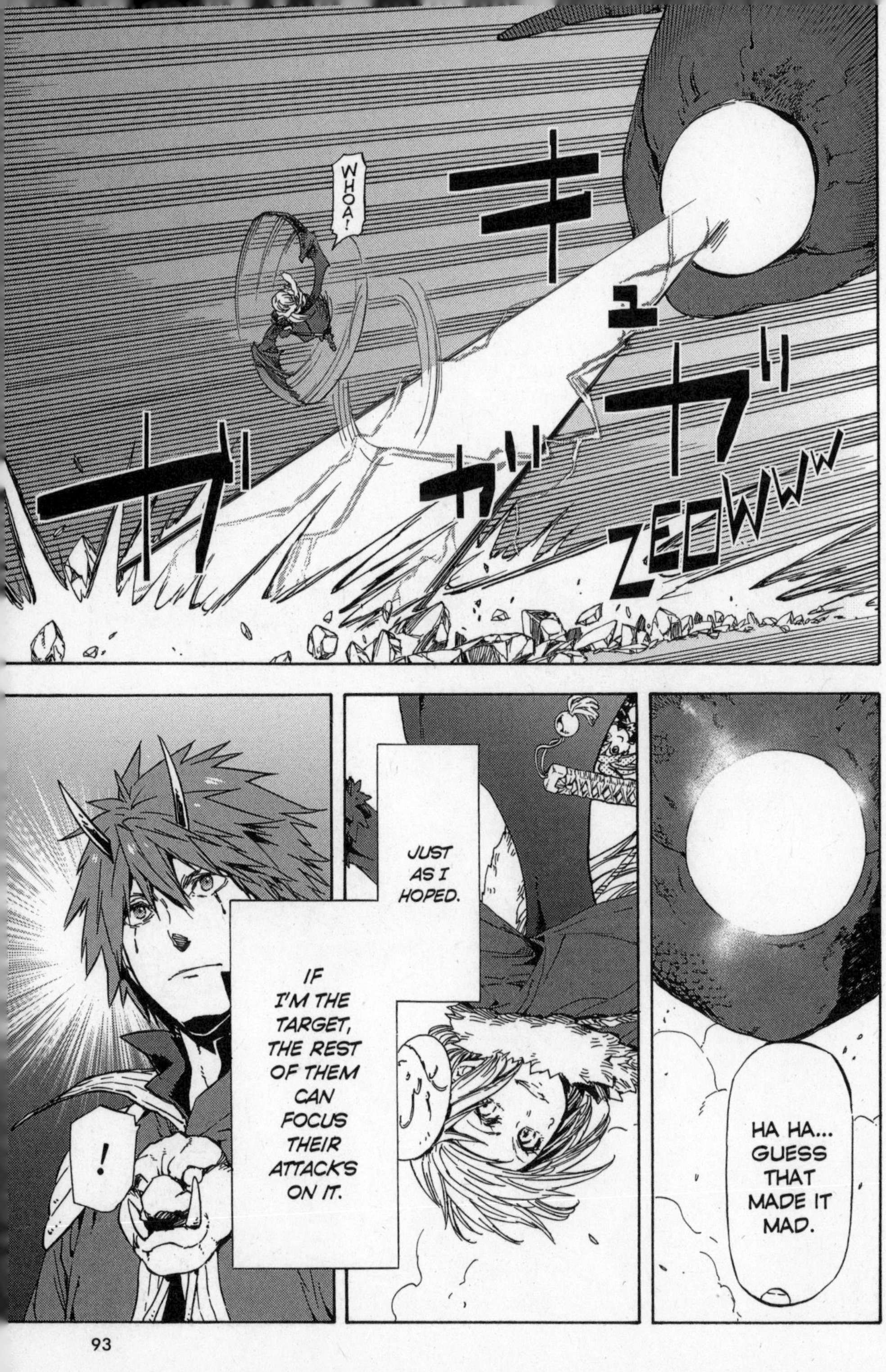
キュ
WHOA!
ZEOWWW
HA HA... GUESS THAT MADE IT MAD.
JUST AS I HOPED.
IF I'M THE TARGET, THE REST OF THEM CAN FOCUS THEIR ATTACKS ON IT.
!

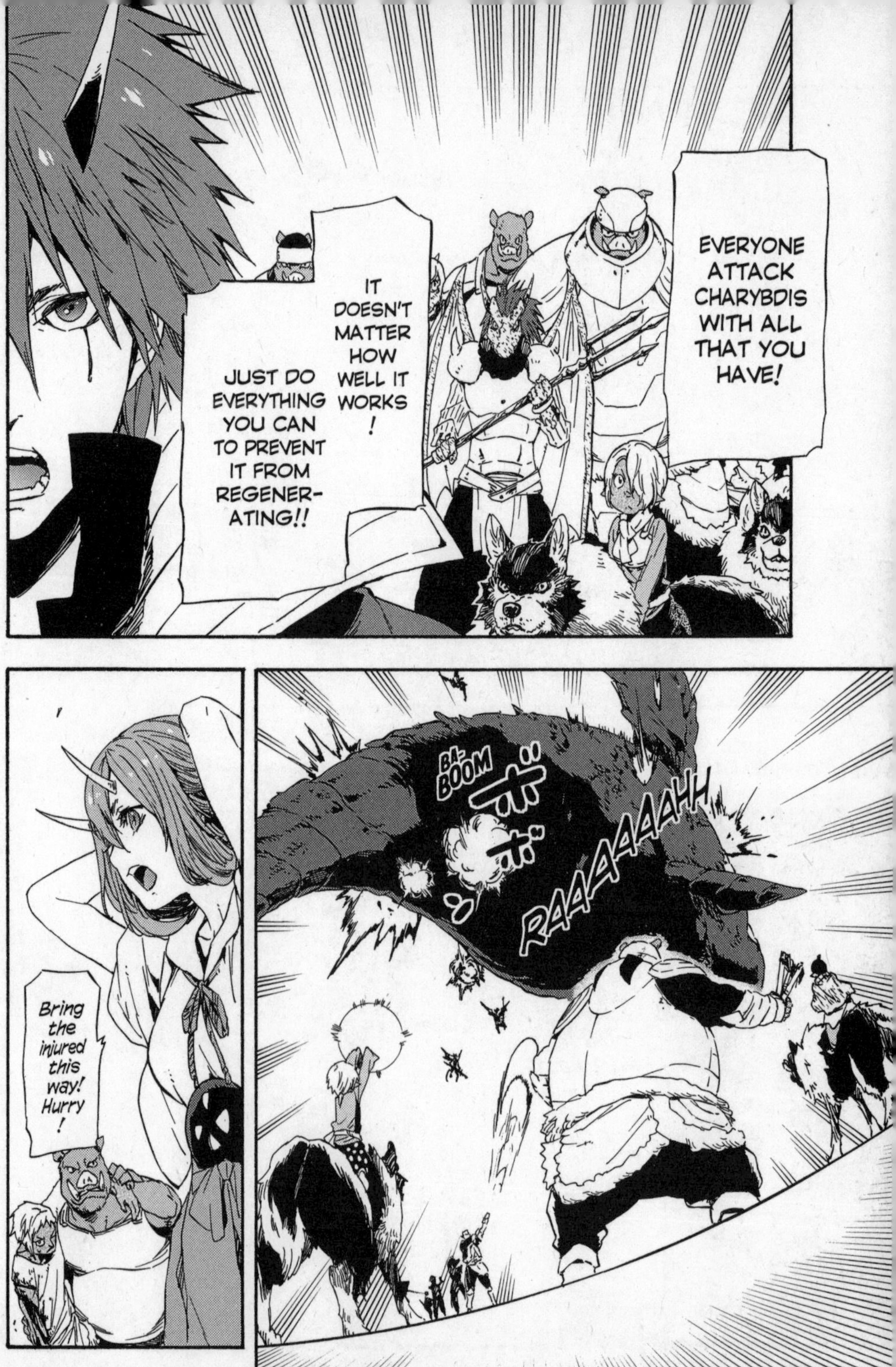
EVERYONE ATTACK CHARYBDIS WITH ALL THAT YOU HAVE!
IT DOESN'T MATTER HOW WELL IT WORKS!
JUST DO EVERYTHING YOU CAN TO PREVENT IT FROM REGENER-ATING!!
BA-BOOM
ボ
ボ
RAAAAAAAHH
Bring the injured this way! Hurry!

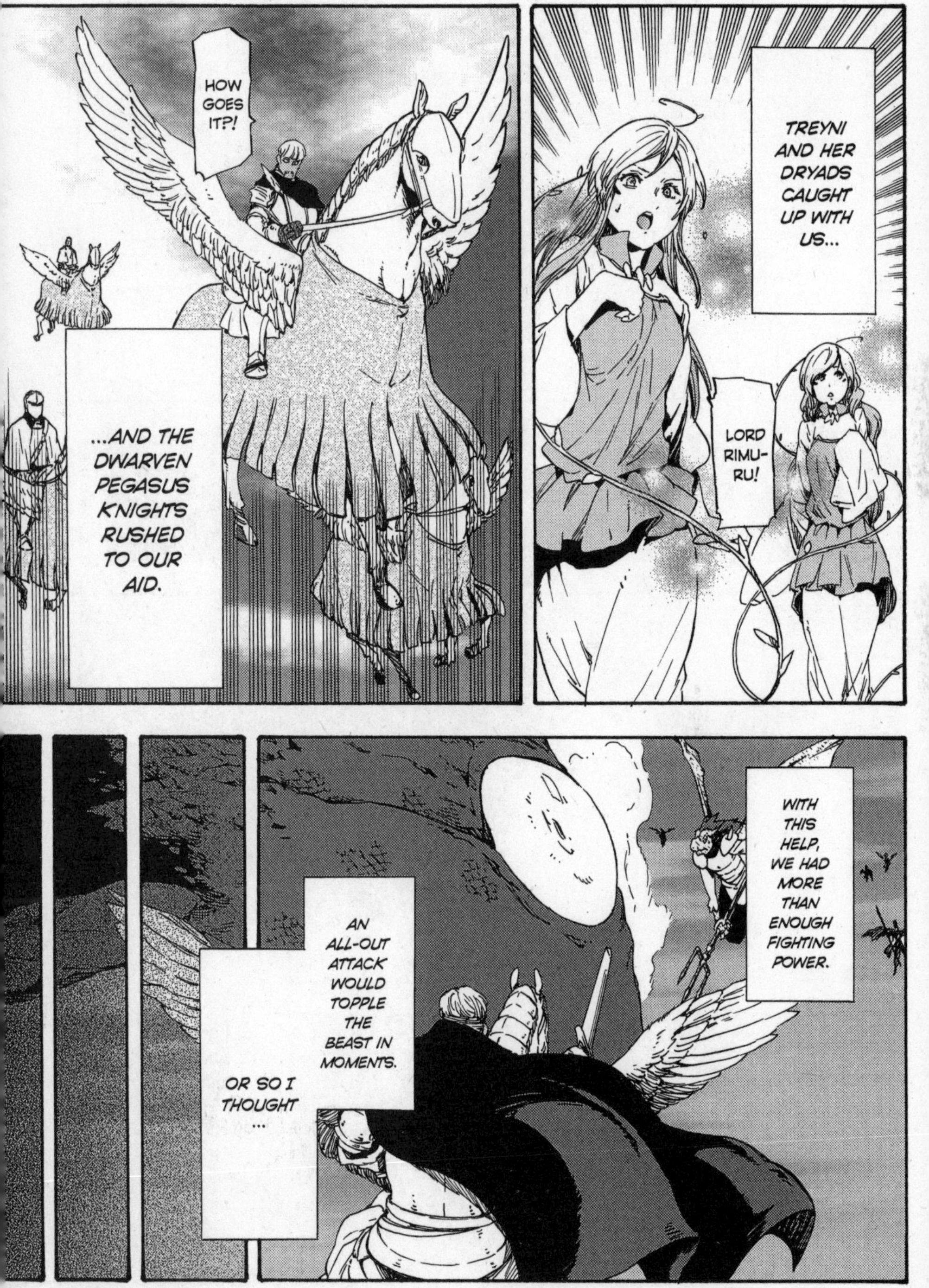
TREYNI AND HER DRYADS CAUGHT UP WITH US...
LORD RIMU-RU!
HOW GOES IT?!
...AND THE DWARVEN PEGASUS KNIGHTS RUSHED TO OUR AID.
WITH THIS HELP, WE HAD MORE THAN ENOUGH FIGHTING POWER.
AN ALL-OUT ATTACK WOULD TOPPLE THE BEAST IN MOMENTS.
OR SO I THOUGHT...

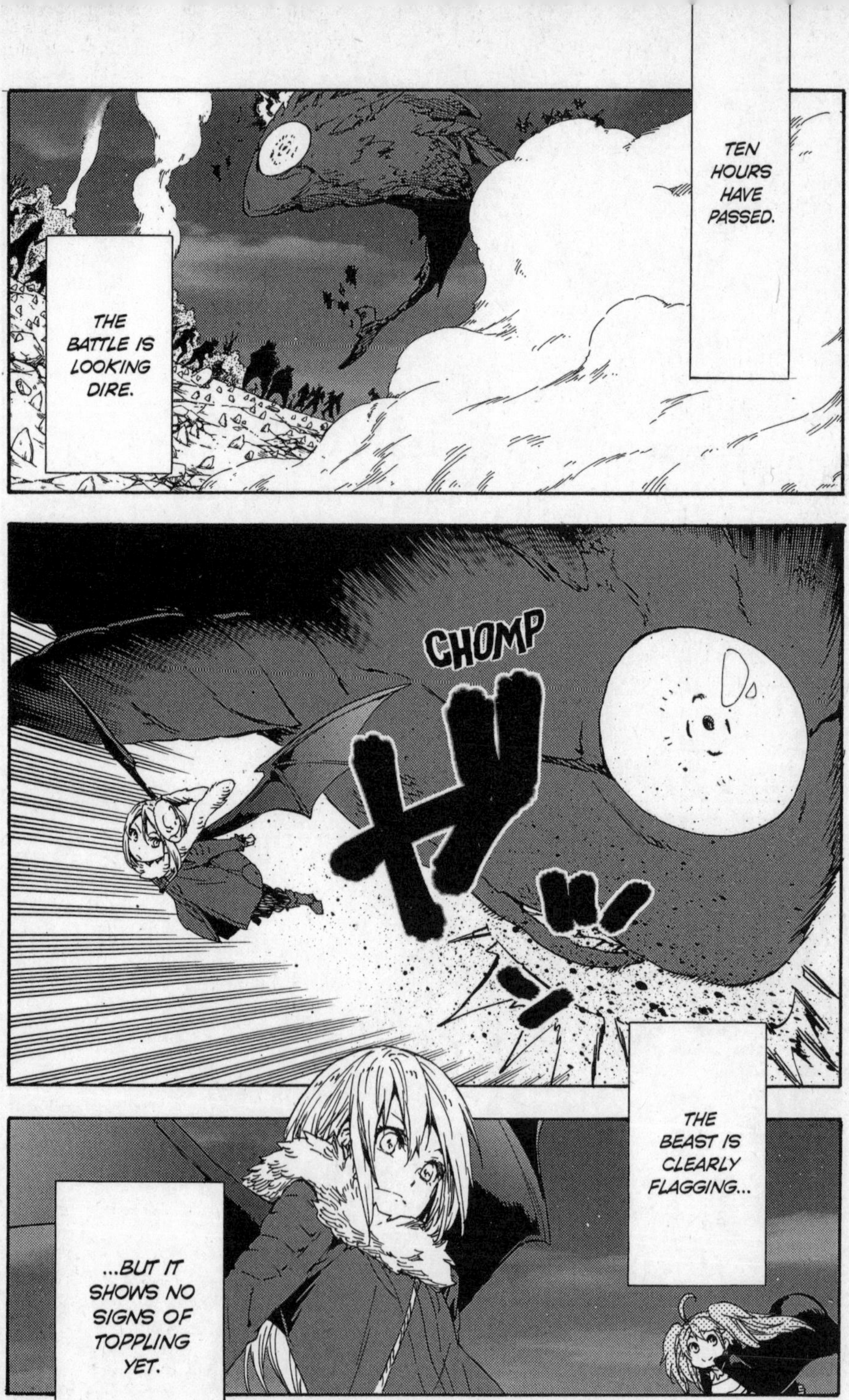
TEN HOURS HAVE PASSED.
THE BATTLE IS LOOKING DIRE.
CHOMP
THE BEAST IS CLEARLY FLAGGING...
...BUT IT SHOWS NO SIGNS OF TOPPLING YET.

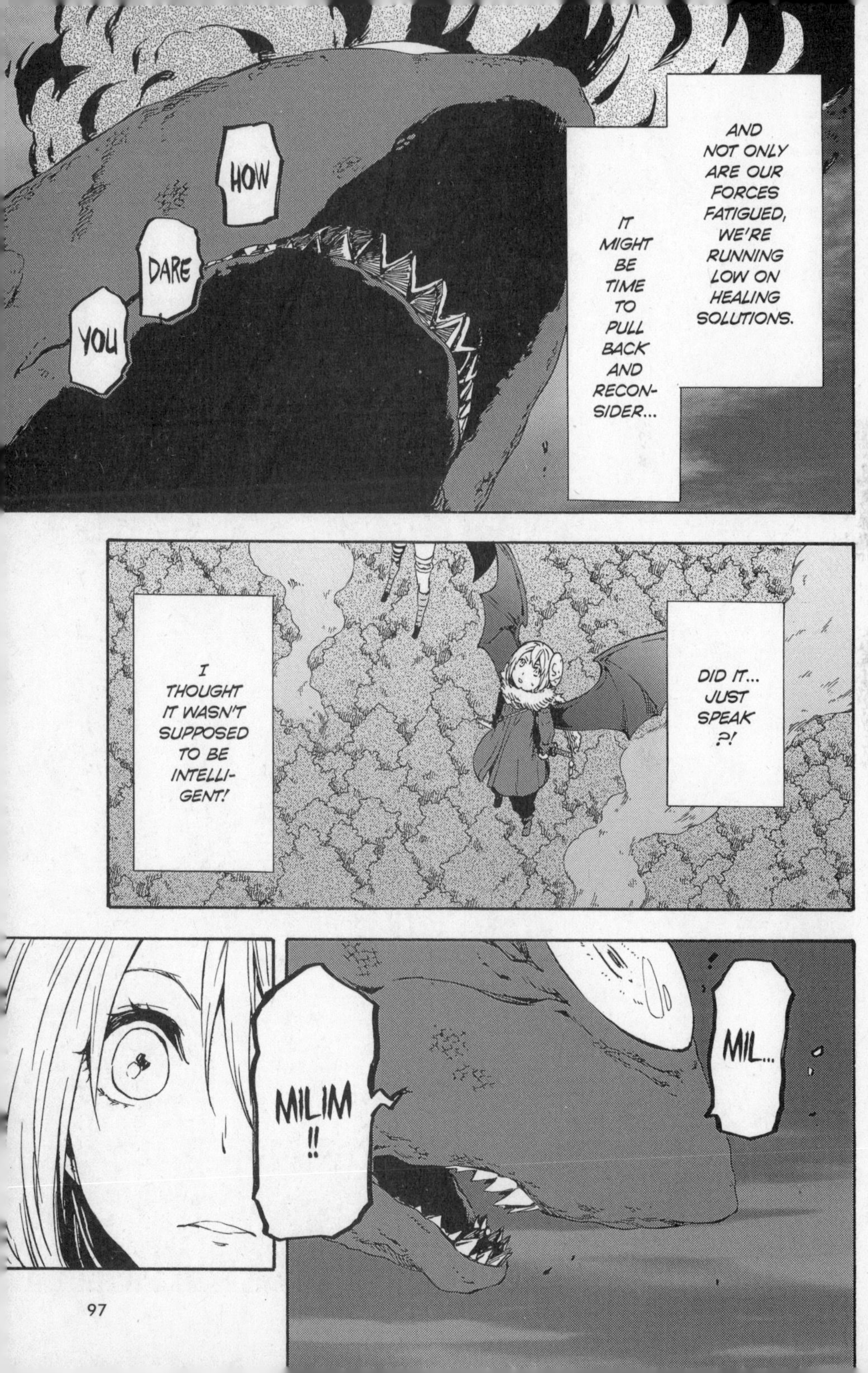
AND NOT ONLY ARE OUR FORCES FATIGUED, WE'RE RUNNING LOW ON HEALING SOLUTIONS.
IT MIGHT BE TIME TO PULL BACK AND RECONSIDER...
HOW
DARE
YOU
DID IT... JUST SPEAK?!
I THOUGHT IT WASN'T SUPPOSED TO BE INTELLIGENT!
MIL...
MILIM!!

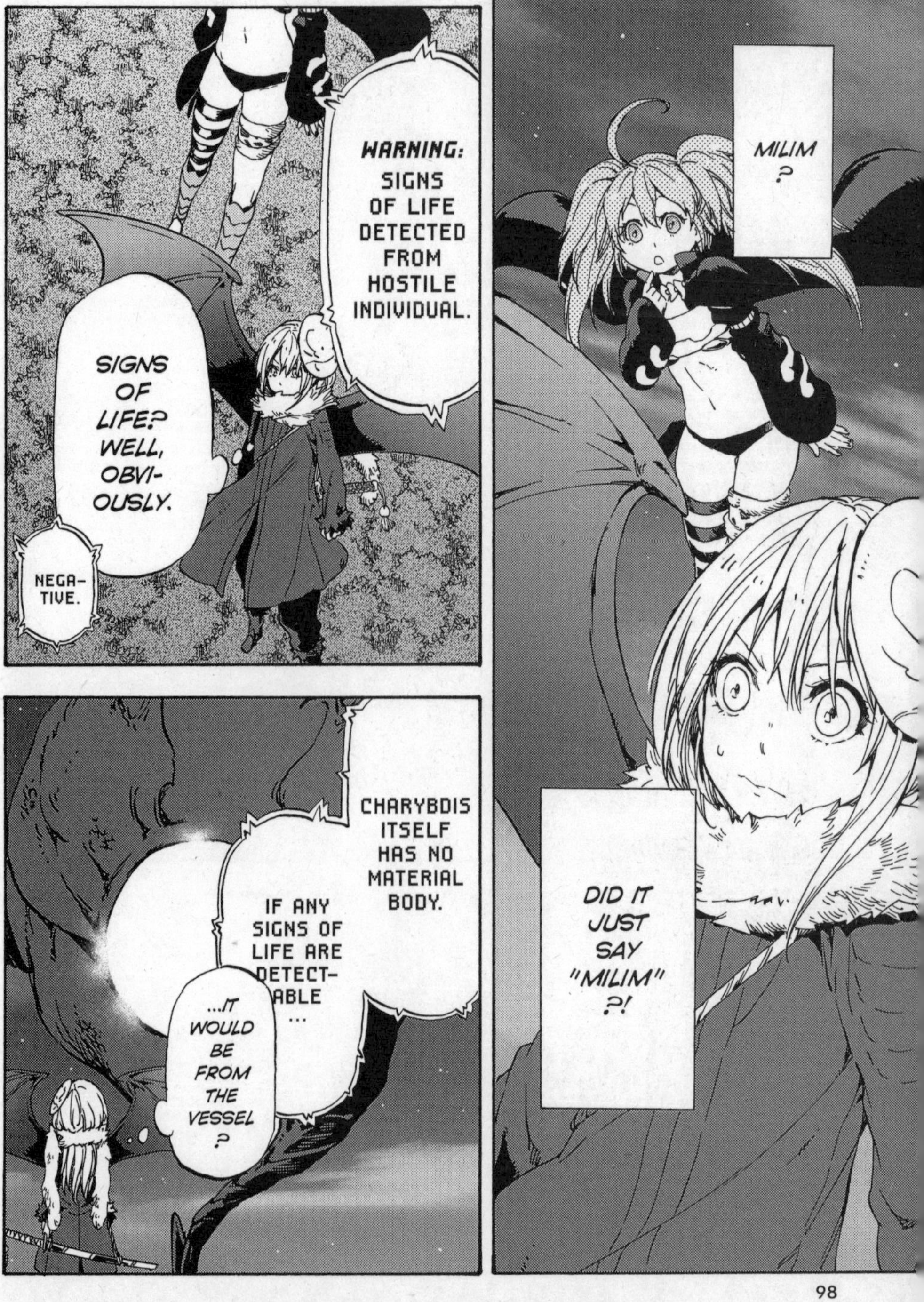
MILIM ?
DID IT JUST SAY "MILIM" ?!
WARNING: SIGNS OF LIFE DETECTED FROM HOSTILE INDIVIDUAL.
SIGNS OF LIFE? WELL, OBVIOUSLY.
NEGATIVE.
CHARYBDIS ITSELF HAS NO MATERIAL BODY.
IF ANY SIGNS OF LIFE ARE DETECTABLE ...
...IT WOULD BE FROM THE VESSEL ?

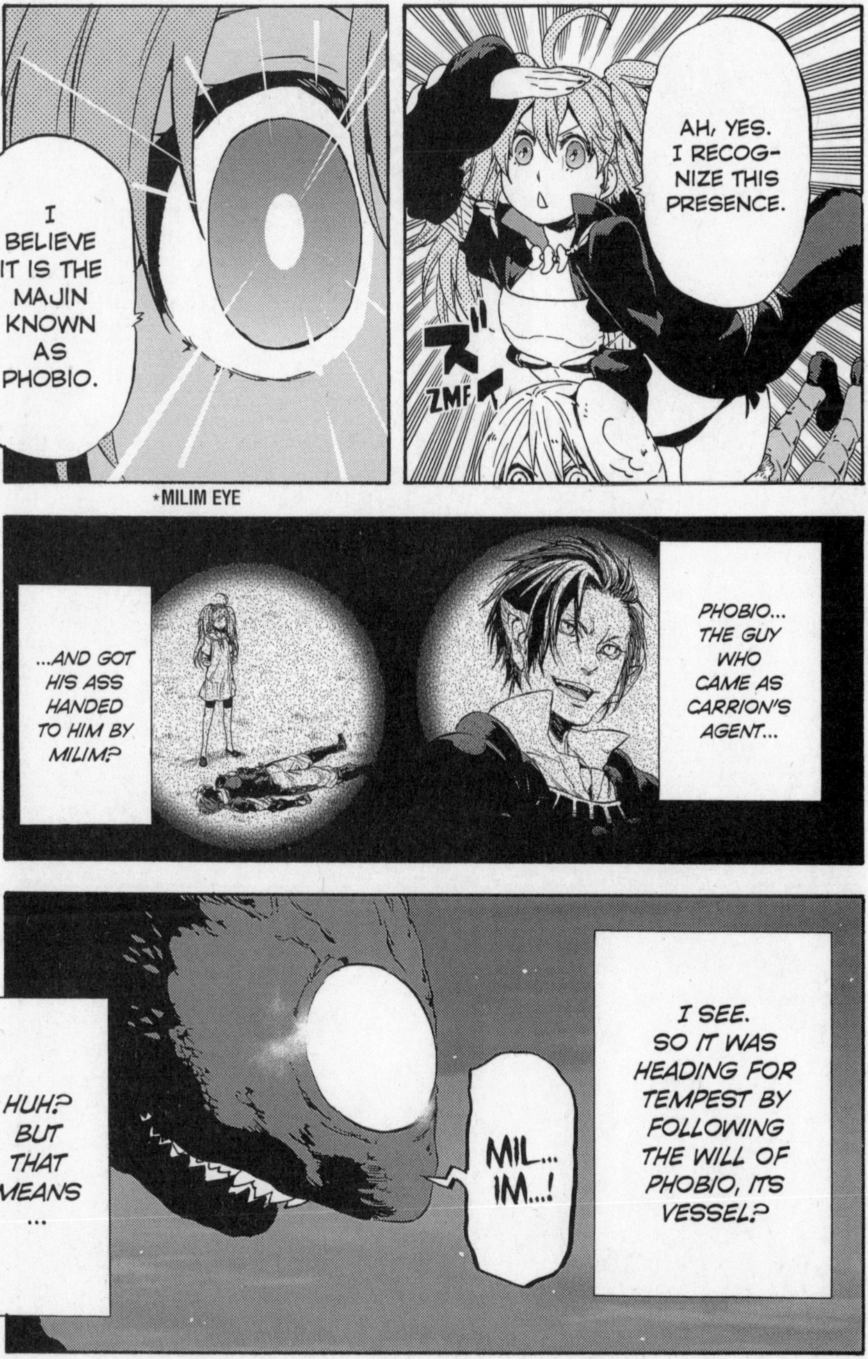
AH, YES. I RECOG-NIZE THIS PRESENCE.
ZMF
I BELIEVE IT IS THE MAJIN KNOWN AS PHOBIO.
*MILIM EYE
PHOBIO... THE GUY WHO CAME AS CARRION'S AGENT...
...AND GOT HIS ASS HANDED TO HIM BY MILIM?
I SEE. SO IT WAS HEADING FOR TEMPEST BY FOLLOWING THE WILL OF PHOBIO, ITS VESSEL?
MIL... IM...!
HUH? BUT THAT MEANS ...

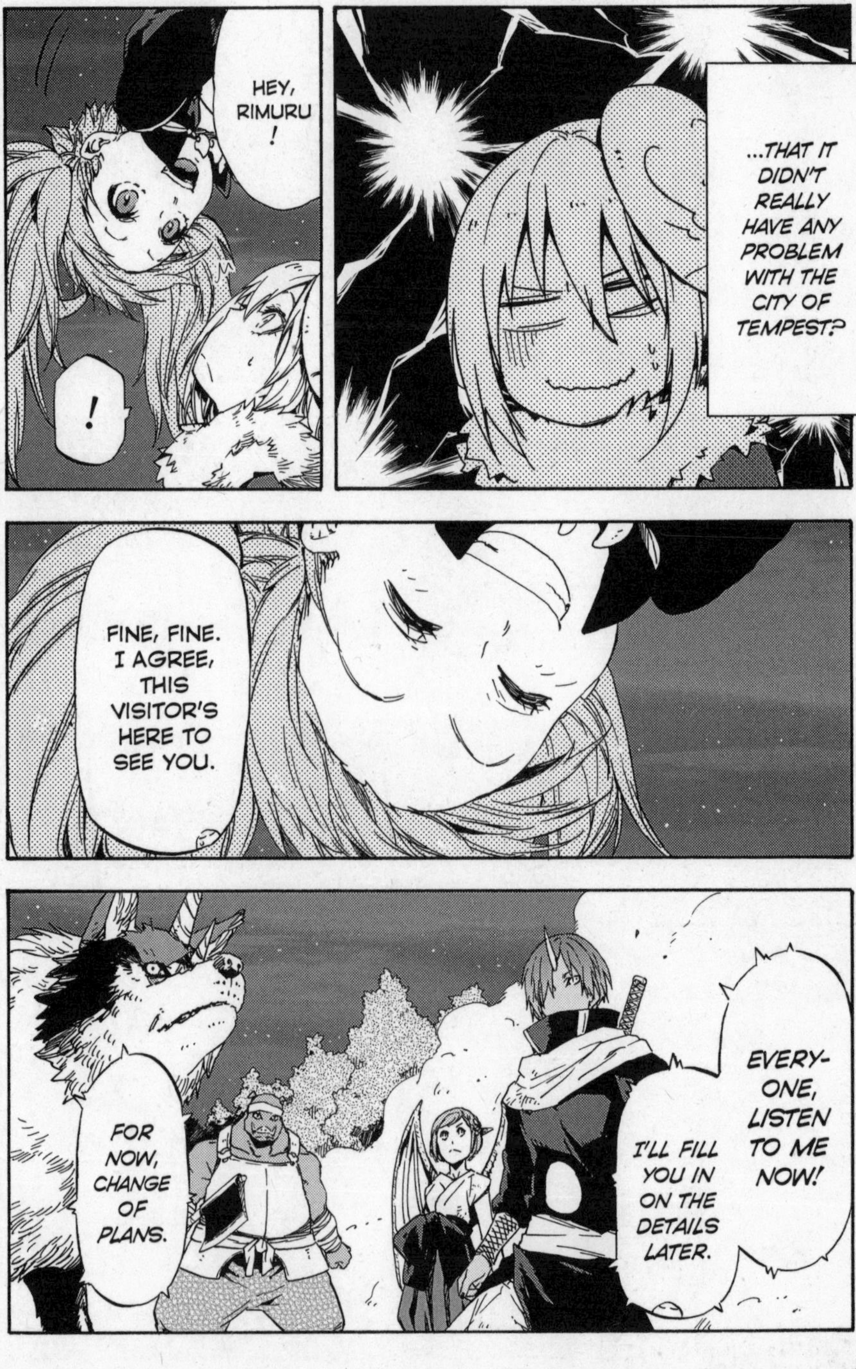
...THAT IT DIDN'T REALLY HAVE ANY PROBLEM WITH THE CITY OF TEMPEST?
HEY, RIMURU!
!
FINE, FINE. I AGREE, THIS VISITOR'S HERE TO SEE YOU.
EVERY-ONE, LISTEN TO ME NOW!
I'LL FILL YOU IN ON THE DETAILS LATER.
FOR NOW, CHANGE OF PLANS.

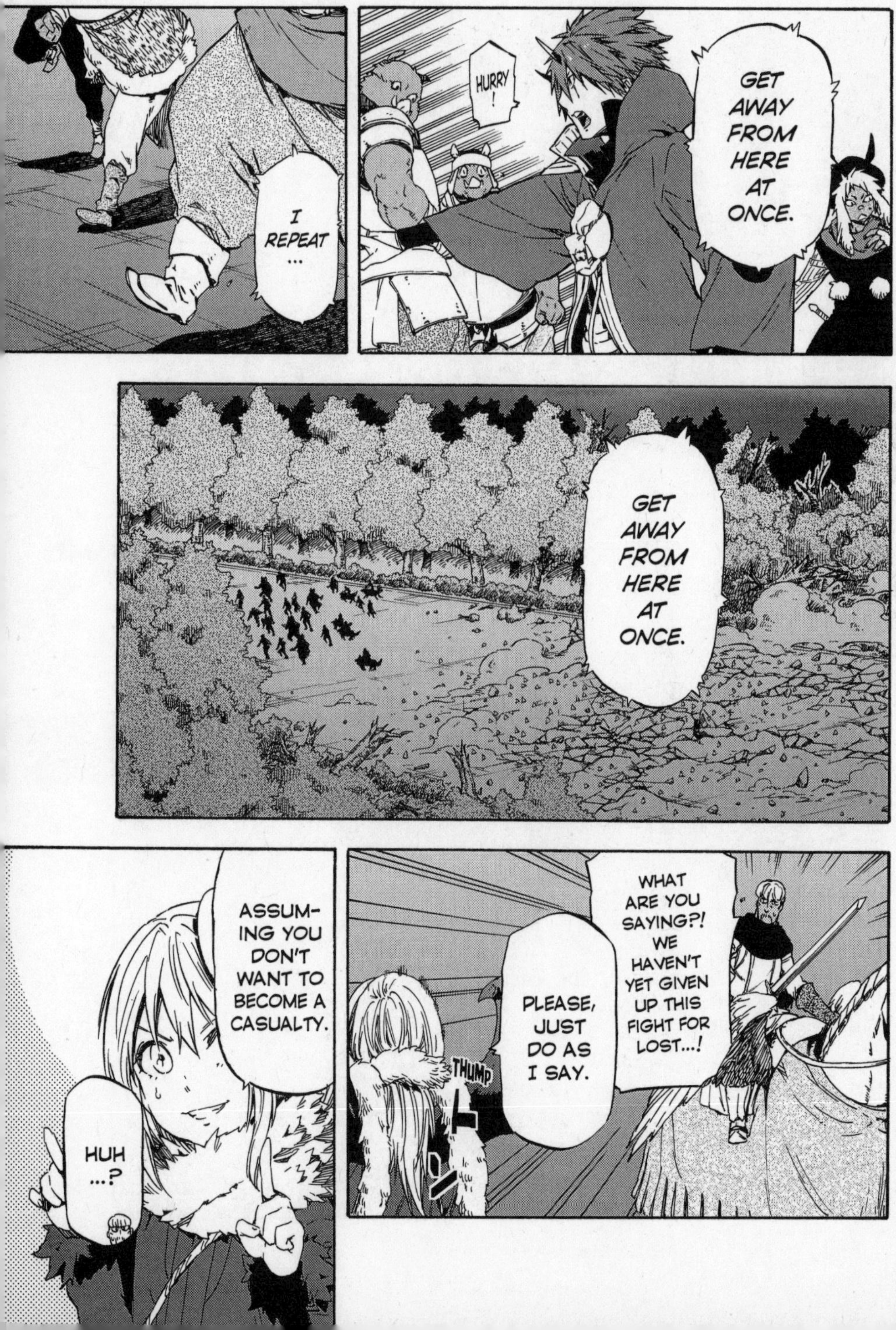
GET AWAY FROM HERE AT ONCE.
HURRY!
I REPEAT...
GET AWAY FROM HERE AT ONCE.
WHAT ARE YOU SAYING?! WE HAVEN'T YET GIVEN UP THIS FIGHT FOR LOST...!
PLEASE, JUST DO AS I SAY.
THUMP
ASSUMING YOU DON'T WANT TO BECOME A CASUALTY.
HUH...?

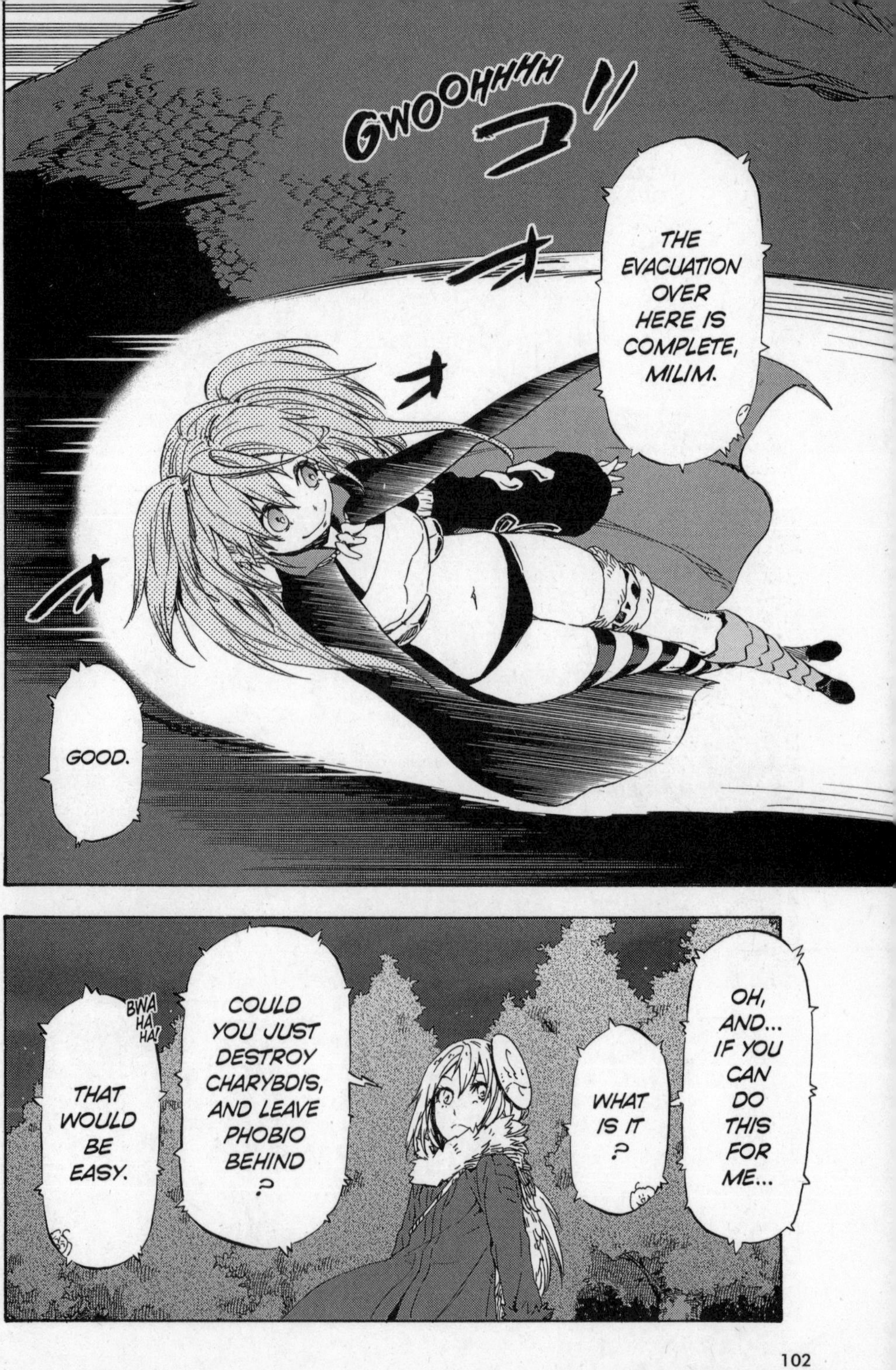
GWOOHHHH
THE EVACUATION OVER HERE IS COMPLETE, MILIM.
GOOD.
OH, AND... IF YOU CAN DO THIS FOR ME...
WHAT IS IT?
COULD YOU JUST DESTROY CHARYBDIS, AND LEAVE PHOBIO BEHIND?
BWA HA HA!
THAT WOULD BE EASY.

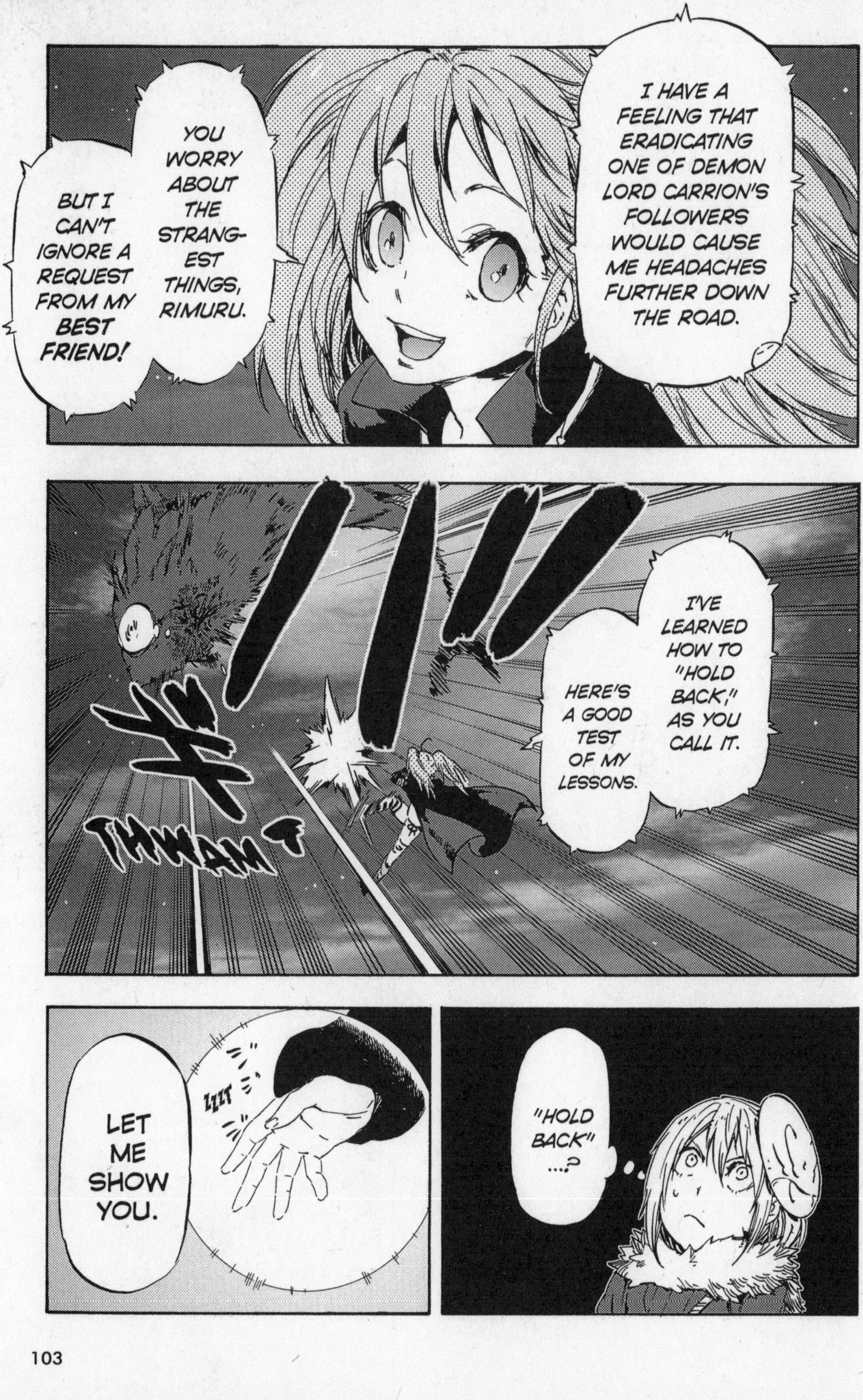
I HAVE A FEELING THAT ERADICATING ONE OF DEMON LORD CARRION'S FOLLOWERS WOULD CAUSE ME HEADACHES FURTHER DOWN THE ROAD.
YOU WORRY ABOUT THE STRANG-EST THINGS, RIMURU.
BUT I CAN'T IGNORE A REQUEST FROM MY BEST FRIEND!
I'VE LEARNED HOW TO "HOLD BACK," AS YOU CALL IT.
HERE'S A GOOD TEST OF MY LESSONS.
THWAM
"HOLD BACK" ...?
ZZZT
LET ME SHOW YOU.

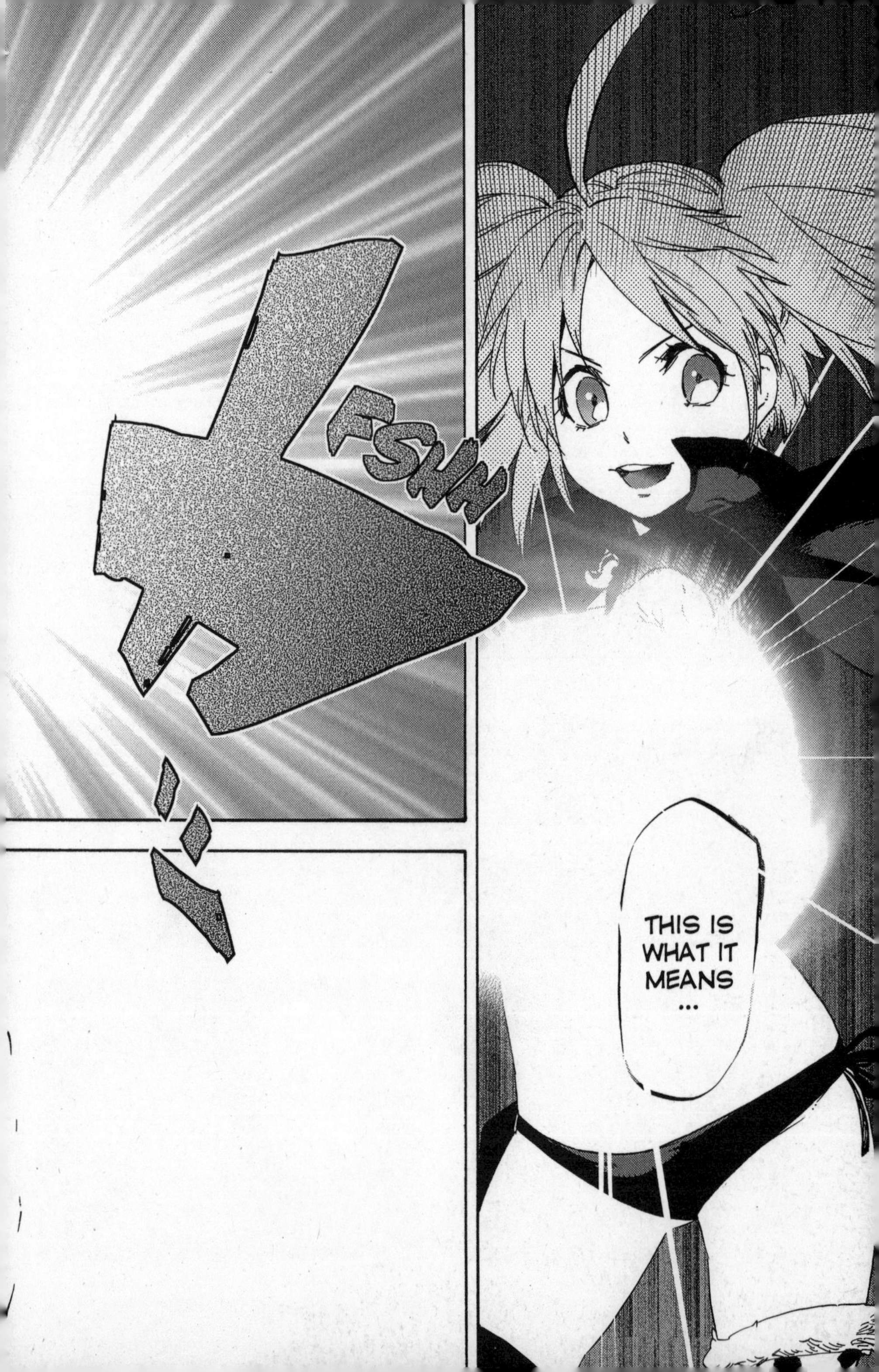
THIS IS WHAT IT MEANS ...
FSHH

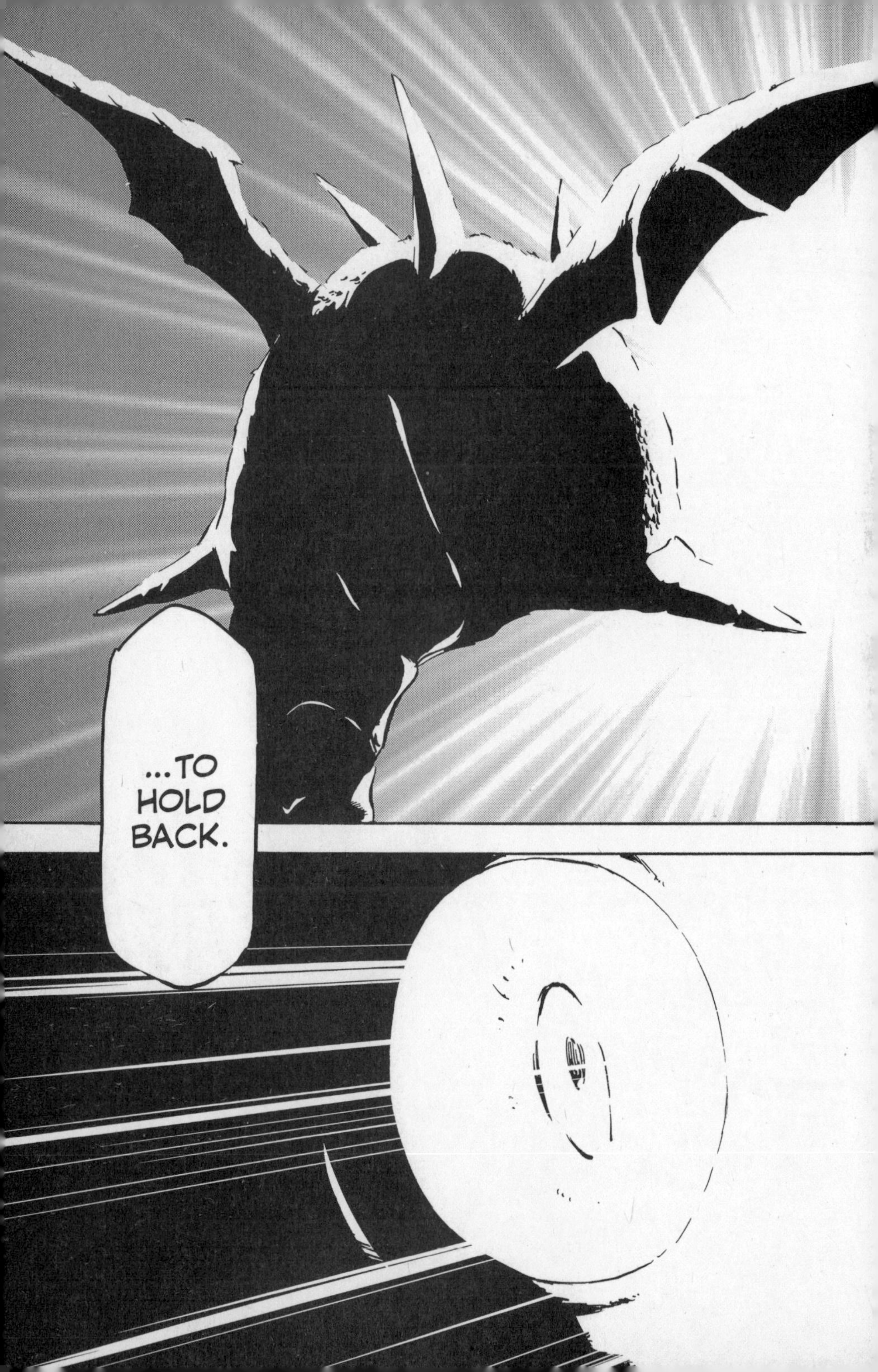
...TO HOLD BACK.

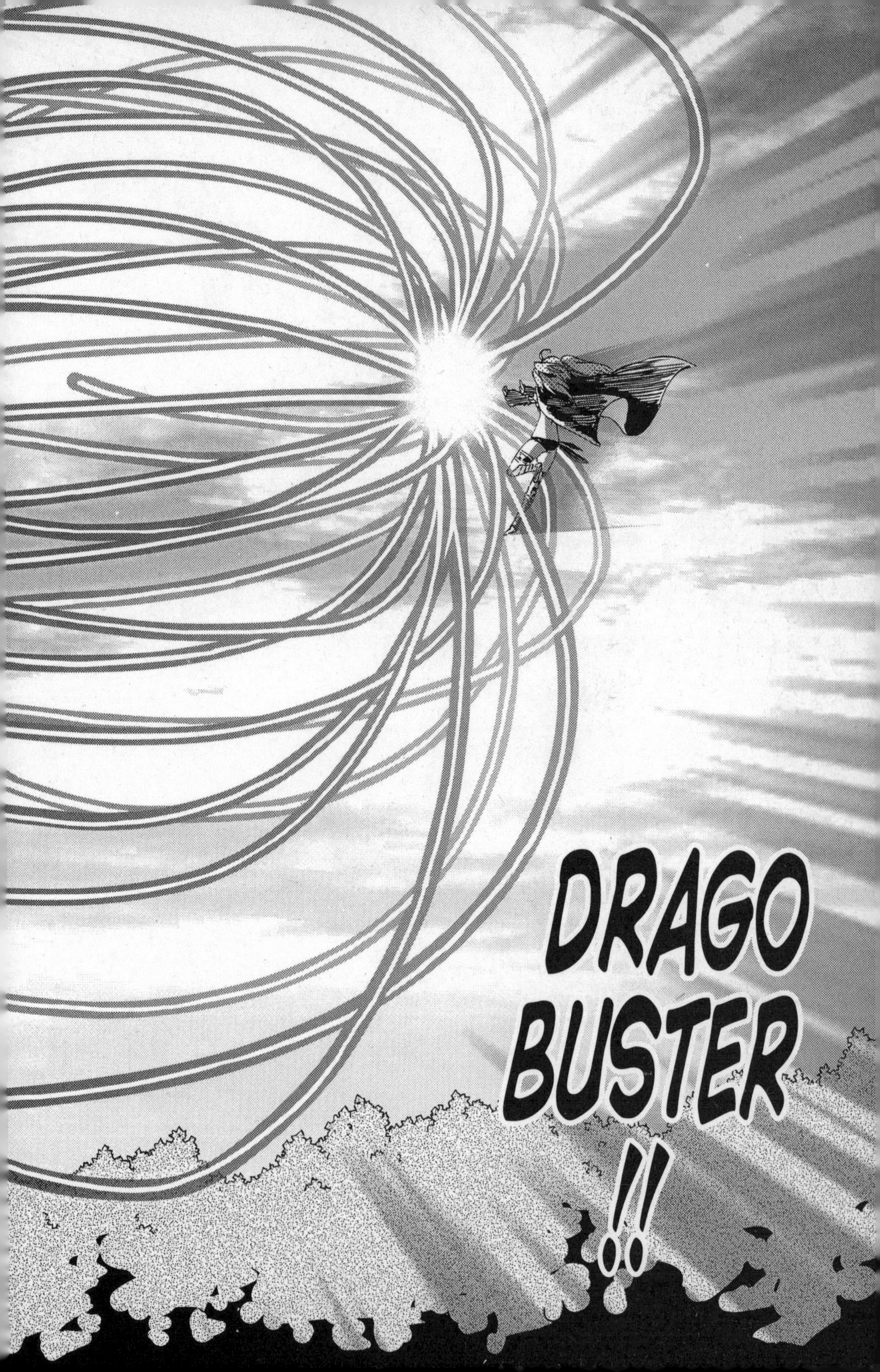
DRAGO BUSTER!!

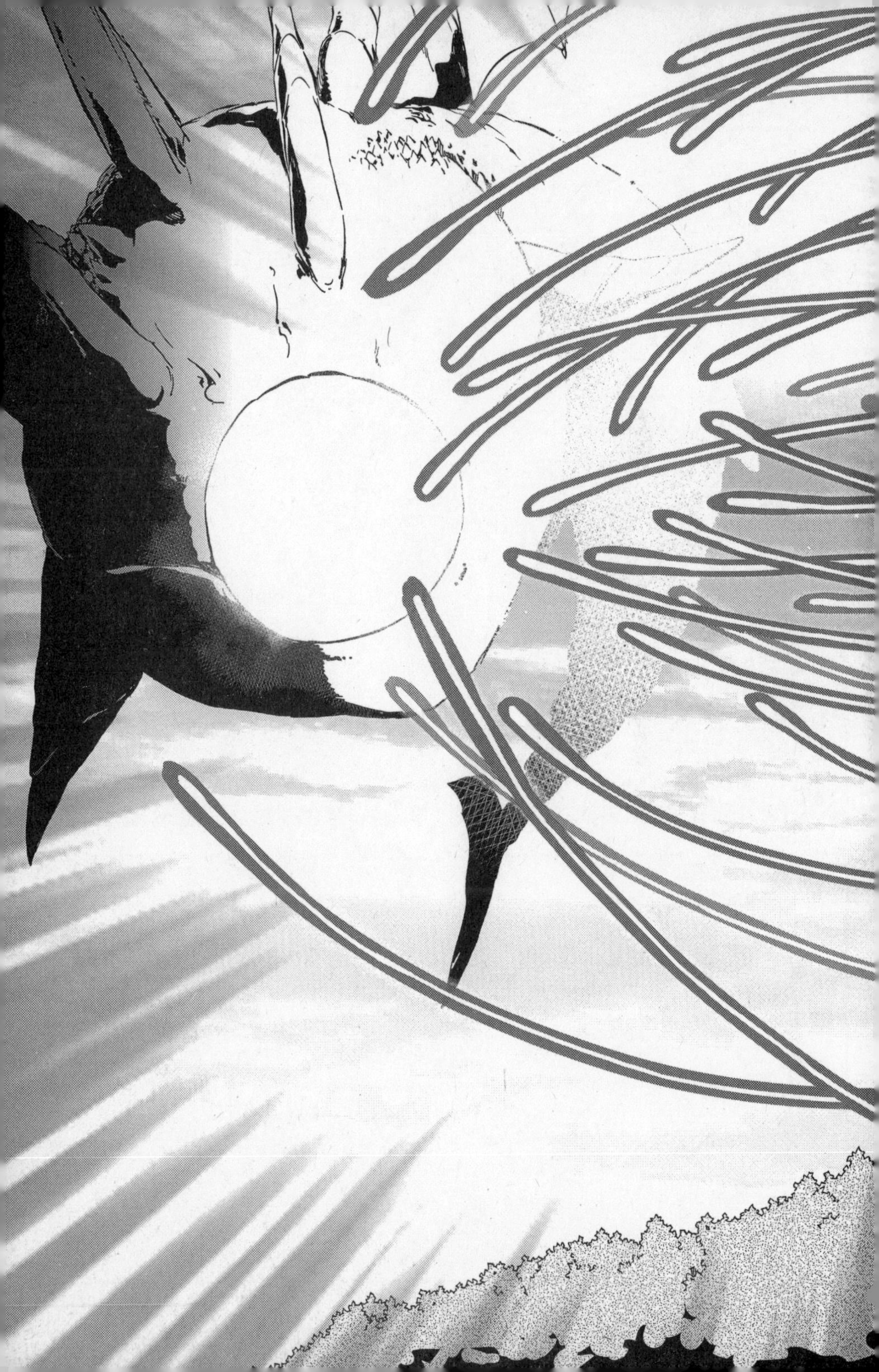

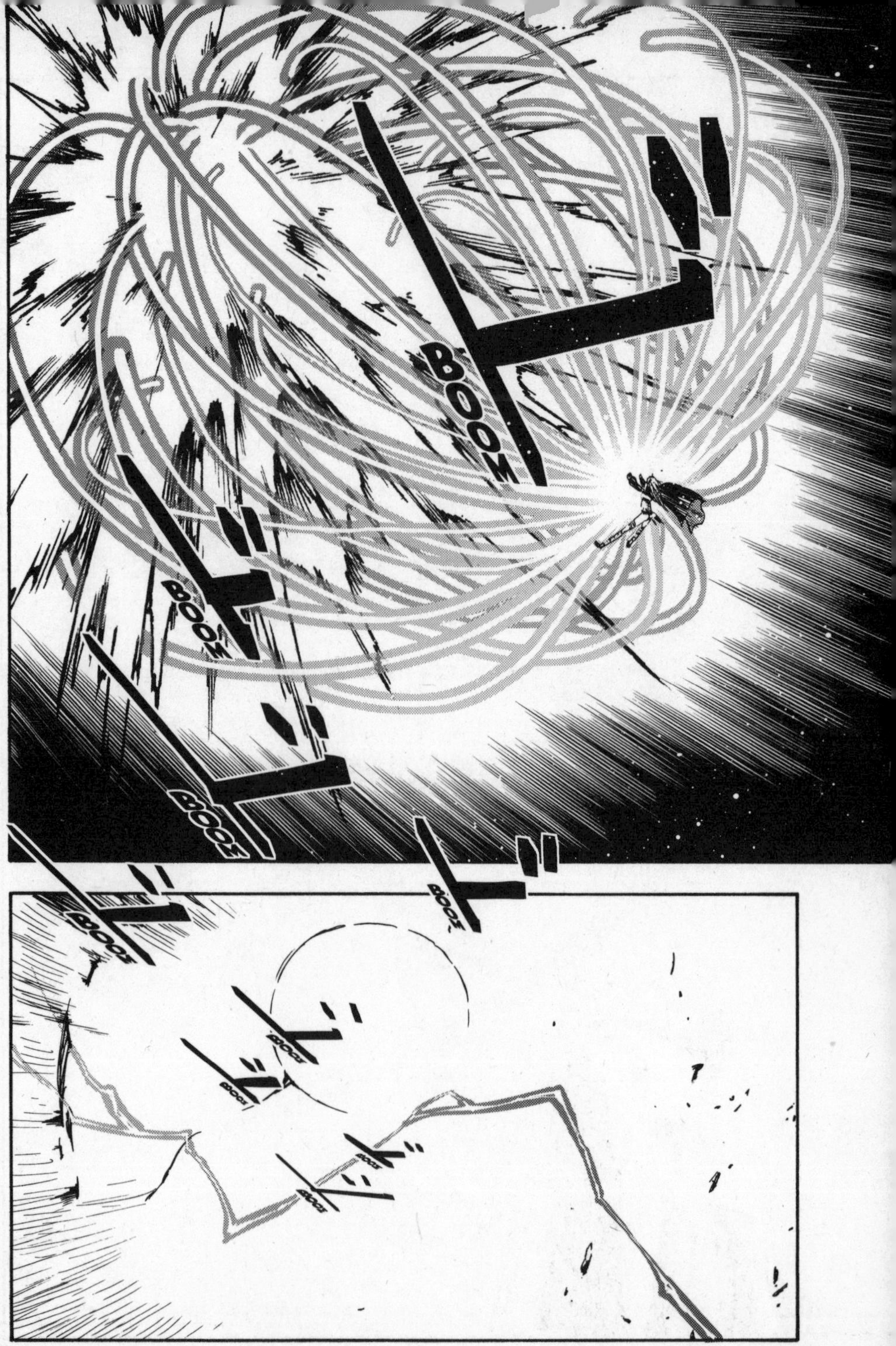
BOOM
BOOM
BOOM
BOOM

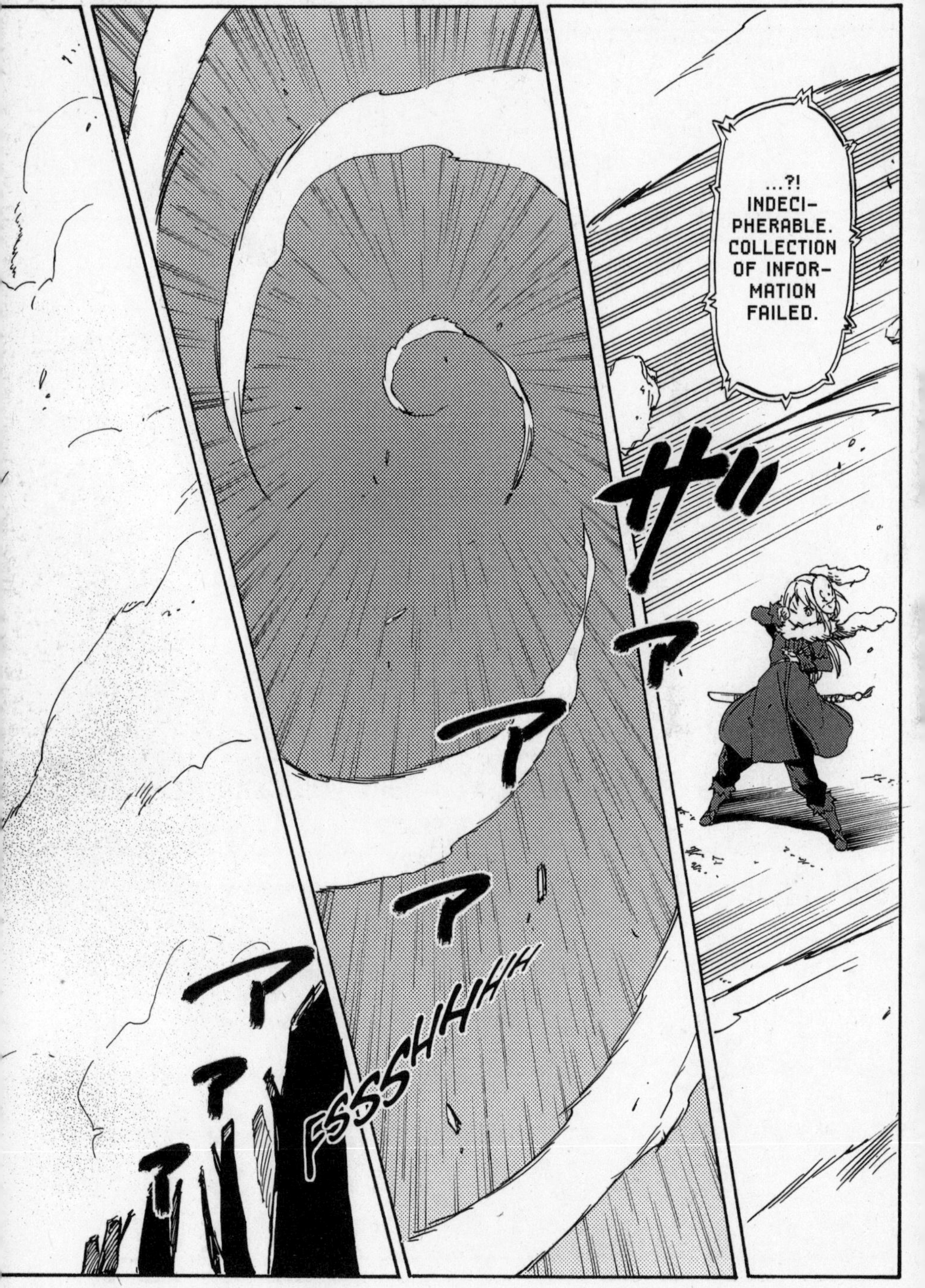
...?! INDECIPHERABLE. COLLECTION OF INFORMATION FAILED.
ザァアアアアア
FSSSHHHH

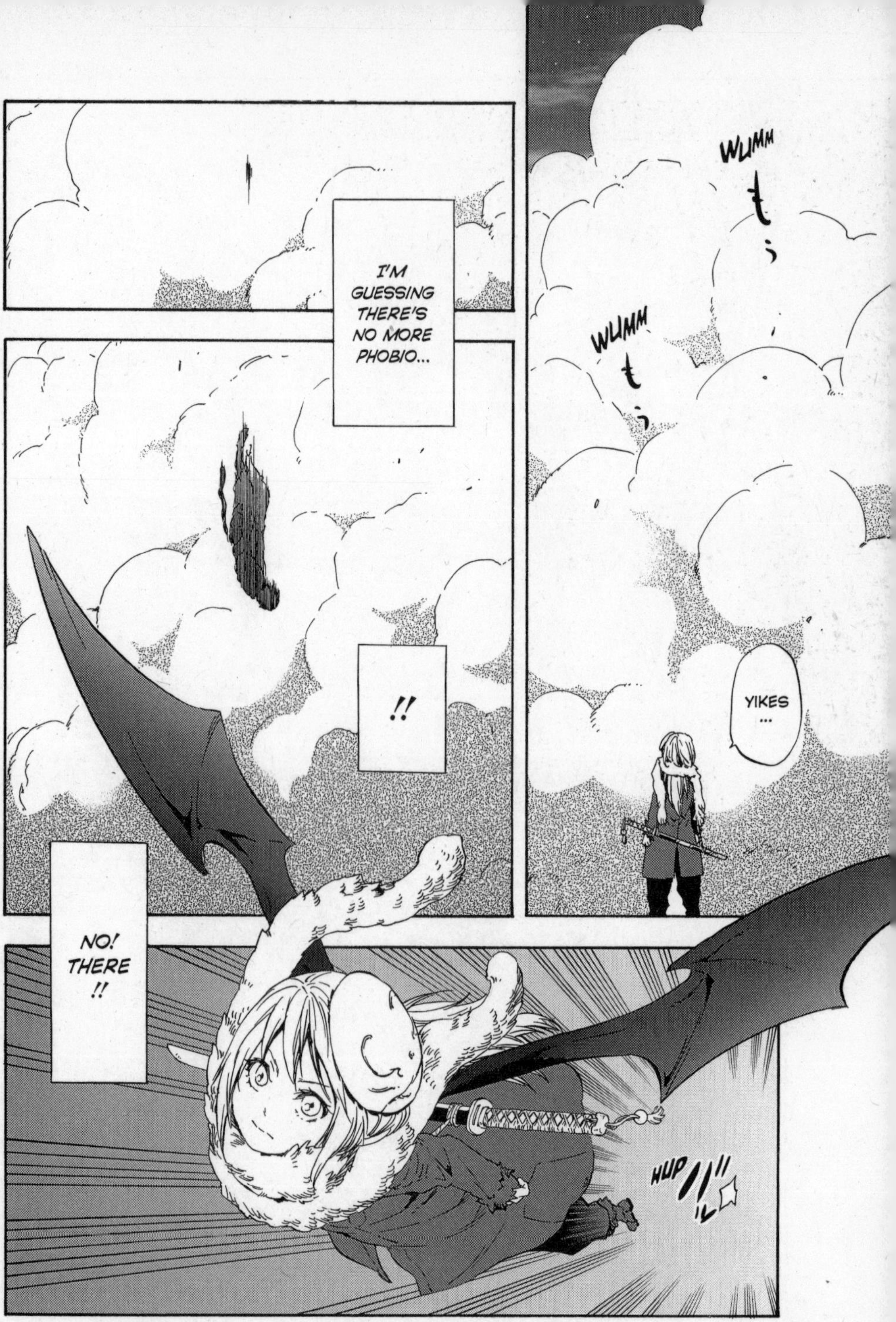
WUMM
WUMM
YIKES ...
I'M GUESSING THERE'S NO MORE PHOBIO...
!!
NO! THERE !!
HUP!!

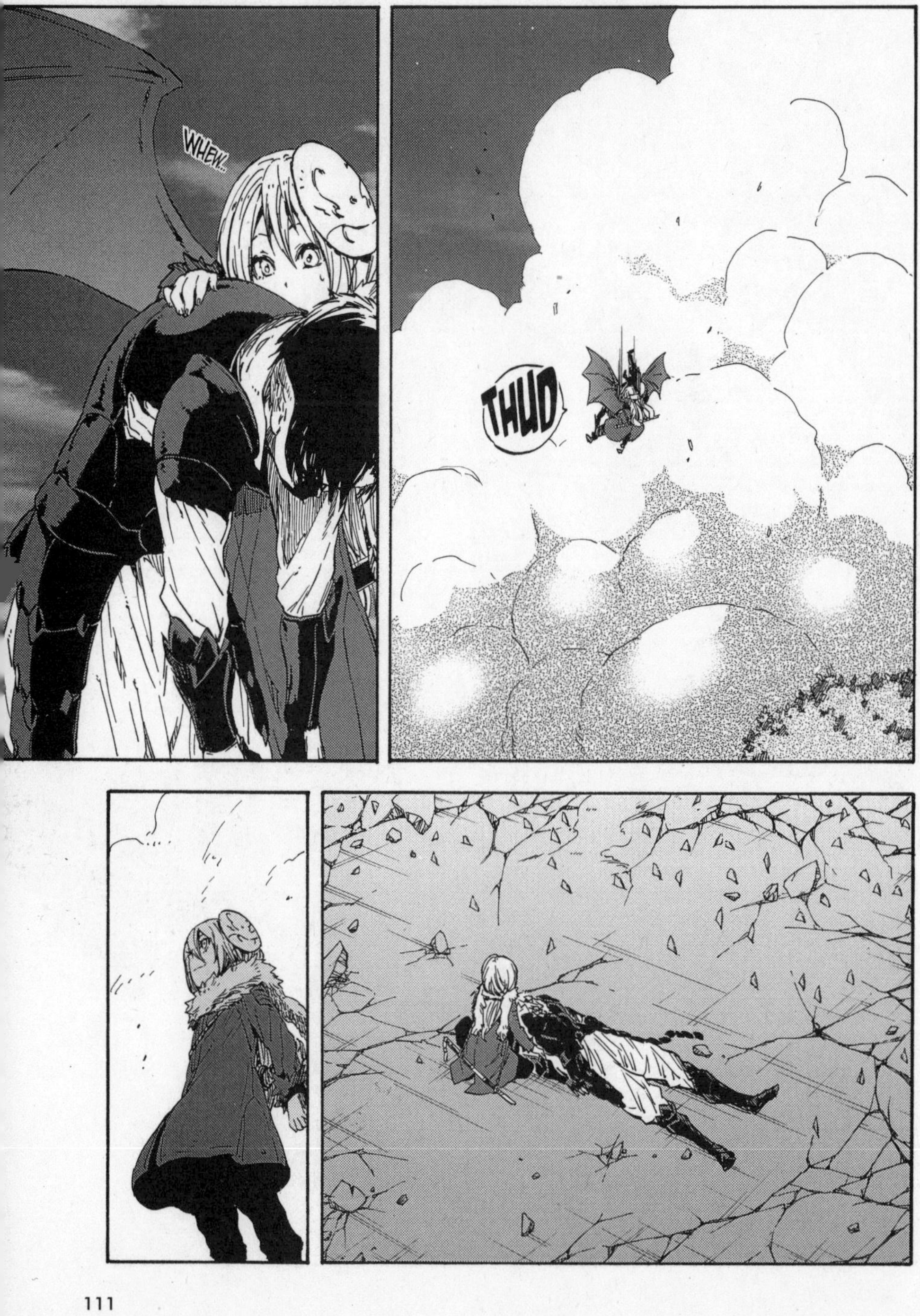
THUD
WHEW...

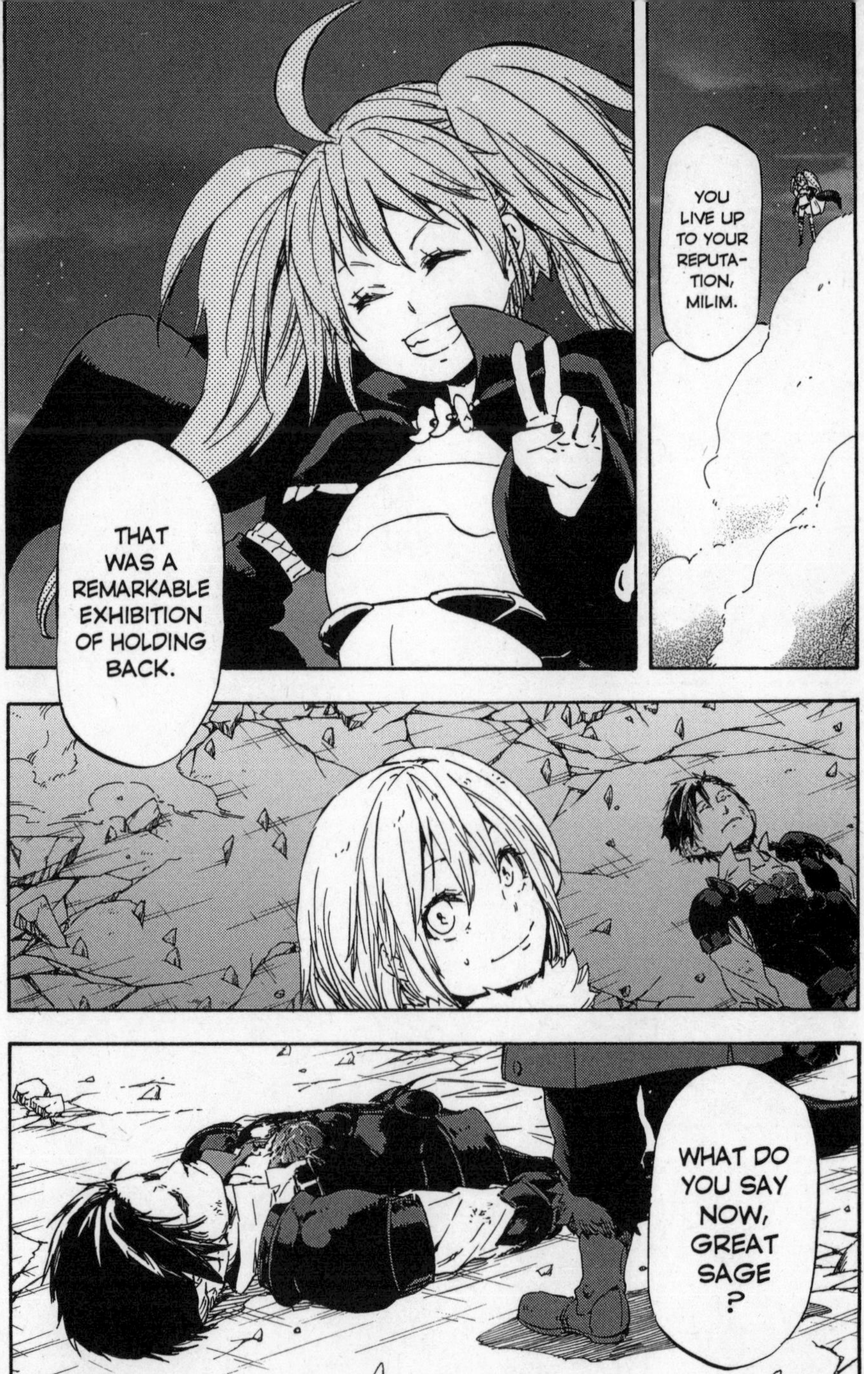
YOU LIVE UP TO YOUR REPUTA-TION, MILIM.
THAT WAS A REMARKABLE EXHIBITION OF HOLDING BACK.
WHAT DO YOU SAY NOW, GREAT SAGE?

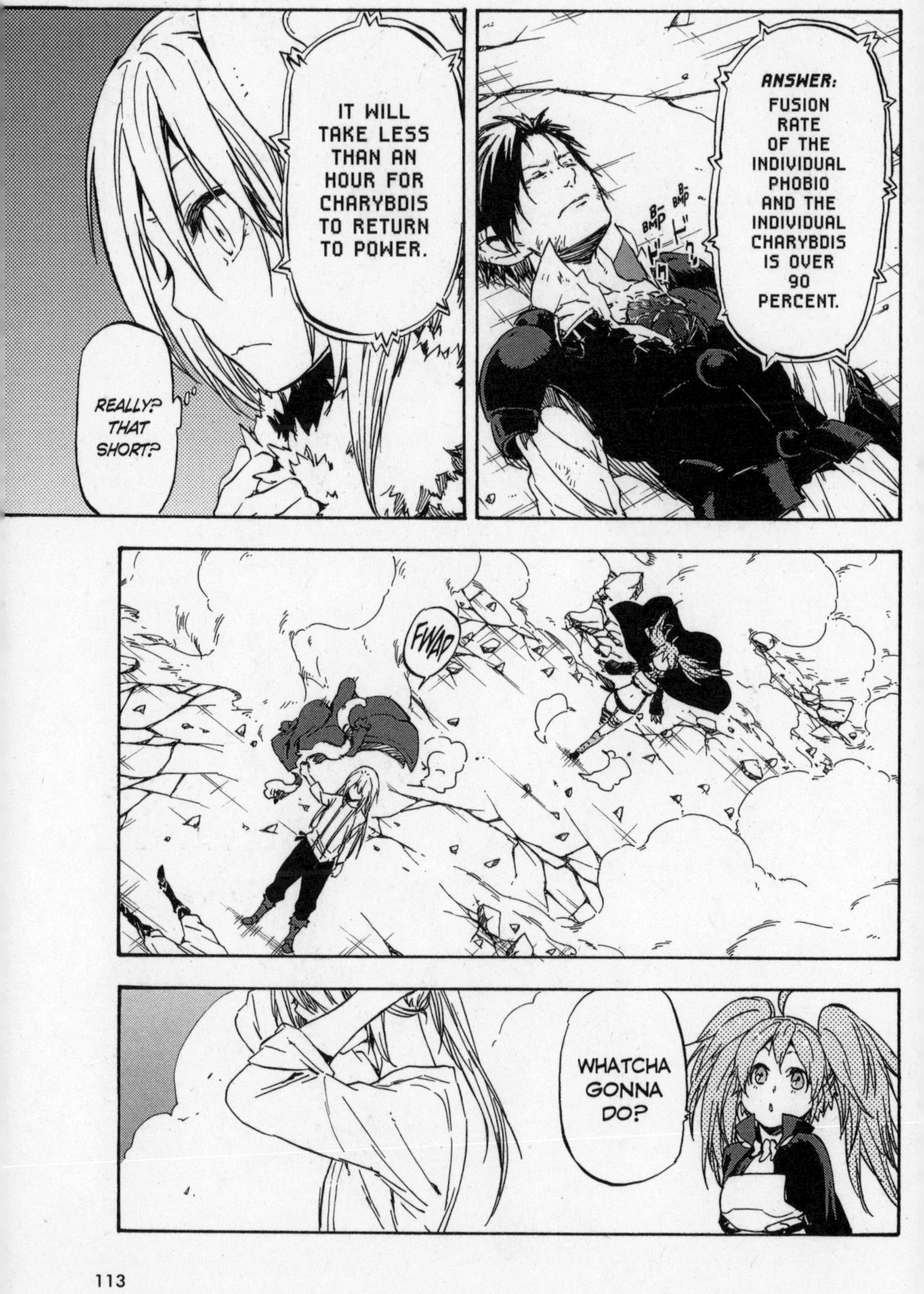
ANSWER: FUSION RATE OF THE INDIVIDUAL PHOBIO AND THE INDIVIDUAL CHARYBDIS IS OVER 90 PERCENT.
B-BMP
B-BMP
IT WILL TAKE LESS THAN AN HOUR FOR CHARYBDIS TO RETURN TO POWER.
REALLY? THAT SHORT?
FWAP
WHATCHA GONNA DO?

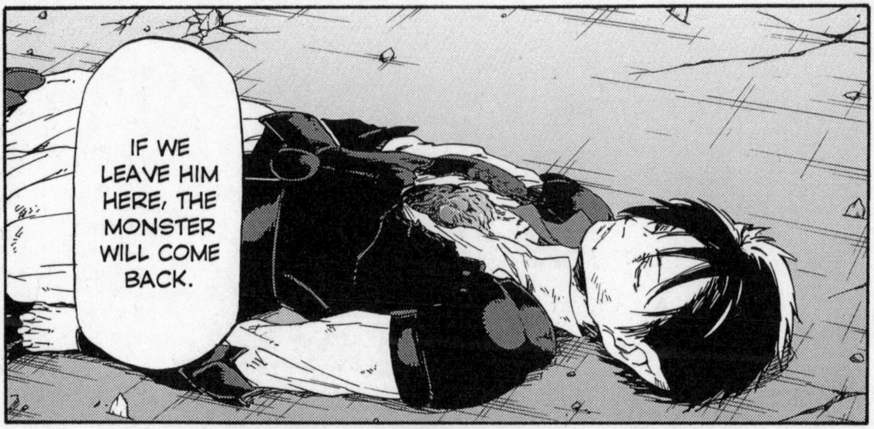
IF WE LEAVE HIM HERE, THE MONSTER WILL COME BACK.

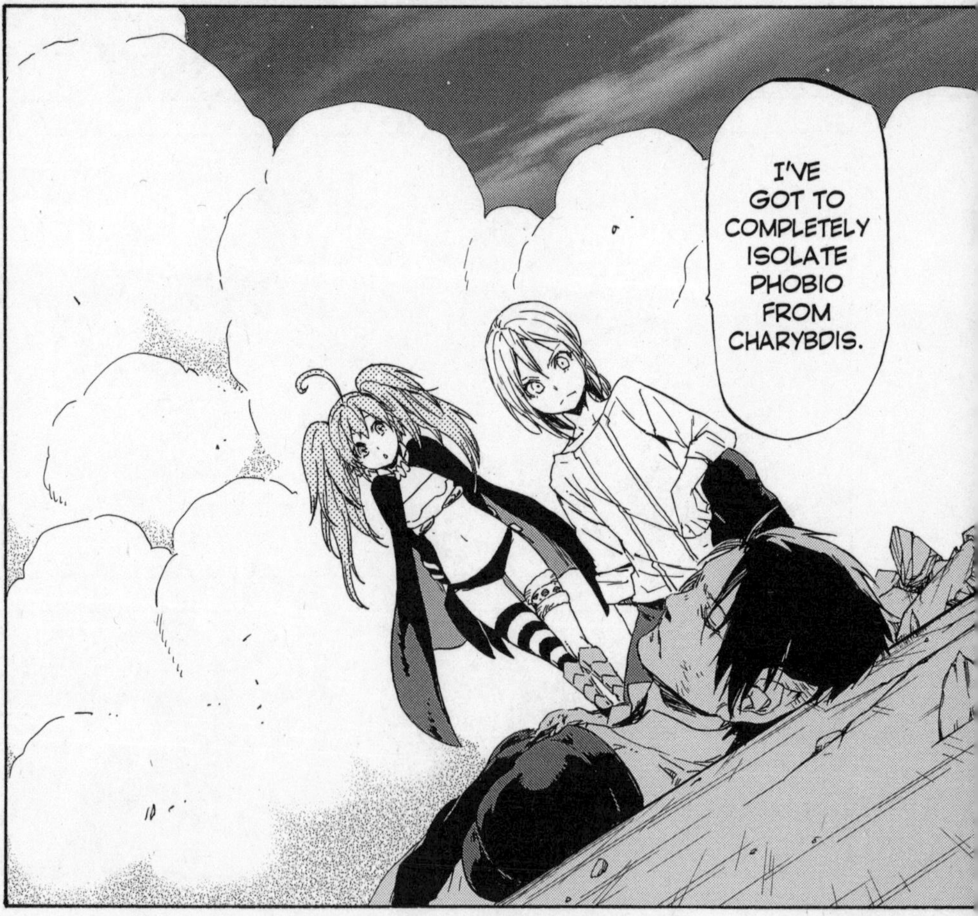
I'VE GOT TO COMPLETELY ISOLATE PHOBIO FROM CHARYBDIS.

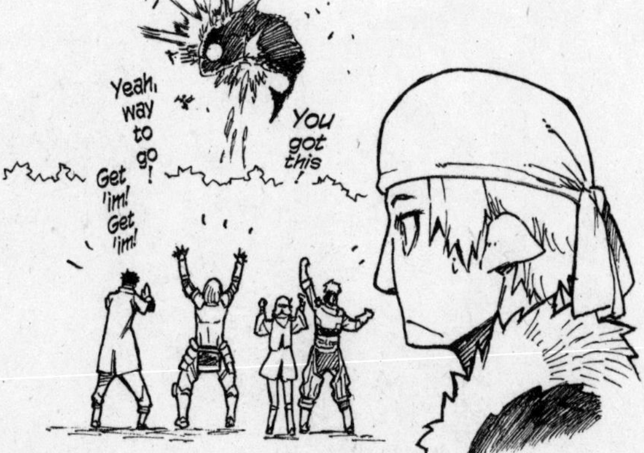
You got this!
Yeah, way to go!
Get 'im! Get 'im!

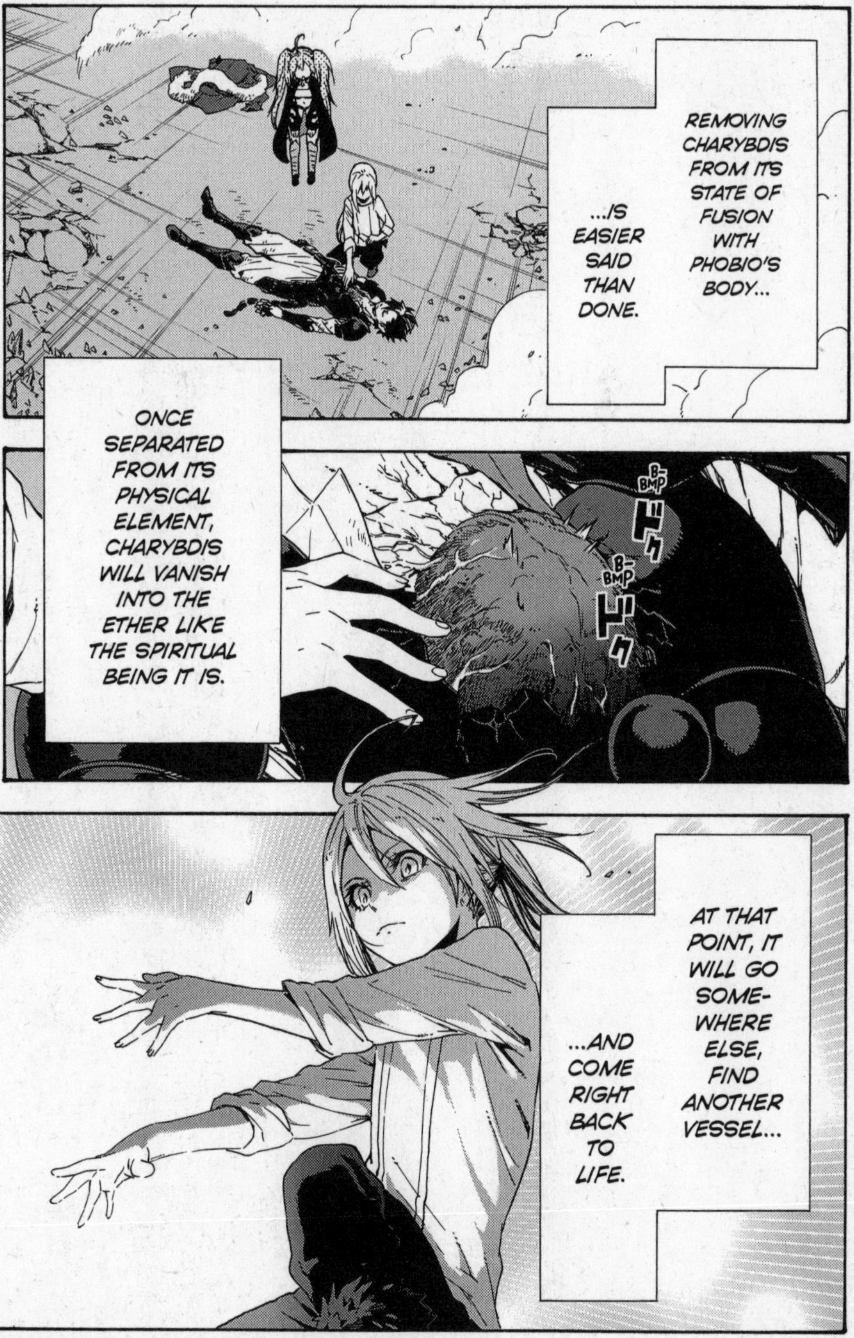
REMOVING CHARYBDIS FROM ITS STATE OF FUSION WITH PHOBIO'S BODY...
...IS EASIER SAID THAN DONE.
ONCE SEPARATED FROM ITS PHYSICAL ELEMENT, CHARYBDIS WILL VANISH INTO THE ETHER LIKE THE SPIRITUAL BEING IT IS.
B-BMP
ドク
B-BMP
ドク
AT THAT POINT, IT WILL GO SOME-WHERE ELSE, FIND ANOTHER VESSEL...
...AND COME RIGHT BACK TO LIFE.

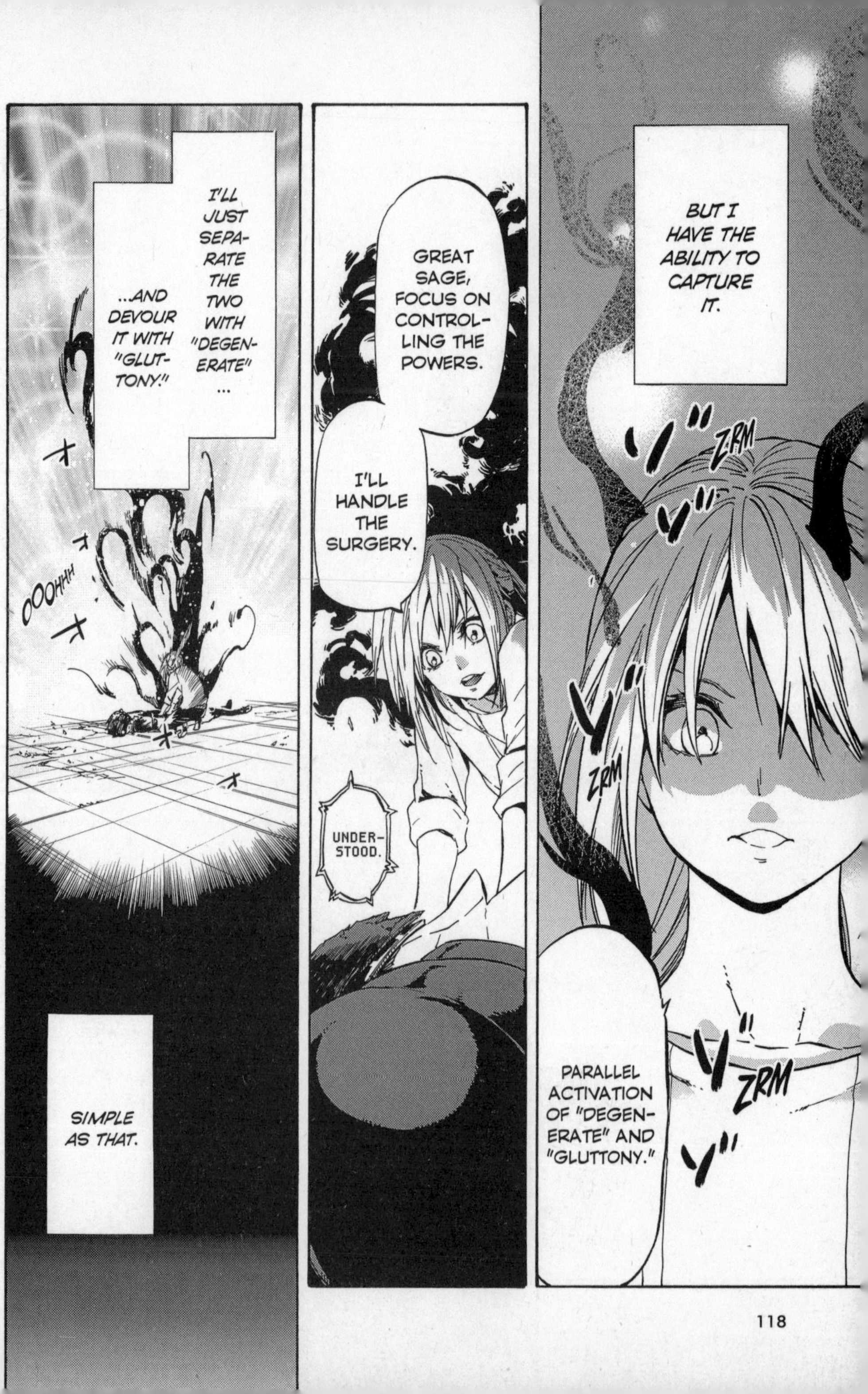
BUT I HAVE THE ABILITY TO CAPTURE IT.
ZRM
ZRM
PARALLEL ACTIVATION OF "DEGEN-ERATE" AND "GLUTTONY."
ZRM
GREAT SAGE, FOCUS ON CONTROL-LING THE POWERS.
I'LL HANDLE THE SURGERY.
UNDER-STOOD.
I'LL JUST SEPA-RATE THE TWO WITH "DEGEN-ERATE" ...
...AND DEVOUR IT WITH "GLUT-TONY."
OOOHHH
SIMPLE AS THAT.

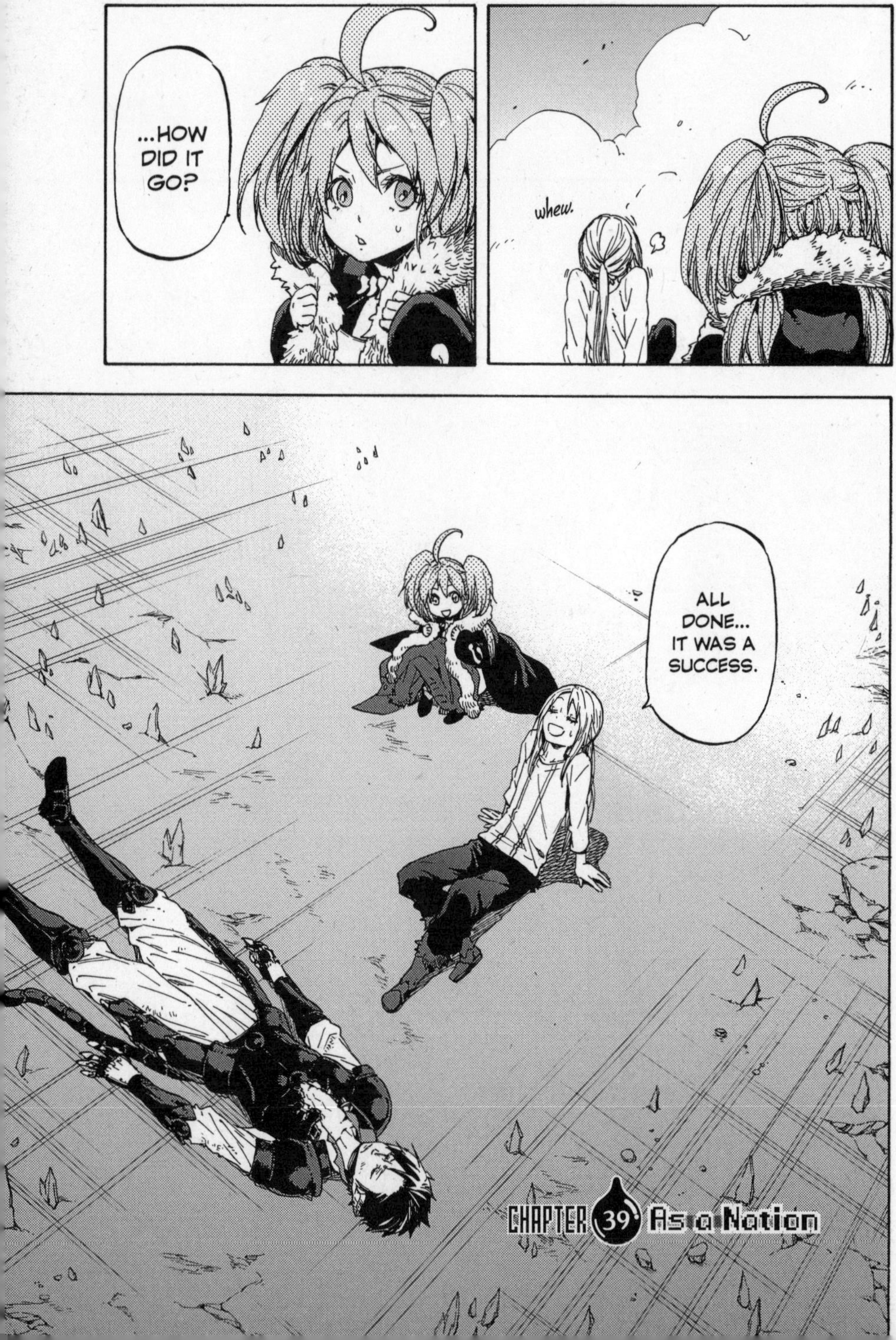
whew.
...HOW DID IT GO?
ALL DONE... IT WAS A SUCCESS.
CHAPTER 39 As a Nation

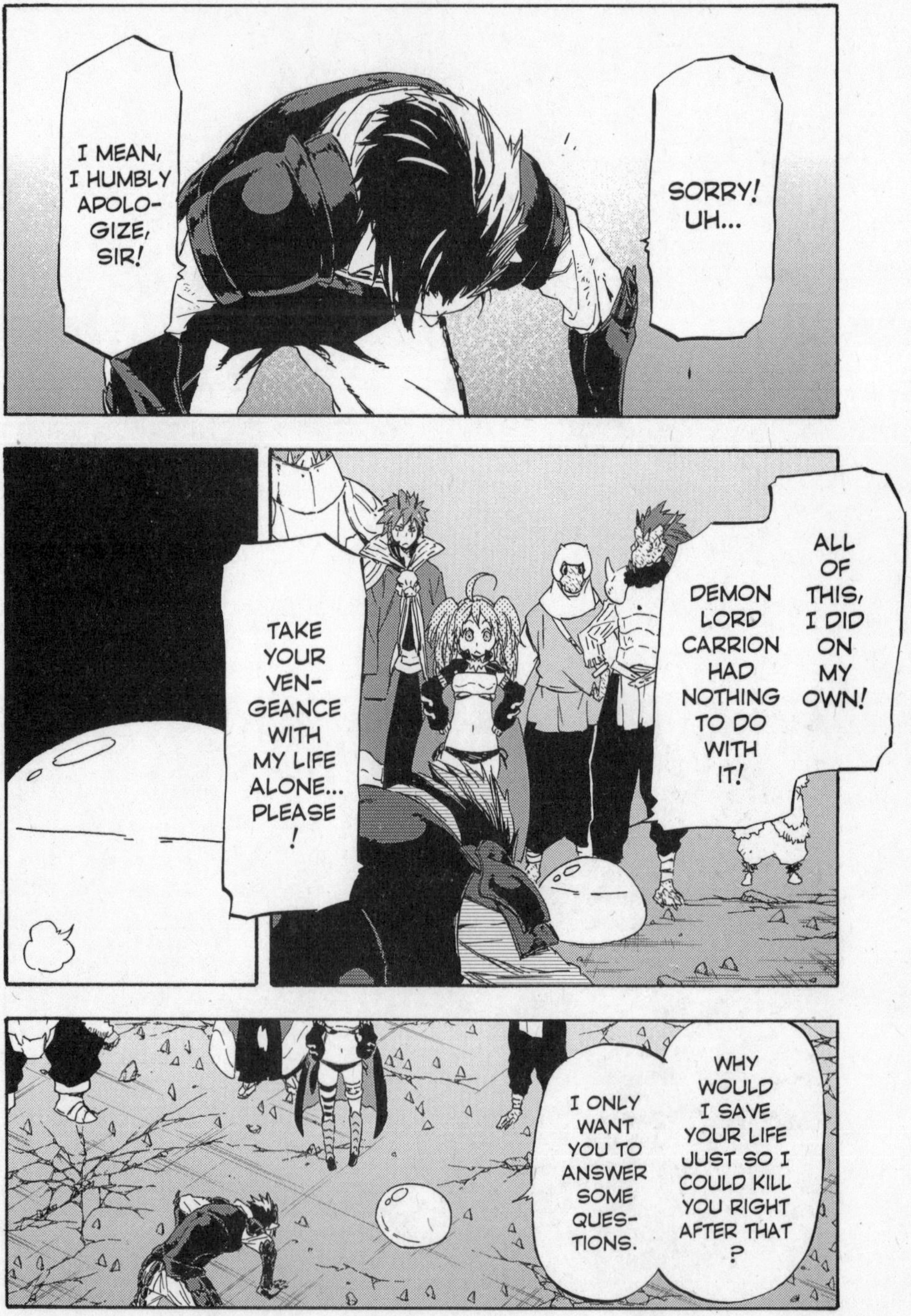
SORRY! UH...
I MEAN, I HUMBLY APOLOGIZE, SIR!
ALL OF THIS, I DID ON MY OWN!
DEMON LORD CARRION HAD NOTHING TO DO WITH IT!
TAKE YOUR VENGEANCE WITH MY LIFE ALONE... PLEASE!
WHY WOULD I SAVE YOUR LIFE JUST SO I COULD KILL YOU RIGHT AFTER THAT?
I ONLY WANT YOU TO ANSWER SOME QUESTIONS.

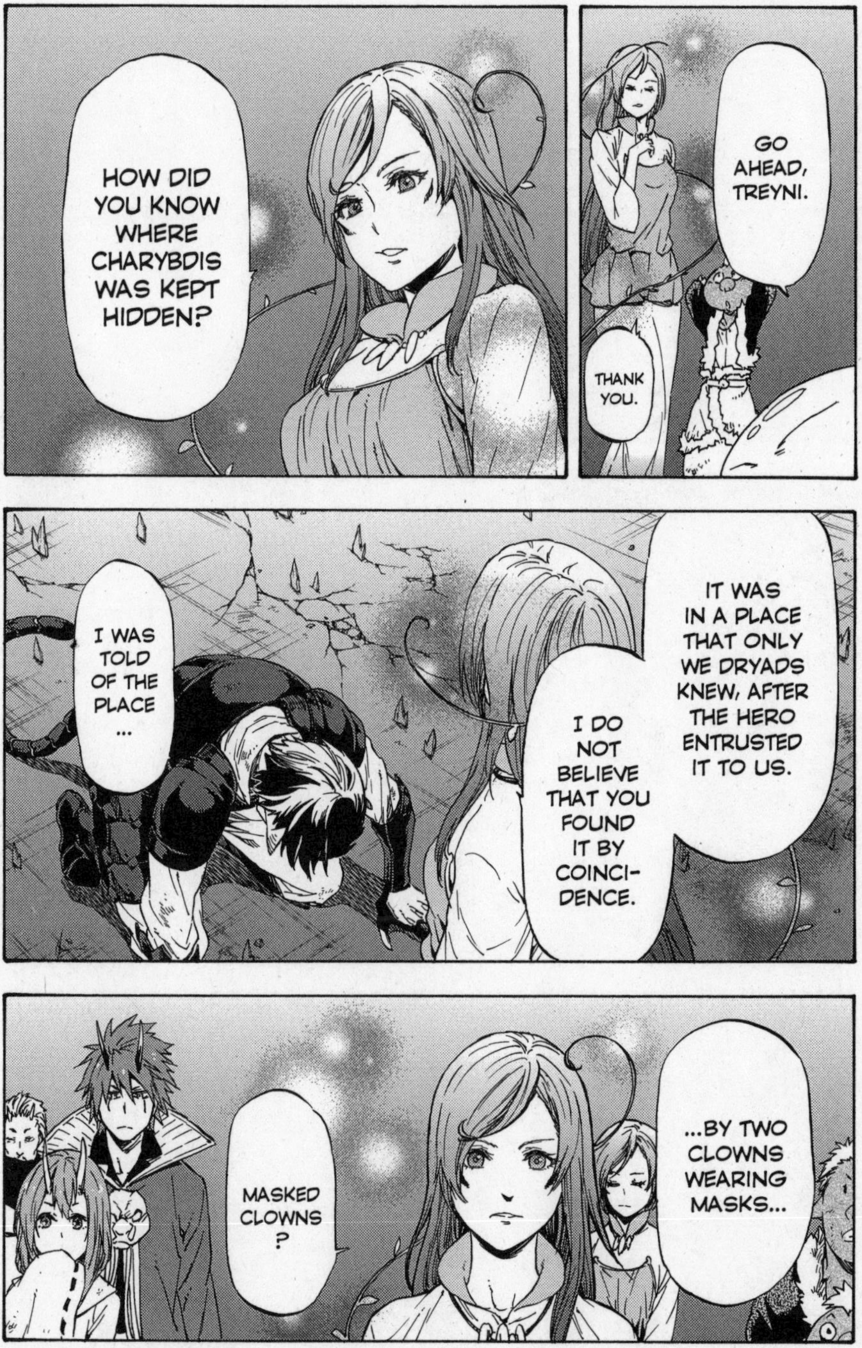
GO AHEAD, TREYNI.
THANK YOU.
HOW DID YOU KNOW WHERE CHARYBDIS WAS KEPT HIDDEN?
IT WAS IN A PLACE THAT ONLY WE DRYADS KNEW, AFTER THE HERO ENTRUSTED IT TO US.
I DO NOT BELIEVE THAT YOU FOUND IT BY COINCI-DENCE.
I WAS TOLD OF THE PLACE ...
...BY TWO CLOWNS WEARING MASKS...
MASKED CLOWNS ?

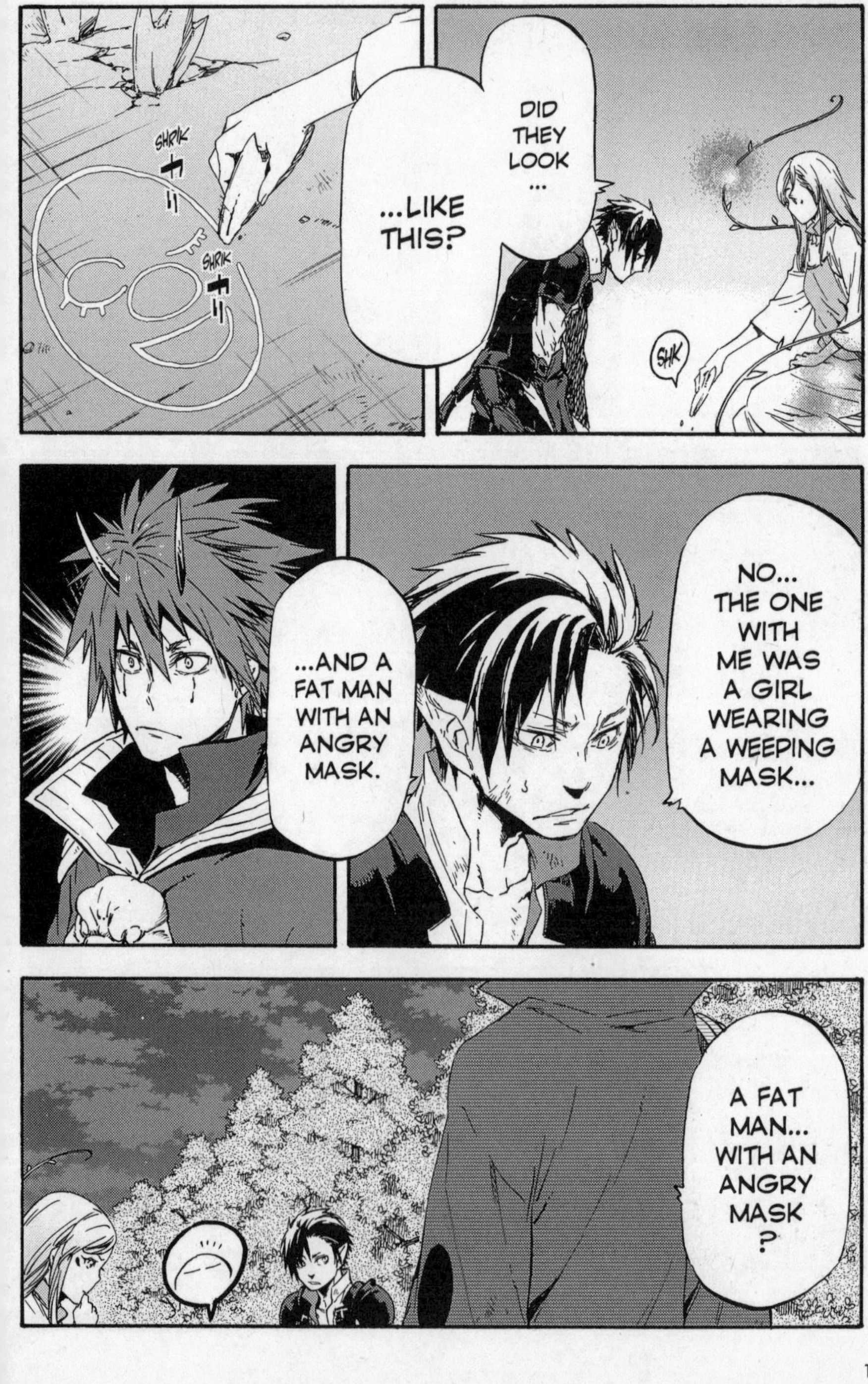
DID THEY LOOK ...
...LIKE THIS?
SHK
SHRIK
SHRIK
NO... THE ONE WITH ME WAS A GIRL WEARING A WEEPING MASK...
...AND A FAT MAN WITH AN ANGRY MASK.
A FAT MAN... WITH AN ANGRY MASK ?

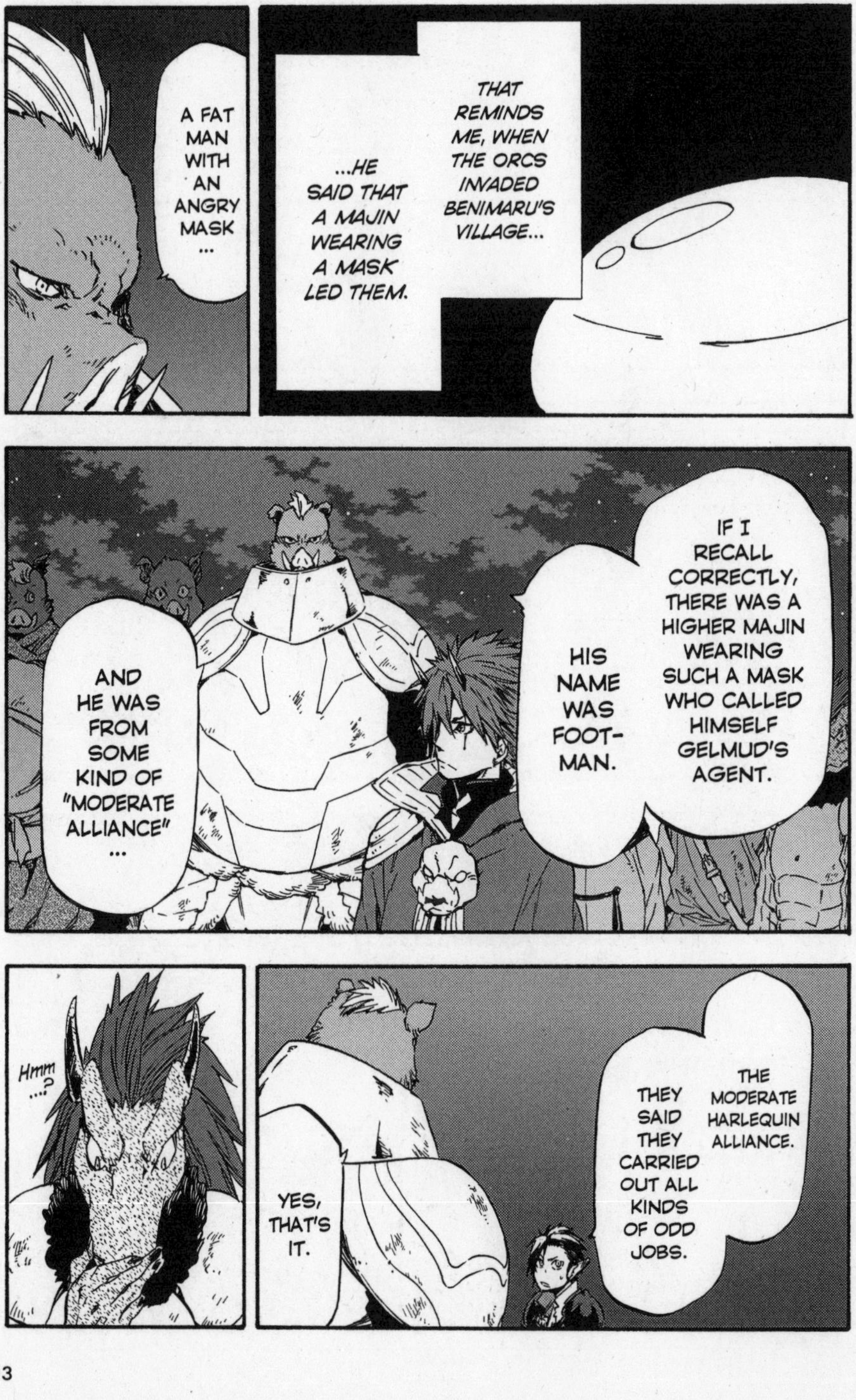
THAT REMINDS ME, WHEN THE ORCS INVADED BENIMARU'S VILLAGE...
...HE SAID THAT A MAJIN WEARING A MASK LED THEM.
A FAT MAN WITH AN ANGRY MASK ...
IF I RECALL CORRECTLY, THERE WAS A HIGHER MAJIN WEARING SUCH A MASK WHO CALLED HIMSELF GELMUD'S AGENT.
HIS NAME WAS FOOT-MAN.
AND HE WAS FROM SOME KIND OF "MODERATE ALLIANCE" ...
THE MODERATE HARLEQUIN ALLIANCE.
THEY SAID THEY CARRIED OUT ALL KINDS OF ODD JOBS.
YES, THAT'S IT.
Hmm ...?

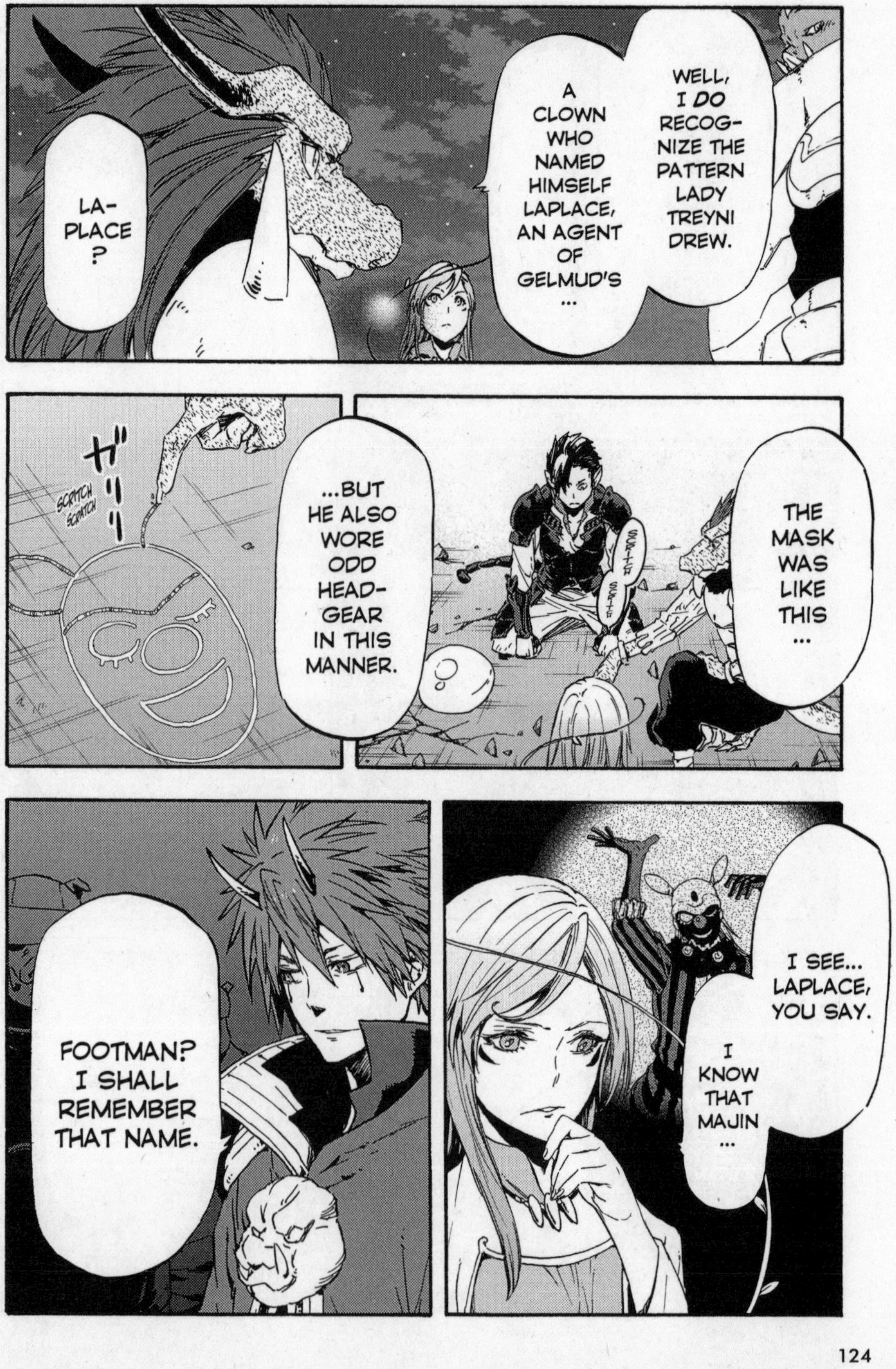
WELL, I DO RECOGNIZE THE PATTERN LADY TREYNI DREW.
A CLOWN WHO NAMED HIMSELF LAPLACE, AN AGENT OF GELMUD'S...
LAPLACE?
THE MASK WAS LIKE THIS...
SCRITCH SCRITCH
...BUT HE ALSO WORE ODD HEADGEAR IN THIS MANNER.
ザリ
SCRATCH SCRATCH
I SEE... LAPLACE, YOU SAY.
I KNOW THAT MAJIN...
FOOTMAN? I SHALL REMEMBER THAT NAME.

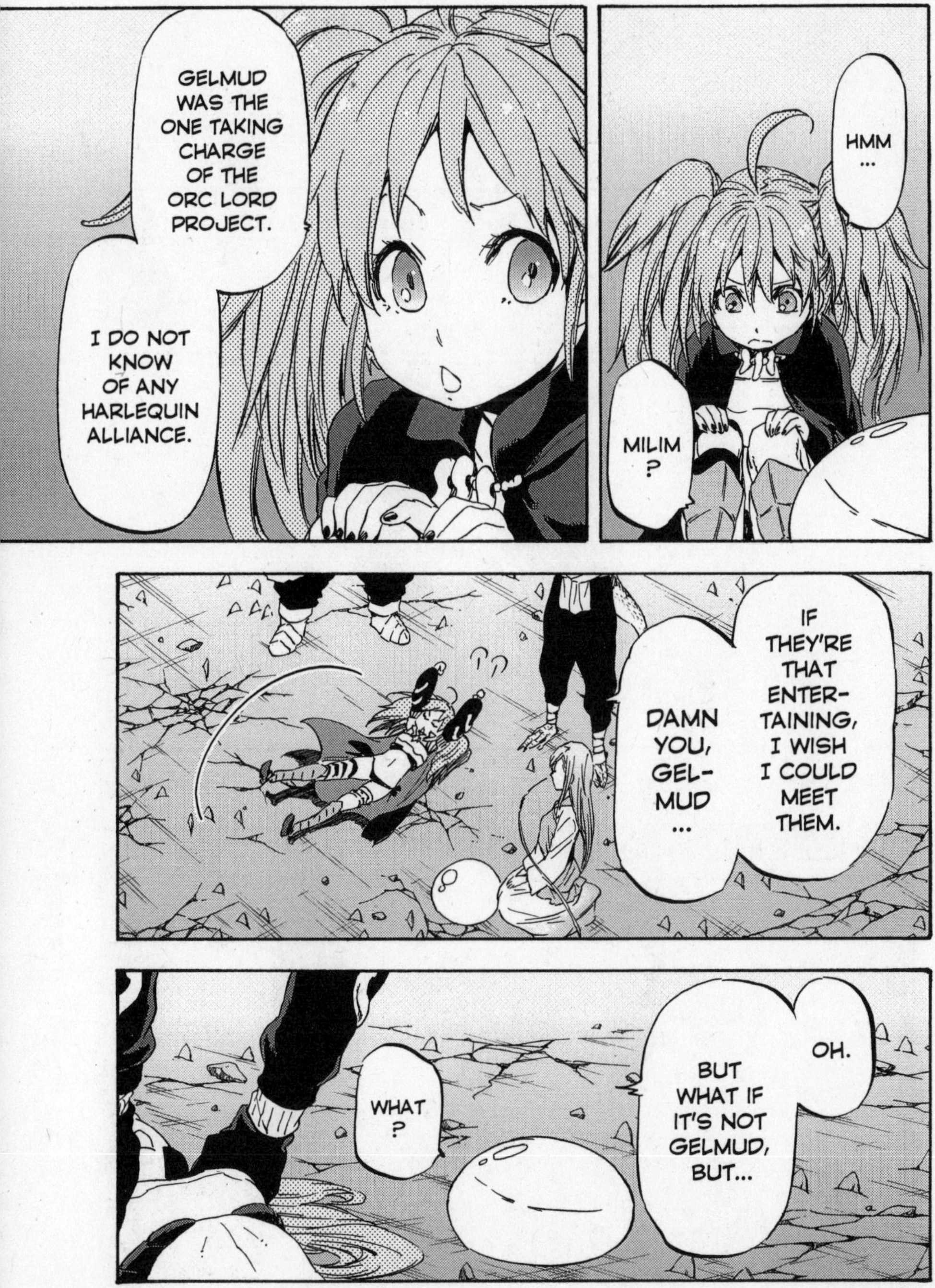
HMM ...
MILIM ?
GELMUD WAS THE ONE TAKING CHARGE OF THE ORC LORD PROJECT.
I DO NOT KNOW OF ANY HARLEQUIN ALLIANCE.
IF THEY'RE THAT ENTERTAINING, I WISH I COULD MEET THEM.
DAMN YOU, GELMUD ...
OH.
BUT WHAT IF IT'S NOT GELMUD, BUT...
WHAT ?

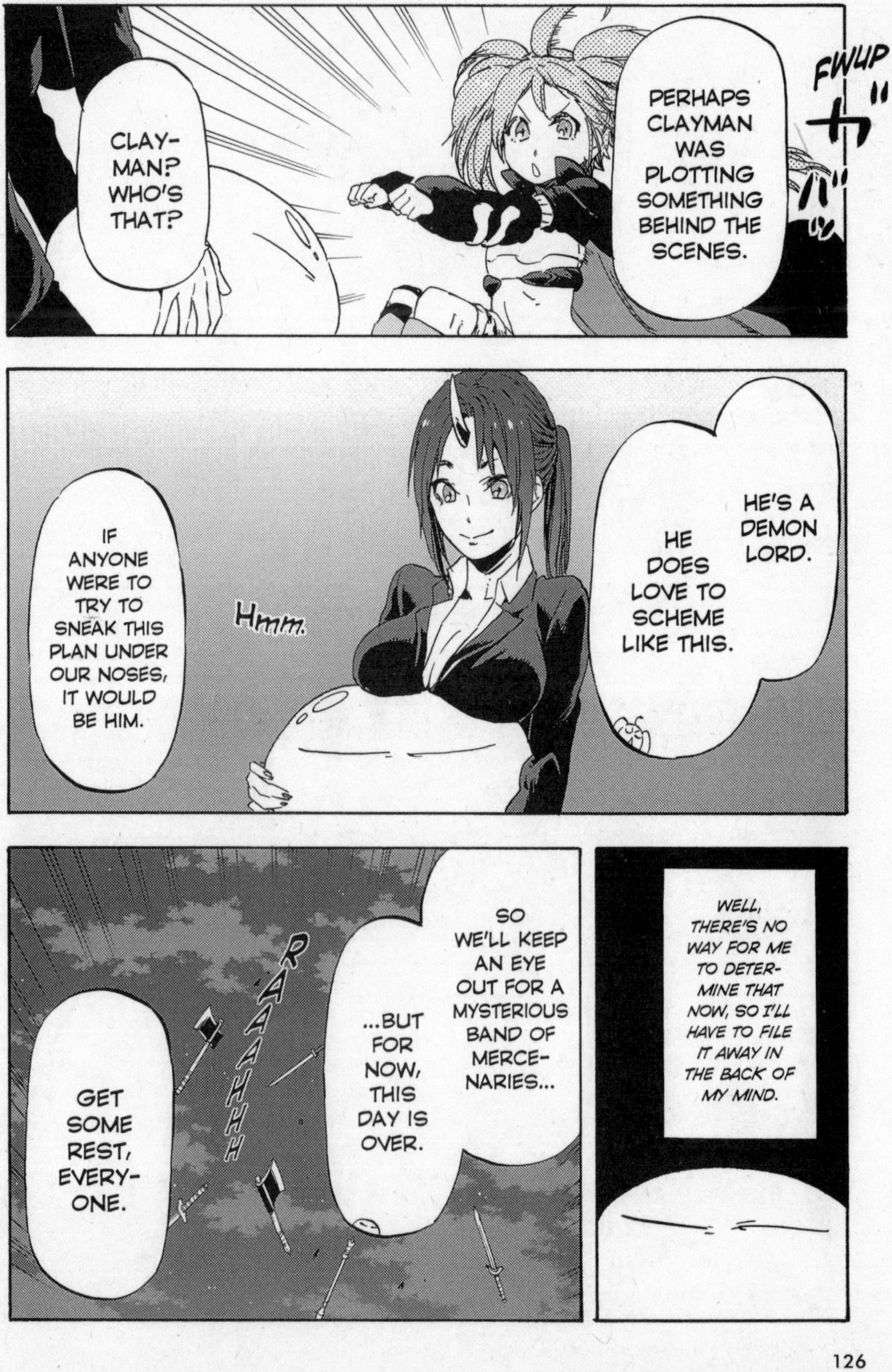
FWUP
PERHAPS CLAYMAN WAS PLOTTING SOMETHING BEHIND THE SCENES.
CLAY-MAN? WHO'S THAT?
HE'S A DEMON LORD.
HE DOES LOVE TO SCHEME LIKE THIS.
Hmm.
IF ANYONE WERE TO TRY TO SNEAK THIS PLAN UNDER OUR NOSES, IT WOULD BE HIM.
WELL, THERE'S NO WAY FOR ME TO DETER-MINE THAT NOW, SO I'LL HAVE TO FILE IT AWAY IN THE BACK OF MY MIND.
SO WE'LL KEEP AN EYE OUT FOR A MYSTERIOUS BAND OF MERCE-NARIES...
...BUT FOR NOW, THIS DAY IS OVER.
RAAAAHHHH
GET SOME REST, EVERY-ONE.

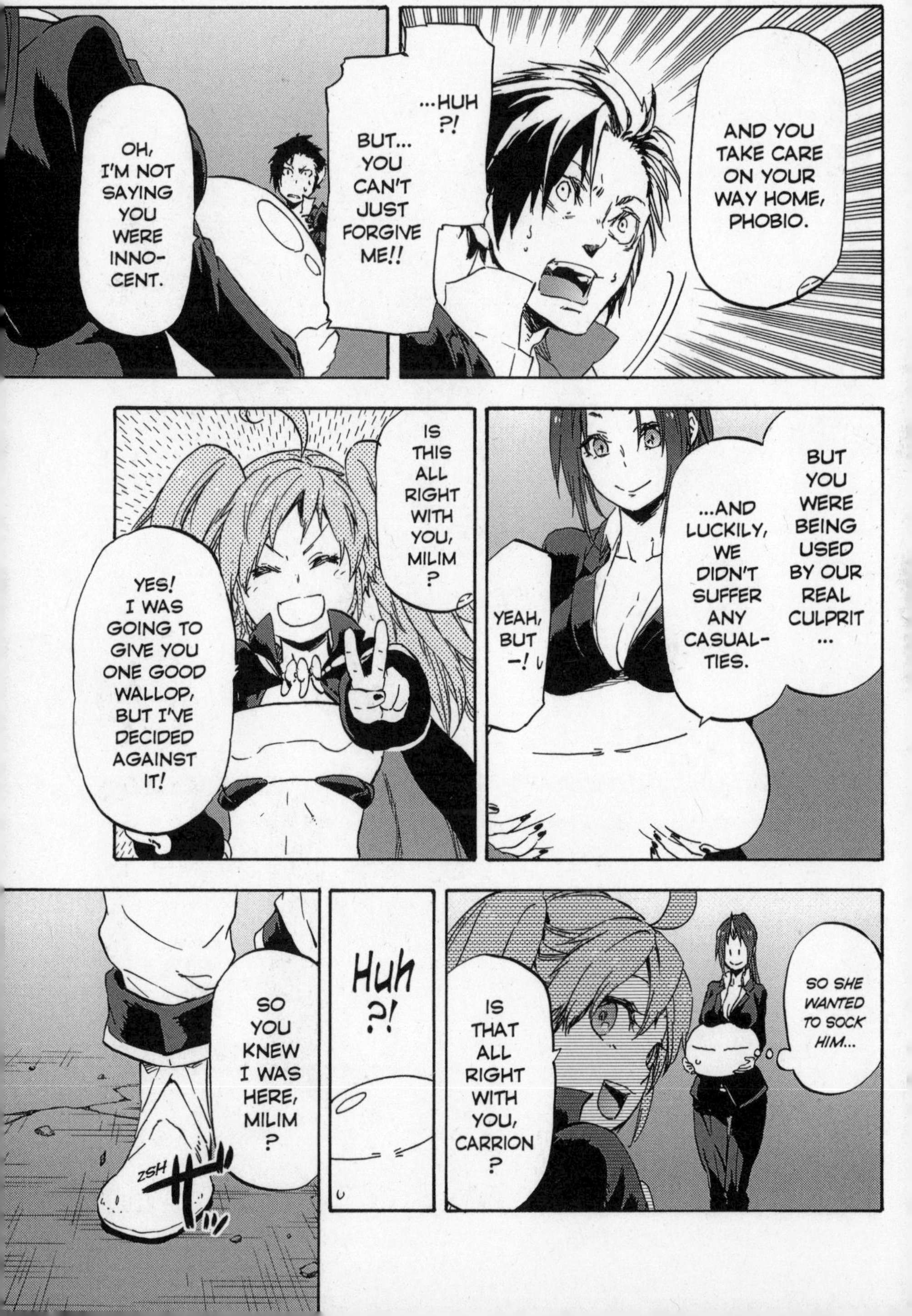
AND YOU TAKE CARE ON YOUR WAY HOME, PHOBIO.
...HUH ?!
BUT... YOU CAN'T JUST FORGIVE ME!!
OH, I'M NOT SAYING YOU WERE INNO-CENT.
BUT YOU WERE BEING USED BY OUR REAL CULPRIT ...
...AND LUCKILY, WE DIDN'T SUFFER ANY CASUAL-TIES.
YEAH, BUT —!
IS THIS ALL RIGHT WITH YOU, MILIM ?
YES! I WAS GOING TO GIVE YOU ONE GOOD WALLOP, BUT I'VE DECIDED AGAINST IT!
SO SHE WANTED TO SOCK HIM...
IS THAT ALL RIGHT WITH YOU, CARRION ?
Huh ?!
SO YOU KNEW I WAS HERE, MILIM ?
ZSH

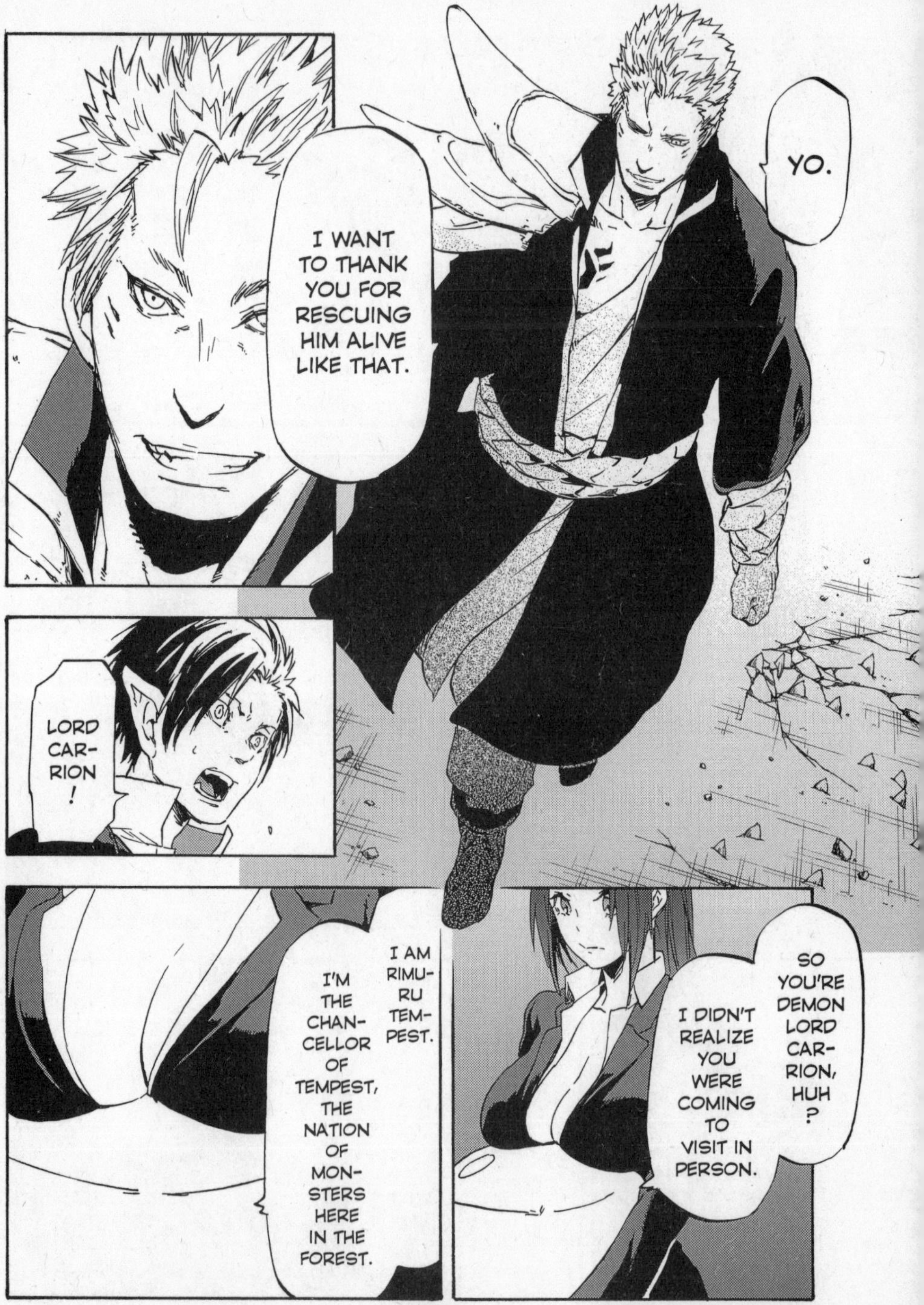
YO.
I WANT TO THANK YOU FOR RESCUING HIM ALIVE LIKE THAT.
LORD CAR-RION!
SO YOU'RE DEMON LORD CAR-RION, HUH?
I DIDN'T REALIZE YOU WERE COMING TO VISIT IN PERSON.
I AM RIMU-RU TEM-PEST.
I'M THE CHAN-CELLOR OF TEMPEST, THE NATION OF MON-STERS HERE IN THE FOREST.

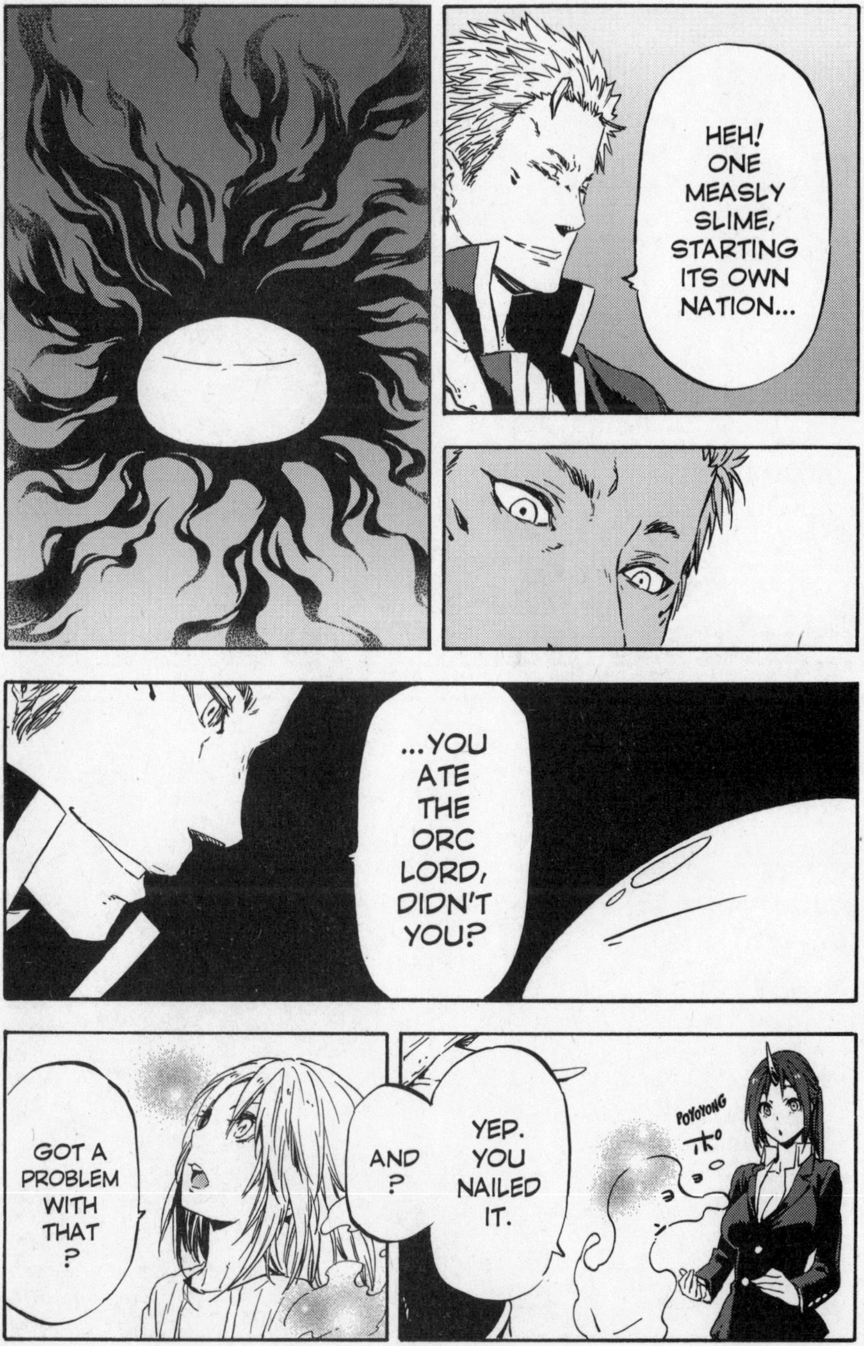
HEH! ONE MEASLY SLIME, STARTING ITS OWN NATION...
...YOU ATE THE ORC LORD, DIDN'T YOU?
POYOYONG
YEP. YOU NAILED IT.
AND ?
GOT A PROBLEM WITH THAT ?

FWA HA HA HA! THAT'S FUNNY!

I CAN SEE WHY MILIM LIKES YOU!

PUH!

I HOPE YOU CAN FORGIVE HIM, AND CHALK THIS UP TO ME NOT PAYING ATTENTION THE WAY I SHOULD.

SORRY FOR LETTING MY SUB-ORDINATE GO OUT OF CONTROL LIKE THAT.

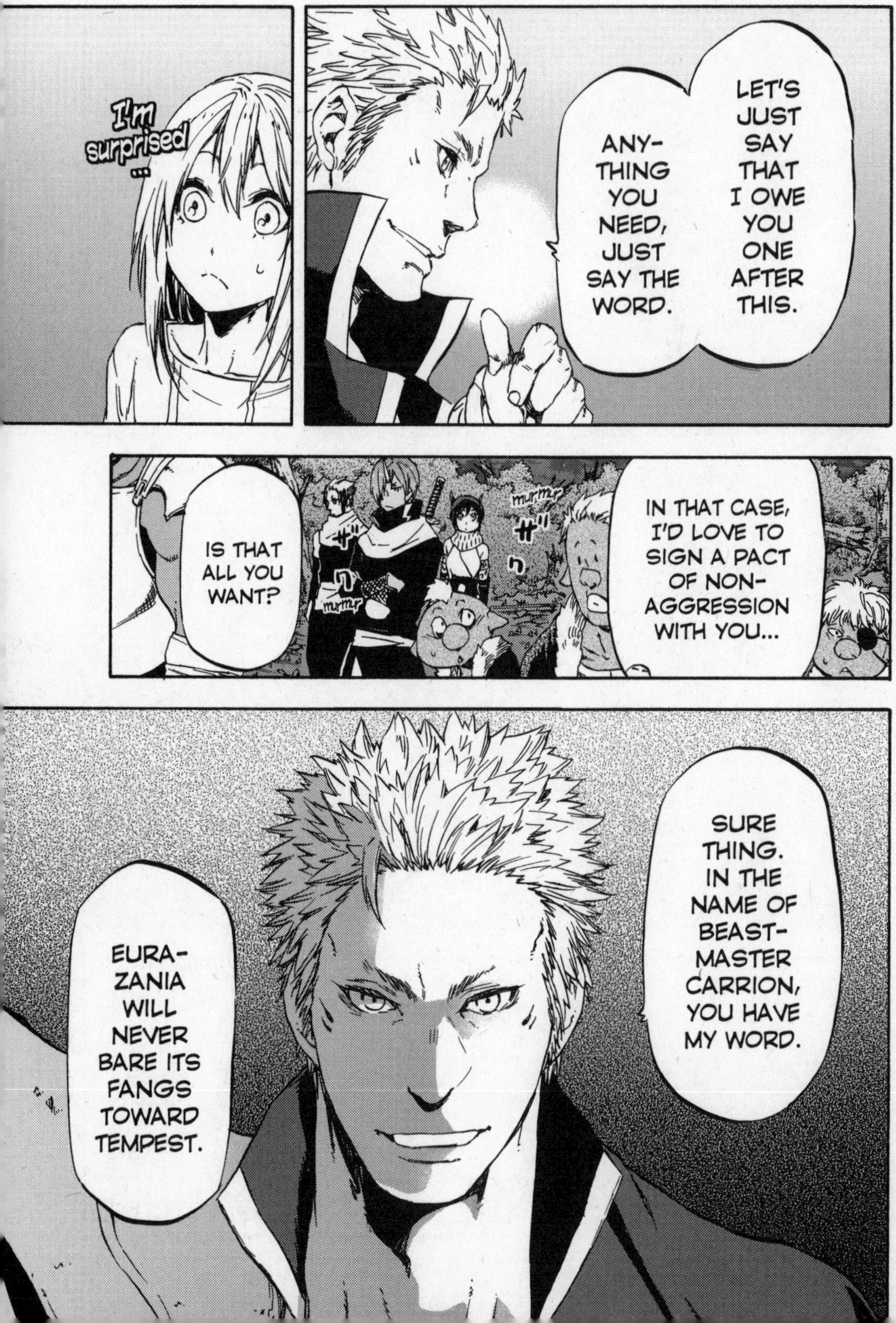
LET'S JUST SAY THAT I OWE YOU ONE AFTER THIS.
ANYTHING YOU NEED, JUST SAY THE WORD.
I'm surprised ...
IN THAT CASE, I'D LOVE TO SIGN A PACT OF NON-AGGRESSION WITH YOU...
murmur
murmur
IS THAT ALL YOU WANT?
SURE THING. IN THE NAME OF BEASTMASTER CARRION, YOU HAVE MY WORD.
EURAZANIA WILL NEVER BARE ITS FANGS TOWARD TEMPEST.

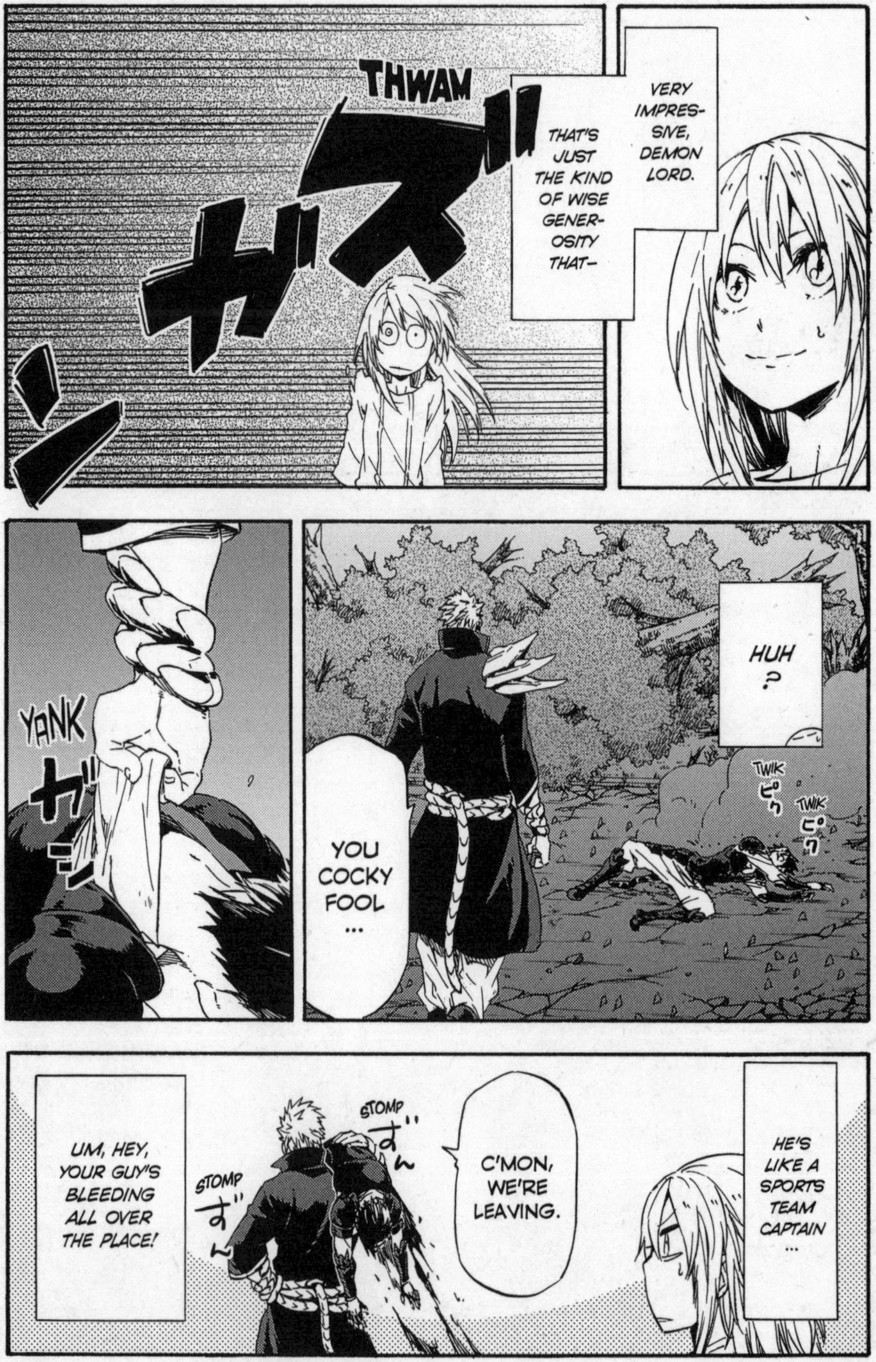
VERY IMPRESSIVE, DEMON LORD.
THAT'S JUST THE KIND OF WISE GENEROSITY THAT—
THWAM
HUH?
TWIK
ピク
TWIK
ピク
YOU COCKY FOOL...
YANK
HE'S LIKE A SPORTS TEAM CAPTAIN...
C'MON, WE'RE LEAVING.
STOMP
ずん
STOMP
ずん
UM, HEY, YOUR GUY'S BLEEDING ALL OVER THE PLACE!

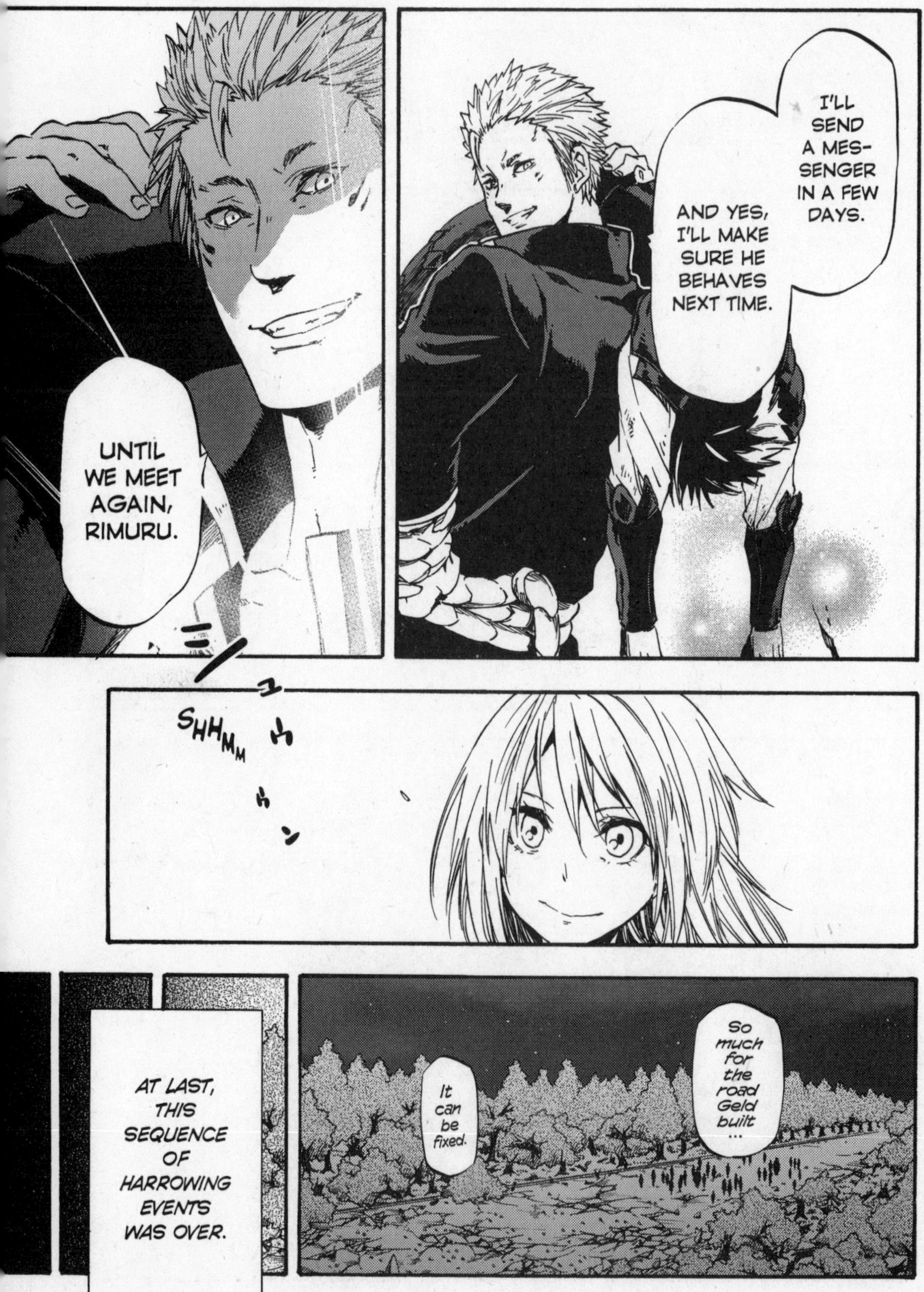
I'LL SEND A MES-SENGER IN A FEW DAYS.
AND YES, I'LL MAKE SURE HE BEHAVES NEXT TIME.
UNTIL WE MEET AGAIN, RIMURU.
SHHMM
So much for the road Geld built...
It can be fixed.
AT LAST, THIS SEQUENCE OF HARROWING EVENTS WAS OVER.

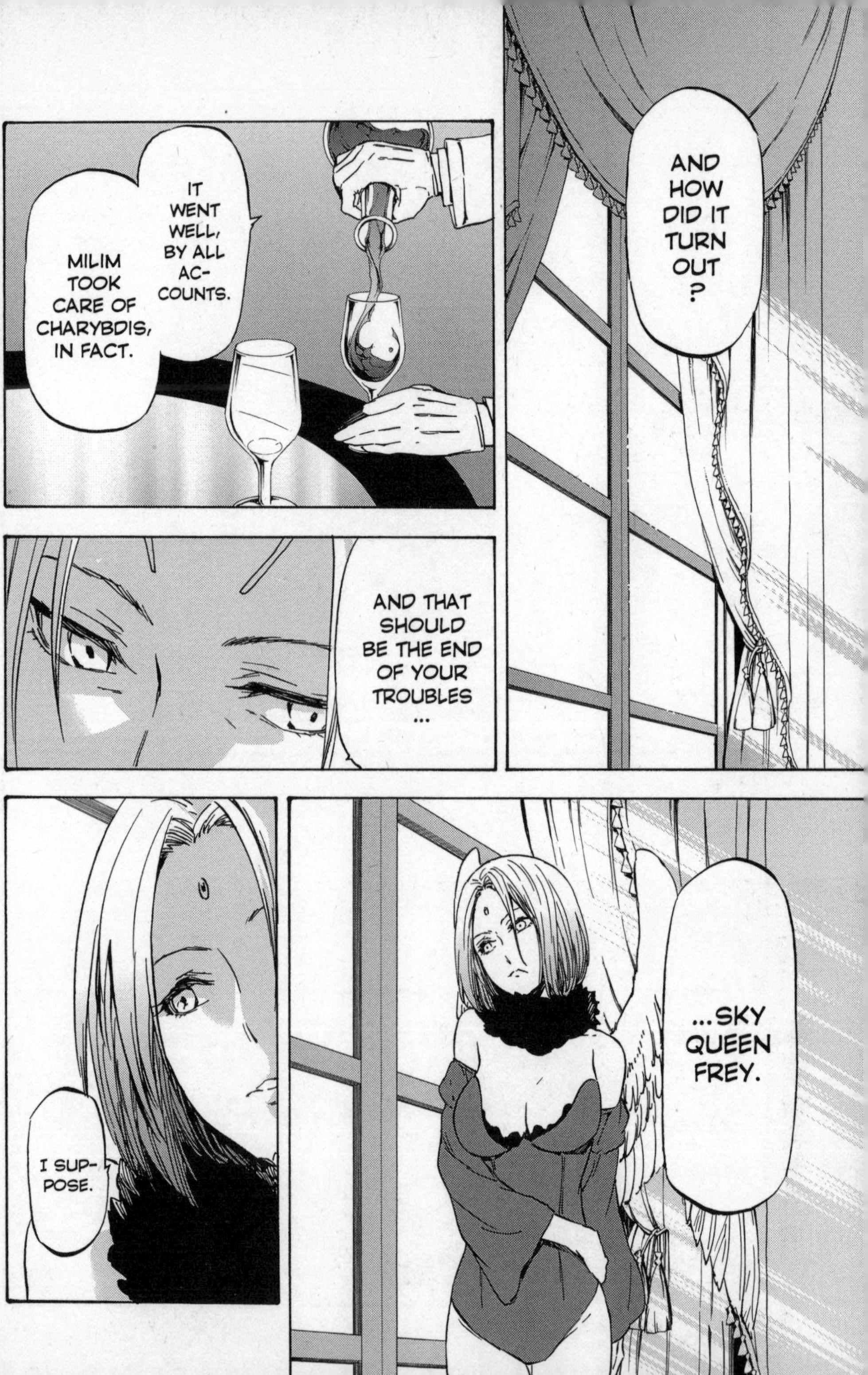
AND HOW DID IT TURN OUT?
IT WENT WELL, BY ALL AC-COUNTS.
MILIM TOOK CARE OF CHARYBDIS, IN FACT.
AND THAT SHOULD BE THE END OF YOUR TROUBLES...
...SKY QUEEN FREY.
I SUP-POSE.

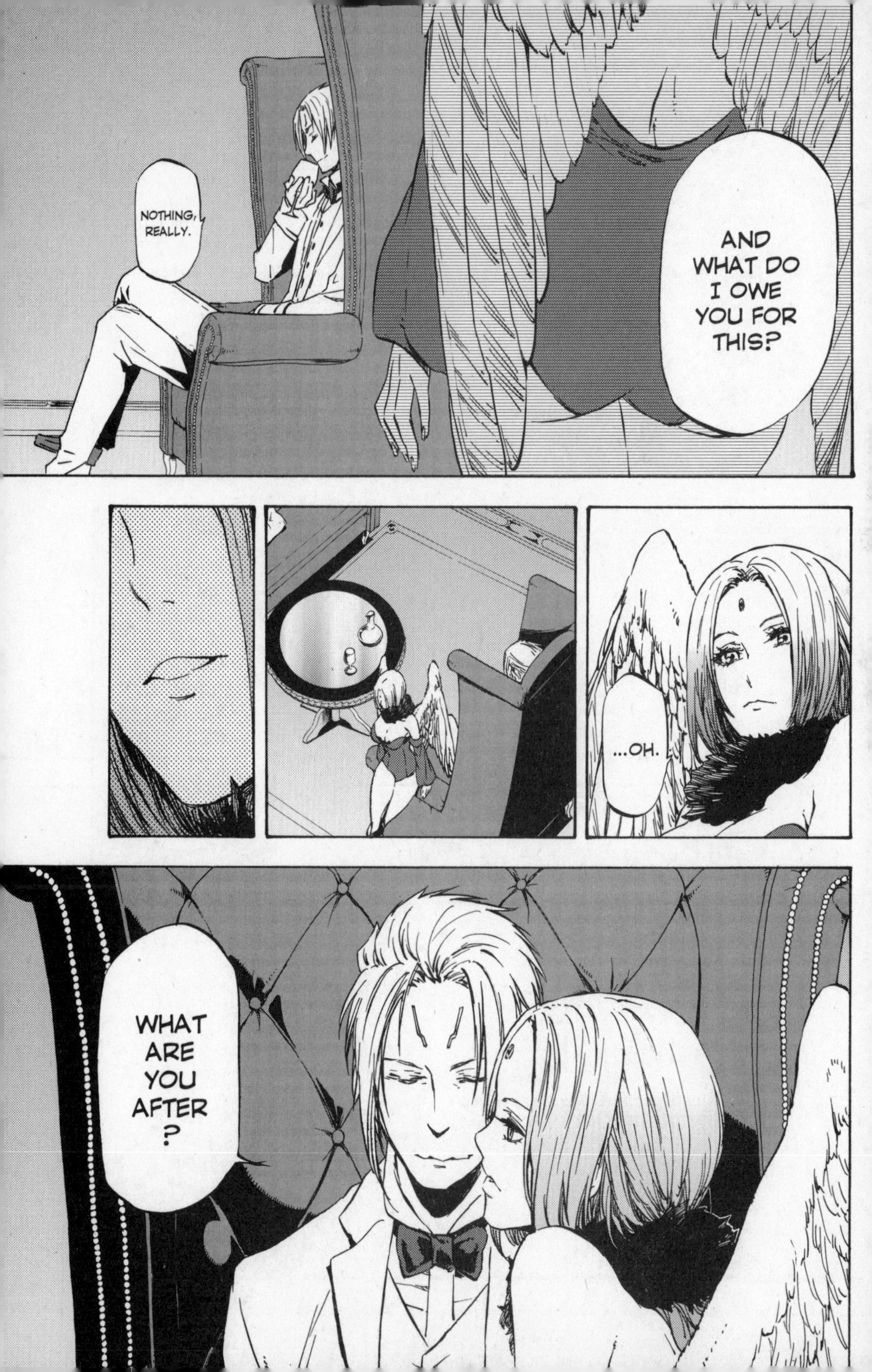
AND WHAT DO I OWE YOU FOR THIS?
NOTHING, REALLY.
...OH.
WHAT ARE YOU AFTER?

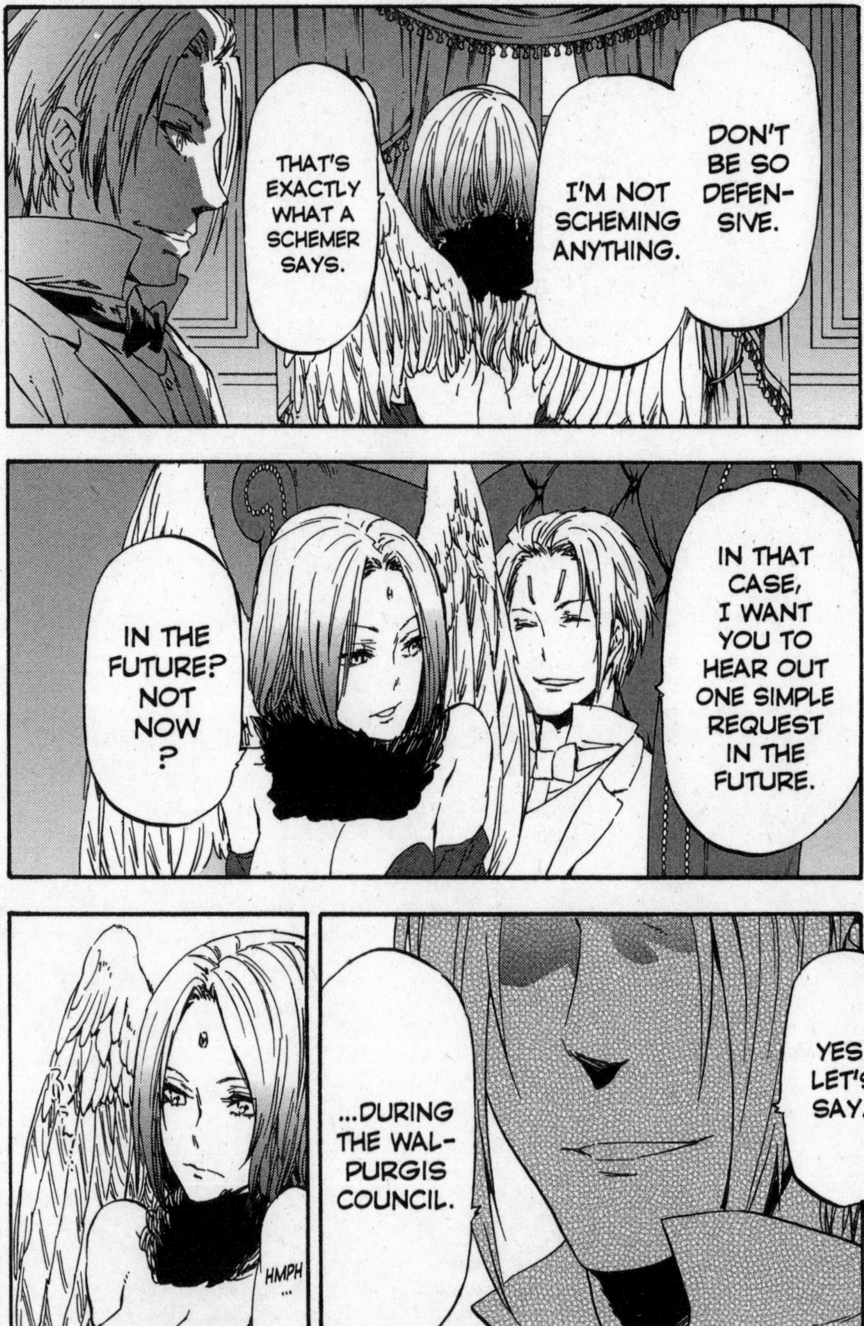
DON'T BE SO DEFENSIVE.
I'M NOT SCHEMING ANYTHING.
THAT'S EXACTLY WHAT A SCHEMER SAYS.
IN THAT CASE, I WANT YOU TO HEAR OUT ONE SIMPLE REQUEST IN THE FUTURE.
IN THE FUTURE? NOT NOW?
YES. LET'S SAY...
...DURING THE WALPURGIS COUNCIL.
HMPH...

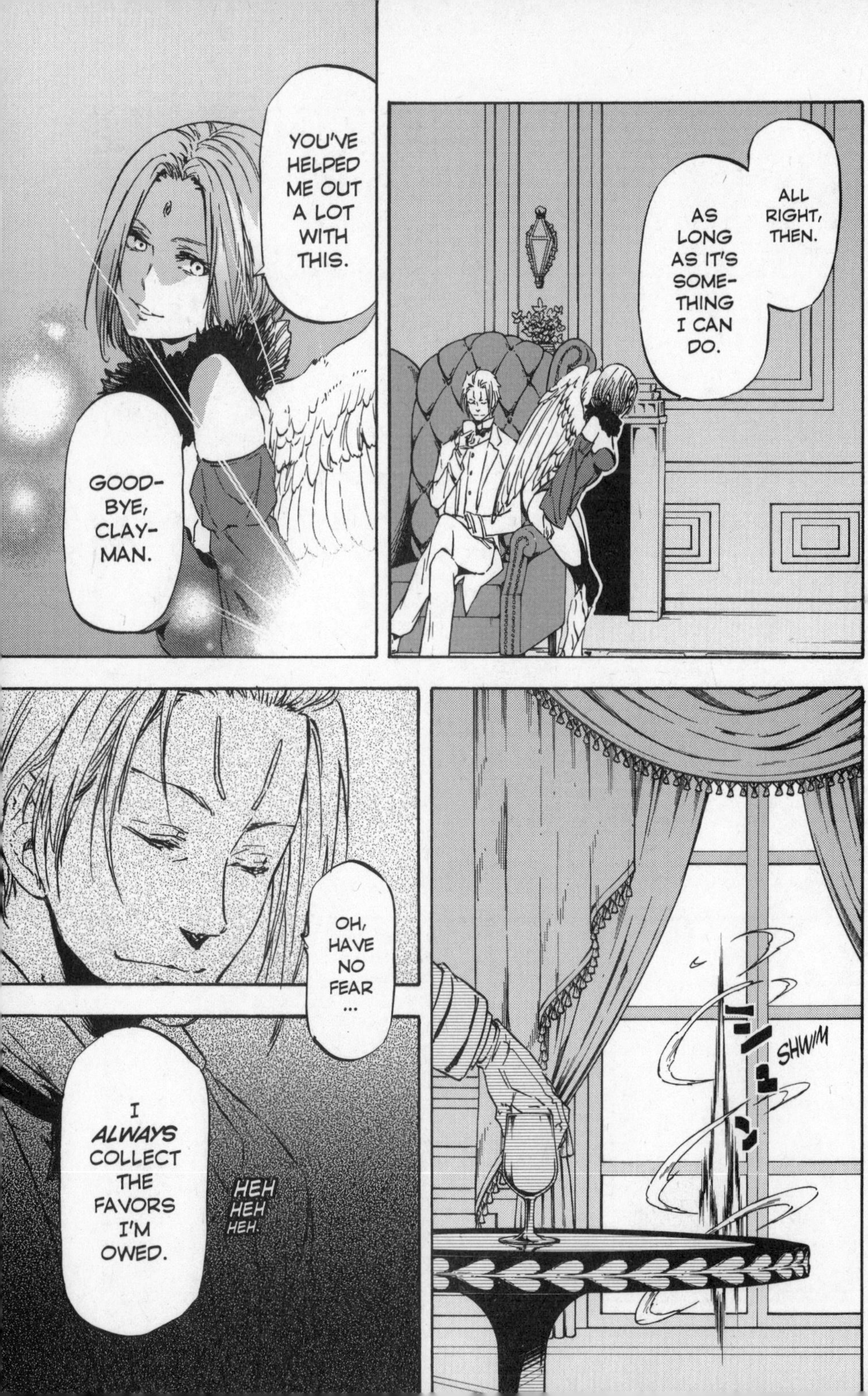
ALL RIGHT, THEN.
AS LONG AS IT'S SOMETHING I CAN DO.
YOU'VE HELPED ME OUT A LOT WITH THIS.
GOOD-BYE, CLAY-MAN.
SHWIM
OH, HAVE NO FEAR...
I *ALWAYS* COLLECT THE FAVORS I'M OWED.
HEH HEH HEH.

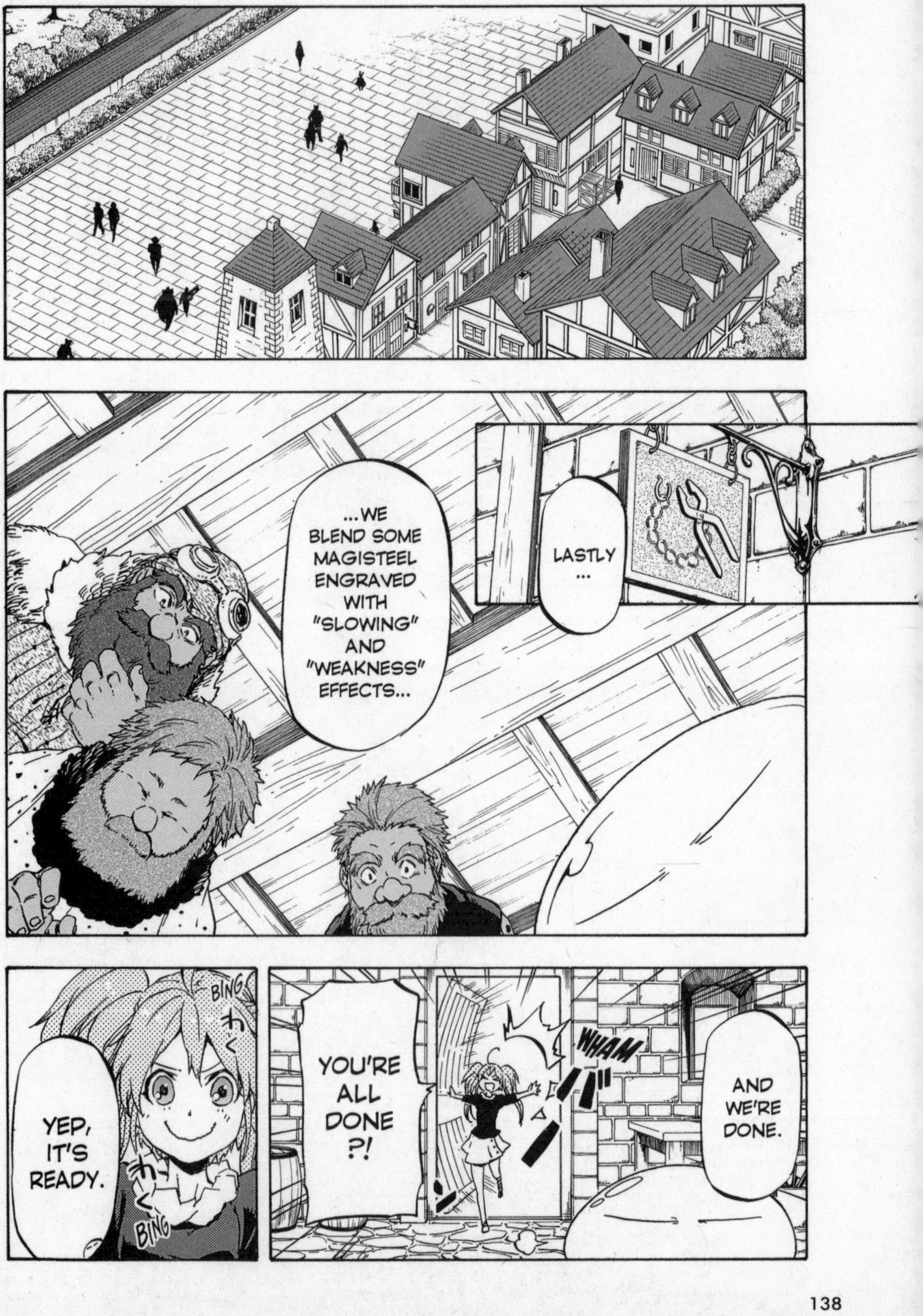
LASTLY ...
...WE BLEND SOME MAGISTEEL ENGRAVED WITH "SLOWING" AND "WEAKNESS" EFFECTS...
AND WE'RE DONE.
WHAM
YOU'RE ALL DONE ?!
BING
わく
YEP, IT'S READY.
わく
BING

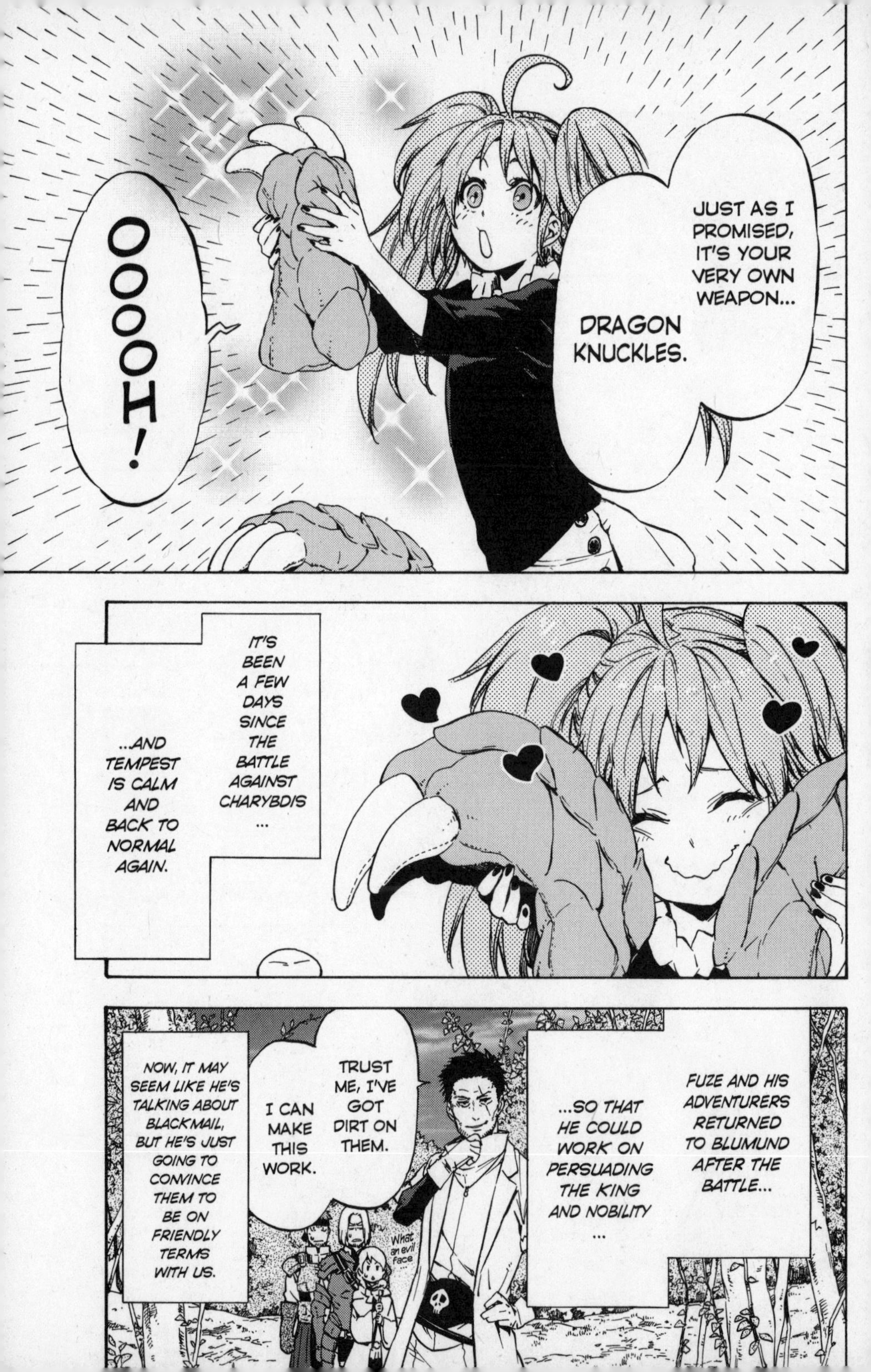
JUST AS I PROMISED, IT'S YOUR VERY OWN WEAPON...
DRAGON KNUCKLES.
OOOOH!
IT'S BEEN A FEW DAYS SINCE THE BATTLE AGAINST CHARYBDIS...
...AND TEMPEST IS CALM AND BACK TO NORMAL AGAIN.
FUZE AND HIS ADVENTURERS RETURNED TO BLUMUND AFTER THE BATTLE...
...SO THAT HE COULD WORK ON PERSUADING THE KING AND NOBILITY...
What an evil face
TRUST ME, I'VE GOT DIRT ON THEM.
I CAN MAKE THIS WORK.
NOW, IT MAY SEEM LIKE HE'S TALKING ABOUT BLACKMAIL, BUT HE'S JUST GOING TO CONVINCE THEM TO BE ON FRIENDLY TERMS WITH US.

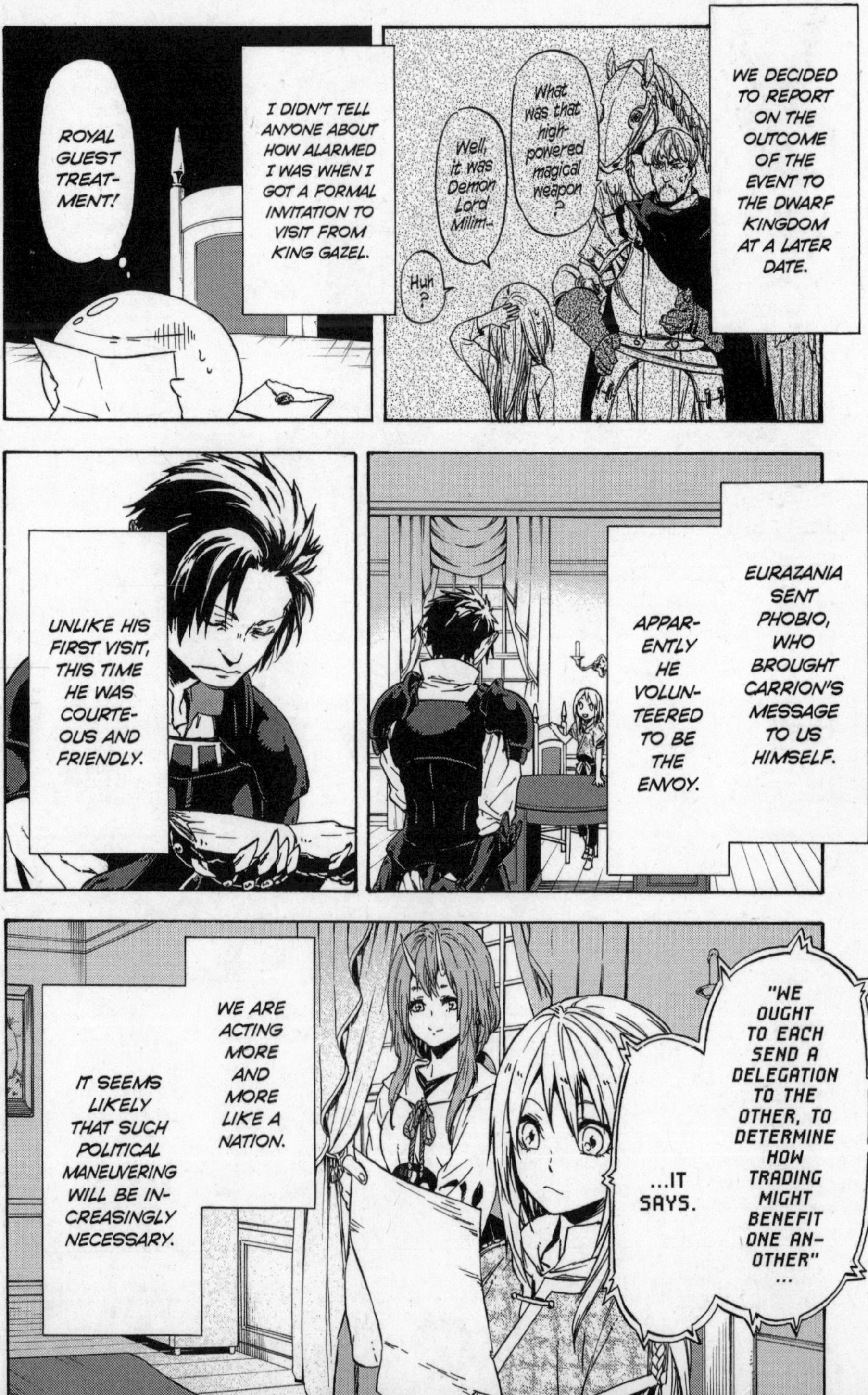
WE DECIDED TO REPORT ON THE OUTCOME OF THE EVENT TO THE DWARF KINGDOM AT A LATER DATE.
What was that high-powered magical weapon?
Well, it was Demon Lord Milim...
Huh?
I DIDN'T TELL ANYONE ABOUT HOW ALARMED I WAS WHEN I GOT A FORMAL INVITATION TO VISIT FROM KING GAZEL.
ROYAL GUEST TREAT-MENT!
EURAZANIA SENT PHOBIO, WHO BROUGHT CARRION'S MESSAGE TO US HIMSELF.
APPAR-ENTLY HE VOLUN-TEERED TO BE THE ENVOY.
UNLIKE HIS FIRST VISIT, THIS TIME HE WAS COURTE-OUS AND FRIENDLY.
"WE OUGHT TO EACH SEND A DELEGATION TO THE OTHER, TO DETERMINE HOW TRADING MIGHT BENEFIT ONE AN-OTHER"...
...IT SAYS.
WE ARE ACTING MORE AND MORE LIKE A NATION.
IT SEEMS LIKELY THAT SUCH POLITICAL MANEUVERING WILL BE IN-CREASINGLY NECESSARY.

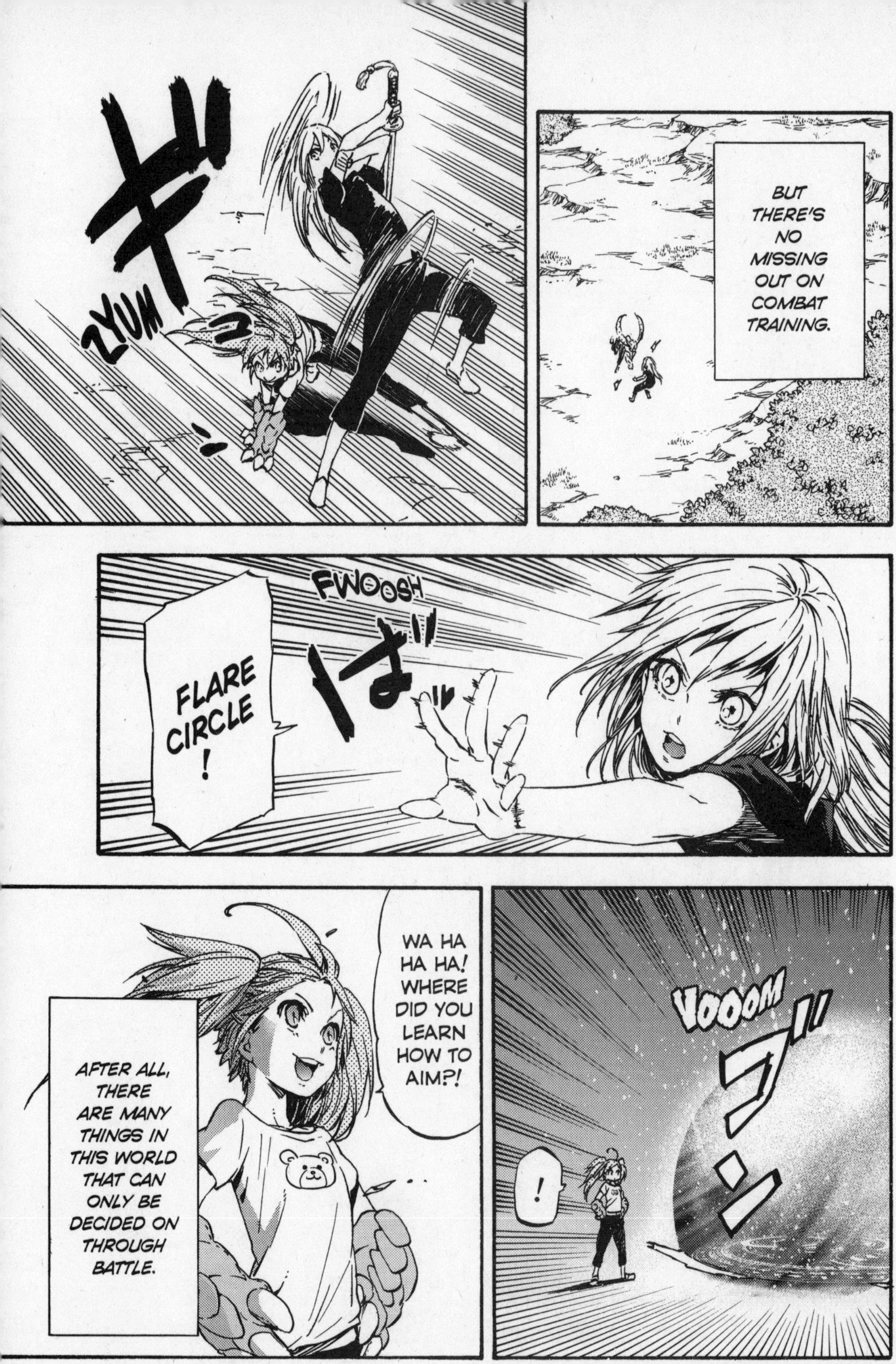
BUT THERE'S NO MISSING OUT ON COMBAT TRAINING.
ZYUM
FWOOSH
FLARE CIRCLE!
VOOOM
!
WA HA HA HA! WHERE DID YOU LEARN HOW TO AIM?!
AFTER ALL, THERE ARE MANY THINGS IN THIS WORLD THAT CAN ONLY BE DECIDED ON THROUGH BATTLE.

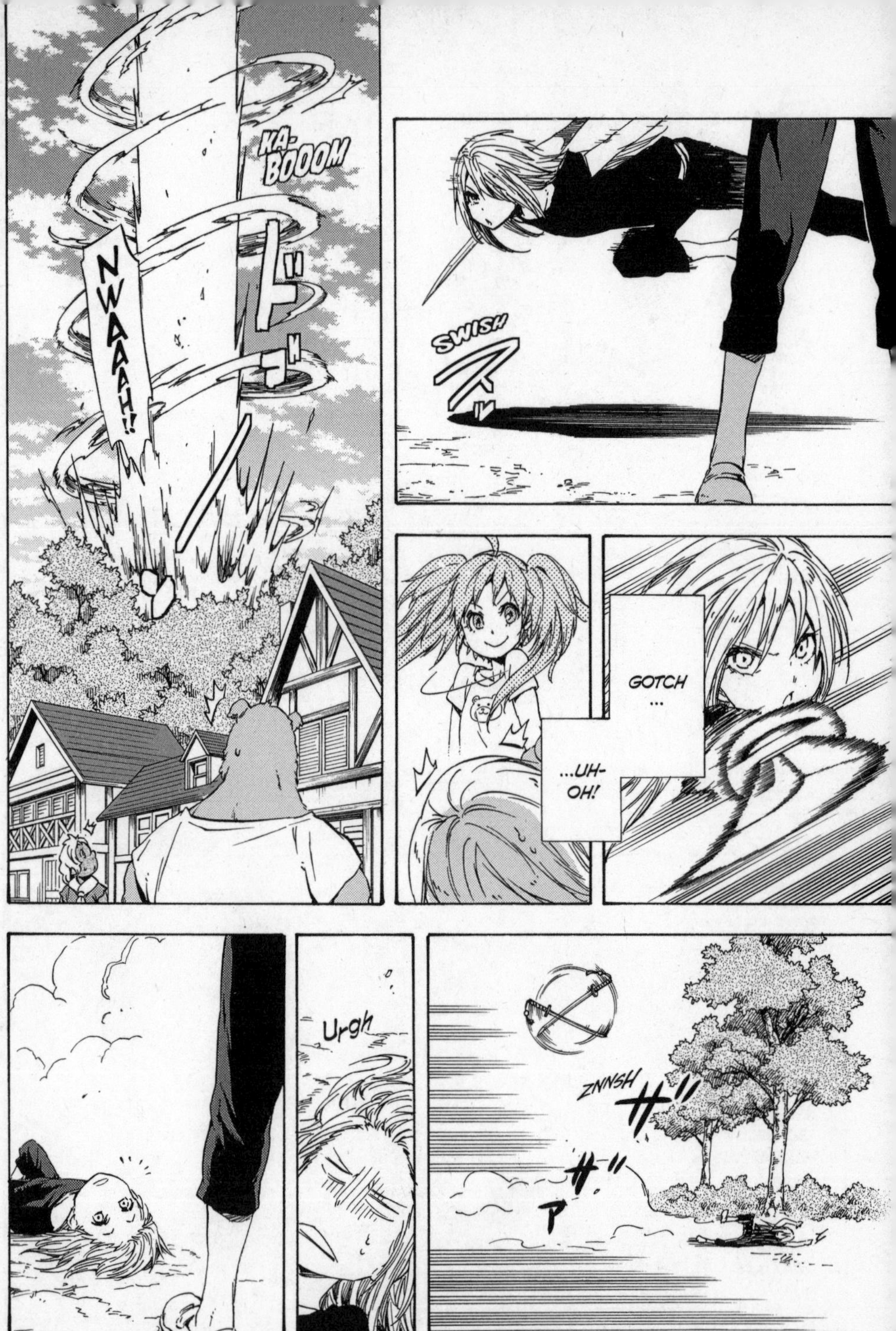
SWISH
GOTCH ...
...UH-OH!
KA-BOOOM
NWAAAH!!
ZNNSH
Urgh

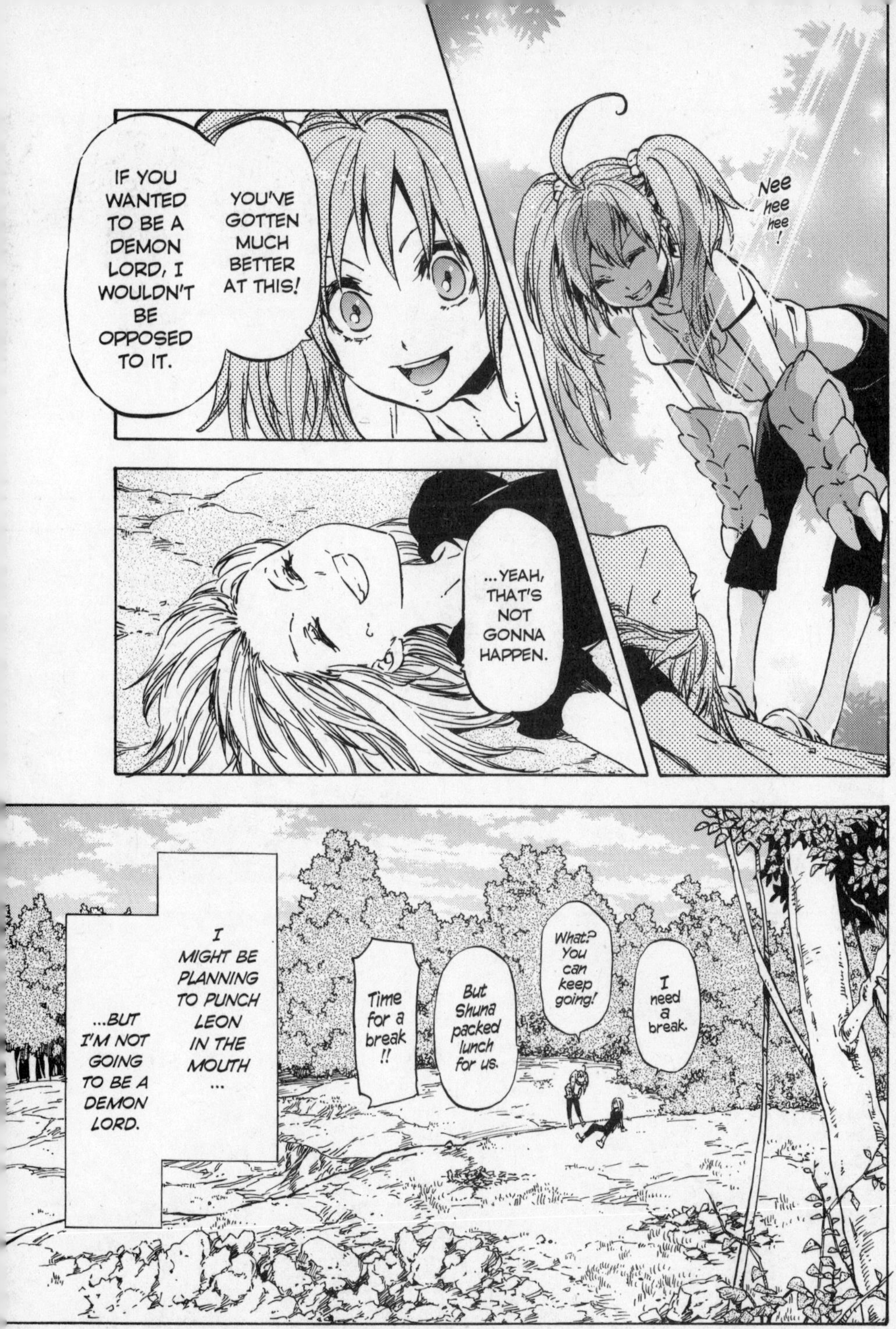
Nee hee hee!
YOU'VE GOTTEN MUCH BETTER AT THIS!
IF YOU WANTED TO BE A DEMON LORD, I WOULDN'T BE OPPOSED TO IT.
...YEAH, THAT'S NOT GONNA HAPPEN.
I need a break.
What? You can keep going!
But Shuna packed lunch for us.
Time for a break!!
I MIGHT BE PLANNING TO PUNCH LEON IN THE MOUTH...
...BUT I'M NOT GOING TO BE A DEMON LORD.

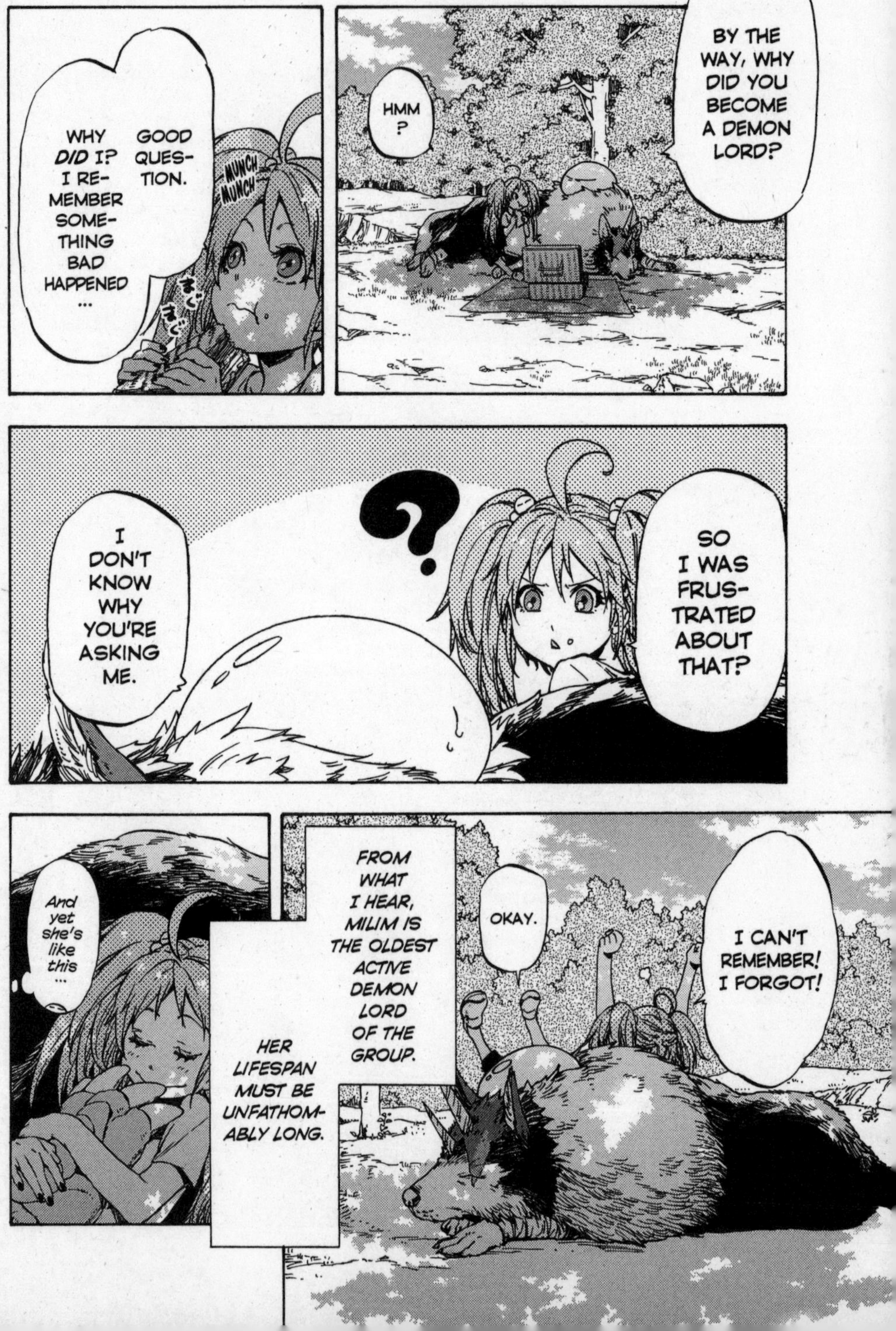
BY THE WAY, WHY DID YOU BECOME A DEMON LORD?
HMM?
MUNCH MUNCH
まぐ まぐ
GOOD QUESTION.
WHY *DID* I? I REMEMBER SOMETHING BAD HAPPENED...
SO I WAS FRUSTRATED ABOUT THAT?
I DON'T KNOW WHY YOU'RE ASKING ME.
I CAN'T REMEMBER! I FORGOT!
OKAY.
FROM WHAT I HEAR, MILIM IS THE OLDEST ACTIVE DEMON LORD OF THE GROUP.
HER LIFESPAN MUST BE UNFATHOMABLY LONG.
And yet she's like this...

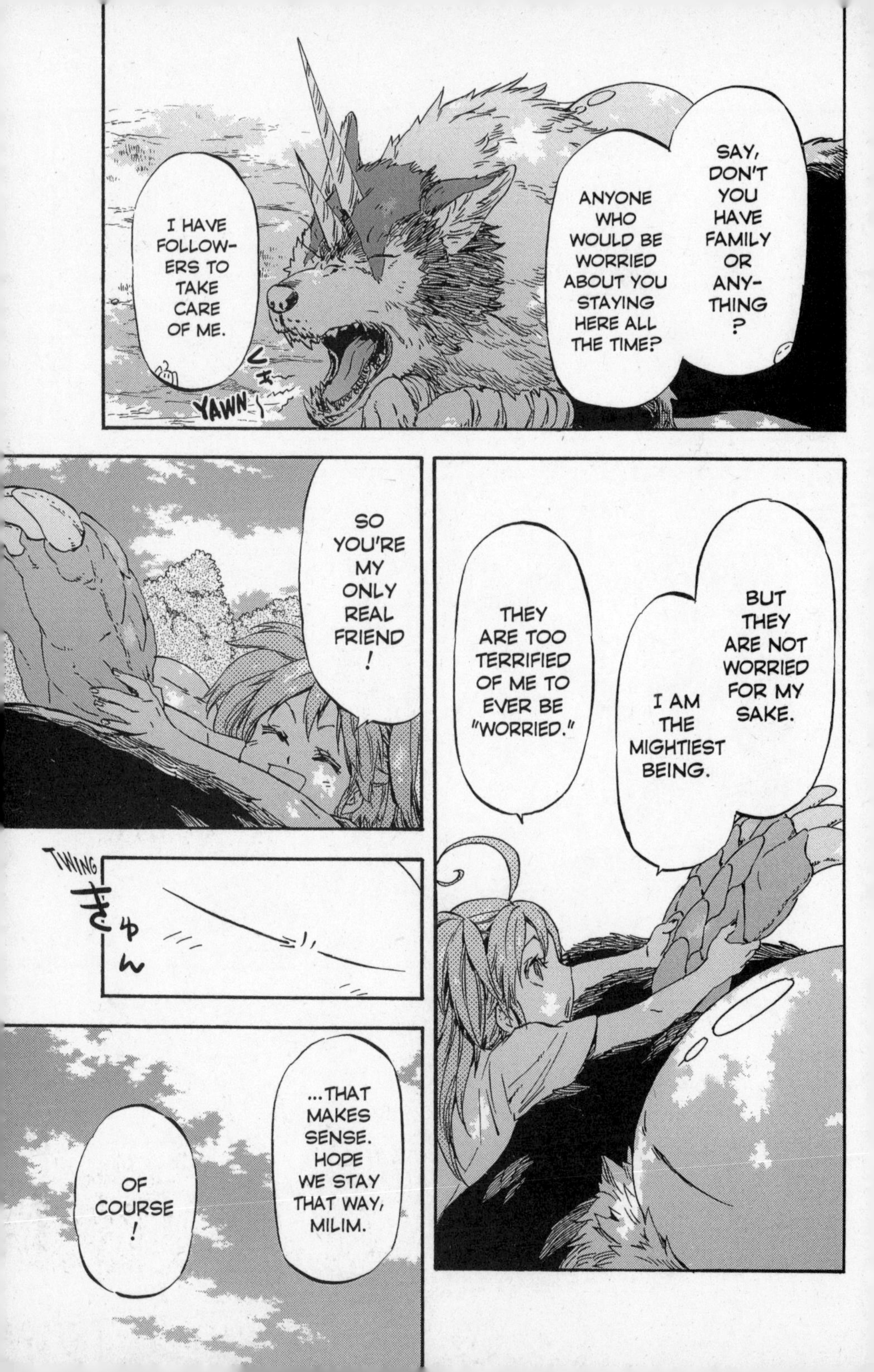
SAY, DON'T YOU HAVE FAMILY OR ANYTHING?
ANYONE WHO WOULD BE WORRIED ABOUT YOU STAYING HERE ALL THE TIME?
I HAVE FOLLOWERS TO TAKE CARE OF ME.
YAWN
BUT THEY ARE NOT WORRIED FOR MY SAKE.
I AM THE MIGHTIEST BEING.
THEY ARE TOO TERRIFIED OF ME TO EVER BE "WORRIED."
SO YOU'RE MY ONLY REAL FRIEND!
TWING
...THAT MAKES SENSE. HOPE WE STAY THAT WAY, MILIM.
OF COURSE!

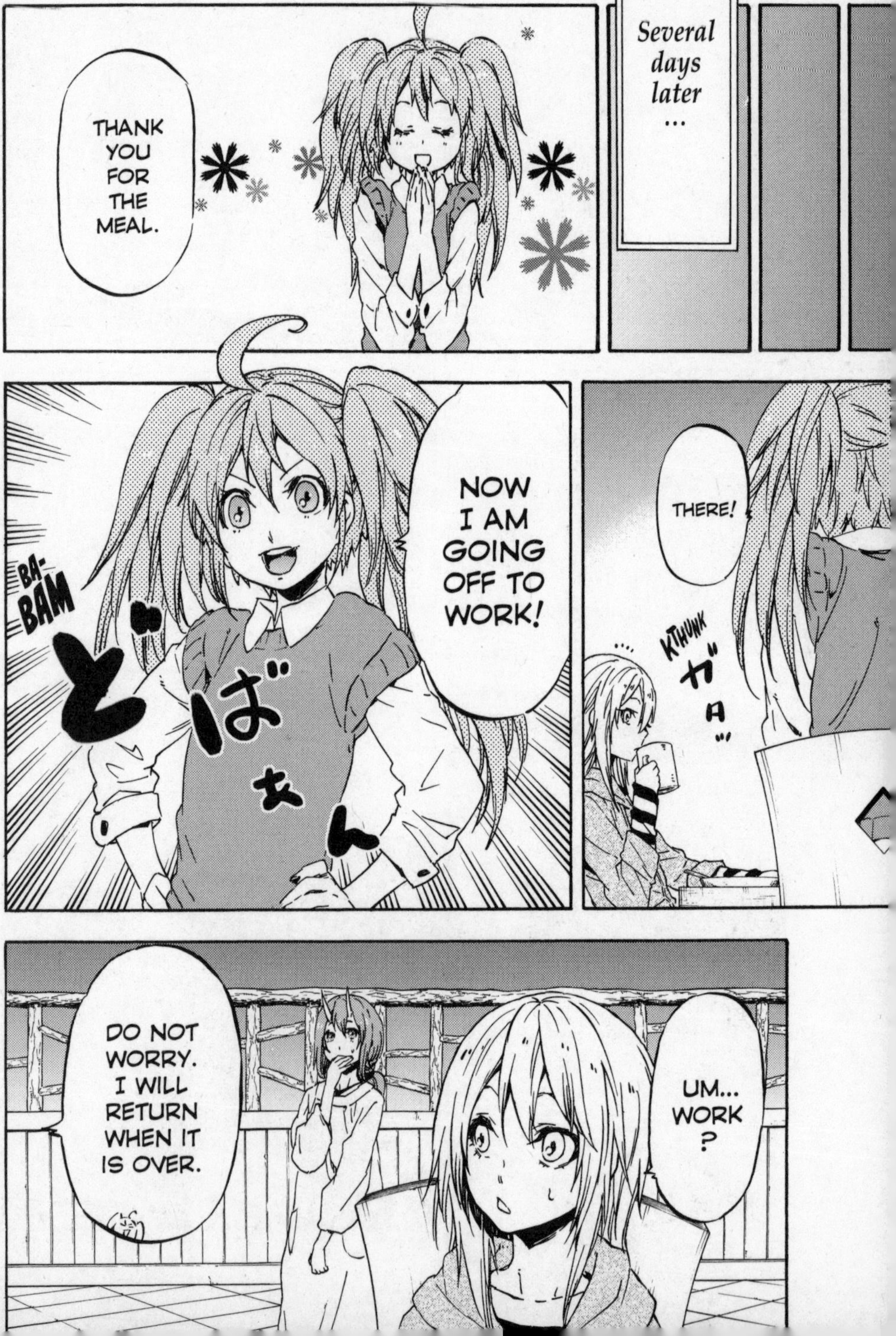
Several days later …
THANK YOU FOR THE MEAL.
THERE!
KTHUNK
ガタ
NOW I AM GOING OFF TO WORK!
BA-BAM
どばぁん
UM... WORK?
DO NOT WORRY. I WILL RETURN WHEN IT IS OVER.

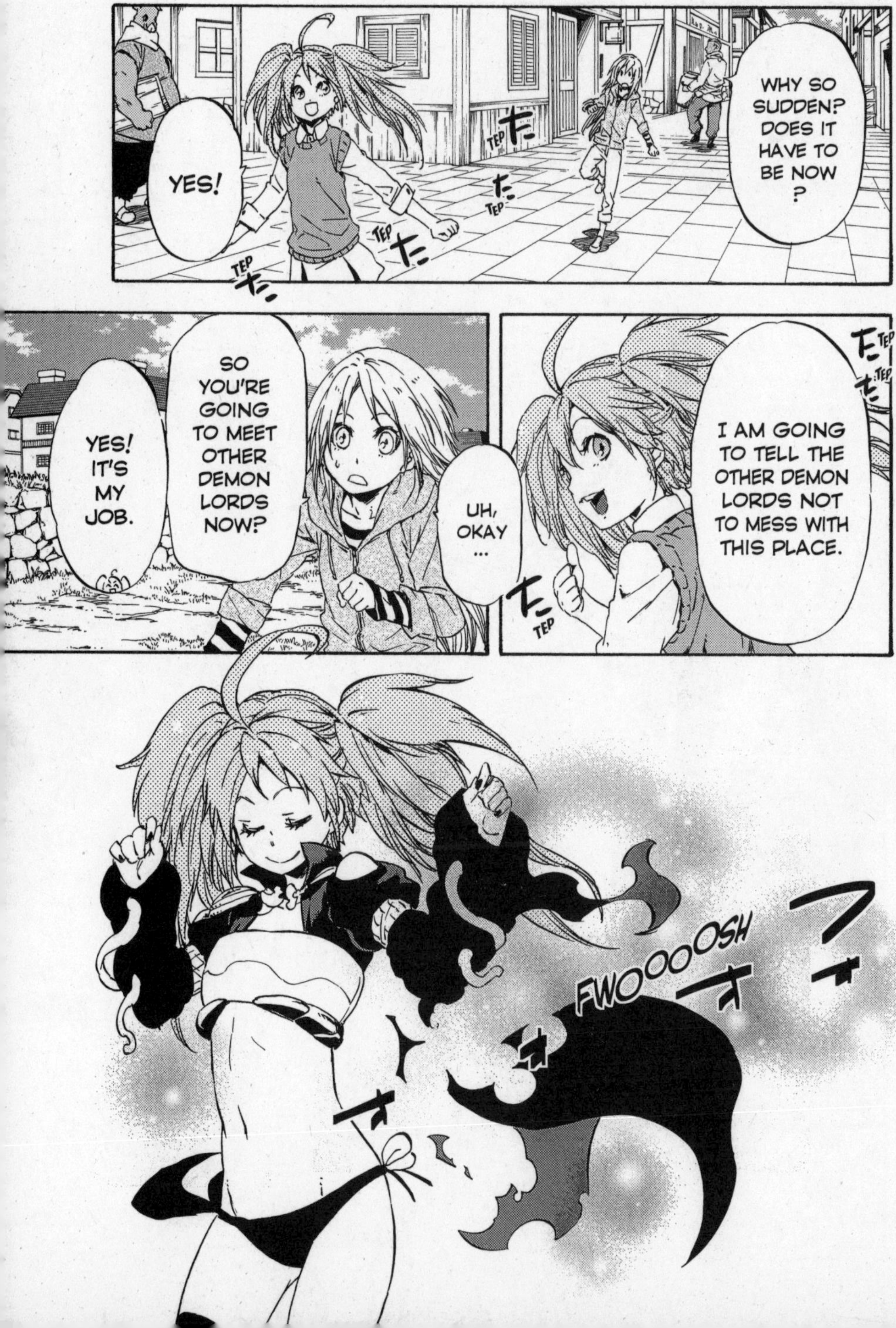
WHY SO SUDDEN? DOES IT HAVE TO BE NOW ?
TEP
TEP
YES!
TEP
TEP
TEP
TEP
I AM GOING TO TELL THE OTHER DEMON LORDS NOT TO MESS WITH THIS PLACE.
TEP
UH, OKAY ...
SO YOU'RE GOING TO MEET OTHER DEMON LORDS NOW?
YES! IT'S MY JOB.
FWOOOOSH

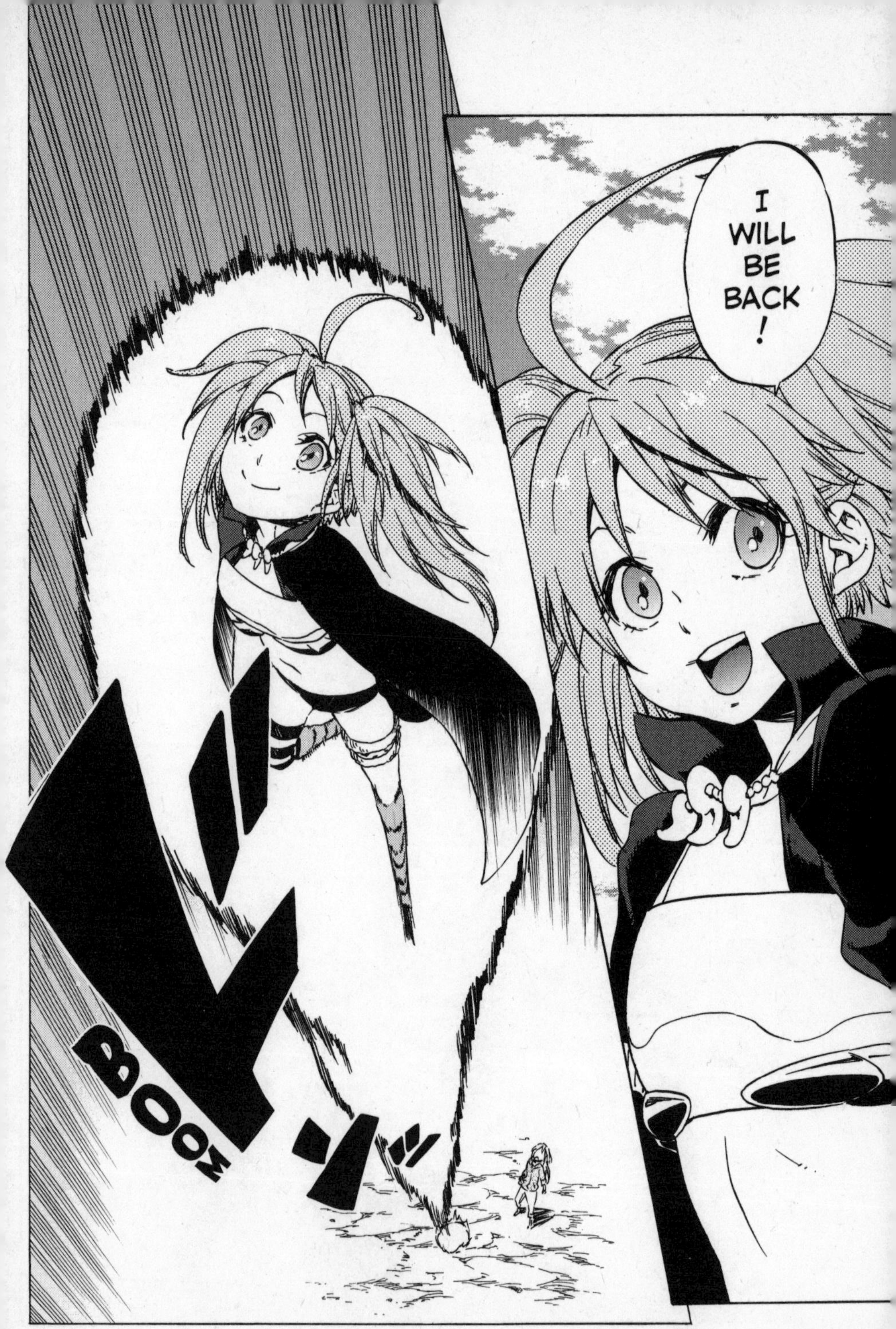
I WILL BE BACK!
BOOM

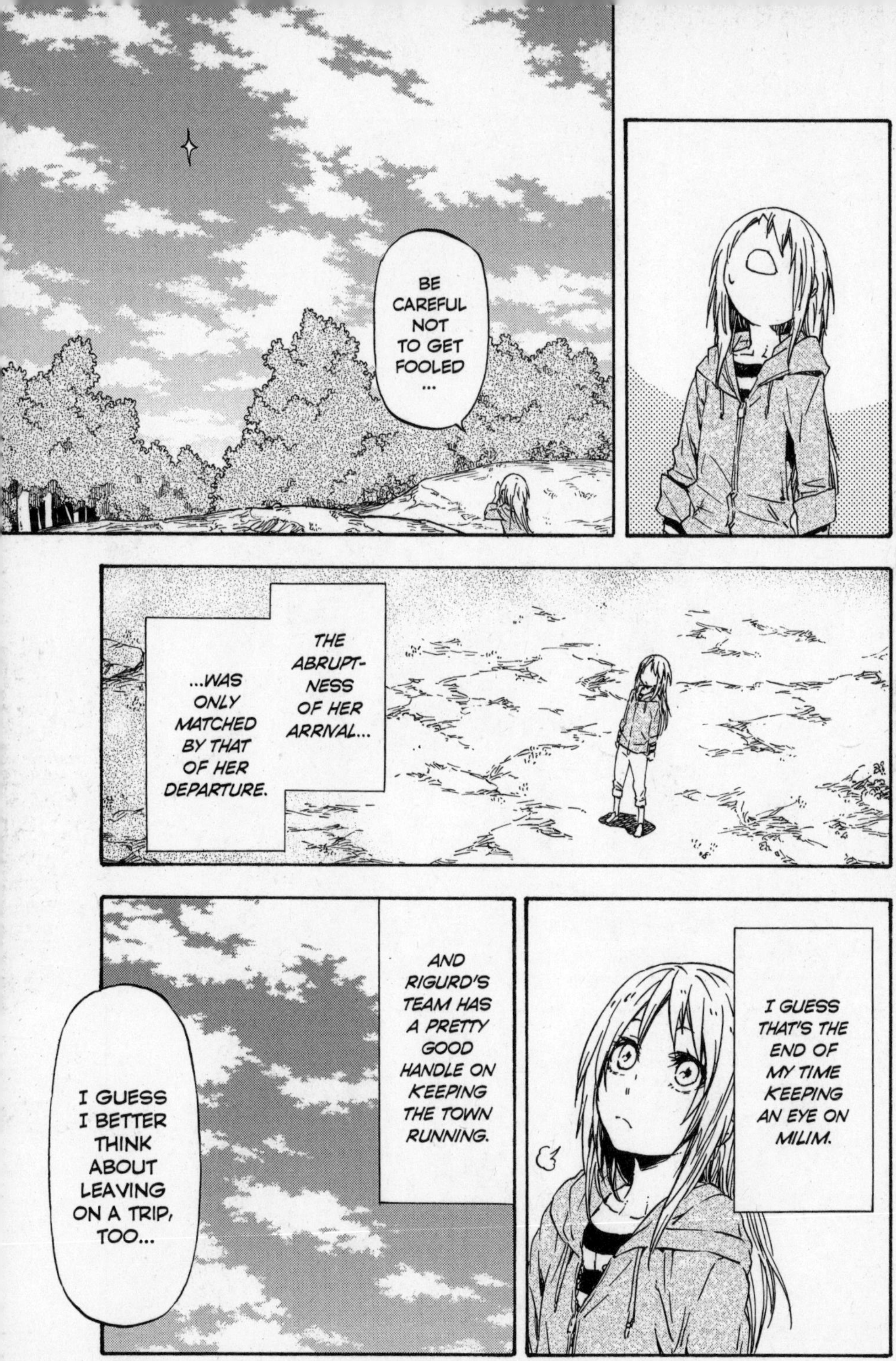
BE CAREFUL NOT TO GET FOOLED ...
THE ABRUPT-NESS OF HER ARRIVAL...
...WAS ONLY MATCHED BY THAT OF HER DEPARTURE.
I GUESS THAT'S THE END OF MY TIME KEEPING AN EYE ON MILIM.
AND RIGURD'S TEAM HAS A PRETTY GOOD HANDLE ON KEEPING THE TOWN RUNNING.
I GUESS I BETTER THINK ABOUT LEAVING ON A TRIP, TOO...

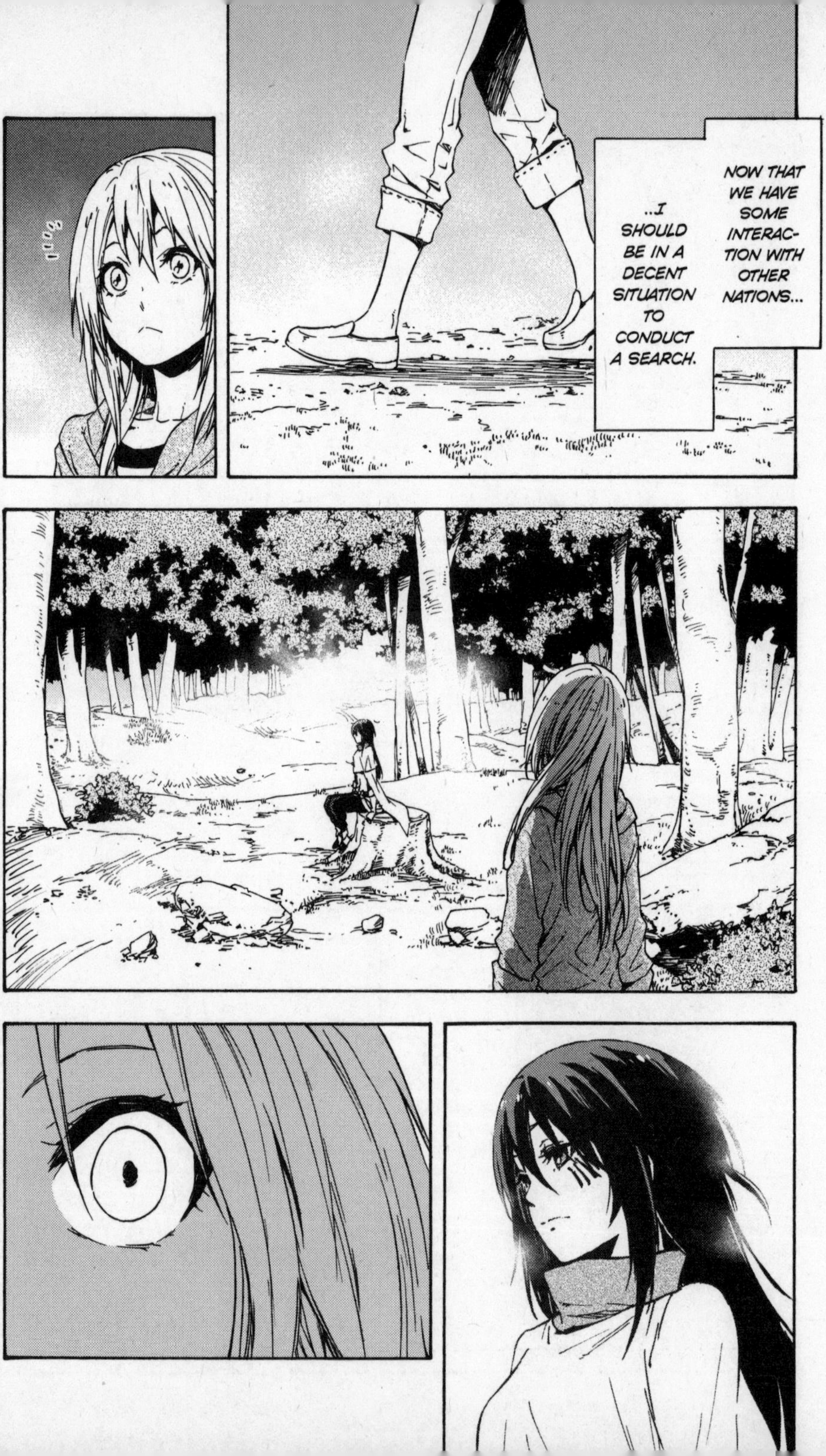
NOW THAT WE HAVE SOME INTERAC-TION WITH OTHER NATIONS...
...I SHOULD BE IN A DECENT SITUATION TO CONDUCT A SEARCH.

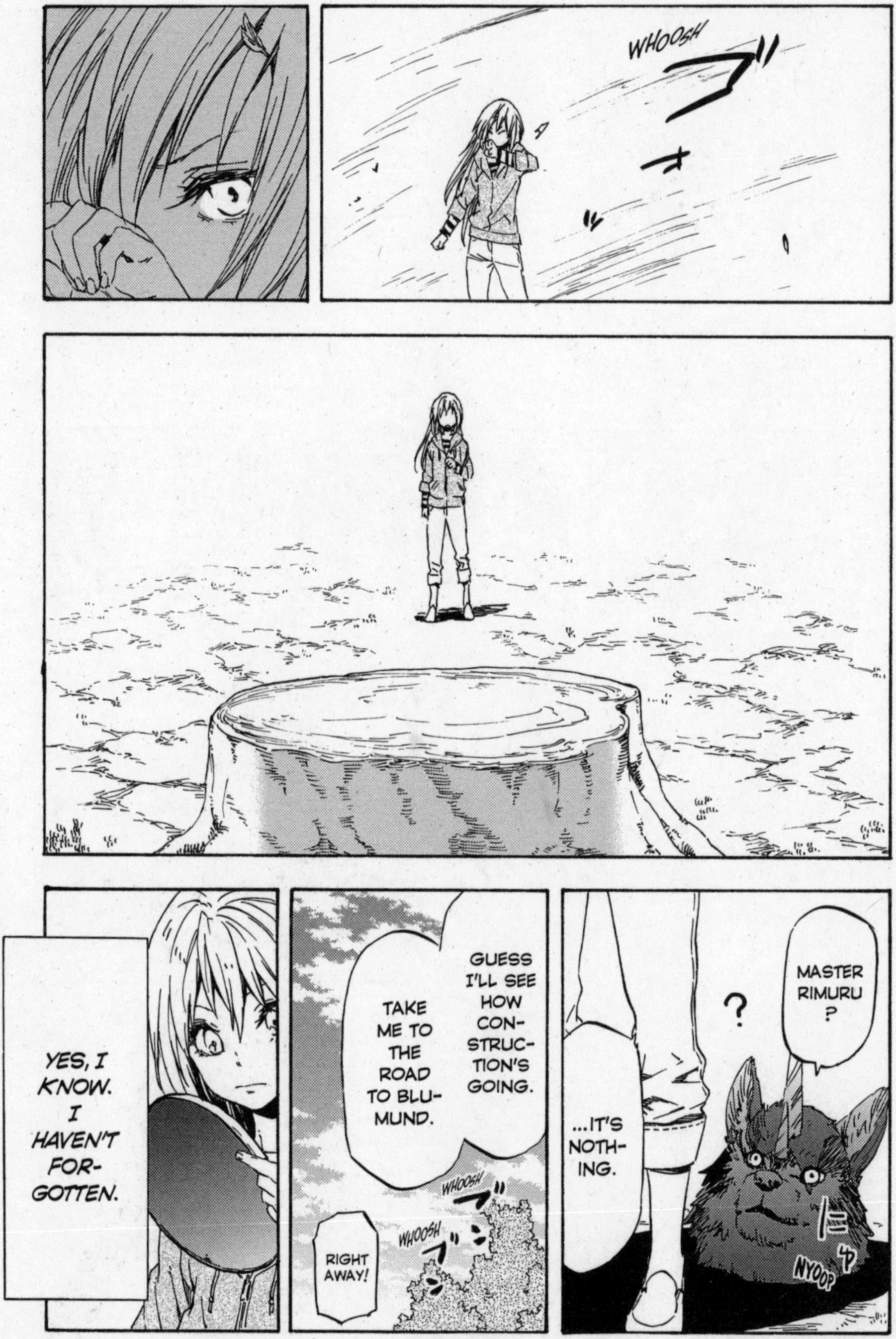
WHOOSH
MASTER RIMURU?
?
...IT'S NOTHING.
NYOOP
GUESS I'LL SEE HOW CONSTRUCTION'S GOING.
TAKE ME TO THE ROAD TO BLUMUND.
WHOOSH
WHOOSH
RIGHT AWAY!
YES, I KNOW. I HAVEN'T FORGOTTEN.

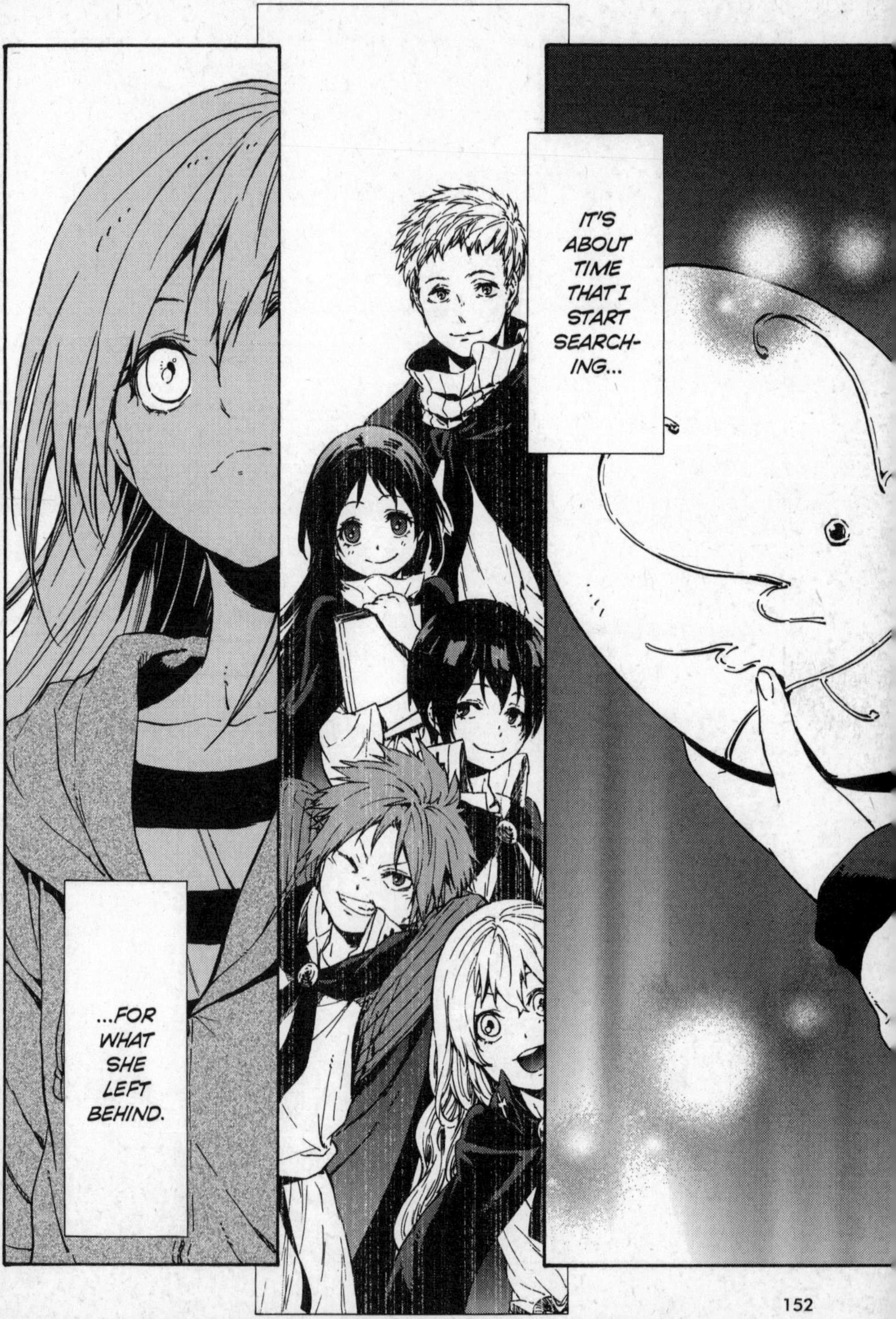
IT'S ABOUT TIME THAT I START SEARCHING...
...FOR WHAT SHE LEFT BEHIND.

Reincarnate
in Volume 9?

→YES

NO

Bonus Short Story

Veldora's Slime Observation Journal

~BIG CATCH~

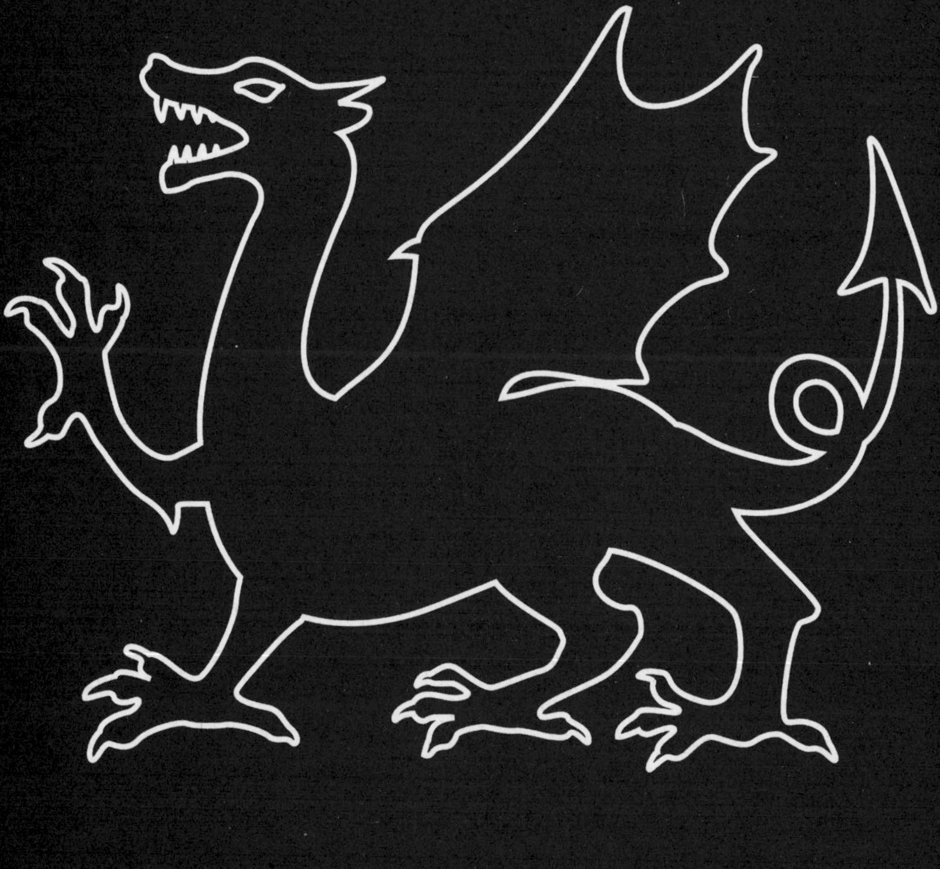

Veldora's Slime Observation Journal
~BIG CATCH~

◆ DISPATCH FROM THE OVERSEER ◆

"Help."

Oops, I allowed the voice of my mind to leak out. As it happens, I am in quite a bind at the moment. Why is that, you ask?

"Warning. Please continue analyzing. Do not slack off."

Heh. Now does it make sense to you?

No mercy. Rimuru abuses me with no mercy whatsoever!

But of course, I do understand that he does it for my sake.

Still...is this really the only way? Is it right to make someone work around the clock, just because they do not require sleep?

If I'd known it would come to this, I'd happily let him keep stealing my magical energy. Just kidding. That's a little dragon humor for you. Don't take it seriously.

No! I said don't take it seriously!

"Gyaiiiiee!!"

What a dreadful state of affairs. It seemed he assumed that I had plenty of power to spare. I've just been given a taste of Rimuru's true cruelty.

But I was not the only one put through the wringer.

"Help me, Master Veldora, help meee!!"

Hmm. Strange. I feel as though I imagined hearing Ifrit's voice in the distance.

"It's not your imagination! It's not your imaginaaatiooon!"

Sadly, Ifrit, there is nothing I can do. For I have already placed the "Ifrit Raising Project" under Rimuru's supervision.

"Forgive me, Ifrit. Do not blame me, but your own immature self!" I answered, with the utmost pity.

Speaking of which, Rimuru's project is a frightening one, indeed. I had thought my pace of strengthening Ifrit was impressive, but I had no idea.

He is pouring the energy he took from me into Ifrit.

"I can't! I can't do this! I'm going to lose control of the energy and go completely berserk!" Ifrit wailed, trying to resist, but Rimuru ignored him.

What? It's not a problem? You say there's no one around for Ifrit to actually harm? I see... It is only Ifrit and I present. The only one who could possibly suffer would be me.

...

Is this acceptable to me?

It is a bit sad to consider, but I do not expect it will be a problem.

Thus Ifrit was forced to learn how to control his magical energy.

Ah, yes. Speaking of training, the human named Youm had a tough time of it as well.

Unlike monsters, humans do not suddenly grow in energy. The shackles of their flesh prevent this, so their bodies are what must be improved. So instead of energy, they improve in "level." Even a fresh set of equipment can bring considerable gains.

For example, a human with just a small knowledge of swordsmanship might be able to defeat most monsters just by having a special, unique-level weapon. As long as the weapon's attack power is high enough, that is adequate to vanquish a monster.

This is what made Hakuro's method of training so effective for them. By improving Youm's instinct, he gave him "Danger Foresight," and upped his reflexes with hellish training. With one of Kurobei's forged weapons on top of that, his power was certain to jump several ranks upward.

The most important tool in battle is the ability to intuit if one is capable of defeating the enemy or not. And the simplest method of judging that is in a test of speed.

If you can act faster than your opponent, and your attacks are effective, you can ultimately triumph, no matter who you are up against. And if your attacks are ineffective, you have the ability to flee.

And on the other hand, when the opponent is faster, one must be prepared to lose the fight. Hakuro is well aware of this, and his training regimen for Youm was built on this logic. Youm himself did not realize this, but he was treated much more kindly than Ifrit ever was.

With his fresh new equipment, he looks every bit the part of a dashing leader. Operation Chump-to-Champ is a resounding success, I dare say.

So trust in Rimuru and do your part, Ifrit!

◆CHARYBDIS◆

Fuze relaxes in the hot bath with a cold drink.

I am jealous. Oh, how jealous I am.

Is he taunting me, picking a fight because he knows I am hard at work? Is this true?

"Warning. Do not slack off."

This. This is what I, the great and fearsome Storm Dragon, must deal with...

I no longer sense the slightest bit of hesitation from Rimuru regarding what he is inflicting upon me. But I suppose I might bear a tiny bit of responsibility for having been slacking all of this time.

"..."

I feel ashamed.

It would not be smart to anger Rimuru any further. So I apologized and resumed the work.

Alas, how boring it is to engage in such a simple, repetitive task. I am calculating with all of my power, but it is mostly just relying upon my Unique Skill, "Inquirer." Though I am trying, as well...

"Warning. Skill usage inefficiency detected. Please stabilize use for greater efficiency."

Brutal. Simply brutal.

But I am the type who performs better when complimented...

It just doesn't make sense. I have been alive far longer, so how is Rimuru so much better at his skills than me? I do not understand. And yet, that is the reality.

Despite my misgivings, I continued the long and arduous process, dreaming of the day when I would be properly praised for my hard work. And there—just like always, fresh trouble has arisen!

There is a report from Trya, the younger sister of Treyni the dryad. She came to warn us of the return of the dread creature Charybdis.

"What?! The Ruler of the Skies has returned?!" said Rigurd. The Goblin King is surprisingly knowledgeable.

At any rate, it is a fresh problem for Rimuru's group to solve—and a windfall for me. I welcome a terrible monster attacking. It means that Rimuru's concentration will finally be spent elsewhere rather than upon me.

I grinned, relieved that the pressure was finally off.

"Whew, that was dreadful. I am thankful that I'm alive and well today," said Ifrit.

"Indeed. No matter where you find yourself, there are those it is better not to cross. I must make my free time carefully, so as not to slack off too much," I agreed. It was a moment that deepened the bond between us.

"So it's Charybdis this time? Perhaps you'll get yelled at again, Master Veldora."

"Huh?"

What is Ifrit talking about?

"I mean, Charybdis was created from a pool of your magicules, wasn't it? So in a way, it's kind of like your child. Doesn't the parent get blamed for the child's poor behavior?"

What? This is *my* fault?

Besides, how could it be my child? Charybdis simply sprang into being, completely outside of my knowledge!

"Shouldn't you be prepared for a scolding? I don't know if they're going to be interested in excuses like that one if the town gets damaged."

"..."

Well, Ifrit seems entirely checked out on this one. He is placing all of the blame on me so that he can escape Rimuru's wrath. What a dastardly schemer. What have I raised him into...?

But I do not have the time to lose my head about this.

"Have no fear. As long as the word does not get out that Charybdis is my offshoot, I have no reason to be scolded. I am just fine," I said, mostly to convince myself that I was safe.

And no sooner had I said that, than: "Veldora's offshoot?"

My cover has been blown! H-how could you betray me, Trya?!

Why would she tell him? Why can't she see this from my perspective?

"Well, Master Veldora, it is a very famous story. I would assume that someone has been talking about it. And it all started because you were such a rampaging tyrant in the distant past, of course."

"..."

Well, that doesn't leave much room for rebuttal.

"Let us pray," Ifrit said blithely. "At this point, we can only pray that no damage befalls the town."

In the face of all this, that is the most concern he can muster? I am sad to consider him my friend. But...I suppose he is correct.

At this point it would be best to hope that Rimuru and his team are able to defeat the beast as quickly as possible. But it will not be a simple matter. Even by my estimate, Charybdis is a most vexing foe.

If they were as ultra-powerful as I am, it would be no problem. But alas, not everyone can be me...

"Charybdis is incredibly rich in energy. I do not appreciate it being known as my 'offshoot,' but in terms of the scale of power, it is certainly a mighty foe. Even you could not best it, Ifrit."

"It's that tough? But I feel as though it should be more than possible to outmaneuver a being with no conscious will..."

Ifrit said, perhaps recalling his previous self. His logic is sound, of course, but it does not apply to Charybdis.

Hmm, how to explain? I shall use Rimuru's words.

Charybdis is a monster with incredible health that quickly regenerates all harm. It also blocks all magic, so only physical methods of attack will hurt it. Since it has such a vast amount of stamina, each cycle of regeneration allows for significant recovery.

In other words, it is impossible to defeat Charybdis if you cannot deliver attacks that outstrip this regenerative speed. It is the very fact that schemes and strategies do not work against this monster that make it so troublesome to deal with.

"...I see. So it's a regenerating creature. No intelligence can outwit it, only sheer firepower will do the trick. If I cannot defeat it, then the kijin named Benimaru will not be able to, either."

"Most likely. He might inflict damage, but not enough to be fatal. And against Charybdis, that effectively renders it useless."

Its simplicity is what makes it fearsome. One questions how far a coalition of the weak will get against this foe.

"It is indeed troublesome, but on the contrary, that reassures me we are fine," said Ifrit.

What is this? What idea does he have? He has yet to lose his aura of confidence, and I would like to know why.

The answer came very quickly, in fact.

"Heh heh heh, have you already forgotten, Master?"

Oh! Of course! *She* is here!

Not even a demon lord is cause for concern when you have Milim Nava, the "Destroyer," eldest of the great demon lords, on your side.

"That fish may be *big,* but it' still just a fish to me."

It is times like these when she can be counted on. It seems the issue will be settled without damage to the town, if you ask me.

But then...

"We cannot allow you to do that, Lady Milim. This is our town and our problem."

"That's right. We can't take advantage of our friendship to have you solve all of our problems for us."

To my shock, both Shion and Shuna rejected her offer to help.

No! You must not do this!

Now I am going to get the blowback!

And what are friends for, if not to lean on for help?!

"I suppose they mean that you must not count on them to do every single thing. It is a good lesson to take to heart," said Ifrit.

This is not the moment for moral lessons!

On the other hand, there is nothing for us to do but watch, anyway.

"Let us pray, Master!"

"..."

For just a moment, I felt a prickle of annoyance at Ifrit.

◆ TYRANT OF DESTRUCTION ◆

The battle has begun.

The first opponents were not Charybdis, but its companions; flying Megalodon sharks. Fearsome opponents in their own right—I suppose? They are so insignificant to me that it is difficult to judge.

Among Rimuru's personal knowledge was a very frightening story about a giant shark. Because of that, he is cautious simply from the fact of a shark floating in the air.

This only affected Rimuru, however. His followers fearlessly dispatched the Megalodons one after the other. Their teamwork is impressive, especially when crossing so many species lines.

The chief officers like Soei, Shion, and Ranga are holding their own. These sharks are nothing to them. Hakuro just used his katana to dice one of them. I am endlessly impressed with the level of his skill.

Quite the big catch, indeed.

Now the opening act is finished. Charybdis has gone into motion.

The air is full of a hideous noise like scraping glass. It is the sound of Charybdis's scales rubbing against each other. The beast launched all of the thousands upon thousands of scales that cover its body at once.

"Ahh. That would be Charybdis's 'Tempest Scales' attack."

"You are so wise and worldly, Master Veldora."

"I suppose."

It is a powerful technique to go to right at the start, but a natural one. The only attacks Charybdis can use are its light beams, its scales, and a body blow. In other words, Tempest Scales is simply an ordinary attack for Charybdis.

The cloud of scales covered the sky, bearing down on Shion and Ranga.

It was Rimuru who saved them.

"Gluttony"!

A new Unique Skill for Rimuru. In fact, this is a combination of the Unique Skill "Starved" and the Unique Skill "Predator," evolved into the Unique Skill "Gluttony."

Can you believe it? Skills evolving! Even I had trouble wrapping my considerable mind around the concept.

There are times when the mold of one's mind and its powerful wishes give shape to skills. This is the nature of what we call "Unique Skills."

The process is impossible without a mighty soul, but among such beings, some can even have two or three of them.

Skills evolving, however, is an entirely different matter.

"Is it that rare?"

"Hrmph. Is it rare? Enough that I now doubt what I once took for granted."

"I see! Well, that's a very important thing to do."

...Hmm? And what exactly do you mean by that, Ifrit?

It felt as though his nuance was slightly different from mine. Ah, well...

"For example, Ifrit. You do not possess any Unique Skills, do you?"

"No."

"Do you know why?"

"...Because my sense of self was thin at best?"

"That would be correct. Strictly speaking, there are finer distinctions, but your understanding of it is not wrong."

As a higher elemental spirit, Ifrit's magical energy alone is impressive. It is far beyond any human—even in comparison to the strengthened soul of an "otherworlder" required to cross over.

The reason that Ifrit still does not possess a Unique Skill is because he lacks personal desire. You cannot gain skills without greed.

Of course, it is more often that one wishes for a skill and does not gain it. But the process will not start without the wishing.

In what situation does a skill evolve, then?

A Common Skill evolves into an Extra Skill when certain proficiency-related conditions are met. But in the case of a Unique Skill that represents the shape of one's desires, evolution through proficiency is not possible.

If there were a way to evolve such a skill...

"A Unique Skill is the shape of the mind itself."

"Meaning?"

"Perhaps a change in the mind..."

"Would allow for the skill to evolve?"

It is the only possibility that I can think of. And yet...

Can the mind itself grow over such a short period of time?

It is one thing to gain a new skill, but the way Rimuru absorbs it, advances it, and makes it his own is simply preposterous. It defies common sense.

In fact, considering how long I have lived, his quick progress just makes me look worse!

And on top of that, he has such a keen and creative use of his skills...

For example, he just used his new skill to devour the entire storm of scales that filled the sky. He has not always utilized his skills correctly, but this one was brilliant.

"I can only speak on conjecture at this time. But I would recommend, Ifrit, that you find your desire and seek to gain your own Unique Skill, just in case."

"Understood. I will take my time and think hard about what I truly wish for."

He has loosened up as of late, but Ifrit still has a very uptight personality. He is just too serious. Surely it is a fault of not possessing a firm identity of his own.

It has led to various failings, but I trust that he can slowly but surely change himself. After all, that is personal growth.

The same could be said of me, too.

I ought to work hard to advance my own skills. And then I will exhibit them in front of Rimuru as though I had no idea they could do that. Then the feisty slime will surely recognize my greatness.

Heh heh heh. I cannot wait for that moment to arrive!

Ifrit and I have secretly found our own grand goals to achieve.

But now, back to Rimuru's battle.

Ten hours have passed, and the fight is locked in a stalemate.

At first, Ifrit and I were enjoying our commentary on the battle.

"And there it is! Charybdis's eerie light beam!!"

"Lord Rimuru nimbly avoided it. That is not an easy maneuver!"

But now we are getting bored. Ten hours is long. Far too long.

It is but an instant compared to the eon that is my existence, but my concentration can only last for so long. I am too much of a genius.

Forgive me, plebeians of the world.

I know that even without trying, I can achieve very high marks.

"If you continue carrying on like that, Lord Rimuru is going to scold you again."

"Ah, yes. I do not want that. I shall have to watch myself."

Meanwhile, something has changed in Charybdis. To my surprise, it turns out that the vessel used to summon Charybdis still contains some of its original mind. It is the majin Phobio, the fellow responsible for causing a stir upon his first arrival here, who forms the core of Charybdis.

And Phobio's target was not Rimuru, but Milim.

"There, you see? This is not all my fault."

"It's true. I guess I was wrong about that."

Much better. Ifrit was threatening me with that accusation earlier, so it had been a concern weighing upon my mind, I will admit.

"In any case, this is a good thing. Now I will not be scolded."

"I always believed you, Master Veldora."

...Pardon me?

That was a highly convenient excuse you just made, Ifrit.
If I recall correctly, it was your statement that started this
whole...

Hmph. This is the sort of growth that I do not need to see.

Milim's Dragon Buster took care of Charybdis.
Tremendous power and fine control. Milim, too, has
achieved significant growth since coming here.

It is a good reminder that I cannot rest on my laurels.

◆ AS A NATION ◆

Charybdis has been evaporated into nothing, but that does
not mean it is gone. It is fused with its vessel, Phobio, and
will return to strength in the matter of an hour.

Now Rimuru is performing an operation to prevent this from
happening. Whatever it is he's doing, it is most unusual.

"What is he...?"

"He appears to be isolating Charybdis and devouring it,
Ifrit."

"Ahh. Wonders never cease when it comes to what Lord
Rimuru is capable of."

No, no, no. It is not possible.

"It's not that simple. This may be hard to believe, but Rimuru
is activating his skills in parallel—in other words, controlling
two or more skills simultaneously."

"What exactly does that mean?"

"Well..."

It is difficult to explain, as Ifrit does not already have a
Unique Skill. However, anyone who does possess one would

understand just how baffling Rimuru's current actions really are.

A Unique Skill is the shape of the mind. How can even the most skilled of individuals have two shapes at once? Perhaps the fact that it is so rare for anyone to have two or more Unique Skills simply means that I do not have enough knowledge of this area.

At any rate, I would not have believed one could be so adept at using skills, had I not witnessed this for myself.

"When you earn your Unique Skill, you too will understand why I was so stunned. Thanks to Rimuru's example, I now have a deeper understanding of the adaptability of skills. I suppose that I can see why I was being scolded for slacking off now."

It was an honest bit of humility. True understanding must exist first if one is to engage in any activity with honest intent.

Starting tomorrow, I shall undertake the decoding of the "Unlimited Imprisonment" that binds me.

"Warning. Starting right now, not tomorrow."

Oh. Right.

I feel as though my stirring intent, summoned at last, has immediately been extinguished.

You see, as soon as someone else tells you to do something, your desire to do it vanishes. But I must do it or face rebuke, so I shall resume with alacrity.

Ifrit followed my lead and has begun doing pushups. He has learned to read the room, so to speak. I am heartened by this.

I do think that it is wrong to work only because you do not wish to be yelled at—but this is the reality we all live in. And I understand this deep working of the world, because I am very smart.

At any rate, I maintained a pose of "working hard to decode." But in the meantime, I was listening in on Rimuru's conversation.

When the dwarven reinforcements were certain that Charybdis was vanquished, they headed back home. Captain Dorf, the leader of the Pegasus Knights, sought an explanation from Rimuru, but because he could not abandon his task, Benimaru took charge of talking him down.

Indeed.

He did witness Milim's Dragon Buster, so he has the right to ask questions about it. But Rimuru was prioritizing the disposal of Charybdis—or more accurately, the rescue of Phobio.

When Phobio was saved at last, he seemed to understand what he had done. As soon as he awoke, he apologized for his actions.

It was befitting of a lycanthrope, the way that he earnestly owned up to his actions. Being able to admit to one's faults is the mark of an admirable soul.

"Perhaps you should try doing that as well, Master Veldora."

...All in good time. All in good time.

For now, I shall return my attention to Phobio. It seems he has traded what he knows with Treyni and Benimaru, and the presence of a sinister mastermind behind this event is coming to light.

Geld recognized it too, and mentioned the name "Footman." Gabiru mentioned a "Laplace."

"I see... Laplace, you say. I know that majin," said Treyni.

"Footman? I shall remember that name," Benimaru swore. It seems that they have some score to settle with these people. They look concerned.

The group asked various questions in an attempt to pool knowledge, but nothing useful was forthcoming, sadly. Even Milim, who seemed as though she would know, did not have any knowledge of these harlequins.

The only thing she offered was the name of Clayman, a demon lord who might have been behind all of this activity. I am not familiar with the recent demon lord situation, but Ifrit did find this to make sense.

"Is this the demon lord you mentioned being steeped in treacherous plotting?"

"Yes, Master. Cruel, baseless rumors were spread about Lord Leon which caused him great vexation."

Hmm. So he likes to use underhanded means. If he does not like someone, he ought to simply go and strike them directly...

"That's not the point..."

I did not understand what there was to be hesitant about— but if anything, Rimuru was on the side of caution. But since he couldn't confirm his suspicions, Rimuru decided to let this one go and released Phobio. Rimuru seems not to want to engage in hostilities with Carrion without good reason. All of the followers who agree with him have been infected by his ways, I feel.

It is a softness that is unbecoming of a monster. But in this case, it is also the correct choice.

As Milim sensed, Demon Lord Carrion himself has come to visit.

Ah, I see. So this is one of the recent demon lords. He hides his presence well, but my eyes cannot be fooled. It is clear that even concealed like this, his energy is over twice that of Ifrit's.

Plus, Carrion is a lycanthrope. Given that he is known as the "Beastmaster," and king of their domain, it would stand to reason that he is a lion type, the strongest of lines.

When he transforms into his true state, Carrion's energy will surely expand threefold. His strength is absolutely worthy of the demon lord moniker.

The fact that he came to visit in person is a sign of how much he cares about this Phobio underling. Perhaps he learned about the incident with Charybdis, and decided to come and assist Rimuru.

Rimuru doesn't seem to have been thinking that far ahead, but ultimately, things turned out well. By returning Phobio alive and well, he's earned Carrion's trust and esteem.

How I wish that I could learn from his good fortune.

This would be the end of the Charybdis incident, at last.

It is now certain that someone was pulling strings behind this, but the identity of our enemy is still unknown. It is not the most satisfying way to end, but at least we can say that the danger has passed.

Peace has returned to Rimuru's town.

Ifrit and I have been diligent and hard at work, so Rimuru's complaints are few and far between.

"Actually...I'm always diligent and hardworking," said Ifrit, who seems not to want to be associated with me. That is nothing new, so I shall ignore him.

I am more concerned with being jealous of Milim's new present. It is a very odd, unique weapon created through much trial and error.

Dragon Knuckles. Well, the name is cheap. But the effects attached to the claws are so varied and impressive that it speaks highly of its makers' efforts.

First, it has excellent toughness to ensure it does not break. Pure magisteel make, of course.

Next, the claws are made of a shock-absorbing material, meaning that the damage done from the impact is less than a hundredth of its natural value.

The attached magical effects are "Slowing" and "Weakness." These make use of the wearer's natural magic power, of course, and inflict their effects upon that wearer.

In other words, all of these things are handicaps to the one wearing the claws. It is an anti-Milim safety device, something that no one else could possibly use. For example, if a hobgoblin were to put them on, it would be unable to even stand. Kaijin tried it out just for fun, and needed help just to move around in them.

Who would want such a thing? As it happens, Milim was delighted with them. Even I wanted them, so I understand her feeling.

The days after this passed peacefully, but they are not fated to do so forever. Things are happening in quick succession on a variety of fronts.

Fuze left for home with the promise of finessing a friendly relationship with Rimuru's nation, and the Dwarf Kingdom sent an invitation for a royal guest. Given the agreement with Dorf, this was perhaps an inevitable outcome.

And from the Animal Kingdom of Eurazania, they sent Phobio. It seems that trade will be opened soon. Demon Lord Carrion makes for a capable sovereign. Not only is he keeping his word to Rimuru, but he is using the agreement for the benefit of his nation.

When it comes to politics, intelligence is more prized than might. Rimuru should be fine, given his cunning nature, but if he is ever careless, he will find himself absorbed into a larger power.

Diplomacy can be a frightening thing, indeed.

But all I am doing is quoting the knowledge I took from Rimuru's past experience. It is not actually my concern!

Kwaaaa ha ha ha ha!

One day, as things were getting busier and busier, Milim suddenly said, "Now I am going off to work!"

"My niece has a job? I did not know this."

"She's doing well for herself. Not even you have a job, Master Veldora."

...Am I the only one who felt spite from that? Perhaps I have taken a wrong turn with Ifrit's education. I shall have to re-examine my choices with raising him, but that is for another time.

With Milim leaving for her trip, Rimuru seems to feel that a weight is off of his shoulders. He's also begun to think on other topics with a wistful air.

Yes, Rimuru is ready to take a new step in his journey.

What will happen next? All I can do is watch, but I am not worried.

I will simply enjoy the new adventure as it unfol—

"Warning. You are currently idle. Please resume decoding."

Oh. Er, right.

Then I shall *secretly* enjoy the new adventure as it unfolds.

To be reincarnated in Volume 9!

COERCION

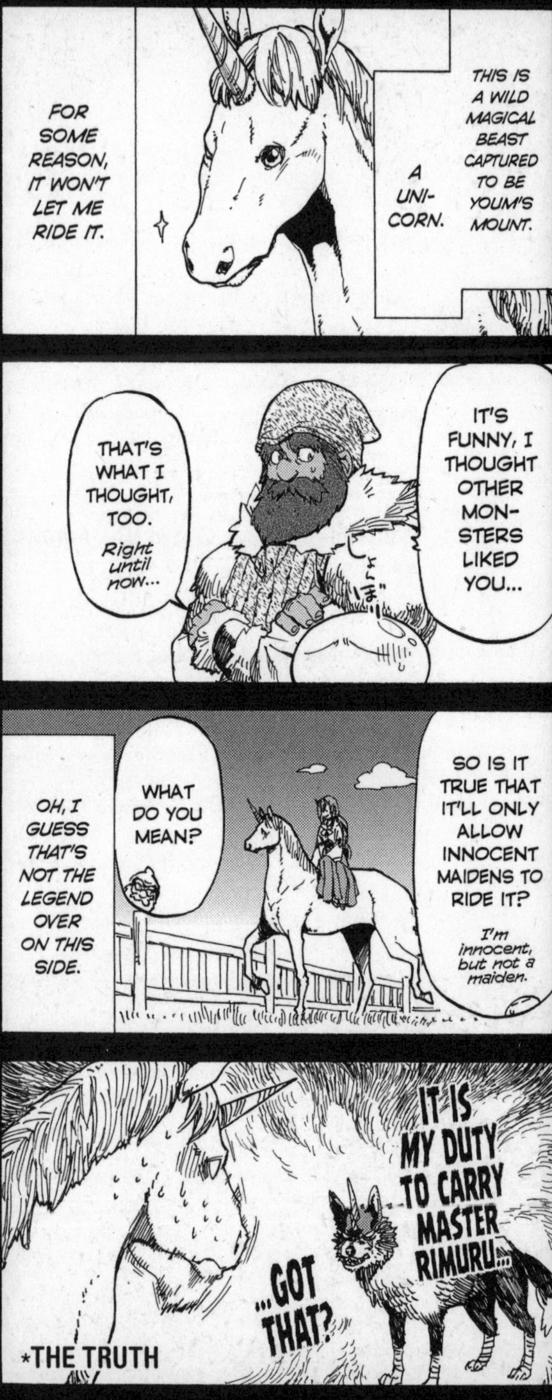

THIS IS A WILD MAGICAL BEAST CAPTURED TO BE YOUM'S MOUNT.
A UNI-CORN.
FOR SOME REASON, IT WON'T LET ME RIDE IT.
IT'S FUNNY, I THOUGHT OTHER MON-STERS LIKED YOU...
THAT'S WHAT I THOUGHT, TOO.
Right until now...
SO IS IT TRUE THAT IT'LL ONLY ALLOW INNOCENT MAIDENS TO RIDE IT?
I'm innocent, but not a maiden.
WHAT DO YOU MEAN?
OH, I GUESS THAT'S NOT THE LEGEND OVER ON THIS SIDE.
IT IS MY DUTY TO CARRY MASTER RIMURU...
...GOT THAT?
*THE TRUTH

LIST OF ACKNOWLEDGMENTS

AUTHOR:
Fuse-sensei

CHARACTER DESIGN:
Mitz Vah-sensei

TRAVEL GUIDE:
Sho Okagiri-sensei

REINCARNATED SLIME DIARY:
Shiba

ASSISTANTS:
Muraichi-san
Daiki Haraguchi-san
Masashi Kiritani-sensei
Taku Arao-sensei

Everyone at the editorial department

And You!!

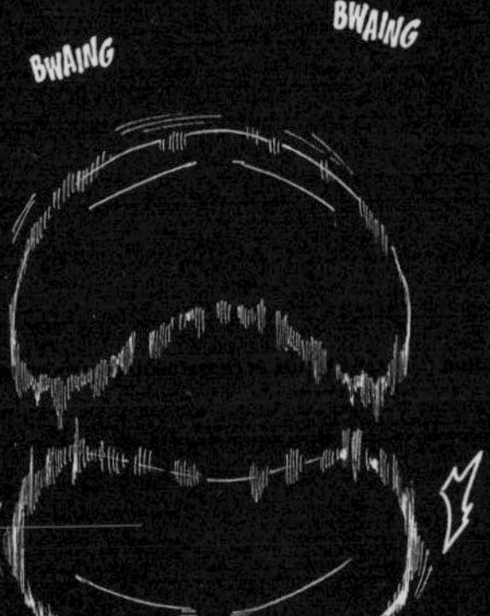

BWAING
BWAING

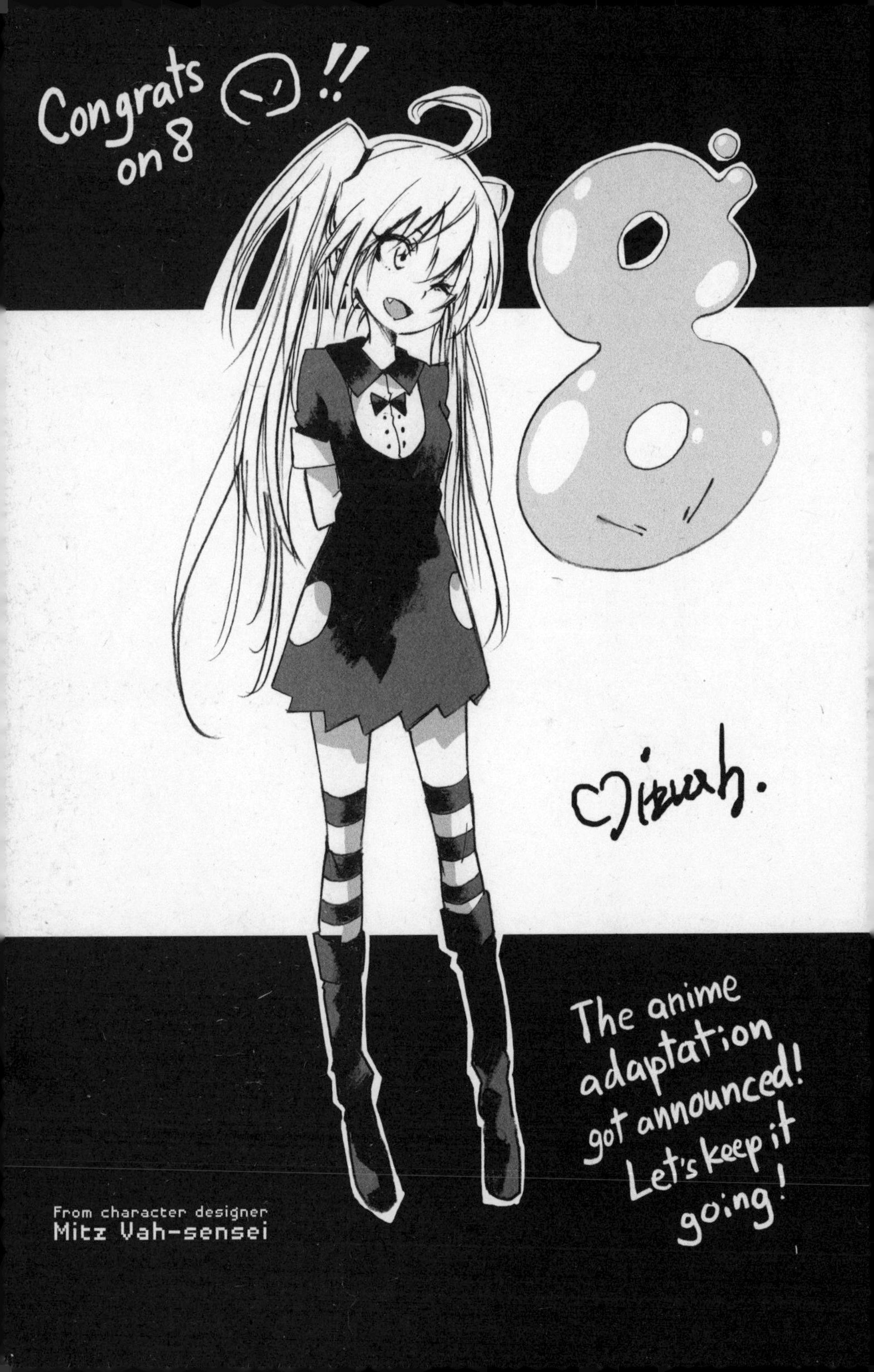
Congrats on 8 !!
The anime adaptation got announced! Let's keep it going!

From character designer
Mitz Vah-sensei

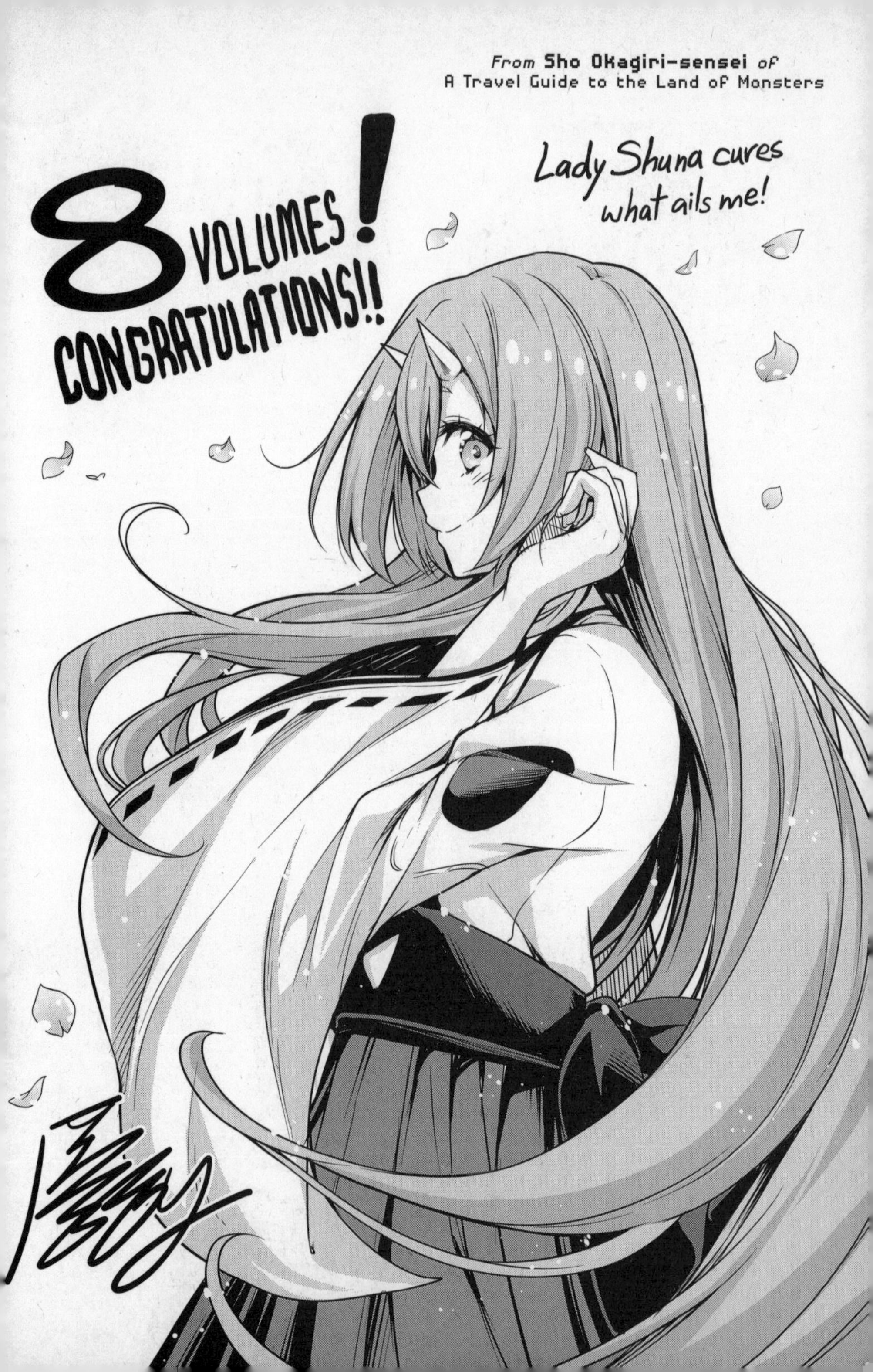
From Sho Okagiri-sensei of
A Travel Guide to the Land of Monsters
8 VOLUMES!
CONGRATULATIONS!!
Lady Shuna cures what ails me!

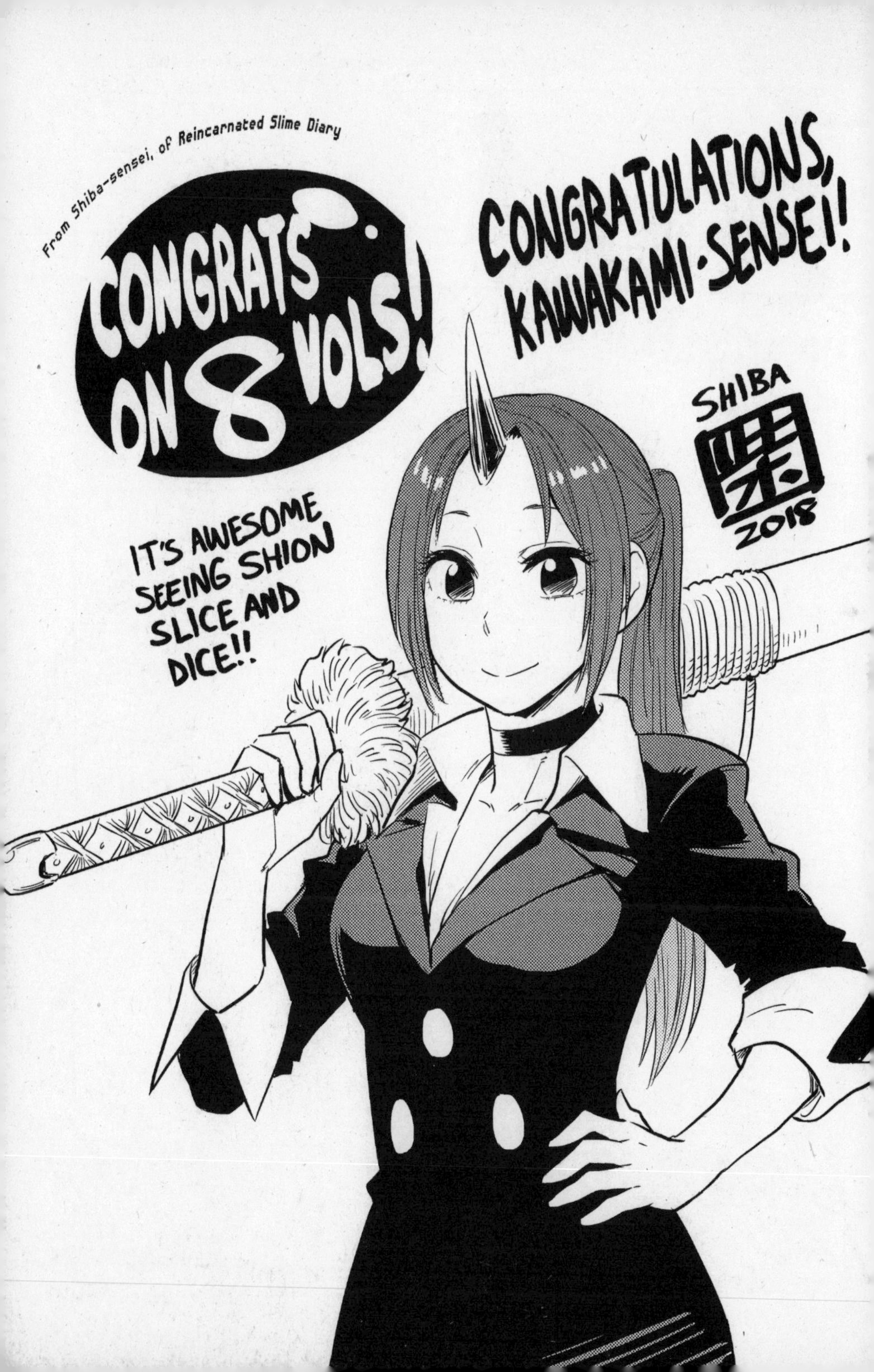
From Shiba-sensei, of Reincarnated Slime Diary
CONGRATS ON 8 VOLS!
CONGRATULATIONS, KAWAKAMI-SENSEI!!
SHIBA 2018
IT'S AWESOME SEEING SHION SLICE AND DICE!!

Learn From Your Forebears

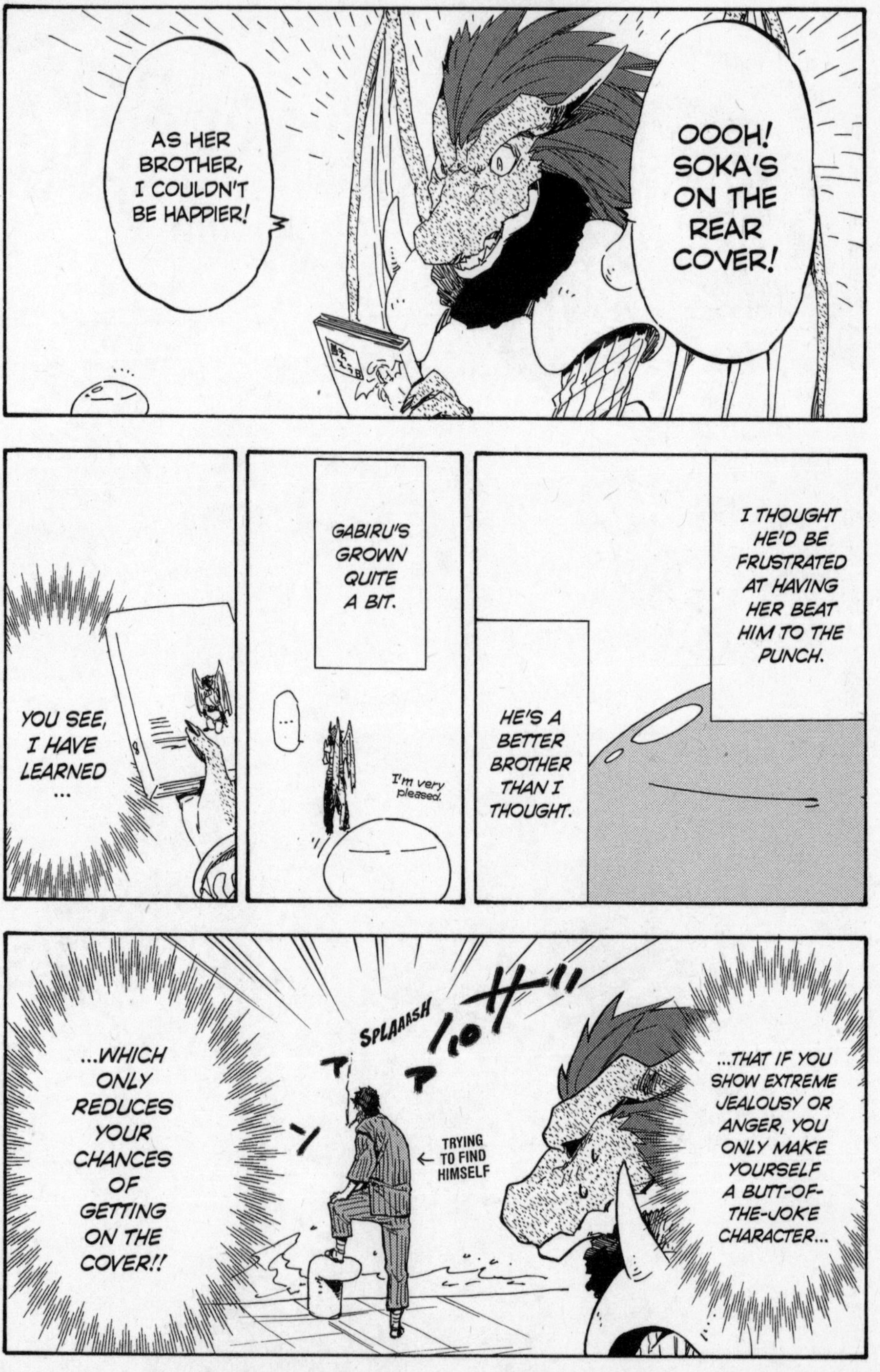
OOOH! SOKA'S ON THE REAR COVER!
AS HER BROTHER, I COULDN'T BE HAPPIER!
I THOUGHT HE'D BE FRUSTRATED AT HAVING HER BEAT HIM TO THE PUNCH.
HE'S A BETTER BROTHER THAN I THOUGHT.
GABIRU'S GROWN QUITE A BIT.
...
I'm very pleased.
YOU SEE, I HAVE LEARNED ...
...THAT IF YOU SHOW EXTREME JEALOUSY OR ANGER, YOU ONLY MAKE YOURSELF A BUTT-OF-THE-JOKE CHARACTER...
SPLAAASH
TRYING TO FIND HIMSELF
...WHICH ONLY REDUCES YOUR CHANCES OF GETTING ON THE COVER!!

Fresh-
cooked
slime.

TRANSLATION NOTES

SHISHI-ODOSHI

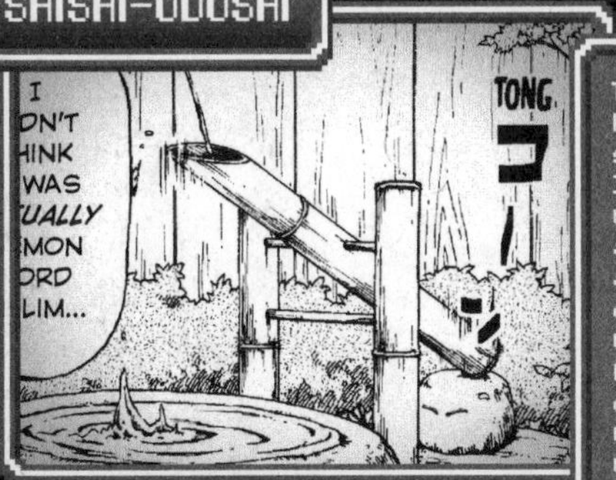
TONG
コ
I ON'T HINK WAS TUALLY EMON ORD LIM...

page 20

The contraption shown in this scene is known as a *shishi odoshi* (literally "deer scarer"). This device is often found in Japanese hot springs and is thus used to setup or introduce bathing scenes in anime and manga. The *shishi odoshi* creates a sound to scare off wildlife that would otherwise eat or damage one's crops and is typically composed of a bamboo tube that fills with water until pushed beyond the center of gravity of its pivot, causing the tube to hit a rock or other hard object. In this case, that hard object is a stone that looks like Rimuru.

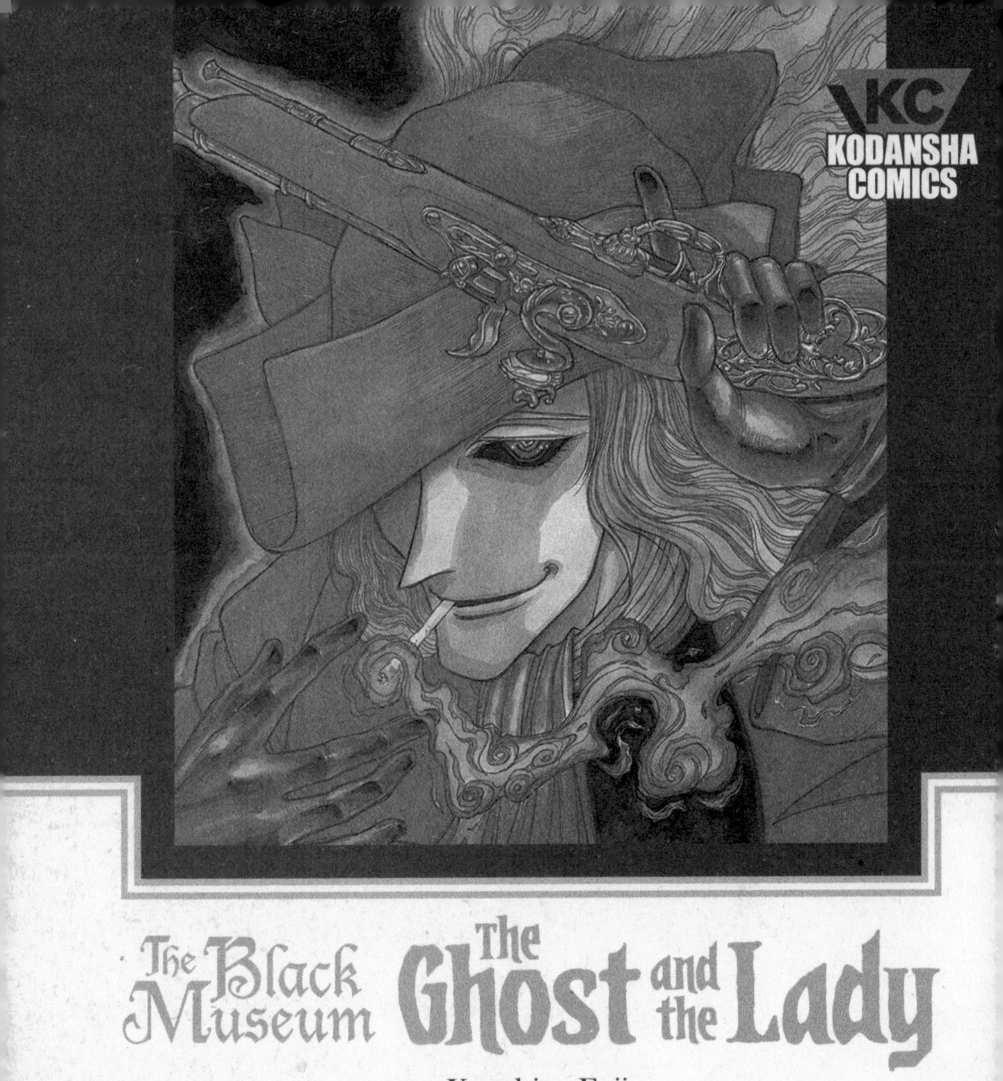
KC
KODANSHA
COMICS

The Black Museum: The Ghost and the Lady

By Kazuhiro Fujita

Deep in Scotland Yard in London sits an evidence room dedicated to the greatest mysteries of British history. In this "Black Museum" sits a misshapen hunk of lead–two bullets fused together–the key to a wartime encounter between Florence Nightingale, the mother of modern nursing, and a supernatural Man in Grey. This story is unknown to most scholars of history, but a special guest of the museum will tell the tale of The Ghost and the Lady...

Praise for Kazuhiro Fujita's *Ushio and Tora*

"A charming revival that combines a classic look with modern depth and pacing... **Essential viewing both for curmudgeons and new fans alike.**" — Anime News Network

"**GREAT!** The first episode of Ushio and Tora captures the essence of '90s anime." — IGN

New action series from Hiroyuki Takei, creator of the classic shonen franchise Shaman King!

In medieval Japan, a bell hanging on the collar is a sign that a cat has a master. Norachiyo's bell hangs from his katana sheath, but he is nonetheless a stray — a ronin. This one-eyed cat samurai travels across a dishonest world, cutting through pretense and deception with his blade.

NEKOGAHARA

STRAY CAT SAMURAI

By
Hiroyuki Takei

DELUXE EDITION

BATTLE ANGEL ALITA

After more than a decade out of print, the original cyberpunk action classic returns in glorious 400-page hardcover deluxe editions, featuring an all-new translation, color pages, and new cover designs!

KC
KODANSHA COMICS

Far beneath the shimmering space-city of Zalem lie the trash-heaps of The Scrapyard... Here, cyber-doctor and bounty hunter Daisuke Ido finds the head and torso of an amnesiac cyborg girl. He names her Alita and vows to fill her life with beauty, but in a moment of desperation, a fragment of Alita's mysterious past awakens in her. She discovers that she possesses uncanny prowess in the legendary martial art known as panzerkunst. With her newfound skills, Alita decides to become a hunter-warrior - tracking down and taking out those who prey on the weak. But can she hold onto her humanity in the dark and gritty world of The Scrapyard?

Having lost his wife, high school teacher Kōhei Inuzuka is doing his best to raise his young daughter Tsumugi as a single father. He's pretty bad at cooking and doesn't have a huge appetite to begin with, but chance brings his little family together with one of his students, the lonely Kotori. The three of them are anything but comfortable in the kitchen, but the healing power of home cooking might just work on their grieving hearts.

"This season's number-one feel-good anime!" —Anime News Network

"A beautifully-drawn story about comfort food and family and grief. Recommended." —Otaku USA Magazine

sweetness & lightning

By Gido Amagakure

The award-winning manga about what happens inside you!

"Far more entertaining than it ought to be... what kid doesn't want to think that every time they sneeze a torpedo shoots out their nose?"
—Anime News Network

Strep throat! Hay fever! Influenza! The world is a dangerous place for a red blood cell just trying to get her deliveries finished. Fortunately, she's not alone...she's got a whole human body's worth of cells ready to help out! The mysterious white blood cells, the buff and brash killer T cells, even the cute little platelets— everyone's got to come together if they want to keep you healthy!

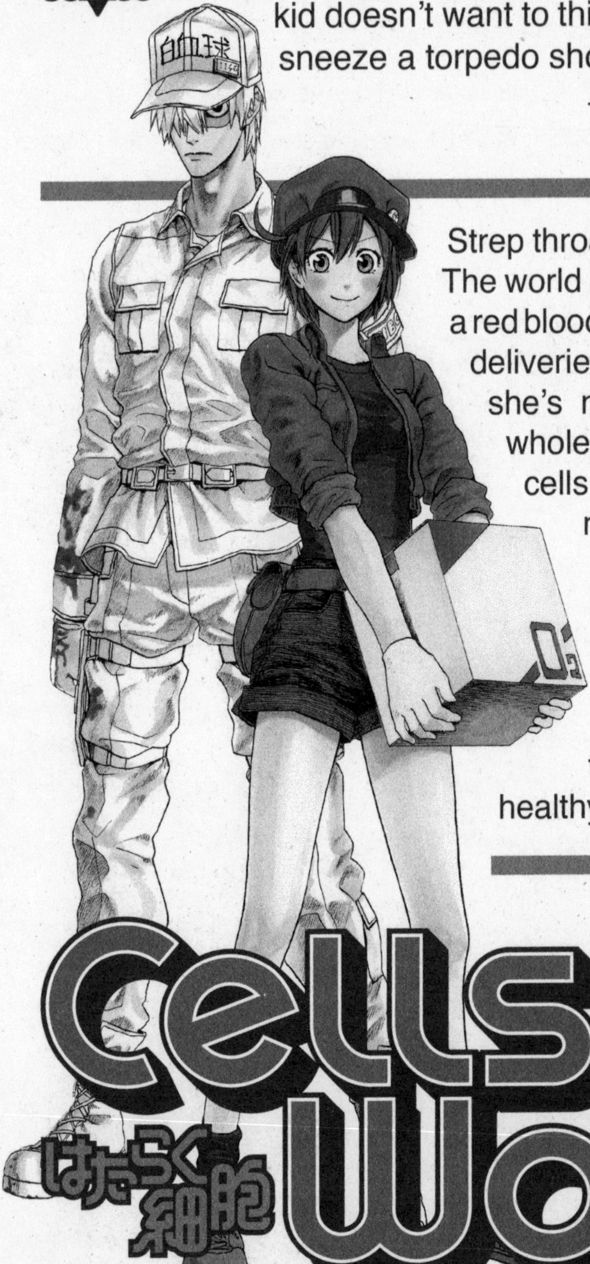

Cells at Work!

はたらく細胞

By Akane Shimizu

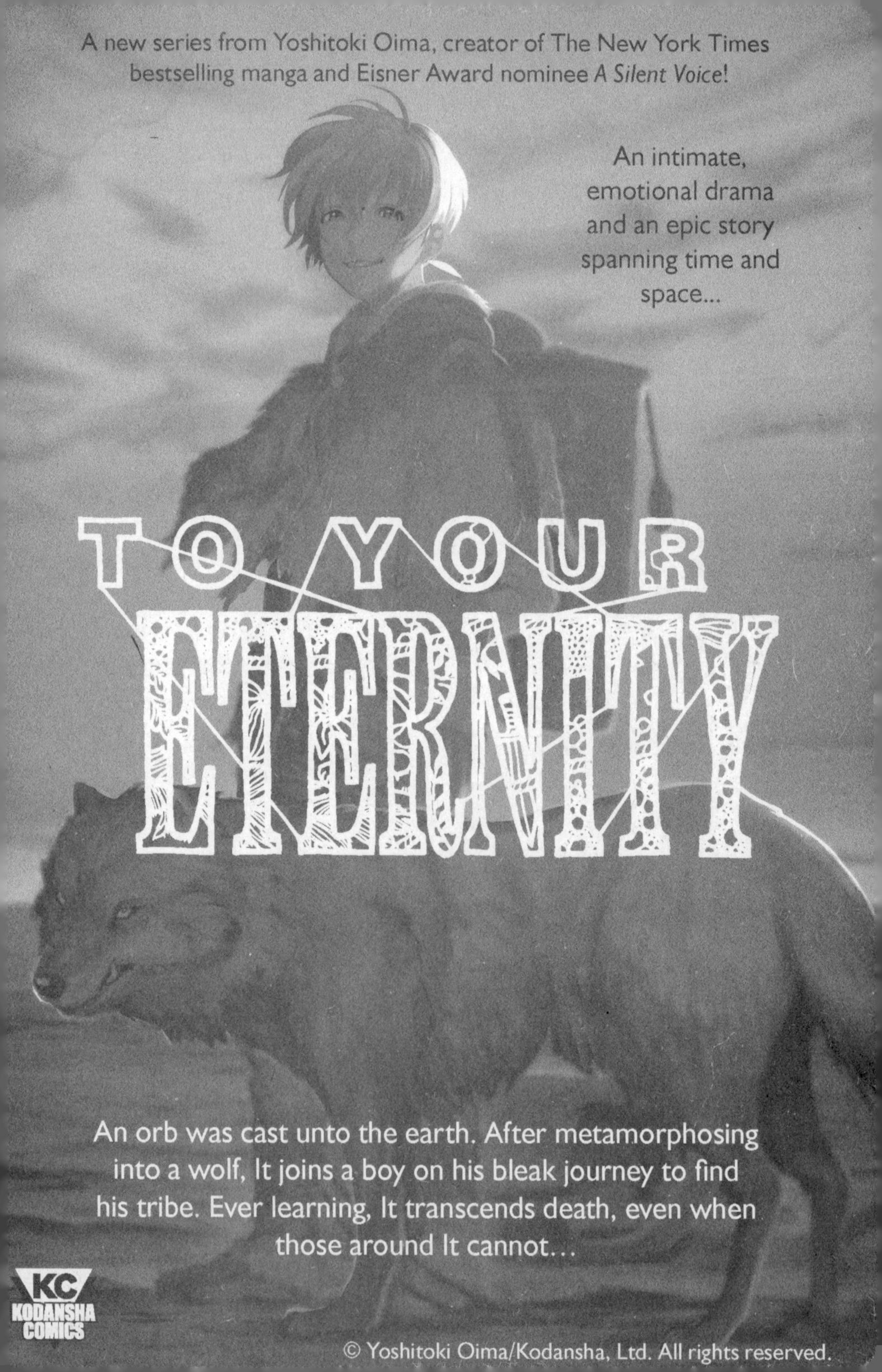
A new series from Yoshitoki Oima, creator of The New York Times bestselling manga and Eisner Award nominee *A Silent Voice*!
An intimate, emotional drama and an epic story spanning time and space...
TO YOUR ETERNITY
An orb was cast unto the earth. After metamorphosing into a wolf, It joins a boy on his bleak journey to find his tribe. Ever learning, It transcends death, even when those around It cannot…
KC KODANSHA COMICS
© Yoshitoki Oima/Kodansha, Ltd. All rights reserved.

Japan's most powerful spirit medium delves into the ghost world's greatest mysteries!

Story by Kyo Shirodaira, famed author of mystery fiction and creator of *Spiral*, *Blast of Tempest*, and *The Record of a Fallen Vampire*.

Both touched by spirits called yôkai, Kotoko and Kurô have gained unique superhuman powers. But to gain her powers Kotoko has given up an eye and a leg, and Kurô's personal life is in shambles. So when Kotoko suggests they team up to deal with renegades from the spirit world, Kurô doesn't have many other choices, but Kotoko might just have a few ulterior motives...

IN/SPECTRE

STORY BY KYO SHIRODAIRA
ART BY CHASHIBA KATASE

A Kodansha Comics Trade Paperback Original.

Published in the United States by Kodansha Comics,
an imprint of Kodansha USA Publishing, LLC, New York.

Publication rights for this English edition arranged through Kodansha Ltd., Tokyo.

First published in Japan in 2018 by Kodansha Ltd., Tokyo, as *Tensei Shitara Suraimu Datta Ken* volume 8.

ISBN 978-1-63236-729-7

Printed in the United States of America.

www.kodanshacomics.com

9 8 7 6 5 4 3 2

Translation: Stephen Paul
Lettering: Evan Hayden
Editing: Ajani Oloye
Kodansha Comics edition cover design: Phil Balsman